C++
from the Ground Up

Third Edition

About the Author

Herbert Schildt is the world's leading programming author. He is an authority on the C, C++, Java, and C# languages, and is a master Windows programmer. His programming books have sold more than 3 million copies worldwide and have been translated into all major foreign languages. He is the author of numerous bestsellers, including *C++: The Complete Reference, C#: The Complete Reference, Java 2: The Complete Reference, C: The Complete Reference, C++ From the Ground Up, C++: A Beginner's Guide, C#: A Beginner's Guide*, and *Java 2: A Beginner's Guide*. Schildt holds a master's degree in computer science from the University of Illinois. He can be reached at his consulting office at (217) 586-4683.

C++
from the Ground Up

Third Edition

Herbert Schildt

McGraw-Hill/Osborne

New York   Chicago   San Francisco
Lisbon   London   Madrid   Mexico City
Milan   New Delhi   San Juan
Seoul   Singapore   Sydney   Toronto

The McGraw·Hill Companies

McGraw-Hill/Osborne
2600 Tenth Street
Berkeley, California 94710
U.S.A.

To arrange bulk purchase discounts for sales promotions, premiums, or fund-raisers, please contact **McGraw-Hill**/Osborne at the above address. For information on translations or book distributors outside the U.S.A., please see the International Contact Information page immediately following the index of this book.

C++ from the Ground Up, Third Edition

1234567890 DOC DOC 019876543

ISBN 0-07-222897-0

Publisher	**Indexer**
Brandon A. Nordin	Sheryl Schildt
Vice President & Associate Publisher	**Computer Designers**
Scott Rogers	Tabitha M. Cagan, Tara A. Davis, John Patrus, Lucie Ericksen
Acquisitions Editor	**Illustrators**
Lisa McClain	Michael Mueller, Lyssa Wald, Melinda Lytle
Project Editors	**Cover Series Design**
Jenn Tust, Elizabeth Seymour	John Nedwidek, emdesign
Proofreader	**Cover Illustration**
Marian M. Selig	Lance Ravella

This book was composed with Corel VENTURA™ Publisher.

Contents

Contents

Contents

Preface

This book teaches you how to program in C++ — the most powerful computer language in use today. No previous programming experience is required. The book starts with the basics, covers the fundamentals, moves on to the core of the language, and concludes with its more advanced features. By the time you finish, you will be an accomplished C++ programmer.

C++ is your gateway to modern, object-oriented programming. It is the preeminent language for the development of high-performance software and is the choice of programmers worldwide. Simply put, to be a top-flight, professional programmer today implies competency in C++.

C++ is more than just a popular language. C++ provides the conceptual substrata that underlie the design of several other languages, and much of modern computing. It is no accident that two other important languages, Java and C#, are descended from C++. There is little in programming that has not been influenced by the syntax, style, and philosophy of C++.

Because C++ was designed for professional programming, C++ is not the easiest programming language to learn. It is, however, the *best* programming language to learn. Once you have mastered C++, you will be able to write professional-quality, high-performance programs. You will also be able to easily learn languages like Java or C# because they share the same basic syntax and design as C++.

What Is New in the Third Edition

In the time that has passed since the previous edition of this book, there have been no changes to the C++ language. There have, however, been big changes to the computing environment. For example, Java became the dominant language for Web programming, the .NET Framework was released, and C# was invented. Through all the changes of the past few years, one thing has remained constant: the staying power of C++. C++ has been, is, and will remain the dominant language of "power programmers" well into the forseeable future.

The overall structure and organization of the third edition is similar to the second edition. Most of the changes involve updating and expanding the coverage throughout. In some cases, additional details were added. In other cases, the presentation of a topic was improved. In still other situations, descriptions were modernized to reflect the current programming environment. Several new sections were also added.

Two appendices were added. One describes the extended keywords defined by Microsoft that are used for creating managed code for the .NET Framework. The second explains how to adapt the code in this book for use with an older, non-standard C++ compiler.

Finally, all code examples were retested against the current crop of compilers, including Microsoft's Visual Studio .NET and Borland's C++ Builder.

What Version of C++

The material in this book describes Standard C++. This is the version of C++ defined by the ANSI/ISO Standard for C++, and it is the one that is currently supported by all major compilers. Therefore, using this book, you can be confident that what you learn today will also apply tomorrow.

How to Use This Book

The best way to learn any programming language, including C++, is by doing. Therefore, after you have read through a section, try the sample programs. Make sure that you understand why they do what they do before moving on. You should also experiment with the programs, changing one or two lines at a time and observing the results. The more you program, the better you become at programming.

If You're Using Windows

If your computer uses Windows and your goal is to write Windows-based programs, then you have chosen the right language to learn. C++ is completely at home with Windows programming. However, none of the programs in this book use the Windows graphical user interface (GUI). Instead, they are console-based programs that can be run under a Windows console session, such as that provided by the Command Prompt window. The reason for this is easy to understand: GUI-based Windows programs are, by their nature, large and complex. They also use many techniques not directly related to the C++ language. Thus, they are not well-suited for teaching a programming language. However, you can still use a Windows-based compiler to compile the programs in this book because the compiler will automatically create a console session in which to execute your program.

Once you have mastered C++, you will be able to apply your knowledge to Windows programming. In fact, Windows programming using C++ allows the use of class libraries such as MFC or the newer .NET Framework, which can greatly simplify the development of a Windows program.

Don't Forget: Code on the Web

Remember, the source code for all of the programs in this book is available free of charge on the Web at **http://www.osborne.com**. Downloading this code prevents you from having to type in the examples.

For Further Study

C++from the Ground Up is your gateway to the Herb Schildt series of programming books. Here are some others that you will find of interest.

To learn more about C++, try

C++: The Complete Reference

C++: A Beginner's Guide

Teach Yourself C++

STL Programming From the Ground Up

C++ Programmer's Reference

To learn about Java programming, we recommend the following:

Java 2: A Beginner's Guide

Java 2: The Complete Reference

Java 2 Programmer's Reference

To learn about C#, Herb offers these books:

C#: A Beginner's Guide

C#: The Complete Reference

To learn about Windows programming we suggest the following Schildt books:

Windows 98 Programming From the Ground Up

Windows 2000 Programming From the Ground Up

MFC Programming From the Ground Up

The Windows Programming Annotated Archives

If you want to learn about the C language, which is the foundation of all modern programming, then the following titles will be of interest.

C: The Complete Reference

Teach Yourself C

When you need solid answers, fast, turn to Herbert Schildt, the recognized authority on programming.

CHAPTER 1

The Story of C++

C++ is the single most important language that any programmer can learn. This is a strong statement, but it is not an exaggeration. C++ is the center of gravity around which all of modern programming revolves. Its syntax and design philosophy define the essence of object-oriented programming. Moreover, C++ charts the course for future language development. For example, both Java and C# are directly descended from C++. C++ is also the universal language of programming; it is the language in which programmers share ideas with one another. To be a professional programmer today implies competency in C++. It is that fundamental and that important. C++ is the gateway to all of modern programming.

Before beginning your study of C++, it is important for you to know how C++ fits into the historical context of computer languages. Understanding the forces that drove its creation, the design philosophy it represents, and the legacy that it inherits makes it easier to appreciate the many innovative and unique features of C++. With this in mind, this chapter presents a brief history of the C++ programming language, its origins, its relationship to its predecessor (C), its uses, and the programming philosophies that it supports. It also puts C++ into perspective relative to other programming languages.

The Origins of C++

The story of C++ begins with C. The reason for this is simple: C++ is built upon the foundation of C. In fact, C++ is a superset of C. (Indeed, all C++ compilers can also be used to compile C programs!) Specifically, C++ is an expanded and enhanced version of C that embodies the philosophy of object-oriented programming (which is described later in this chapter). C++ also includes several other improvements to the C language, including an extended set of library routines. However, much of the spirit and flavor of C++ is inherited directly from C. To fully understand and appreciate C++, you need to understand the "how and why" behind C.

The Creation of C

The C language shook the computer world. Its impact should not be underestimated because it fundamentally changed the way programming was approached and thought about. C is considered by many to be the first modern "programmer's language." Prior to the invention of C, computer languages were generally designed either as academic exercises or by bureaucratic committees. C is different. C was designed, implemented, and developed by real, working programmers, and it reflected the way they approached the job of programming. Its features were honed, tested, thought about, and rethought by the people who actually used the language. The result of this process was a language that programmers liked to use. Indeed, C quickly attracted many followers who had a near-religious zeal for it, and it found wide and rapid acceptance in the programmer community. In short, C is a language designed by and for programmers.

C was invented and first implemented by Dennis Ritchie on a DEC PDP-11 using the UNIX operating system. C is the result of a development process that started with an older language called BCPL, which was developed by Martin Richards. BCPL influenced a language called B, invented by Ken Thompson, which led to the development of C in the 1970s.

For many years, the de facto standard for C was the one supplied with the Unix operating system and described in *The C Programming Language,* by Brian Kernighan and Dennis Ritchie (Prentice-Hall, 1978). However, because no formal standard existed, there were discrepancies between different implementations of C. To alter this situation, a committee was established in the beginning of the summer of 1983 to work on the creation of an ANSI (American National Standards Institute) standard that would define—once and for all—the C language. The final version of the standard was adopted in December 1989, the first copies of which became available in early 1990. This version of C is commonly referred to as *C89,* and it is the foundation upon which C++ is built.

NOTE: The C standard was updated in 1999 and this version of C is usually referred to as *C99*. This version contains some new features, including a few borrowed from C++, but, overall, it is compatible with the original C89 standard. At the time of this writing, no widely available compiler supports C99 and it is still C89 that defines what is commonly thought of as the C language. Furthermore, it is C89 that is the basis for C++. It is possible that a future standard for C++ will include the features added by C99, but they are not part of C++ at this time.

It may seem hard to understand at first, but C is often called a "middle-level" computer language. As it is applied to C, middle-level does not have a negative connotation; it does not mean that C is less powerful, harder to use, or less developed than a "high-level" language, or that it is as difficult to use as assembly language. (*Assembly language,* or *assembler,* as it is often called, is simply a symbolic representation of the actual machine code that a computer can execute.) C is thought of as a middle-level language because it combines elements of high-level languages, such as Pascal, Modula-2, or Visual Basic, with the functionality of assembler.

From a theoretical point of view, a *high-level language* attempts to give the programmer everything he or she could possibly want, already built into the language. A *low-level language* provides nothing other than access to the actual machine instructions. A *middle-level language* gives the programmer a concise set of tools and allows the programmer to develop higher-level constructs on his or her own. A middle-level language offers the programmer built-in power, coupled with flexibility.

Being a middle-level language, C allows you to manipulate bits, bytes, and addresses— the basic elements with which a computer functions. Thus, C does not attempt to buffer the hardware of the machine from your program to any significant extent. For example, the size of an integer in C is directly related to the word size of the CPU. In most high-level languages there are built-in statements for reading and writing disk files. In C, all of these procedures are performed by calls to library routines and not by keywords defined by the language. This approach increases C's flexibility.

C allows—indeed, needs—the programmer to define routines for performing high-level operations. These routines are called *functions,* and they are very important to the C language. In fact, functions are the building blocks of both C and C++. You can easily tailor a library of functions to perform various tasks that are used by your program. In this sense, you can personalize C to fit your needs.

There is another aspect of C that you must understand, because it is also important to C++: C is a structured language. The most distinguishing feature of a structured language is that it uses blocks. A *block* is a set of statements that are logically connected. For example, imagine an IF statement that, if successful, will execute five discrete statements. If these statements can be grouped together and referenced as an indivisible unit, then they form a block.

A structured language supports the concept of subroutines with local variables. A *local variable* is simply a variable that is known only to the subroutine in which it is defined. A structured language also supports several loop constructs, such as **while**, **do-while,** and **for.** The use of the **goto** statement, however, is either prohibited or discouraged, and is not the common form of program control in the same way that it is in traditional BASIC or FORTRAN. A structured language allows you to indent statements and does not require a strict field concept (as did early versions of FORTRAN).

Finally, and perhaps most importantly, C is a language that stays out of the way. The underlying philosophy of C is that the programmer, not the language, is in charge. Therefore, C will let you do virtually anything that you want, even if what you tell it to do is unorthodox, highly unusual, or suspicious. C gives you nearly complete control over the machine. Of course, with this power comes considerable responsibility, which you, the programmer, must shoulder.

Understanding the Need for C++

Given the preceding discussion of C, you might be wondering why C++ was invented. Since C is a successful and useful computer programming language, why was there a need for something else? The answer is complexity. Throughout the history of programming, the increasing complexity of programs has driven the need for better ways to manage that complexity. C++ is a response to that need. To better understand this correlation, consider the following.

Approaches to programming have changed dramatically since the invention of the computer. The primary reason for change has been to accommodate the increasing complexity of programs. For example, when computers were first invented, programming was done by toggling in the binary machine instructions using the computer's front panel. As long as programs were just a few hundred instructions long, this approach worked. As programs grew, assembly language was invented so that programmers could deal with larger, increasingly complex programs by using symbolic representations of the machine instructions. As programs continued to grow, high-level languages were developed to give programmers more tools with which to handle complexity.

The first widespread language was, of course, FORTRAN. While FORTRAN was a very impressive first step, it is hardly a language that encourages clear, easy-to-understand programs. The 1960s gave birth to structured programming. This is the method of programming supported by languages such as C. With structured languages, it was, for the first time, possible to write moderately complex programs fairly easily. However, even with structured programming methods, once a project reaches a certain size, its complexity exceeds what a programmer can manage. By the late 1970s, many projects were near or at this point. To solve this problem, a new way to program began to emerge. This method is called *object-oriented programming* (OOP for short). Using OOP, a programmer could handle larger programs. The trouble was that C did not support object-oriented programming. The desire for an object-oriented version of C ultimately led to the creation of C++.

In the final analysis, although C is one of the most liked and widely used professional programming languages in the world, there comes a time when its ability to handle complexity reaches its limit. The purpose of C++ is to allow this barrier to be broken and to help the programmer comprehend and manage larger, more complex programs.

C++ Is Born

In response to the need to manage greater complexity, C++ was born. It was invented by Bjarne Stroustrup in 1979 at Bell Laboratories in Murray Hill, New Jersey. He initially called the new language "C with Classes." However, in 1983 the name was changed to C++.

C++ contains the entire C language. As stated earlier, C is the foundation upon which C++ is built. C++ includes all of C's features, attributes, and benefits. It also adheres to C's philosophy that the programmer, not the language, is in charge. At this point, it is critical to understand that the invention of C++ was not an attempt to create a new programming language. Instead, it was an enhancement to an already highly successful language.

Most of the additions that Stroustrup made to C were designed to support object-oriented programming. In essence, C++ is the object-oriented version of C. By building upon the foundation of C, Stroustrup provided a smooth migration path to OOP. Instead of having to learn an entirely new language, a C programmer needed to learn only a few new features to reap the benefits of the object-oriented methodology.

But C is not the only language that influenced C++. Stroustrup states that some of its object-oriented features were inspired by another object-oriented language called Simula67. Therefore, C++ represents the blending of two powerful programming methods.

When creating C++, Stroustrup knew that it was important to maintain the original spirit of C, including its efficiency, flexibility, and philosophy, while at the same time adding support for object-oriented programming. Happily, his goal was accomplished. C++ still provides the programmer with the freedom and control of C, coupled with the power of objects.

Although C++ was initially designed to aid in the management of very large programs, it is in no way limited to this use. In fact, the object-oriented attributes of C++ can be effectively applied to virtually any programming task. It is not uncommon to see C++ used for projects such as compilers, editors, programmer tools, games, and networking programs. Because C++ shares C's efficiency, much high-performance systems software is constructed using C++. Also, C++ is frequently the language of choice for Windows programming.

One important point to remember is this: Because C++ is a superset of C, once you can program in C++, you can also program in C! Thus, you will actually be learning two programming languages at the same time, with the same effort that you would use to learn only one.

The Evolution of C++

Since C++ was first invented, it has undergone three major revisions, with each revision adding to and altering the language. The first revision was in 1985 and the second occurred in 1990. The third revision occurred during the C++ standardization process. In the early 1990s, work began on a standard for C++. Towards that end, a joint ANSI and ISO (International Standards Organization) standardization committee was formed. The first draft of the proposed standard was created on January 25, 1994. In that draft, the ANSI/ISO C++ committee (of which I was a member) kept the features first defined by Stroustrup and added some new ones as well. But, in general, this initial draft reflected the state of C++ at the time.

Soon after the completion of the first draft of the C++ standard, an event occurred that caused the standard to expand greatly: the creation of the Standard Template Library (STL) by Alexander Stepanov. As you will learn, the STL is a set of generic routines that you can use to manipulate data. It is both powerful and elegant. But the STL is also quite large. Subsequent to the first draft, the committee voted to include the STL in the specification for C++. The addition of the STL expanded the scope of C++ well beyond its original definition. While important, the inclusion of the STL, among other things, slowed the standardization of C++.

It is fair to say that the standardization of C++ took far longer than any one had expected when it began. In the process, many new features were added to the language and many small changes were made. In fact, the version of C++ defined by the C++ committee is much larger and more complex than Stroustrup's original design. The final draft was passed out of committee on November 14, 1997, and an ANSI/ISO standard for C++ became a reality in 1998. This specification for C++ is commonly referred to as *Standard C++*.

The material in this book describes Standard C++. This is the version of C++ supported by all mainstream C++ compilers, including Microsoft's Visual C++ and Borland's C++ Builder. Therefore, the code and information in this book is fully applicable to all modern C++ environments.

What Is Object-Oriented Programming?

Since object-oriented programming was fundamental to the development of C++, it is important to define precisely what object-oriented programming is. Object-oriented programming has taken the best ideas of structured programming and has combined them with several powerful concepts that allow you to organize your programs more effectively. In general, when programming in an object-oriented fashion, you decompose a problem into its constituent parts. Each component becomes a self-contained object that contains its own instructions and data related to that object. Through this process, complexity is reduced and you can manage larger programs.

All object-oriented programming languages have three things in common: encapsulation, polymorphism, and inheritance. Although we will examine these concepts in detail later in this book, let's take a brief look at them now.

Encapsulation

As you probably know, all programs are composed of two fundamental elements: program statements (code) and data. *Code* is that part of a program that performs actions, and *data* is the information affected by those actions. *Encapsulation* is a programming mechanism that binds together code and the data it manipulates, and that keeps both safe from outside interference and misuse.

In an object-oriented language, code and data may be bound together in such a way that a self-contained *black box* is created. Within the box are all necessary data and code. When code and data are linked together in this fashion, an object is created. In other words, an *object* is the device that supports encapsulation.

Within an object, the code, data, or both may be private to that object or public. *Private* code or data is known to, and accessible only by, another part of the object. That is, private code or data may not be accessed by a piece of the program that exists outside the object. When code or data is *public,* other parts of your program may access it, even though it is defined within an object. Typically, the public parts of an object are used to provide a controlled interface to the private elements of the object.

Polymorphism

Polymorphism (from the Greek, meaning "many forms") is the quality that allows one interface to be used for a general class of actions. The specific action is determined by the exact nature of the situation. A simple example of polymorphism is found in the steering wheel of an automobile. The steering wheel (i.e., the interface) is the same no matter what type of actual steering mechanism is used. That is, the steering wheel works the same whether your car has manual steering, power steering, or rack-and-pinion steering. Therefore, once you know how to operate the steering wheel, you can drive any type of car. The same principle can also apply to programming. For example, consider a stack (which is a first-in, last-out list). You might have a program that requires three different types of stacks. One stack is used for integer values, one for floating-point values, and one for characters. In this case, the algorithm that implements each stack is the same, even though the data being stored differs. In a non-object-oriented language, you would be required to create three different sets of stack routines, calling each set by a different name, with each set having its own interface. However, because of polymorphism, in C++ you can create one general set of stack routines (one interface) that works for all three specific situations. This way, once you know how to use one stack, you can use them all.

More generally, the concept of polymorphism is often expressed by the phrase "one interface, multiple methods." This means that it is possible to design a generic interface to a group of related activities. Polymorphism helps reduce complexity by allowing the same interface to be used to specify a general class of action. It is the compiler's job to select the *specific action* (i.e., method) as it applies to each situation. You, the programmer, don't need to do this selection manually. You need only remember and utilize the general interface.

The first object-oriented programming languages were interpreters, so polymorphism was, of course, supported at run time. However, C++ is a compiled language. Therefore, in C++, both run-time and compile-time polymorphism are supported.

Inheritance

Inheritance is the process by which one object can acquire the properties of another object. The reason this is important is that it supports the concept of hierarchical classification. If you think about it, most knowledge is made manageable by hierarchical (i.e., top-down) classifications. For example, a Red Delicious apple is part of the classification *apple,* which in turn is part of the *fruit* class, which is under the larger class *food.* That is, the *food* class possesses certain qualities (edible, nutritious, etc.) that also apply, logically, to its *fruit* subclass. In addition to these qualities, the *fruit* class has specific characteristics (juicy, sweet, etc.) that distinguish it from other food. The *apple* class defines those qualities specific to an apple (grows on trees, not tropical, etc.). A Red Delicious apple would, in turn, inherit all the qualities of all preceding classes, and would define only those qualities that make it unique.

Without the use of hierarchies, each object would have to explicitly define all of its characteristics. However, using inheritance, an object needs to define only those qualities that make it unique within its class. It can inherit its general attributes from its parent. Thus, it is the inheritance mechanism that makes it possible for one object to be a specific instance of a more general case.

C++ Implements OOP

As you will see as you progress through this book, many of the features of C++ exist to provide support for encapsulation, polymorphism, and inheritance. Remember, however, that you can use C++ to write any type of program, using any type of approach. The fact that C++ supports object-oriented programming does not mean that you can only write object-oriented programs. As with its predecessor, C, one of C++'s strongest advantages is its flexibility.

How C++ Relates to Java and C#

As most readers will know, there are two other computer languages that are having a strong impact on programming: Java and C#. Java was developed by Sun Microsystems and C# was created by Microsoft. Because there is sometimes confusion about how these two languages relate to C++, a brief discussion of their relationship is in order.

C++ is the parent for both Java and C#. Although Java and C# added, removed, and modified various features, in total the syntax for all three languages is nearly identical. Furthermore, the object model used by C++ is similar to the ones used by Java and C#. Finally, the overall "look and feel" of these languages is very similar. This means that once you know C++, you can easily learn Java or C#. This is one reason that Java and C# borrowed C++'s syntax and object model; it facilitated their rapid adoption by legions of experienced C++ programmers. The reverse case is also true. If you know Java or C#, learning C++ is easy.

The main difference between C++, Java, and C# is the type of computing environment for which each is designed. C++ was created to produce high-performance programs for a specific type of CPU and operating system. For example, if you want to write a high-performance program that runs on an Intel Pentium under the Windows operating system, then C++ is the best language to use.

1

Java and C# were developed in response to the unique programming needs of the highly distributed networked environment that typifies much of contemporary computing. Java was designed to enable the creation of cross-platform portable code for the Internet. Using Java, it is possible to write a program that runs in a wide variety of environments, on a wide range of operating systems and CPUs. Thus, a Java program can move about freely on the Internet. C# was designed for Microsoft's .NET Framework, which supports mixed-language, component-based code that works in a networked environment.

Although both Java and C# enable the creation of portable code that works in a highly distributed environment, the price one pays for this portability is efficiency. Java programs execute slower than do C++ programs. The same is true for C#. Thus, if you want to create high-performance software, use C++. If you need to create highly portable software, use Java or C#.

One final point: C++, Java, and C# are designed to solve different sets of problems. It is not an issue of which language is best in and of itself. Rather, it is a question of which language is right for the job at hand.

CHAPTER 2

An Overview
of C++

One of the hardest things about learning a programming language is the fact that no element exists in isolation. Rather, the components of the language work together. It is this interrelatedness that makes it difficult to discuss one aspect of C++ without involving another. To help overcome this problem, this chapter provides a brief overview of several core C++ features, including the general form of a C++ program, some simple control statements, variables, and operators. It does not go into too many details, but rather concentrates on the general concepts common to all C++ programs. Most of the topics presented here are examined more closely in later chapters.

Since learning is best accomplished by doing, it is recommended that you work through the examples using your computer.

Your First C++ Program

Before getting into any theory, let's look at a simple C++ program. We will start by entering, compiling, and running the following program.

```
/* Program #1 - A first C++ program.

   Enter this program, then compile and run it.
*/

#include <iostream>
using namespace std;

// main() is where program execution begins.
int main()
{
  cout << "This is my first C++ program.";

  return 0;
}
```

You will follow these steps.

1. Enter the program.
2. Compile the program.
3. Execute the program.

Source code is the form of your program that you create. Object code is the form of your program that the computer executes.

Before beginning, it is necessary to define two terms. The first is *source code*. Source code is the version of your program that humans can read. The preceding listing is an example of source code. The executable version of your program is called *object code* or *executable code*. Object code is created by the compiler when it compiles your program.

Entering the Program

The programs shown in this book are available from Osborne's Web site: **www.osborne.com.** However, if you want to enter the programs by hand, you are free to do so. Typing in the programs yourself often helps you remember the key concepts. If you choose to enter a program by hand, you must use a text editor not a word processor. Word processors typically store format information along with text. The problem is that this format information will confuse the C++ compiler. If you are using a Windows platform, then you can use WordPad, or any other programming editor that you like.

The name of the file that holds the source code for the program is technically arbitrary. However, C++ programs are normally contained in files that use the file extension **.cpp**. Thus, you can call a C++ program file by any name, but it should use the **.cpp** extension. For this example, call the source file **MyProg.cpp** so that you can follow along. For most of the other programs in this book, simply use a name of your own choosing.

2

Compiling the Program

How you will compile **MyProg.cpp** depends upon your compiler, and what options you are using. Furthermore, many compilers, such as Microsoft's Visual C++ and Borland's C++ Builder, provide two different ways for compiling a program: the command line compiler and the Integrated Development Environment (IDE). Thus, it is not possible to give generalized instructions for compiling a C++ program that will work for all compilers. You must consult your compiler's instructions.

The preceding paragraph not withstanding, two of the most popular compilers are Visual C++ and C++ Builder. For the benefit of readers using one of these compilers, brief compilation instructions are provided here. For both Visual C++ or C++ Builder, the easiest way to compile and run the programs in this book is to the use the command-line compilers offered by these environments, and that is the method described.

To compile **MyProg.cpp** using Visual C++, you will use this command line.

```
C:\...>cl -GX MyProg.cpp
```

The –GX option enhances compilation. To use the Visual C++ command-line compiler, you must first execute the batch file VCVARS32.BAT, which is provided by Visual C++. (You will want to consult your Visual C++ documentation for details.) To compile **MyProg.cpp** using C++ Builder, use this command line.

```
C:\...>bcc32 Sample.cpp
```

The output from a C++ compiler is executable object code. For a Windows environment, the executable file will use the same name as the source file, but have the **.exe** extension. Thus, the executable version of **MyProg.cpp** will be in **MyProg.exe**.

NOTE: If you are receiving error messages when you try to compile the first sample program and are positive that you have entered it correctly, then you may be using an older C++ compiler that predates the ANSI/ISO standard for C++. If this is the case, refer to Appendix B for instructions on using an older compiler.

Run the Program

After a C++ program has been compiled, it is ready to be run. Since the output from a C++ compiler is executable object code, to run the program, simply enter its name at the command prompt. For example, to run **MyProg.exe** use this command line:

```
C:\...>MyProg
```

When run, the program displays the following output.

```
This is my first C++ program.
```

If you are using an Integrated Development Environment, then you can run a program by selecting Run from a menu. Consult the instructions for your specific compiler. As mentioned earlier, for the programs in this book, it is usually easier to compile and run from the command line.

One last point: The programs in this book are console-based, not window-based. That is, they run in a Command Prompt session. C++ is completely at home with Windows programming. Indeed, it is the most commonly used language for Windows development. However, none of the programs in this book use the Windows Graphic User Interface (GUI). The reason for this is easy to understand: Windows is a complicated environment to write programs for, involving many side issues unrelated to the C++ language. In contrast, console-based programs are much shorter and are the type of programs normally used to teach programming. Once you have mastered C++, you will be able to apply your knowledge to Windows programming with no trouble.

A Line-by-Line Explanation

Now that you have successfully compiled and run the first sample program it is time to understand how it works. Towards this end, we will examine the program line by line. The program begins with the lines

```
/* Program #1 - A first C++ program.

   Enter this program, then compile and run it.
*/
```

A comment is a remark that is embedded in your program.

This is a *comment*. Like most other programming languages, C++ lets you enter a remark into a program's source code. The contents of a comment are ignored by the compiler. The purpose of a comment is to describe or explain the operation of a program to anyone reading its source code. In the case of this comment, it identifies the program. In more complex programs, you will use comments to help explain what each feature of the program is for and how it goes about doing its work. In other words, you can use comments to provide a "play-by-play" description of what your program does.

In C++, there are two types of comments. The one you've just seen is called a *multiline comment*. This type of comment begins with a */*/ (a slash followed by an asterisk). It ends only when a **/* is encountered. Anything between these two comment symbols is completely ignored by the compiler. Multiline comments may be one or more lines long. The second type of comment is found a little further on in the program; we'll be discussing it shortly.

The next line of code looks like this:

```
#include <iostream>
```

The C++ language defines several *headers*, which contain information that is either necessary or useful to your program. For this program, the header **<iostream>** is needed. (It is used to support the C++ I/O system.) This header is provided with your compiler. A header is included in your program by using the **#include** directive. Later in this book, you will learn more about headers and why they are important.

The next line in the program is

```
using namespace std;
```

This tells the compiler to use the **std** namespace. Namespaces are a relatively recent addition to C++. Although namespaces are discussed in detail later in this book, here is a brief description. A *namespace* creates a declarative region in which various program elements can be placed. Elements declared in one namespace are separate from elements declared in another. Namespaces help in the organization of large programs. The **using** statement informs the compiler that you want to use the **std** namespace. This is the namespace in which the entire Standard C++ library is declared. By using the **std** namespace, you simplify access to the standard library.

The next line in the program is

```
// main() is where program execution begins.
```

This line shows you the second type of comment available in C++: the *single-line comment*. Single-line comments begin with **//** and stop at the end of the line. Typically, C++ programmers use multiline comments when writing larger, more detailed commentaries, and they use single-line comments when short remarks are needed. However, this is a matter of personal style.

The next line, as the preceding comment indicates, is where program execution begins:

```
int main()
```

main( ) is where
a C++ program
begins execution.

All C++ programs are composed of one or more functions. (Loosely speaking, a *function* is a subroutine.) Every C++ function must have a name, and the only function that any C++ program *must* include is the one shown here, called **main( )**. The **main( )** function is where program execution begins and (most commonly) ends. (Technically speaking, a C++ program begins with a call to **main( )** and, in most cases, ends when **main( )** returns.) The opening curly brace on the line that follows **main( )** marks the start of the **main( )** function's code. The **int** that precedes **main( )** specifies the type of data returned by **main( )**. As you will learn, C++ supports several built-in data types and **int** is one of them. It stands for *integer*.

The next line in the program is

```
cout << "This is my first C++ program.";
```

This is a console output statement. It causes the message **This is my first C++ program.** to be displayed on the screen. It accomplishes this by using the output operator <<. The << operator causes whatever expression is on its right side to be output to the device specified on its left side. **cout** is a predefined identifier that stands for *console output,* which (most generally) refers to the computer's screen. Thus, this statement causes the message to be output to the screen. Notice that this statement ends with a semicolon. In fact, all C++ statements end with a semicolon.

The message "This is my first C++ program." is a *string*. In C++, a string is a sequence of characters enclosed between double quotes. As you will see, strings are used frequently in C++.

The next line in the program is

```
return 0;
```

This line terminates **main( )** and causes it to return the value 0 to the calling process (which is typically the operating system). For most operating systems, a return value of 0 signifies that the program is terminating normally. Other values indicate that the program is terminating because of some error. **return** is one of C++'s keywords, and it is used to return a value from a function. All of your programs should return 0 when they terminate normally (that is, without error).

The closing curly brace at the end of the program formally concludes the program. Although the brace is not actually part of the object code of the program, conceptually you can think of a C++ program ending when the closing curly brace of **main( )** is executed. In fact, if the **return** statement were not part of this sample program, the program would automatically end when the closing curly brace was encountered.

Handling Syntax Errors

As you may know from your previous programming experience, it is quite easy to accidentally type something incorrectly when entering code into your computer. Fortunately, if you enter something incorrectly into your program, the compiler will report a *syntax error* message when it tries to compile it. Most C++ compilers attempt to make sense out of your source code no matter what you have written. For this reason, the error that is reported may not always reflect the actual cause of the problem. In the preceding program, for example, an accidental omission of the opening curly brace after **main( )** will cause some compilers to report the **cout** statement as the source of a syntax error. Therefore, when you receive a syntax error message, be prepared to look at the two or three lines of code that precede the point at which the error is flagged.

Many C++ compilers report not only actual errors, but also warnings. The C++ language was designed to be very forgiving, and to allow virtually anything that is syntactically correct to be compiled. However, some things, even though syntactically correct, are suspicious. When the compiler encounters one of these situations, it prints a warning. You, as the programmer, then decide whether its suspicions are justified. Frankly, some compilers are a bit too helpful and flag warnings on perfectly correct C++ statements. There are also compilers that allow you to turn on various options that report information about your program that you might like to know. Sometimes this information is reported in the form of a warning message even though there is nothing to be "warned" about. The programs in this book are in compliance with Standard C++, and when entered correctly, they will not generate any troublesome warning messages.

TIP: Most C++ compilers offer several levels of error (and warning) reporting. Generally, you can select the specific type of error reporting that you want. For example, most compilers offer options that report such things as inefficient constructs or the use of obsolete features. For the examples in this book, you will want to use your compiler's default (or "normal") error reporting. However, you should examine your compiler's documentation to see what options you have at your disposal. Many compilers have sophisticated features that can help you spot subtle errors before they become big problems. Understanding your compiler's error reporting system is worth the time and effort that you spend.

A Second Simple Program

Perhaps no other construct is as important to a programming language as the assignment of a value to a variable. A *variable* is a named memory location that may be assigned a value. Further, the value of a variable can be changed one or more times during the execution of a program. That is, the content of a variable is changeable, not fixed.

The following program creates a variable called **x,** gives it the value 1023, and then displays the message **This program prints the value of x: 1023** on the screen.

```
// Program #2 - Using a variable

#include <iostream>
using namespace std;

int main()
{
  int x; // this declares a variable

  x = 1023; // this assigns 1023 to x

  cout << "This program prints the value of x: ";
  cout << x; // This displays 1023

  return 0;
}
```

This program introduces two new concepts. First, the statement

```
int x;  // this declares a variable
```

The type of a variable determines the values it may hold.

declares a variable called **x** of type integer. In C++, all variables must be declared before they are used. Further, the type of values that the variable can hold must also be specified. This is called the *type* of the variable. In this case, **x** may hold integer values. These are whole-number values whose range will be at least –32,768 to 32,767. In C++, to declare a variable to be of type integer, precede its name with the keyword **int**. Later, you will see that C++ supports a wide variety of built-in variable types. (You can create your own data types, too.)

The second new feature is found in the next line of code:

```
x = 1023; // this assigns 1023 to x
```

As the comment suggests, this assigns the value 1023 to **x**. In C++, the assignment operator is the single equal sign. It copies the value on its right side into the variable on its left. After the assignment, the variable **x** will contain the number 1023.

The two **cout** statements display the output generated by the program. Notice how the following statement is used to display the value of **x**:

```
cout << x; // This displays 1023
```

In general, if you want to display the value of a variable, simply put it on the right side of **<<** in a **cout** statement. In this specific case, because **x** contains the number 1023, it is this number that is displayed on the screen. Before moving on, you might want to try giving **x** other values and watching the results.

A More Practical Example

Your first two sample programs, while illustrating several important features of the C++ language, are not very useful. The next sample program actually performs a meaningful task: It converts gallons to liters. It also shows how to input information.

```
// This program converts gallons to liters.

#include <iostream>
using namespace std;

int main()
{
  int gallons, liters;

  cout << "Enter number of gallons: ";
  cin >> gallons; // this inputs from the user

  liters = gallons * 4; // convert to liters
```

2

```
    cout << "Liters: " << liters;

    return 0;
}
```

This program first displays a prompting message on the screen, and then waits for you to enter a whole number amount of gallons. (Remember, integer types cannot have fractional components.) The program then displays the approximate liter equivalent. There are actually 3.7854 liters in a gallon, but since integers are used in this example, the conversion is rounded to 4 liters per gallon. For example, if you enter 1 gallon, the program responds with the metric equivalent of 4 liters.

The first new thing you see in this program is that two variables, **gallons** and **liters**, are declared following the **int** keyword, in the form of a comma-separated list. In general, you can declare any number of variables of the same type by separating them with commas. (As an alternative, the program could have used multiple **int** statements to accomplish the same thing.)

The function uses this statement to actually input a value entered by the user:

```
cin >> gallons; // this inputs from the user
```

cin is another predefined identifier that is provided with your C++ compiler. **cin** stands for *console input* (which generally means input from the keyboard). The input operator is the **>>** symbol. The value entered by the user (which must be an integer, in this case) is put into the variable that is on the right side of the **>>** (in this case, **gallons**).

There is one more new thing in this program. Examine this line:

```
cout << "Liters: " << liters;
```

It uses two output operators within the same output statement. Specifically, it outputs the string "Liters: " followed by the value of **liters**. In general, you can chain together as many output operations as you like within one output statement. Just use a separate **<<** for each item.

A New Data Type

Although the gallons-to-liters program is fine for rough approximations, because it uses integers, it leaves something to be desired when a more accurate answer is needed. As stated, integer data types cannot represent any fractional value. If you need fractions, then you must use a floating-point data type. One of these is called **double**, which represents double-precision floating-point. Data of this type will typically be in the range 1.7E–308 to 1.7E+308. Operations on floating-point numbers preserve any fractional part of the outcome and, hence, provide a more accurate conversion.

The following version of the conversion program uses floating-point values:

```
/* This program converts gallons to liters using
   floating point numbers. */
```

```
#include <iostream>
using namespace std;

int main()
{
  double gallons, liters;

  cout << "Enter number of gallons: ";
  cin >> gallons; // this inputs from the user

  liters = gallons * 3.7854; // convert to liters

  cout << "Liters: " << liters;

  return 0;
}
```

There are two changes to this program from the previous version. First, **gallons** and **liters** are declared as **double**. Second, the conversion coefficient is now specified as 3.7854, allowing a more accurate conversion. Whenever C++ encounters a number that contains a decimal point, it automatically knows that it is a floating-point constant. One other thing: notice that the **cout** and **cin** statements are unchanged from the previous version of this program that used **int** variables. C++'s I/O system automatically adjusts to whatever type of data you give it.

Try the program at this time. Enter 1 gallon when prompted. The equivalent number of liters is now 3.7854.

A Quick Review

Before proceeding, let's review the most important things that you have learned:

1. All C++ programs must have a **main( )** function, and it is there that program execution begins.
2. All variables must be declared before they are used.
3. C++ supports a variety of data types, including integer and floating point.
4. The output operator is **<<**, and when used with **cout**, it causes information to be displayed on the screen.
5. The input operator is **>>**, and when used with **cin**, it reads information from the keyboard.
6. Program execution stops at the end of **main( )**.

Functions

A C++ program is constructed from building blocks called *functions*. A function is a subroutine that contains one or more C++ statements and performs one or more tasks. In well-written C++ code, each function performs only one task.

Each function has a name, and it is this name that is used to call the function. In general, you can give a function whatever name you please. However, remember that **main( )** is reserved for the function that begins execution of your program.

In C++, one function cannot be embedded within another function. Unlike Pascal, Modula-2, and some other programming languages that allow the nesting of functions, C++ considers all functions to be separate entities. (Of course, one function may call another.)

When denoting functions in text, this book uses a convention that has become common when writing about C++: A function will have parentheses after its name. For example, if a function's name is **getval**, then it will be written **getval( )** when its name is used in a sentence. This notation will help you distinguish variable names from function names in this book.

In your first programs, **main( )** was the only function. As stated earlier, **main( )** is the first function executed when your program begins to run, and it must be included in all C++ programs. There are two types of functions that will be used by your programs. The first type is written by you. **main( )** is an example of this type of function. The other type of function is implemented by the compiler and is found in the compiler's *standard library*. (The standard library is discussed shortly, but in general terms, it is a collection of predefined functions.) Programs that you write will usually contain a mix of functions that you create and those supplied by the compiler.

Since functions form the foundation of C++, let's take a closer look at them now.

A Program with Two Functions

The following program contains two functions: **main( )** and **myfunc( )**. Before running this program (or reading the description that follows), examine it closely and try to figure out exactly what it displays on the screen.

```
/* This program contains two functions: main()
   and myfunc().
*/
#include <iostream>
using namespace std;

void myfunc(); // myfunc's prototype

int main()
{
  cout << "In main()";
  myfunc(); // call myfunc()
  cout << "Back in main()";

  return 0;
}

void myfunc()
{
  cout << " Inside myfunc() ";
}
```

The program works like this. First, **main( )** begins, and it executes the first **cout** statement. Next, **main( )** calls **myfunc( )**. Notice how this is achieved: the function's name, **myfunc**, appears, followed by parentheses, and finally by a semicolon. A function call is a C++ statement and, therefore, must end with a semicolon. Next, **myfunc( )** executes its **cout** statement, and then returns to **main( )** at the line of code immediately following the call. Finally, **main( )** executes its second **cout** statement, and then terminates. The output on the screen is this:

```
In main() Inside myfunc() Back in main()
```

There is one other important statement in the preceding program:

```
void myfunc(); // myfunc's prototype
```

A prototype declares a function prior to its first use.

As the comment states, this is the *prototype* for **myfunc( )**. Although we will discuss prototypes in detail later, a few words are necessary now. A *function prototype* declares the function prior to its definition. The prototype allows the compiler to know the function's return type, as well as the number and type of any parameters that the function may have. The compiler needs to know this information prior to the first time the function is called. This is why the prototype occurs before **main( )**. The only function that does not require a prototype is **main( )**, because it is predefined by C++.

As you can see, **myfunc( )** does not contain a **return** statement. The keyword **void**, which precedes both the prototype for **myfunc( )** and its definition, formally states that **myfunc( )** does not return a value. In C++, functions that don't return values are declared as **void**.

Function Arguments

It is possible to pass one or more values to a function. A value passed to a function is called an *argument*. In the programs that you have studied so far, none of the functions take any arguments. Specifically, neither **main( )** nor **myfunc( )** in the preceding examples have an argument. However, functions in C++ can have one or more arguments. The upper limit is determined by the compiler you are using, but Standard C++ specifies that at least 256 arguments will be allowed.

An argument is a value passed to a function when it is called.

Here is a short program that uses one of C++'s standard library (i.e., built-in) functions, called **abs( )**, to display the absolute value of a number. The **abs( )** function takes one argument, converts it into its absolute value, and returns the result.

```
// Use the abs() function.
#include <iostream>
#include <cstdlib>
using namespace std;

int main()
{
  cout << abs(-10);

  return 0;
}
```

Here, the value –10 is passed as an argument to **abs( )**. The **abs( )** function receives the argument that it is called with and returns its absolute value, which is 10 in this case. Although **abs( )** takes only one argument, other functions can have several. The key point here is that when a function requires an argument, it is passed by specifying it between the parentheses that follow the function's name.

2

The return value of **abs( )** is used by the **cout** statement to display the absolute value of –10 on the screen. The reason this works is that whenever a function is part of a larger expression, it is automatically called so that its return value can be obtained. In this case, the return value of **abs( )** becomes the value of the right side of the **<<** operator, and is therefore displayed on the screen.

Notice one other thing about the preceding program: it also includes the header **<cstdlib>**. This is the header required by **abs( )**. In general, whenever you use a library function, you must include its header. The header provides the prototype for the library function, among other things.

A parameter is a variable defined by a function that receives an argument.

When you create a function that takes one or more arguments, the variables that will receive those arguments must also be declared. These variables are called the *parameters* of the function. For example, the function shown next prints the product of the two integer arguments passed to the function when it is called.

```
void mul(int x, int y)
{
  cout << x * y << " ";
}
```

Each time **mul( )** is called, it will multiply the value passed to **x** by the value passed to **y**. Remember, however, that **x** and **y** are simply the operational variables that receive the values you use when calling the function.

Consider the following short program, which illustrates how to call **mul( )**:

```
// A simple program that demonstrates mul().

#include <iostream>
using namespace std;

void mul(int x, int y); // mul()'s prototype

int main()
{
  mul(10, 20);
  mul(5, 6);
  mul(8, 9);

  return 0;
}

void mul(int x, int y)
{
  cout << x * y << " ";
}
```

This program will print 200, 30, and 72 on the screen. When **mul( )** is called, the C++ compiler copies the value of each argument into the matching parameter. That is, in the first call to **mul( )**, 10 is copied into **x** and 20 is copied into **y**. In the second call, 5 is copied into **x** and 6 into **y**. In the third call, 8 is copied into **x** and 9 into **y**.

If you have never worked with a language that allows parameterized functions, then the preceding process may seem a bit strange. Don't worry; as you see more examples of C++ programs, the concept of arguments, parameters, and functions will become clear.

REMEMBER: The term *argument* refers to the value that is used to call a function. The variable that receives the value of an argument is called a *parameter*. In fact, functions that take arguments are called parameterized functions.

In C++ functions, when there are two or more arguments, they are separated by commas. In this book, the term *argument list* refers to comma-separated arguments. The argument list for **mul( )** is x,y.

Functions Returning Values

Many of the C++ library functions that you use will return values. For example, the **abs( )** function used earlier returned the absolute value of its argument. Functions you write may also return values to the calling routine. In C++, a function uses a **return** statement to return a value. The general form of **return** is

   return *value*;

where *value* is the value being returned.

To illustrate the process of functions returning values, the foregoing program can be rewritten, as shown next. In this version, **mul( )** returns the product of its arguments. Notice that the placement of the function on the right side of an assignment statement assigns the return value to a variable.

```
// Returning a value.

#include <iostream>
using namespace std;

int mul(int x, int y); // mul()'s prototype

int main()
{
  int answer;

  answer = mul(10, 11); // assign return value
  cout << "The answer is " <<  answer;

  return 0;
```

```
}

// This function returns a value.
int mul(int x, int y)
{
  return x * y; // return product of x and y
}
```

In this example, **mul( )** returns the value of **x*y** by using the **return** statement. This value is then assigned to **answer**. That is, the value returned by the **return** statement becomes **mul( )**'s value in the calling routine.

Since **mul( )** now returns a value, it is not preceded by the keyword **void**. (Remember, **void** is used only when a function does *not* return a value.) Just as there are different types of variables, there are also different types of return values. Here, **mul( )** returns an integer. The return type of a function precedes its name in both its prototype and its definition.

Before moving on, a short historical note is in order. For early versions of C++, if no return type is specified, then a function is assumed to return an integer value. For example, in old code you might find **mul( )** written like this:

```
// An old-style way to code mul().
mul(int x, int y) // default to int return type
{
  return x * y; // return product of x and y
}
```

Here, the type returned by **mul( )** is integer by default, since no other return type is specified. However, the "default-to-int" rule was dropped by Standard C++. Although most compilers will continue to support the "default-to-int" rule for the sake of backward compatibility, you should explicitly specify the return type of every function that you write. Since older code frequently made use of the default integer return type, this change is also something to keep in mind when working on legacy code.

When a **return** statement is encountered, the function returns immediately, skipping any remaining code. It is possible to cause a function to return by using the **return** statement without any value attached to it, but this form of **return** can be used only with functions that have no return values and that are declared as **void**. Also, there can be more than one **return** in a function.

The main( ) Function

As you know, the **main( )** function is special because it is the first function called when your program executes. It signifies the beginning of your program. Unlike some programming languages that always begin execution at the "top" of the program, C++ begins every program with a call to the **main( )** function, no matter where that function is located in the program. (However, it is common for **main( )** to be the first function in your program so that it can be easily found.)

There can be only one **main( )** in a program. If you try to include more than one, your program will not know where to begin execution. Actually, most compilers will catch this type of error and report it. As mentioned earlier, since **main( )** is predefined by C++, it does not require a prototype.

The General Form of C++ Functions

The preceding examples have shown some specific types of functions. However, all C++ functions share a common form, which is shown here:

```
return-type function-name(parameter list)
{
  .
  . body of the function
  .
}
```

Let's look closely at the different parts that make up a function.

The return type of a function determines the type of data that the function will return. As you will see later in this book, you can specify nearly any return type you like. Keep in mind, however, that no function has to return a value. If it does not return a value, its return type is **void**. But if it does return a value, that value must be of a type that is compatible with the function's return type.

Every function must have a name. After the name is a parenthesized parameter list. The *parameter list* specifies the names and types of variables that will be passed information. If a function has no parameters, the parentheses are empty.

Next, braces surround the body of the function. The body of the function is composed of the C++ statements that define what the function does. The function terminates and returns to the calling procedure when the closing curly brace is reached or when a **return** statement is encountered.

Some Output Options

Up to this point, there has been no occasion to advance output to the next line—that is, to execute a carriage return-linefeed sequence. However, the need for this will arise very soon. In C++, the carriage return-linefeed sequence is generated using the *newline* character. To put a newline character into a string, use this code: **\n** (a backslash followed by a lowercase n). To see an example of a carriage return-linefeed sequence, try the following program:

```
/* This program demonstrates the \n code, which
   generates a new line.
*/
#include <iostream>
using namespace std;

int main()
{
  cout << "one\n";
  cout << "two\n";
  cout << "three";
```

```
   cout << "four";

   return 0;
}
```

This program produces the following output:

```
one
two
threefour
```

The newline character can be placed anywhere in the string, not just at the end. You might want to try experimenting with the newline character now, just to make sure you understand exactly what it does.

Two Simple Commands

So that meaningful examples can be developed in the next chapter, it is necessary for you to understand, in their simplest form, two C++ commands: the **if** and the **for**. Later, these commands will be explored completely.

The if Statement

if selects between two paths of execution.

The C++ **if** statement operates in much the same way that an IF statement operates in any other language. Its simplest form is

> if(*condition*) *statement*;

where *condition* is an expression that is evaluated to be either true or false. In C++, true is non-zero and false is zero. If the condition is true, then the statement will execute. If it is false, then the statement will not execute. The following fragment displays the phrase **10 is less than 11** on the screen.

```
if(10 < 11) cout << "10 is less than 11";
```

The comparison operators, such as **<** (less than) and **>=** (greater than or equal), are similar to those in other languages. However, in C++, the equality operator is **==**. The following **cout** statement will not execute, because the condition of equality is false; that is, because 10 is not equal to 11, the statement will not display **hello** on the screen.

```
if(10==11) cout << "hello";
```

Of course, the operands inside an **if** statement need not be constants. They can also be variables, or even calls to functions.

The following program shows an example of the **if** statement. It prompts the user for two numbers and reports if the first value is less than the second.

```
// This program illustrates the if statement.

#include <iostream>
```

```
using namespace std;

int main()
{
  int a, b;

  cout << "Enter first number: ";
  cin >> a;
  cout << "Enter second number: ";
  cin >> b;

  if(a < b) cout << "First number is less than second.";

  return 0;
}
```

The for Loop

for is one of the loop statements provided by C++.

The **for** loop repeats a statement a specified number of times. The **for** loop can operate much like the FOR loop in other languages, including Java, C#, Pascal, and BASIC. Its simplest form is

for(*initialization, condition, increment*) *statement*;

Here, *initialization* sets a loop control variable to an initial value. *condition* is an expression that is tested each time the loop repeats. As long as *condition* is true (non-zero), the loop keeps running. The *increment* is an expression that determines how the loop control variable is incremented each time the loop repeats.

For example, the following program prints the numbers 1 through 100 on the screen.

```
// A program that illustrates the for loop.

#include <iostream>
using namespace std;

int main()
{
  int count;

  for(count=1; count<=100; count=count+1)
    cout << count << " ";

  return 0;
}
```

Figure 2-1 illustrates the execution of the **for** loop in this example. As you can see, **count** is initialized to 1. Each time the loop repeats, the condition **count<=100** is tested. If it is true, the value is output and **count** is increased by one. When **count** reaches a value greater than 100, the condition becomes false, and the loop stops running.

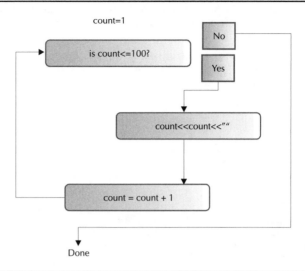

How the **for**
loop works.
Figure 2-1.

In professionally written C++ code, you will seldom see a statement like
count=count+1, because for this sort of statement, C++ supports a special
shorthand that looks like this: **count++**. The **++** is the *increment* operator. It
increases its operand by 1. The complement of **++** is **– –**, the *decrement* operator,
which decreases its operand by 1. For example, the preceding **for** statement will
generally be written like this:

```
for(count=1; count<=100; count++)
  cout << count << " ";
```

This is the form that will be used throughout the rest of this book.

Blocks of Code

Because C++ is a structured (as well as an object-oriented) language, it supports
the creation of blocks of code. A *block* is a logically connected group of program
statements that is treated as a unit. In C++, a code block is created by placing a
sequence of statements between opening and closing curly braces. In this example,

```
if(x<10) {
  cout << "too low, try again";
  cin >> x;
}
```

A block is
a logically
connected unit
of statements.

the two statements after the **if** and between the curly braces are both executed only if
x is less than 10. These two statements, together with the braces, represent a block of
code. They are a logical unit: One of the statements cannot execute without the other
also executing. In C++, the target of most commands can be either a single statement

or a code block. Code blocks allow many algorithms to be implemented with greater clarity and efficiency. They can also help you better conceptualize the true nature of an algorithm.

The program that follows uses a block of code. Enter and run the program so that you can see the effect of the block.

```cpp
// This program demonstrates a block of code.

#include <iostream>
using namespace std;

int main()
{
  int a, b;

  cout << "Enter first number: ";
  cin >> a;
  cout << "Enter second number: ";
  cin >> b;

  if(a < b) {
    cout << "First number is less than second.\n";
    cout << "Their difference is: " << b-a;
  }

  return 0;
}
```

This program prompts the user to enter two numbers from the keyboard. If the first number is less than the second number, then both **cout** statements are executed. Otherwise, both are skipped. At no time can just one of them execute.

Semicolons and Positioning

In C++, the semicolon is a statement *terminator*. That is, each individual statement must be ended with a semicolon. It indicates the end of one logical entity.

As you know, a block is a set of logically connected statements that are surrounded by opening and closing braces. A block is *not* terminated with a semicolon. Since a block is a group of statements, with a semicolon after each statement, it makes sense that a block is not terminated by a semicolon; instead, the end of the block is indicated by the closing brace. This is also the reason that there is no semicolon following the closing brace of a function.

C++ does not recognize the end of the line as a terminator. For this reason, it does not matter where on a line you put a statement. For example,

```cpp
x = y;
y = y+1;
mul(x, y);
```

is the same as

```
x = y;   y = y+1;   mul(x, y);
```

to a C++ compiler.

2

Indentation Practices

You may have noticed in the previous examples that certain statements were indented. C++ is a free-form language, meaning that it does not matter where you place statements relative to each other on a line. However, over the years, a common and accepted indentation style has developed that provides very readable programs. This book follows that style, and it is recommended that you do so as well. Using this style, you indent one level after each opening brace, and move back out one level after each closing brace. There are certain statements that encourage some additional indenting; these will be covered later.

C++ Keywords

There are 63 keywords currently defined for Standard C++. These are shown in Table 2-1. Together with the formal C++ syntax, they form the C++ programming language. Also, early versions of C++ defined the **overload** keyword, but it is now obsolete.

asm	else	new	this
auto	enum	operator	throw
bool	explicit	private	true
break	export	protected	try
case	extern	public	typedef
catch	false	register	typeid
char	float	reinterpret_cast	typename
class	for	return	union
const	friend	short	unsigned
const_cast	goto	signed	using
continue	if	sizeof	virtual
default	inline	static	void
delete	int	static_cast	volatile
do	long	struct	wchar_t
double	mutable	switch	while
dynamic_cast	namespace	template	

The C++
Keywords
Table 2-1.

Keep in mind that the case of the keywords is significant. C++ is a case-sensitive language, and it requires that all keywords be in lowercase. For example, **RETURN** will *not* be recognized as the keyword **return**.

Identifiers in C++

In C++ an *identifier* is a name assigned to a function, a variable, or any other user-defined item. Identifiers can be from one to several characters long. The first 1024 characters will be significant. Variable names may start with any letter of the alphabet or with an underscore. Next may be either a letter, a digit, or an underscore. The underscore can be used to enhance the readability of a variable name, as in **first_name**. Uppercase and lowercase are different; that is, to C++, **count** and **COUNT** are separate names. Here are some examples of acceptable identifiers:

```
first    last    Addr1    top_of_file
name23    _temp    t    s23e3    MyVar
```

You cannot use any of the C++ keywords as identifier names. Also, you should not use the name of any standard function, such as **abs**, for an identifier. Beyond these two restrictions, good programming practice dictates that you use identifier names that reflect the meaning or usage of the items being named.

The Standard C++ Library

In the discussion of the sample programs earlier in this chapter, it was mentioned that **abs( )** is provided with your C++ compiler. **abs( )** is not part of the C++ language per se, yet you will find it included with every C++ compiler. This function, and many others, are found in the *standard library*. We will be making extensive use of library functions in the example programs throughout this book.

The C++ standard library contains many predefined functions that you can use in your programs.

C++ defines a rather large set of functions that will be contained in the standard library. These functions are designed to perform many commonly needed tasks, including I/O operations, mathematical computations, and string handling. When you use a library function, the C++ compiler automatically links the object code for that function to the object code of your program.

Because the C++ standard library is so large, it already contains many of the functions that you will need to use in your programs. The library functions act as building blocks that you simply assemble. You should explore your compiler's library documentation. You may be surprised at how varied the library functions are. If you write a function that you will use again and again, it too can be stored in a library.

In addition to providing library functions, every C++ compiler also contains a *class library*, which is an object-oriented library. Finally, C++ defines the Standard Template Library (STL), which provides reusable routines that can be configured to meet your specific requirements. However, you will need to wait until you learn about classes, objects, and templates before you can make use of the class library or the STL.

CHAPTER 3

The Basic Data Types

As you saw in Chapter 2, all variables in C++ must be declared prior to their use. This is necessary because the compiler must know what type of data a variable contains before it can properly compile any statement that uses the variable. In C++ there are seven basic data types: character, wide character, integer, floating point, double floating point, Boolean, and somewhat surprisingly, valueless. The keywords used to declare variables of these types are **char**, **wchar_t**, **int**, **float**, **double**, **bool**, and **void**, respectively. Common sizes and ranges of each data type are shown in Table 3-1. Remember, the sizes and ranges used by your compiler may vary from those listed here. The most common variance occurs between 16-bit and 32-bit environments. In general, an integer in a 16-bit environment is 16 bits wide. In a 32-bit environment, an integer is usually 32 bits wide.

Variables of type **char** are used to hold 8-bit ASCII characters such as A, B, or C, or any other 8-bit quantity. To specify a character, you must enclose it between single quotes. The type **wchar_t** is designed to hold characters that are part of large character sets. As you may know, many human languages, such as Chinese, define a large number of characters, more than will fit within the 8 bits provided by the **char** type. The **wchar_t** type was added to C++ to accommodate this situation. While we won't be making much use of **wchar_t** in this book, it is something that you will want to look into if you are tailoring programs for the international market.

Variables of type **int** can hold integer quantities that do not require fractional components. Variables of this type are often used for controlling loops and conditional statements. Variables of the types **float** and **double** are employed either when a fractional component is required or when your application requires very large or small numbers. The difference between a **float** and a **double** variable is the magnitude of the largest (and smallest) number that each one can hold. As shown in Table 3-1, a **double** in C++ can store a number approximately ten times larger than a **float**.

Type	Typical Bit Width	Typical Range
char	8	–128 to 127
wchar_t	16	0 to 65,535
int (16-bit environments)	16	–32,768 to 32,767
int (32-bit environments)	32	–2,147,483,648 to 2,147,483,647
float	32	3.4E–38 to 3.4E+38
double	64	1.7E–308 to 1.7E+308
bool	N/A	true or false
void	N/A	valueless

Common Sizes and Ranges of the Basic Types in C++

Table 3-1.

The **bool** type stores Boolean (i.e., true/false) values. C++ defines two Boolean constants: **true** and **false**, which are the only values that a **bool** variable may have.

As you have seen, **void** is used to declare any function that does not return a value. Other purposes of **void** are discussed later in this book.

Declaration of Variables

The general form of a variable declaration statement is shown here:

> *type variable_list;*

Here, *type* must be a valid C++ data type, and *variable_list* may consist of one or more identifier names separated by commas. Some declarations are shown here, for example:

```
int i, j, k;

char ch, chr;

float f, balance;

double d;
```

In C++, the name of a variable has nothing to do with its type.

Standard C++ states that at least the first 1,024 characters of any identifier name (including variable names) will be significant. This means that if two variable names differ in at least one character within the first 1,024 characters, then the compiler will consider them to be different names.

There are three places where variables will be declared: inside functions, in the definition of function parameters, and outside of all functions. These variables are called *local variables, formal parameters,* and *global variables,* respectively. Although we will examine the importance of these three different types of variables in greater detail later in this book, let's take a brief look at them now.

Local Variables

Variables that are declared inside a function are local variables. They can be used only by statements that are inside that function. Local variables are not known to functions outside their own. Consider this example:

```
#include <iostream>
using namespace std;

void func();

int main()
```

```
{
  int x; // local to main()

  x = 10;
  func();
  cout << "\n";
  cout << x; // displays 10

  return 0;
}

void func()
{
  int x; // local to func()

  x = -199;
  cout << x; // displays -199
}
```

A local variable is known only to the function in which it is declared.

Here, the integer variable **x** is declared twice, once in **main( )** and once in **func( )**. The **x** in **main( )** has no bearing on, or relationship to, the **x** in **func( )**. Specifically, changes to the **x** inside **func( )** will not affect the **x** inside **main( )**. Therefore, this program will print –199 and 10 on the screen.

In C++, local variables are created when the function is called and are destroyed when the function is exited. Correspondingly, the storage for these local variables is created and destroyed in the same way. For these reasons, local variables do not maintain their values between function calls. (That is, the value of a local variable is lost each time its function returns.)

In some C++ literature, a local variable is called a *dynamic variable* or an *automatic variable*. However, this book will continue to use the term *local variable* because it is the more common term.

Formal Parameters

A formal parameter is a local variable that receives the value of an argument passed to a function.

As you saw in Chapter 2, if a function has arguments, then those arguments must be declared. These are called the *formal parameters* of the function. As shown in the following fragment, this declaration occurs after the function name, inside the parentheses:

```
int func1(int first, int last, char ch)
{
  .
  .
  .
}
```

The **func1( )** function has three arguments, called **first**, **last**, and **ch**. You must tell C++ what type of variables these are by declaring them, as shown above. Once this has been done, these arguments receive information passed to the function. They may also be used inside the function as normal local variables. For example, you may make assignments to a function's formal parameters or use them in any allowable C++ expression. Even though these variables perform the special task of receiving the value of the arguments passed to the function, they can be used like any other local variable. Like other local variables, their value is lost once the function terminates.

Global Variables

Global variables are known throughout your entire program.

3

You may be wondering how to make a variable and its data stay in existence throughout the entire execution of your program. You can do this in C++ by using a global variable. Unlike local variables, *global variables* will hold their value throughout the lifetime of your program. You create global variables by declaring them outside of all functions. A global variable can be accessed by any function. That is, a global variable is available for use throughout your entire program.

In the following program, you can see that the variable **count** has been declared outside of all functions. Its declaration is before the **main( )** function. However, it could have been placed anywhere, as long as it was not in a function. Remember, though, that since you must declare a variable before you use it, it is best to declare global variables at the top of the program.

```cpp
#include <iostream>
using namespace std;

void func1();
void func2();

int count; // this is a global variable

int main()
{
  int i; // this is a local variable

  for(i=0; i<10; i++) {
    count = i * 2;
    func1();
  }

  return 0;
}

void func1()
{
  cout << "count: " << count; // access global count
  cout << '\n'; // output a newline
  func2();
}

void func2()
```

```
{
  int count; // this is a local variable

  for(count=0; count<3; count++) cout << '.';
}
```

Looking closely at this program, it should be clear that although neither **main( )** nor **func1( )** has declared the variable **count**, both may use it. In **func2( )**, however, a local variable called **count** is declared. When **func2( )** uses **count**, it is referring to its local variable, not the global one. It is important to remember that if a global variable and a local variable have the same name, all references to that variable name inside the function in which the local variable is declared will refer to the local variable and not to the global variable.

Some Type Modifiers

C++ allows the **char**, **int**, and **double** data types to have *modifiers* preceding them. A modifier is used to alter the meaning of the base type so that it more precisely fits the needs of various situations. The data type modifiers are listed here:

signed

unsigned

long

short

The modifiers **signed**, **unsigned**, **long**, and **short** can be applied to integer base types. In addition, **signed** and **unsigned** can be applied to **char**, and **long** can be applied to **double**. Tables 3-2a and 3-2b show all the allowed combinations of the basic types and the type modifiers for both 16- and 32-bit environments. The tables also show the most common size and range for each type. You should check your compiler's documentation for the actual range supported by your compiler.

As you look at the tables, pay special attention to the size of a short integer, an integer, and a long integer. Notice that in most 16-bit environments, the size of an integer is the same as a short integer. Also notice that in most 32-bit environments, the size of an integer is the same as a long integer. The reason for this is found in C++'s definition of its basic types. Standard C++ states that a long integer will be at least as large as an integer, and that an integer will be at least as large as a short integer. Further, the size of an integer should be based upon the execution environment. This means that for 16-bit environments, integers are 16 bits, and for 32-bit environments, integers are 32 bits. However, the smallest allowable size for an integer in any environment is 16 bits. Since C++ defines only the relationship and a set of guidelines for the size of the integer types, there is no requirement (or guarantee) that one type will be larger than another. However, the sizes shown in both tables hold true for many compilers.

Type	Bit Width	Common Range
char	8	–128 to 127
unsigned char	8	0 to 255
signed char	8	–128 to 127
int	16	–32,768 to 32,767
unsigned int	16	0 to 65,535
signed int	16	–32,768 to 32,767
short int	16	same as int
unsigned short int	16	same as unsigned int
signed short int	16	same as short int
long int	32	–2,147,483,648 to 2,147,483,647
unsigned long int	32	0 to 4,294,967,295
signed long int	32	–2,147,483,648 to 2,147,483,647
float	32	3.4E–38 to 3.4E+38
double	64	1.7E–308 to 1.7E+308
long double	80	3.4E–4932 to 1.1E+4932
bool	N/A	true or false
wchar_t	16	0 to 65,535

All Possible Combinations of the Basic Types and Modifiers in C++, Along With Their Common Bit Lengths and Ranges for a 16-bit Environment
Table 3-2a.

3

Although it is allowed, the use of **signed** on integers is redundant because the default declaration assumes a signed value. Technically, whether **char** is signed or unsigned by default is implementation-defined. However, for most compilers, **char** is signed. In these environments, the use of **signed** on **char** is also redundant. For the rest of this book, it will be assumed that **char**s are signed entities.

The difference between signed and unsigned integers is in the way the high-order bit of the integer is interpreted. If a signed integer is specified, then the C++ compiler will generate code that assumes that the high-order bit of an integer is to be used as a *sign flag*. If the sign flag is 0, then the number is positive; if it is 1, then the number is negative. Negative numbers are almost always represented using the *two's complement* approach. In this method, all bits in the number are reversed, and then 1 is added to this number.

Signed integers are important for a great many algorithms, but they have only half the absolute magnitude of their unsigned relatives. For example, assuming 16-bit integers, here is 32,767:

```
0 1 1 1 1 1 1 1   1 1 1 1 1 1 1 1
```

Type	Bit Width	Common Range
char	8	–128 to 127
unsigned char	8	0 to 255
signed char	8	–128 to 127
int	32	–2,147,483,648 to 2,147,483,647
unsigned int	32	0 to 4,294,967,295
signed int	32	–2,147,483,648 to 2,147,483,647
short int	16	–32,768 to 32,767
unsigned short int	16	0 to 65,535
signed short int	16	–32,768 to 32,767
long int	32	Same as int
unsigned long int	32	Same as unsigned int
signed long int	32	Same as signed int
float	32	3.4E–38 to 3.4E+38
double	64	1.7E–308 to 1.7E+308
long double	80	3.4E–4932 to 1.1E+4932
bool	N/A	true or false
wchar_t	16	0 to 65,535

All Possible Combinations of the Basic Types and Modifiers in C++, Along With Their Common Bit Lengths and Ranges for a 32-bit Environment
Table 3-2b.

For a signed value, if the high-order bit were set to 1, the number would then be interpreted as –1 (assuming the two's complement format). However, if you declared this to be an **unsigned int**, then when the high-order bit was set to 1, the number would become 65,535.

To understand the difference between the way that signed and unsigned integers are interpreted by C++, you should run this short program now:

```
#include <iostream>
using namespace std;

/* This program shows the difference between
   signed and unsigned integers.
*/
int main()
{
  short int i; // a signed short integer
  short unsigned int j; // an unsigned short integer

  j = 60000;
```

```
   i = j;
   cout << i << " " << j;

   return 0;
}
```

When this program is run, the output is **–5536 60000**. This is because the bit pattern that represents 60,000 as a short unsigned integer is interpreted as –5,536 by a short signed integer.

3

C++ allows a shorthand notation for declaring **unsigned**, **short**, or **long** integers. You can simply use the word **unsigned**, **short**, or **long**, without the **int**. The **int** is implied. For example, the following two statements both declare unsigned integer variables.

```
unsigned x;
unsigned int y;
```

Variables of type **char** can be used to hold values other than just the ASCII character set. A **char** variable can also be used as a "small" integer with the range –128 through 127, and it can be used in place of an integer when the situation does not require larger numbers. For example, the following program uses a **char** variable to control the loop that prints the alphabet on the screen:

```
// This program prints the alphabet in reverse order.

#include <iostream>
using namespace std;

int main()
{
  char letter;

  for(letter = 'Z'; letter >= 'A'; letter--)
    cout << letter;

  return 0;
}
```

If the **for** loop seems weird to you, keep in mind that the character A is represented inside the computer as a number, and that the values from A to Z are sequential, in ascending order.

Literals

In C++, *literals* (also called *constants*) refer to fixed values that cannot be altered by the program. For the most part, literals and their usage are so intuitive that they have been used in one form or another by all the preceding sample programs. Now, the time has come to explain them formally.

C++ literals can be of any of the basic data types. The way each literal is represented depends upon its type. Character literals are enclosed between single quotes. For example, 'a' and '%' are both character literals. As some of the examples thus far have shown, if you want to assign a character to a variable of type **char**, you will use a statement similar to this one:

```
ch = 'Z';
```

To specify a wide character literal (i.e., one that is of type **wchar_t**), precede the character with an **L**. For example,

```
wchar_t wc;
wc = L'A';
```

Here, **wc** is assigned the wide-character constant equivalent of A.

Integer literals are specified as numbers without fractional components. For example, 10 and –100 are integer literals. Floating-point literals require the use of the decimal point, followed by the number's fractional component. For example, 11.123 is a floating-point constant. C++ also allows you to use scientific notation for floating-point numbers.

There are two floating-point types: **float** and **double**. There are also several flavors of the basic types that can be generated with the type modifiers. The question is this: How does the compiler determine the type of a literal? For example, is 123.23 a **float** or a **double**? The answer to this question has two parts. First, the C++ compiler automatically makes certain assumptions about literals; second, you can explicitly specify the type of a literal, if you like.

By default, the C++ compiler fits an integer literal into the smallest compatible data type that will hold it, beginning with **int**. Therefore, assuming 16-bit integers, 10 is **int** by default, but 103,000 is **long**. Even though the value 10 could be fit into a character, the compiler will not do this, because it means crossing type boundaries.

An exception to the smallest-type rule is a floating-point constant, which is assumed to be **double**. For virtually all programs you will write as a beginner, the compiler defaults are perfectly adequate. However, it is possible to specify precisely the type of literal you want.

In cases where the default assumption that C++ makes about a numeric literal is not what you want, C++ allows you to specify the exact type by using a suffix. For floating-point types, if you follow the number with an F, the number is treated as a **float**. If you follow it with an L, the number becomes a **long double**. For integer types, the U suffix stands for **unsigned** and the L for **long**. (Both the U and the L must be used to specify an **unsigned long**.) Some examples are shown here:

Data Type	Examples of Literals
int	1 123 21000 –234
long int	35000L –34L
unsigned int	10000U 987U 40000U
unsigned long	12323UL 900000UL
float	123.23F 4.34e–3F
double	23.23 123123.33 –0.9876324
long double	1001.2L

3

Hexadecimal and Octal Literals

As you probably know, in programming it is sometimes easier to use a number system based on 8 or 16 instead of 10. The number system based on 8 is called *octal,* and it uses the digits 0 through 7. In octal, the number 10 is the same as 8 in decimal. The base-16 number system is called *hexadecimal,* and it uses the digits 0 through 9, plus the letters A through F, which stand for 10, 11, 12, 13, 14, and 15. For example, the hexadecimal number 10 is 16 in decimal. Because of the frequency with which these two number systems are used, C++ allows you to specify integer literals in hexadecimal or octal instead of decimal. A hexadecimal literal must begin with 0x (a zero followed by an x). An octal literal begins with a zero. Here are some examples:

```
hex = 0xFF; // 255 in decimal
oct = 011; // 9 in decimal
```

String Literals

C++ supports one other type of literal in addition to those of the predefined data types: the string. A *string* is a set of characters enclosed by double quotes. For example, "this is a test" is a string. You have seen examples of strings in some of the **cout** statements in the preceding sample programs. Keep in mind one important fact: although C++ allows you to define a string literal, it does not have a built-in string data type. Instead, as you will see a little later in this book, strings are supported in C++ as character arrays. (However, Standard C++ does provide a string type in its class library, which you will also learn about later in this book.)

CAUTION: You must not confuse strings with characters. A single character literal is enclosed by single quotes, as with 'a'. However, "a" is a string containing only one letter.

Character Escape Sequences

Enclosing character literals in single quotes works for most printing characters, but a few characters, such as the carriage return, pose a special problem when a text editor is used. In addition, certain other characters, such as the single and double quotes, have special meaning in C++, so you cannot use them directly. For these reasons, C++ provides the *character escape sequences* shown in Table 3-3. These sequences are also referred to as *backslash character constants*.

The following sample program illustrates the use of backslash codes. When this program is run, it outputs a newline, a backslash, and a backspace.

```
#include <iostream>
using namespace std;

int main()
{
  cout << "\n\\\b";

  return 0;
}
```

Code	Meaning
\b	backspace
\f	form feed
\n	newline
\r	carriage return
\t	horizontal tab
\"	double quote
\'	single quote character
\\	backslash
\v	vertical tab
\a	alert
\?	?
\N	octal constant (where *N* is an octal constant)
\xN	hexadecimal constant (where *N* is a hexadecimal constant)

The Character
Escape
Sequences
Table 3-3.

Variable Initializations

You can assign a value to a variable at the same time that it is declared by placing an equal sign and the value after the variable name. The general form of initialization is:

type variable_name = value;

Some examples are:

```
char ch = 'a';
int first = 0;
float balance = 123.23F;
```

Although variables are frequently initialized by constants, you can initialize a variable by using any expression valid at the time of the initialization. As you will see, initialization plays an important role when you are working with objects.

Global variables are initialized only at the start of the program. Local variables are initialized each time the function in which they are declared is entered. All global variables are initialized to zero if no other initializer is specified. Local variables that are not initialized will have unknown values before the first assignment is made to them.

Here is a simple example of variable initialization. This program uses the **total( )** function to compute the summation of the value that it is passed. In other words, **total( )** sums the digits from 1 to the value. For example, the summation of 3 is 1 + 2 + 3, or 6. In the process, **total( )** displays a running total. Notice the use of the **sum** variable in **total( )**.

```
// An example that uses variable initialization.

#include <iostream>
using namespace std;

void total(int x);

int main()
{
  cout << "Computing summation of 5.\n";
  total(5);

  cout << "\nComputing summation of 6.\n";
  total(6);

  return 0;
}

void total(int x)
```

3

```
{
  int sum=0; // initialize sum
  int i, count;

  for(i=1; i<=x; i++) {
    sum = sum + i;
    for(count=0; count<10; count++) cout << '.';
    cout << "The current sum is " << sum << '\n';
  }
}
```

Here is the output produced by the program.

```
Computing summation of 5.
..........The current sum is 1
..........The current sum is 3
..........The current sum is 6
..........The current sum is 10
..........The current sum is 15

Computing summation of 6.
..........The current sum is 1
..........The current sum is 3
..........The current sum is 6
..........The current sum is 10
..........The current sum is 15
..........The current sum is 21
```

As you can see, each time **total( )** is called, **sum** is initialized to zero.

Operators

C++ is rich in built-in operators. An *operator* is a symbol that tells the compiler to perform specific mathematical or logical manipulations. C++ has three general classes of operators: *arithmetic, relational* and *logical,* and *bitwise.* In addition, C++ has some special operators for particular tasks. This chapter will examine the arithmetic, relational, and logical operators, reserving the more advanced bitwise operators for later.

Arithmetic Operators

Table 3-4 lists the arithmetic operators allowed in C++. The operators +, –, *, and / all work the same way in C++ as they do in any other computer language (or algebra, for that matter). These can be applied to any built-in data type allowed by C++. When / is applied to an integer or a character, any remainder will be truncated; for example, 10/3 will equal 3 in integer division.

Operator	Action
–	subtraction, also unary minus
+	addition
*	multiplication
/	division
%	modulus
– –	decrement
++	increment

Arithmetic
Operators
Table 3-4.

The modulus operator **%** also works in C++ in the same way that it does in other languages. Remember that the modulus operation yields the remainder of an integer division. This means that the **%** cannot be used on type **float** or **double**. The following program illustrates its use:

```
#include <iostream>
using namespace std;

int main()
{
  int x, y;

  x = 10;
  y = 3;
  cout << x/y; // will display 3
  cout << "\n";
  cout << x%y; /* will display 1, the remainder of
                  the integer division */
  cout << "\n";

  x = 1;
  y = 2;
  cout << x/y << " " << x%y; // will display 0 1

  return 0;
}
```

The reason the last line prints a 0 and 1 is because 1/2 in integer division is 0, with a remainder of 1. Thus, 1%2 yields the remainder 1.

The unary minus, in effect, multiplies its single operand by –1. That is, any number preceded by a minus sign switches its sign.

Increment and Decrement

C++ has two operators not found in some other computer languages. These are the increment and decrement operators, **++** and **– –**. These operators were mentioned in passing in Chapter 2, when the **for** loop was introduced. The **++** operator adds 1 to its operand, and **– –** subtracts 1. Therefore,

```
x = x+1;
```

is the same as

```
++x;
```

and

```
x = x-1;
```

is the same as

```
--x;
```

Both the increment and decrement operators can either precede (prefix) or follow (postfix) the operand. For example:

```
x = x+1;
```

can be written as

```
++x; // prefix form
```

or as

```
x++; // postfix form
```

In the foregoing example, there is no difference whether the increment is applied as a prefix or a postfix. However, when an increment or decrement is used as part of a larger expression, there is an important difference. When an increment or decrement operator precedes its operand, C++ will perform the corresponding operation prior to obtaining the operand's value for use by the rest of the expression. If the operator follows its operand, then C++ will obtain the operand's value before incrementing or decrementing it. Consider the following:

```
x = 10;
y = ++x;
```

In this case, **y** will be set to 11. However, if the code is written as

```
x = 10;
y = x++;
```

then **y** will be set to 10. In both cases, **x** is still set to 11; the difference is when it happens. There are significant advantages in being able to control when the increment or decrement operation takes place.

Most C++ compilers create very fast, efficient object code for increment and decrement operations that is better than the code generated when the corresponding assignment statement is used. Therefore, it is a good idea to use increment and decrement operators when you can.

3

The precedence of the arithmetic operators is shown here:

highest	++ – –
	– (unary minus)
	* / %
lowest	+ –

Operators on the same precedence level are evaluated by the compiler from left to right. Of course, parentheses may be used to alter the order of evaluation. Parentheses are treated by C++ in the same way that they are by virtually all other computer languages: They force an operation, or a set of operations, to have a higher precedence level.

IN DEPTH

How C++ Got Its Name

Now that you understand the full meaning behind the **++** operator, you can probably guess how C++ got its name. As you know, C++ is built upon the C language. C++ adds several enhancements to C, most of which support object-oriented programming. Thus, C++ represents an *incremental* improvement to C, making the addition of the **++** (the *increment* operator) to the name C a fitting name for C++.

Bjarne Stroustrup initially named C++ "C with Classes." However, at the suggestion of Rick Mascitti, Stroustrup later changed the name to C++. While the new language was already destined for success, the adoption of the name C++ virtually guaranteed its place in history because it was a name that every C programmer would instantly recognize!

Relational and Logical Operators

In the terms *relational operator* and *logical operator, relational* refers to the relationships that values can have with one another, and *logical* refers to the ways in which true and false values can be connected together. Since the relational operators produce true or false results, they often work with the logical operators. For this reason, these operators will be discussed together here.

The relational and logical operators are shown in Table 3-5. Notice that in C++, *not equal* is represented by **!=** and *equal* is represented by the double equal sign, **==**. In Standard C++, the outcome of a relational or logical expression produces a **bool** result. That is, the outcome of a relational or logical expression is either **true** or **false**. For older compilers, the outcome of a relational or logical expression will be an integer value of either 0 or 1. This difference is mostly academic, though, because C++ automatically converts **true** into 1 and **false** into 0, and vice versa.

The operands for a relational operator can be of nearly any type, as long as they can be compared. The operands to the logical operators must produce a true or false result. Because any non-zero value is true and zero is false, the logical operators can be used with any expression that evaluates to a zero or non-zero result.

Relational Operators	
Operator	**Meaning**
>	greater than
>=	greater than or equal to
<	less than
<=	less than or equal to
==	equal to
!=	not equal to
Logical Operators	
Operator	**Meaning**
&&	AND
||	OR
!	NOT

The Relational and Logical Operators in C++
Table 3-5.

Remember, in C++,
any non-zero value
is true. Zero is
false.

The logical operators are used to support the basic logical operations AND, OR, and NOT, according to the following truth table. The table uses 1 for true and 0 for false.

p	q	p AND q	p OR q	NOT p
0	0	0	0	1
0	1	0	1	1
1	1	1	1	0
1	0	0	1	0

Although C++ does not contain a built-in exclusive-OR (XOR) logical operator, it is easy to construct one. The XOR operation uses this truth table:

p	q	XOR
0	0	0
0	1	1
1	0	1
1	1	0

In words, the XOR operation produces a true result when one, and only one, operand is true. The following function uses the **&&** and II operators to construct an XOR operation. The result is returned by the function.

```
bool xor(bool a, bool b)
{
  return (a || b) && !(a && b);
}
```

The following program uses this function. It displays the results of an AND, OR, and XOR on the values you enter. (Remember, one will be treated as true and zero is false.)

```
// This program demonstrates the xor() function.
#include <iostream>
using namespace std;

bool xor(bool a, bool b);

int main()
{
  bool p, q;

  cout << "Enter P (0 or 1): ";
  cin >> p;
  cout << "Enter Q (0 or 1): ";
  cin >> q;
```

```
cout << "P AND Q: " << (p && q) << '\n';
cout << "P OR Q: " << (p || q) << '\n';
cout << "P XOR Q: " << xor(p, q) << '\n';

    return 0;
}

bool xor(bool a, bool b)
{
    return (a || b) && !(a && b);
}
```

Here is a sample run produced by the program:

```
Enter P (0 or 1): 1
Enter Q (0 or 1): 1
P AND Q: 1
P OR Q: 1
P XOR Q: 0
```

In the program, notice that although the parameters to **xor( )** are specified as type **bool**, integer values are entered by the user. As was just explained, this is allowed because C++ automatically converts 1 values into true and 0 into false. When the **bool** return value of **xor( )** is output, it is automatically converted into either 1 or 0, depending upon whether the outcome of the operation is true or false. As a point of interest, it is also possible to specify the return type and parameters of **xor( )** as **int**, and the function would work exactly the same. Again, this is because of C++'s automatic conversions between integer values and Boolean values.

Both the relational and logical operators are lower in precedence than the arithmetic operators. This means that an expression like 10 > 1+12 is evaluated as if it were written 10 > (1+12). The result is, of course, false. Also, the parentheses surrounding **p && q** and **p || q** in the preceding program are necessary because the **&&** and **||** operators are lower in precedence than the output operator.

You can link any number of relational operations together by using logical operators. For example, this expression joins three relational operations:

```
var>15 || !(10<count) && 3<=item
```

The following table shows the relative precedence of the relational and logical operators:

highest	!
	> >= < <=
	== !=
	&&
lowest	||

Expressions

Operators, literals, and variables are constituents of *expressions*. You probably already know the general form of expressions from your other programming experience or from algebra. However, there are a few aspects of expressions that relate specifically to C++; these will be discussed now.

Type Conversion in Expressions

When literals and variables of different types are mixed in an expression, they are converted to the same type. First, all **char** and **short int** values are automatically elevated to **int**. This process is called *integral promotion*. Next, all operands are converted "up" to the type of the largest operand. This is called *type promotion,* and is done on an operation-by-operation basis. For example, if one operand is a **int** and the other a **long int**, then the **int** is promoted to **long int**. Or, if either operand is a **double**, the other operand is promoted to **double**. This means that conversions such as that from a **char** to a **double** are perfectly valid. Once a conversion has been applied, each pair of operands will be of the same type, and the result of each operation will be the same as the type of both operands.

For example, consider the type conversions that occur in Figure 3-1. First, the character **ch** is promoted to **int**. Then the outcome of **ch/i** is converted to a **double** because **f*d** is a **double**. The final result is **double** because, by this time, both operands are **double**.

Converting to and from bool

As mentioned earlier, values of type **bool** are automatically converted into the integers 0 or 1 when used in an integer expression. When an integer result is converted to type **bool**, 0 becomes **false** and a non-zero value becomes **true**. Although **bool** is a fairly

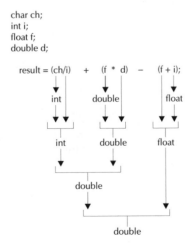

A type
conversion
example
Figure 3-1.

recent addition to C++, the automatic conversions to and from integers mean that it has virtually no impact on older code. Furthermore, the automatic conversions allow C++ to maintain its original definition of true and false as zero and non-zero. Thus, **bool** is mostly a convenience to the programmer.

Casts

It is possible to force an expression to be of a specific type by using a construct called a *cast*. C++ defines five types of casts. Four allow detailed and sophisticated control over casting, and are described later in this book after objects have been explained. However, there is one type of cast that you can use now. It is C++'s most general cast because it can be used to transform any type into any other type. It was also the only type of cast that early versions of C++ supported. The general form of this cast is

(type) expression

where *type* is the target type into which you want to convert the expression. For example, if you want to make sure the expression **x/2** is evaluated to type **float,** you can write

```
(float) x / 2
```

Casts are often considered operators. As an operator, a cast is unary and has the same precedence as any other unary operator.

There are times when a cast can be very useful. For example, you may want to use an integer for loop control, but also perform a computation on it that requires a fractional part, as in the program shown here:

```
#include <iostream>
using namespace std;

int main() // print i and i/2 with fractions
{
  int i;

  for(i=1; i<=100; ++i )
    cout << i << "/ 2 is: " << (float) i / 2 << '\n';

  return 0;
}
```

Without the cast **(float)** in this example, only an integer division would be performed. The cast ensures that the fractional part of the answer will be displayed on the screen.

Spacing and Parentheses

An expression in C++ may have tabs and spaces in it to make it more readable. For example, the following two expressions are the same, but the second is easier to read:

```
x=10/y*(127/x);

x = 10 / y * (127/x);
```

3

Use of redundant or additional parentheses will not cause errors or slow down the execution of the expression. You are encouraged to use parentheses to make clear the exact order of evaluation, both for yourself and for others who may have to figure out your program later. For example, which of the following two expressions is easier to read?

```
x = y/3-34*temp+127;

x = (y/3) - (34*temp) + 127;
```

CHAPTER 4

Program Control
Statements

In this chapter you will learn about the statements that control a program's flow of execution. There are three specific categories of program control statements: *selection* statements, which include the **if** and the **switch**; *iteration* statements, which include the **for**, **while**, and **do-while** loops; and *jump* statements, which include **break**, **continue**, **return**, and **goto**. (However, a discussion of the **return** statement is deferred until later in this book.)

This chapter begins with a thorough examination of the **if** and **for** statements, to which you have already had a brief introduction in Chapter 2. It then discusses the other program control statements.

The if Statement

if selects between two paths of execution.

Chapter 2 introduced the **if** statement. Now it is time to examine it in detail. The complete form of the **if** statement is

    if(*expression*) *statement*;
    else *statement*;

where the targets of the **if** and **else** are single statements. The **else** clause is optional. The targets of both the **if** and **else** can be blocks of statements. The general form of the **if** using blocks of statements is

    if(*expression*)
    {
      statement sequence
    }
    else
    {
      statement sequence
    }

If the conditional expression is true, the target of the **if** will be executed; otherwise, if it exists, the target of the **else** will be executed. At no time will both of them be executed. The conditional expression controlling the **if** may be any type of valid C++ expression that produces a true or false result.

The following program demonstrates the **if** by playing a simple version of the "guess the magic number" game. The program generates a random number, prompts for your guess, and prints the message ** **Right** ** if you guess the magic number. This program also introduces another standard C++ library function, called **rand( )**, which returns a randomly selected integer value. It requires the header called **<cstdlib>**.

```
// Magic Number program.
#include <iostream>
#include <cstdlib>
using namespace std;

int main()
{
```

```
    int magic;   // magic number
    int guess;   // user's guess

    magic = rand(); // get a random number

    cout << "Enter your guess: ";
    cin >> guess;

    if(guess == magic) cout << "** Right **";

    return 0;
}
```

4

This program uses the relational operator **==** to determine whether the guess matches the magic number. If it does, the message is printed on the screen.

Taking the Magic Number program further, the next version uses the **else** to print a message when the wrong number is picked.

```
// Magic Number program: 1st improvement.

#include <iostream>
#include <cstdlib>
using namespace std;

int main()
{
    int magic;   // magic number
    int guess;   // user's guess

    magic = rand(); // get a random number

    cout << "Enter your guess: ";
    cin >> guess;

    if(guess == magic) cout << "** Right **";
    else cout << "...Sorry, you're wrong.";

    return 0;
}
```

The Conditional Expression

Sometimes newcomers to C++ are confused by the fact that any valid C++ expression can be used to control the **if**. That is, the type of expression need not be restricted to only those involving the relational and logical operators or to operands of type **bool**. All that is required is that the controlling expression evaluate to either a true or false result. As you should recall from the previous chapter, a value of zero is automatically converted into **false**, and all non-zero values are converted to **true**. Thus, any expression that results in a zero or non-zero value can be used to control the **if**. For example, the following program reads two integers from the keyboard and displays the quotient.

In order to avoid a divide-by-zero error, an **if** statement, controlled by the second number, is used.

```
// Divide the first number by the second.

#include <iostream>
using namespace std;

int main()
{
  int a, b;

  cout << "Enter two numbers: ";
  cin >> a >> b;

  if(b) cout << a/b << '\n';
  else cout << "Cannot divide by zero.\n";

  return 0;
}
```

Notice that **b** (the divisor) is tested for zero by using **if(b)**. This approach works because when **b** is zero, the condition controlling the **if** is false and the **else** executes. Otherwise, the condition is true (non-zero) and the division takes place. It is not necessary (and would be considered bad style by most C++ programmers) to write this **if** as shown here:

```
if(b != 0) cout << a/b << '\n';
```

This form of the statement is redundant and potentially inefficient.

Nested ifs

A *nested if* is an **if** statement that is the target of another **if** or an **else**. Nested **if**s are very common in programming. The main thing to remember about nested **if**s in C++ is that an **else** statement always refers to the nearest **if** statement that is within the same block as the **else** and not already associated with an **else**. Here is an example:

```
if(i) {
  if(j) statement1;
  if(k) statement2; // this if
  else statement3; // is associated with this else
}
else statement4; // associated with if(i)
```

A nested **if** is an **if** statement that is the target of either another **if** or an **else**.

As the comments indicate, the final **else** is not associated with **if(j)** (even though it is the closest **if** without an **else**), because it is not in the same block. Rather, the final **else** is associated with **if(i)**. The inner **else** is associated with **if(k)** because that is the nearest **if**.

C++ allows at least 256 levels of nesting. In practice, you will seldom need to nest **if** statements this deeply.

We can use a nested **if** to add a further improvement to the Magic Number program. This addition provides the player with feedback about a wrong guess.

```cpp
// Magic Number program: 2nd improvement.

#include <iostream>
#include <cstdlib>
using namespace std;

int main()
{
  int magic;  // magic number
  int guess;  // user's guess

  magic = rand(); // get a random number

  cout << "Enter your guess: ";
  cin >> guess;

  if (guess == magic) {
    cout << "** Right **\n";
    cout << magic << " is the magic number.\n";
  }
  else {
    cout << "...Sorry, you're wrong.";

    // use a nested if statement
    if(guess > magic)
      cout <<" Your guess is too high.\n";
    else
      cout << " Your guess is too low.\n";
  }

  return 0;
}
```

The if-else-if Ladder

A common programming construct that is based upon nested **if**s is the **if-else-if** ladder. It looks like this:

```
if(condition)
  statement;
else if(condition)
  statement;
else if(condition)
  statement;
.
.
.
else
  statement;
```

An **if-else-if** ladder is a series of nested **if/else** statements.

The conditional expressions are evaluated from the top downward. As soon as a true condition is found, the statement associated with it is executed, and the rest of the ladder is bypassed. If none of the conditions is true, then the final **else** statement will be executed. The final **else** often acts as a default condition; that is, if all other conditional tests fail, then the last **else** statement is performed. If there is no final **else** and all other conditions are false, then no action will take place.

The following program demonstrates the **if-else-if** ladder.

```cpp
// Demonstrate an if-else-if ladder.
#include <iostream>
using namespace std;

int main()
{
  int x;

  for(x=0; x<6; x++) {
    if(x==1) cout << "x is one\n";
    else if(x==2) cout << "x is two\n";
    else if(x==3) cout << "x is three\n";
    else if(x==4) cout << "x is four\n";
    else cout << "x is not between 1 and 4\n";
  }

  return 0;
}
```

The program produces the following output:

```
x is not between 1 and 4
x is one
x is two
x is three
x is four
x is not between 1 and 4
```

As you can see, the default **else** is executed only if none of the preceding **if** statements succeed.

The for Loop

The **for** is C++'s most versatile loop.

You were introduced to a simple form of the **for** loop in Chapter 2. You might be surprised just how powerful and flexible the **for** loop is. Let's begin by reviewing the basics, starting with the most traditional forms of the **for** loop.

The general form of the **for** loop for repeating a single statement is

    for(*initialization; expression; increment*) *statement;*

For repeating a block, the general form is

```
for(initialization; expression; increment)
{
    statement sequence
}
```

The *initialization* is usually an assignment statement that sets the initial value of the *loop control variable,* which acts as the counter that controls the loop. The *expression* is a conditional expression that determines whether or not the loop will repeat. The *increment* defines the amount by which the loop control variable will change each time the loop is repeated. Notice that these three major sections of the loop must be separated by semicolons. The **for** loop will continue to execute as long as the conditional expression tests true. Once the condition becomes false, the loop will exit, and program execution will resume on the statement following the **for** block.

4

The following program uses a **for** loop to print the square roots of the numbers between 1 and 99. Notice that in this example, the loop control variable is called **num**.

```cpp
#include <iostream>
#include <cmath>
using namespace std;

int main()
{
  int num;
  double sq_root;

  for(num=1; num < 100; num++) {
    sq_root = sqrt((double) num);
    cout << num << " " << sq_root << '\n';
  }

  return 0;
}
```

Here are the first few lines of output displayed by the program:

```
1 1
2 1.41421
3 1.73205
4 2
5 2.23607
6 2.44949
7 2.64575
8 2.82843
9 3
10 3.16228
```

This program introduces another of C++'s standard functions: **sqrt( )**. The **sqrt( )** function returns the square root of its argument. The argument must be of type **double** and this is why **num** is cast to **double** when **sqrt( )** is called. The function returns a value of type **double**. Notice that the header **<cmath>** has been included. This file is needed to support the **sqrt( )** function.

TIP: In addition to **sqrt( )**, C++ supports an extensive set of mathematical library functions. For example, **sin( )**, **cos( )**, **tan( )**, **log( )**, **ceil( )**, and **floor( )** are a few. If mathematical programming is your interest, you will want to explore the C++ math functions. Remember, they all require the header **<cmath>**.

The **for** loop can proceed in a positive or negative fashion, and it can increment the loop control variable by any amount. For example, the following program prints the numbers 100 to –100, in decrements of 5.

```cpp
#include <iostream>
using namespace std;

int main()
{
  int i;

  for(i=100; i >= -100; i = i-5) cout << i << ' ';

  return 0;
}
```

An important point about **for** loops is that the conditional expression is always tested at the top of the loop. This means that the code inside the loop may not be executed at all if the condition is false to begin with. Here is an example:

```cpp
for(count=10; count < 5; count++)
  cout << count; // this statement will not execute
```

This loop will never execute, because its control variable, **count**, is greater than 5 when the loop is first entered. This makes the conditional expression, **count<5**, false from the outset; thus, not even one iteration of the loop will occur.

Some Variations on the for Loop

The **for** is one of the most versatile statements in the C++ language because it allows a wide range of variations from its traditional use. For example, multiple loop control variables can be used. Consider the following fragment of code:

```cpp
for(x=0, y=10; x<=10; ++x, --y)
  cout << x << ' ' << y << '\n';
```

Here, commas separate the two initialization statements and the two increment expressions. This is necessary in order for the compiler to understand that there are two initialization and two increment statements. In C++, the comma is an operator that essentially means "do this and this." We will look at other uses for the comma operator later in this book, but its most common use is in the **for** loop. You can have any number of initialization and increment statements, but in practice, more than two or three make the **for** loop unwieldy.

The condition controlling the loop may be any valid C++ expression. It does not need to involve the loop control variable. In the next example, the loop continues to execute until the user presses a key at the keyboard. The example also introduces an important library function: **kbhit( )**. This function returns false if no key has been pressed or true if a key has been struck. It does not wait for a keypress, thus allowing the loop to continue execution. The **kbhit( )** function is not defined by Standard C++, but is a common extension that is provided by most compilers. It uses the header file **conio.h**. (This header must be supplied using the **.h** extension, as shown below, since it is not defined by Standard C++.)

```
#include <iostream>
#include <conio.h>
using namespace std;

int main()
{
  int i;

  // print numbers until a key is pressed
  for(i=0; !kbhit(); i++) cout << i << ' ';

  return 0;
}
```

Each time through the loop, **kbhit( )** is called. If a key has been pressed, then a true value is returned, which causes **!kbhit( )** to be false, so the loop stops. However, if no key has been pressed, **kbhit( )** returns false, and **!kbhit( )** is true, allowing the loop to continue.

TIP: The **kbhit( )** function is not part of the C++ standard library. This is because the C++ standard library defines only a minimum set of functions that all C++ compilers must have. **kbhit( )** is not included in this minimal set, because not all environments can support keyboard interactivity. However, **kbhit( )** is supported by virtually all mainstream C++ compilers, although it might be called something slightly different. A compiler manufacturer is free—in fact, encouraged—to provide more library functions than are required to meet the minimum requirements of the standard C++ library. These extra functions are included so that you can fully access and utilize your programming environment. You should feel free to use all the functions supplied by your compiler unless portability to another environment is an issue.

Missing Pieces

Another aspect of the **for** loop that is different in C++ than in many computer languages is that pieces of the loop definition need not be there. For example, if you want to write a loop that runs until the number 123 is typed in at the keyboard, it could look like this:

```
#include <iostream>
using namespace std;

int main()
{
  int x;

  for(x=0; x != 123; ) {
    cout << "Enter a number: ";
    cin >> x;
  }

  return 0;
}
```

The increment portion of the **for** definition is blank. This means that each time the loop repeats, **x** is tested to see whether it equals 123, but no further action takes place. If, however, you type 123 at the keyboard, the loop condition becomes false and the loop exits. The C++ **for** loop will not modify the loop control variable if no increment portion of the loop is present.

Another variation on the **for** is to move the initialization section outside of the loop, as shown in this fragment:

```
cout << "Enter position: ";
cin >> x;

for( ; x < limit; x++) cout << ' ';
```

Here, the initialization section has been left blank, and **x** is initialized by a value entered by the user before the loop is entered .

Placing the initialization outside of the loop is generally done only when the initial value is derived through a process that does not lend itself to containment within the **for** statement, such as when the variable is set by keyboard input. Another situation in which the initialization portion of the **for** might be empty is when you control the loop with a function parameter, using the value the parameter receives when the function is called as the starting point.

The Infinite Loop

An infinite loop is a loop that never terminates.

You can create an *infinite loop* (a loop that never terminates) by using this **for** construct:

```
for(;;)
{
```

```
    //...
}
```

This loop will run forever. Although there are some programming tasks, such as operating system command processors, that require an infinite loop, most "infinite loops" are really just loops with special termination requirements. Near the end of this chapter, you will see how to halt a loop of this type. (Hint: it's done using the **break** statement.)

Time Delay Loops

Time delay loops are often used in programs. These are loops that have no other purpose than to kill time. Delay loops can be created by specifying an empty target statement. For example:

```
for(x=0; x<1000; x++) ;
```

This loop increments **x** one thousand times, but does nothing else. The semicolon that terminates the line is necessary because the **for** expects a statement, which can be empty.

Before moving on, you might want to experiment with your own variations on the **for** loop. As you will find, it is a fascinating loop.

The switch Statement

switch is C++'s
multiway decision
statement.

Before looking at C++'s other loop constructs, let's examine its other selection statement: the **switch**. Although a series of nested **if** statements can perform multiway tests, for many situations, a more efficient approach can be used. C++ has a built-in multiple-branch decision statement called **switch**. It works like this: the value of an expression is successively tested against a list of integer or character constants. When a match is found, the statement sequence associated with that match is executed. The general form of the **switch** statement is

```
switch(expression) {
    case constant1:
        statement sequence
        break;
    case constant2:
        statement sequence
        break;
    case constant3:
        statement sequence
        break;
    .
    .
    .
    default:
        statement sequence
}
```

4

The **switch** expression must evaluate to either a character or an integer value. (Floating-point expressions, for example, are not allowed.) Frequently, the expression controlling the **switch** is simply a variable.

The **default** statement sequence is performed if no matches are found. The **default** is optional; if it is not present, no action takes place if all matches fail. When a match is found, the statements associated with that **case** are executed until the **break** is encountered or, in the case of the **default** or the last **case**, the end of the **switch** is reached.

There are four important things to know about the **switch** statement:

◆ The **switch** differs from the **if** in that **switch** can test only for equality (i.e., for matches between the **switch** expression and the **case** constants), whereas the **if** conditional expression can be of any type.

◆ No two **case** constants in the same **switch** can have identical values. Of course, a **switch** statement enclosed by an outer **switch** may have **case** constants in common.

◆ A **switch** statement is usually more efficient than nested **if**s.

◆ The statement sequences associated with each **case** are *not* blocks. However, the entire **switch** statement *does* define a block. The importance of this will become apparent as you learn more about C++.

Standard C++ specifies that a **switch** can have at least 16,384 **case** statements. In practice, you will want to limit the number of **case** statements to a much smaller total, for reasons of efficiency.

The following program demonstrates the **switch**. It creates a simple "help" system that describes the meaning of the **for**, **if**, and **switch** statements. It displays the help topics and then waits for the user to enter his or her choice. This choice is then used by the **switch** to display information about the requested topic. (You might find it fun to expand the information in this program. You can also add new topics as you learn about them.)

```
// Demonstrate the switch using a simple "help" program.
#include <iostream>
using namespace std;

int main()
{
  int choice;

  cout << "Help on:\n\n";
  cout << "1. for\n";
  cout << "2. if\n";
  cout << "3. switch\n\n";

  cout << "Enter choice (1-3): ";
  cin >> choice;
  cout << "\n";
```

4

```
switch(choice) {
  case 1:
    cout << "for is C++'s most versatile loop.\n";
    break;
  case 2:
    cout << "if is C++'s conditional branch statement.\n";
    break;
  case 3:
    cout << "switch is C++'s multiway branch statement.\n";
    break;
  default:
    cout << "You must enter a number between 1 and 3.\n";
}

  return 0;
}
```

Here is a sample run:

```
Help on:

1. for
2. if
3. switch

Enter choice (1-3): 2

if is C++'s conditional branch statement.
```

Technically, the **break** statement is optional, although most applications of the **switch** will use it. When encountered within the statement sequence of a **case**, the **break** statement causes program flow to exit from the entire **switch** statement and resume at the next statement outside the **switch**. However, if a **break** statement does not end the statement sequence associated with a **case**, then all the statements *at and below* the matching **case** will be executed until a **break** (or the end of the **switch**) is encountered.

For example, study the following program carefully. Can you figure out what it will display on the screen?

```
#include <iostream>
using namespace std;

int main()
{
  int i;

  for(i=0; i<5; i++) {
    switch(i) {
      case 0: cout << "less than 1\n";
      case 1: cout << "less than 2\n";
      case 2: cout << "less than 3\n";
```

```
      case 3: cout << "less than 4\n";
      case 4: cout << "less than 5\n";
    }
    cout << '\n';
  }

  return 0;
}
```

This program displays the following output:

```
less than 1
less than 2
less than 3
less than 4
less than 5

less than 2
less than 3
less than 4
less than 5

less than 3
less than 4
less than 5

less than 4
less than 5

less than 5
```

As this program illustrates, execution will continue into the next **case** if no **break** statement is present.

You can have empty **case**s, as shown in this example:

```
switch(i) {
  case 1:
  case 2:
  case 3: do_something();
    break;
  case 4: do_something_else();
    break;
```

In this fragment, if **i** has the value 1, 2, or 3, then **do_something( )** is called. If **i** has the value 4, then **do_something_else( )** is called. The "stacking" of **case**s, as shown in this example, is very common when several **case**s share common code.

Nested switch Statements

It is possible to have a **switch** as part of the statement sequence of an outer **switch**. Even if the **case** constants of the inner and outer **switch** contain common values, no conflicts will arise. For example, the following code fragment is perfectly acceptable:

```
switch(ch1) {
  case 'A': cout << "This A is part of outer switch";
    switch(ch2) {
      case 'A':
        cout << "This A is part of inner switch";
        break;
      case 'B': // ...
    }
    break;
  case 'B': // ...
```

4

C++ specifies that at least 256 levels of nesting be allowed for **switch** statements. Frankly, few programs ever require anywhere near 256 levels of nesting.

The while Loop

while is another of C++'s loop statements.

Another loop is the **while**. The general form of the **while** loop is

> while(*expression*) *statement*;

where *statement* may be a single statement or a block of statements. The *expression* defines the condition that controls the loop, and it may be any valid expression. The statement is performed while the condition is true. When the condition becomes false, program control passes to the line immediately following the loop.

The next program illustrates the **while** in a short but sometimes fascinating program. Virtually all computers support an extended character set beyond that defined by ASCII. The extended characters, if they exist, often include special characters such as foreign language symbols and scientific notations. The ASCII characters use values that are less than 128. The extended character set begins at 128 and continues to 255. This program prints all characters between 32 (which is a space) and 255. When you run this program, you will most likely see some very interesting characters.

```
/* This program displays all printable characters,
   including the extended character set, if one exists.
*/

#include <iostream>
using namespace std;

int main()
{
  unsigned char ch;
```

```
  ch = 32;
  while(ch) {
     cout << ch;
     ch++;
  }

  return 0;
}
```

Examine the loop expression in the preceding program. You might be wondering why only **ch** is used to control the **while**. The answer is quite easy. Since **ch** is an unsigned character, it can only hold the values 0 through 255. When it holds the value 255 and is then incremented, its value will "wrap around" to zero. Therefore, the test for **ch** being zero serves as a convenient stopping condition.

As with the **for** loop, the **while** checks the conditional expression at the top of the loop, which means that the loop code may not execute at all. This eliminates the need for performing a separate test before the loop. The following program illustrates this characteristic of the **while** loop. It displays a line of periods. The number of periods displayed is equal to the value entered by the user. The program does not allow lines longer than 80 characters. The test for a permissible number of periods is performed inside the loop's conditional expression, not outside of it.

```
#include <iostream>
using namespace std;

int main()
{
  int len;

  cout << "Enter length (1 to 79): ";
  cin >> len;

  while(len>0 && len<80)  {
    cout << '.';
    len--;
  }

  return 0;
}
```

There need not be any statements at all in the body of the **while** loop. Here is an example:

```
while(rand() != 100) ;
```

This loop iterates until the random number generated by **rand( )** equals 100.

The do-while Loop

The **do-while** is the only loop that will always iterate at least once.

Unlike the **for** and the **while** loops, in which the condition is tested at the top of the loop, the **do-while** loop checks its condition at the bottom of the loop. This means that a **do-while** loop will always execute at least once. The general form of the **do-while** loop is

```
do {
    statements;
} while(expression);
```

Although the braces are not necessary when only one statement is present, they are often used to improve readability of the **do-while** construct, thus preventing confusion with the **while**. The **do-while** loop executes as long as the conditional expression is true.

The following program loops until the number 100 is entered.

```cpp
#include <iostream>
using namespace std;

int main()
{
  int num;

  do {
    cout << "Enter a number (100 to stop): ";
    cin >> num;
  } while(num != 100);

  return 0;
}
```

Using a **do-while** loop, we can further improve the Magic Number program. This time, the program loops until you guess the number.

```cpp
// Magic Number program: 3rd improvement.

#include <iostream>
#include <cstdlib>
using namespace std;

int main()
{
  int magic; // magic number
  int guess; // user's guess

  magic = rand(); // get a random number

  do {
```

4

```
   cout << "Enter your guess: ";
   cin >> guess;
   if(guess == magic) {
     cout << "** Right ** ";
     cout << magic << " is the magic number.\n";
   }
   else {
     cout << "...Sorry, you're wrong.";
     if(guess > magic)
        cout << " Your guess is too high.\n";
     else
        cout << " Your guess is too low.\n";
   }
 } while(guess != magic);

 return 0;
}
```

Using continue

continue
immediately causes the next iteration of a loop.

It is possible to force an early iteration of a loop, bypassing the loop's normal control structure. This is accomplished by using **continue**. The **continue** statement forces the next iteration of the loop to take place, skipping any code between itself and the conditional expression that controls the loop. For example, the following program prints the even numbers between 0 and 100:

```
#include <iostream>
using namespace std;

int main()
{
  int x;

  for(x=0; x<=100; x++) {
    if(x%2) continue;
    cout << x << ' ';
  }

  return 0;
}
```

Only even numbers are printed, because an odd one will cause the loop to iterate early, bypassing the **cout** statement.

In **while** and **do-while** loops, a **continue** statement will cause control to go directly to the conditional expression and then continue the looping process. In the case of the **for**, the increment part of the loop is performed, next the conditional expression is executed, and then the loop continues.

Using break to Exit Loops

break *causes immediate termination of a loop.*

It is possible to force an immediate exit from a loop, bypassing the loop's conditional test, by using the **break** statement. When the **break** statement is encountered inside a loop, the loop is immediately terminated, and program control resumes at the next statement following the loop. Here is a simple example:

```cpp
#include <iostream>
using namespace std;

int main()
{
  int t;

  // Loops from 0 to 9, not to 100!
  for(t=0; t<100; t++) {
    if(t==10) break;
    cout << t << ' ';
  }

  return 0;
}
```

4

This program will print the numbers 0 through 9 on the screen before ending. It will not go to 100, because the **break** statement will cause it to terminate early.

The **break** statement is commonly used in loops in which a special condition can cause immediate termination. The following fragment contains an example of such a situation, where a keypress can stop the execution of the loop:

```cpp
for(i=0; i<1000; i++) {
  // do something
  if(kbhit()) break;
}
```

A **break** will cause an exit from only the innermost loop. Here is an example:

```cpp
#include <iostream>
using namespace std;

int main()
{
  int t, count;

  for(t=0; t<100; t++) {
    count = 1;
    for(;;) {
      cout << count << ' ';
      count++;
      if(count==10) break;
    }
```

```
      cout << '\n';
  }

  return 0;
}
```

This program will print the numbers 1 through 9 on the screen 100 times. Each time the **break** is encountered, control is passed back to the outer **for** loop.

NOTE: A **break** used in a **switch** statement will affect only that **switch**, and not any loop the **switch** happens to be in.

As you have seen, it is possible to create an infinite loop in C++ by using the **for** statement. (You can also create infinite loops by using the **while** and the **do-while**, but the **for** is the traditional method.) In order to exit from an infinite loop, you must use the **break** statement. Of course, you can also use **break** to terminate a non-infinite loop.

Nested Loops

As you have seen in some of the preceding examples, one loop can be nested inside of another. C++ allows at least 256 levels of nesting. Nested loops are used to solve a wide variety of programming problems. For example, the following program uses a nested **for** loop to find the prime numbers from 2 to 1000:

```
/* This program finds the prime numbers from
   2 to 1000.
*/

#include <iostream>
using namespace std;

int main()
{
  int i, j;

  for(i=2; i<1000; i++) {
    for(j=2; j <= (i/j); j++)
      if(!(i%j)) break; // if factor found, not prime
    if(j > (i/j)) cout << i << " is prime\n";
  }

  return 0;
}
```

This program determines if the number contained in **i** is prime by successively dividing it by the values between 2 and the result of **i / j**. (You can stop at the value of **i / j** because a number that is larger than **i / j** cannot be a factor of **i**.) If any division is even, the number is not prime. However, if the loop completes, the number is, indeed, prime.

Using the goto Statement

goto is C++'s
unconditional
branch
statement.

The **goto** statement fell out of favor with programmers many years ago because it encouraged the creation of "spaghetti code." However, it is still occasionally—and sometimes effectively—used. This book will not make a judgment regarding its validity as a form of program control. It should be stated, however, that there are no programming situations that require the use of the **goto** statement—it is not an item necessary for making the language complete. Rather, it is a convenience that, if used wisely, can be of benefit in certain programming situations. As such, the **goto** is not used in this book outside of this section. The chief concern most programmers have about the **goto** is its tendency to clutter a program and render it nearly unreadable. However, there are times when the use of the **goto** will actually clarify program flow rather than confuse it.

4

A label is an
identifier
followed by
a colon.

The **goto** requires a label for operation. A *label* is a valid C++ identifier followed by a colon. Furthermore, the label must be in the same function as the **goto** that uses it. For example, a loop from 1 to 100 could be written using a **goto** and a label, as shown here:

```
x = 1;
loop1:
  x++;
  if(x < 100) goto loop1;
```

One good use for the **goto** is to exit from a deeply nested routine. For example, consider the following code fragment:

```
for(...) {
  for(...) {
    while(...) {
      if(...) goto stop;
      .
      .
      .
    }
  }
}
stop:
  cout << "Error in program.\n";
```

Eliminating the **goto** would force a number of additional tests to be performed. A simple **break** statement would not work here, because it would only cause the program to exit from the innermost loop.

TIP: You should use the **goto** sparingly. But if your code would otherwise be much more difficult to read, or if execution speed of the code is critical, then by all means use the **goto**.

Putting Together the Pieces

This next example shows the final version of the Magic Number game. It uses many of the concepts that were presented in this chapter, and you should make sure that you understand all of its elements before you go on to the next chapter. The program allows you to generate a new number, to play the game, and to quit.

```cpp
// Magic Number program: Final improvement.

#include <iostream>
#include <cstdlib>
using namespace std;

void play(int m);

int main()
{
  int option;
  int magic;

  magic = rand();

  do {
    cout << "1. Get a new magic number\n";
    cout << "2. Play\n";
    cout << "3. Quit\n";
    do {
      cout << "Enter your choice: ";
      cin >> option;
    } while(option<1 || option>3);

    switch(option) {
      case 1:
        magic = rand();
        break;
      case 2:
        play(magic);
        break;
      case 3:
        cout << "Goodbye\n";
        break;
    }
  } while(option!=3);
```

```
      return 0;
}

// Play the game.
void play(int m)
{
  int t, x;

  for(t=0; t < 100; t++) {
    cout << "Guess the number: ";
    cin >> x;
    if(x == m) {
      cout << "** Right **\n";
      return;
    }
    else
      if(x < m) cout << "Too low.\n";
      else cout << "Too high.\n";
  }
  cout << "You've used up all your guesses. Try again.\n";
}
```

4

CHAPTER 5

Arrays and Strings

This chapter discusses the array. An *array* is a collection of variables of the same type that are referred to by a common name. In C++, arrays may have from one to several dimensions, although the one-dimensional array is the most common. Arrays offer a convenient means of grouping together several related variables.

The array that you will probably use most often is the character array because it is used to hold strings. As explained earlier, the C++ language does not define a built-in string data type. Instead, strings are implemented as arrays of characters. This approach to strings allows greater power and flexibility than are available in languages that use a distinct string type.

One-Dimensional Arrays

A one-dimensional array is a list of related variables. The general form of a one-dimensional array declaration is

> *type var_name[size]*;

Here, *type* declares the base type of the array. The base type determines the data type of each element that comprises the array. *size* defines how many elements the array will hold. For example, the following declares an integer array named **sample** that is ten elements long:

```
int sample[10];
```

An index identifies a specific element within an array.

An individual element within an array is accessed by use of an index. An *index* describes the position of an element within an array. In C++, all arrays have zero as the index of their first element. Because **sample** has ten elements, it has index values of 0 through 9. You access an array element by indexing the array, using the number of the element you are seeking. To index an array, specify the number of the element you want, surrounded by square brackets. Thus, the first element in **sample** is **sample[0]**, and the last element is **sample[9]**. For example, the following program loads **sample** with the numbers 0 through 9:

```
#include <iostream>
using namespace std;

int main()
{
  int sample[10]; // this reserves 10 integer elements
  int t;

  // load the array
  for(t=0; t<10; ++t) sample[t]=t;

  // display the array
  for(t=0; t<10; ++t) cout << sample[t] << ' ';

  return 0;
}
```

In C++, all arrays consist of contiguous memory locations. (That is, the array elements reside next to each other in memory.) The lowest address corresponds to the first element, and the highest address to the last element. For example, after this fragment is run,

```
int i[7];
int j;

for(j=0; j<7; j++) i[j] = j;
```

i looks like this:

i[0]	i[1]	i[2]	i[3]	i[4]	i[5]	i[6]
0	1	2	3	4	5	6

For a one-dimensional array, the total size of an array in bytes is computed as shown here:

total bytes = number of bytes in type × number of elements

5

Arrays are common in programming because they let you deal easily with large numbers of related variables. For example, the following program creates an array of ten elements, assigns each element a random value, and then displays the minimum and maximum values.

```cpp
#include <iostream>
#include <cstdlib>
using namespace std;

int main()
{
  int i, min_value, max_value;
  int list[10];

  for(i=0; i<10; i++) list[i] = rand();

  // find minimum value
  min_value = list[0];
  for(i=1; i<10; i++)
    if(min_value > list[i]) min_value = list[i];

  cout << "minimum value: " << min_value << '\n';

  // find maximum value
  max_value = list[0];
  for(i=1; i<10; i++)
    if(max_value < list[i]) max_value = list[i];

  cout << "maximum value: " <<  max_value << '\n';

  return 0;
}
```

In C++, you cannot assign one array to another. For example, the following is illegal:

```
int a[10], b[10];

// ...

a = b; // error -- illegal
```

To transfer the contents of one array into another, you must assign each value individually.

No Bounds Checking

C++ performs no bounds checking on arrays; nothing stops you from overrunning the end of an array. If this happens during an assignment operation, you will be assigning values to some other variable's data, or even into a piece of the program's code. In other words, you can index an array of size N beyond N without causing any compile- or run-time error messages, even though doing so will probably cause your program to crash. As the programmer, it is your job both to ensure that all arrays are large enough to hold what the program will put in them and to provide bounds checking whenever necessary.

For example, C++ will compile and run the following program even though the array **crash** is being overrun.

CAUTION: Do not try the following example. It might crash your system!

```
// An incorrect program.  Do Not Execute!

int main()
{
  int crash[10], i;

  for(i=0; i<100; i++) crash[i] = i; // Error! array overrun

  return 1;
}
```

In this case, the loop will iterate 100 times, even though **crash** is only ten elements long! This might cause important information to be overwritten, resulting in a program failure.

You might be wondering why C++ does not provide boundary checks on arrays. The answer is that C++ was designed to give professional programmers the capability to create the fastest, most efficient code possible. Towards this end, virtually no run-time error checking is included because it slows (often dramatically) the execution of a program. Instead, C++ expects you, the programmer, to be responsible enough to prevent array overruns in the first place and to add appropriate error checking on your own, as needed. Also, as you will learn later in this book, it is possible for you to define array types of your own that perform bounds checking, if your program actually requires this feature.

IN DEPTH

Sorting an Array

One common operation performed upon an array is to sort it. As you may know, there are a number of different sorting algorithms. There are the Quicksort, the shaker sort, and the shell sort, to name just three. However, the best-known, simplest, and easiest-to-understand sorting algorithm is called the bubble sort. While the bubble sort is not very efficient—in fact, its performance is unacceptable for sorting large arrays—it may be used effectively for sorting small ones.

The bubble sort gets its name from the way it performs the sorting operation. It uses the repeated comparison and, if necessary, exchange of adjacent elements in the array. In this process, small values move toward one end and large ones toward the other end. The process is conceptually similar to bubbles finding their own level in a tank of water. The bubble sort operates by making several passes through the array, exchanging out-of-place elements when necessary. The number of passes required to ensure that the array is sorted is equal to one less than the number of elements in the array.

The following program sorts an array of integers that contains random values. If you carefully examine the sort, you will find its operation easy to understand.

```cpp
// Using the bubble sort to order an array.
#include <iostream>
#include <cstdlib>
using namespace std;

int main()
{
  int nums[10];
  int a, b, t;
  int size;

  size = 10; // number of elements to sort

  // Give the array some random initial values.
  for(t=0; t<size; t++) nums[t] = rand();

  // Display original array.
  cout << "Original array is: ";
```

5

```
for(t=0; t<size; t++) cout << nums[t] << ' ';
cout << '\n';

// This is the bubble sort.
for(a=1; a<size; a++)
  for(b=size-1; b>=a; b--) {
    if(nums[b-1] > nums[b]) { // if out of order
      // exchange elements
      t = nums[b-1];
      nums[b-1] = nums[b];
      nums[b] = t;
    }
  }
// This is the end of the bubble sort.

// Display sorted array.
cout << "Sorted array is: ";
for(t=0; t<size; t++) cout << nums[t] << ' ';

return 0;
}
```

Although the bubble sort is good for small arrays, it is not efficient when used on larger ones. The best general-purpose sorting algorithm is the Quicksort. The C++ standard library contains a function called **qsort( )** that implements a version of the Quicksort. However, you will need to know more about C++ before you can use it. Chapter 20 of this book discusses the **qsort( )** function in detail.

Strings

By far, the most common use for one-dimensional arrays is to create character strings. In C++, a *string* is defined as a character array that is terminated by a null. A null character is specified using '**\0**', and is zero. Because of the null terminator, it is necessary to declare a character array to be one character longer than the largest string that it will hold.

For example, if you want to declare an array **str** that could hold a 10-character string, you would write:

```
char str[11];
```

A string is a
null-terminated
character array.

Specifying the size as 11 makes room for the null at the end of the string.

As you learned earlier in this book, C++ allows you to define a string literal. Recall that a *string literal* is a list of characters enclosed in double quotes. Here are some examples:

```
"hello there"    "I like C++"
"#$%@@#$"        ""
```

The last string shown is "". This is called a *null string*. It contains only the null terminator, and no other characters. Null strings are useful because they represent the empty string.

It is not necessary to manually add the null onto the end of string constants; the C++ compiler does this for you automatically. Therefore, the string "Hello" will appear in memory like this:

Reading a String from the Keyboard

The easiest way to read a string entered from the keyboard is to make the array that will receive the string the target of a **cin** statement. For example, the following program reads a string entered by the user:

```cpp
// Using cin to read a string from the keyboard.

#include <iostream>
using namespace std;

int main()
{
  char str[80];

  cout << "Enter a string: ";
  cin >> str; // read string from keyboard
  cout << "Here is your string: ";
  cout << str;

  return 0;
}
```

Although this program is technically correct, there is still a problem. To see what it is, examine the following sample run.

```
Enter a string: This is a test
Here is your string: This
```

As you can see, when the program redisplays the string, it shows only the word "This", not the entire sentence that was entered. The reason for this is that the **>>** operator stops reading a string when the first *whitespace* character is encountered. Whitespace characters include spaces, tabs, and newlines.

One way to solve the whitespace problem is to use another of C++'s library functions, **gets( )**. The general form of a **gets( )** call is:

    gets(*array-name*);

If you need your program to read a string, call **gets( )** with the name of the array, without any index, as its argument. Upon return from **gets( )**, the array will hold the string input from the keyboard. The **gets( )** function will continue to read characters until you press ENTER. The header used by **gets( )** is **<cstdio>**.

This version of the preceding program uses **gets( )** to allow the entry of strings containing spaces.

```
// Using gets() to read a string from the keyboard.

#include <iostream>
#include <cstdio>
using namespace std;

int main()
{
  char str[80];

  cout << "Enter a string: ";
  gets(str); // read a string from the keyboard
  cout << "Here is your string: ";
  cout << str;

  return 0;
}
```

Now, when you run the program and enter the string "This is a test", the entire sentence is read and then displayed, as this sample run shows.

```
Enter a string: This is a test
Here is your string: This is a test
```

There is one other point of interest in the preceding programs. Notice that in the **cout** statement, **str** is used directly. For reasons that will be clear after you have read a few more chapters, the name of a character array that holds a string can be used any place that a string literal can be used.

Keep in mind that neither **>>** nor **gets( )** performs any bounds checking on the array. Therefore, if the user enters a string longer than the size of the array, the array will be overwritten. This makes both methods of reading a string potentially dangerous. Later, when I/O is examined in detail in Chapter 18, you will learn ways around this problem.

Some String Library Functions

C++ supports a wide range of string-manipulation functions. The most common are

    strcpy( )
    strcat( )
    strlen( )
    strcmp( )

The string functions all use the same header, **<cstring>**. Let's take a look at these functions now.

strcpy

A call to **strcpy( )** takes this general form:

    strcpy(*to, from*);

The **strcpy( )** function copies the contents of the string *from* into *to*. Remember, the array that forms *to* must be large enough to hold the string contained in *from*. If it isn't, the *to* array will be overrun, which will probably crash your program.

The following program will copy "hello" into string **str**:

```
#include <iostream>
#include <cstring>
using namespace std;

int main()
{
  char str[80];

  strcpy(str, "hello");
  cout << str;

  return 0;
}
```

strcat

A call to **strcat( )** takes this form:

    strcat(*s1, s2*);

The **strcat( )** function appends *s2* to the end of *s1*; *s2* is unchanged. Both strings must be null-terminated, and the result is null-terminated. For example, the following program will print **hello there** on the screen:

```
#include <iostream>
#include <cstring>
using namespace std;
```

5

```
int main()
{
  char s1[20], s2[10];

  strcpy(s1, "hello");
  strcpy(s2, " there");
  strcat(s1, s2);
  cout << s1;

  return 0;
}
```

strcmp

A call to **strcmp( )** takes this general form:

strcmp(*s1*, *s2*);

The **strcmp( )** function compares two strings and returns 0 if they are equal. If *s1* is greater than *s2* lexicographically (i.e., according to dictionary order), then a positive number is returned; if it is less than *s2*, a negative number is returned.

The **password( )** function, shown in the following program, is a password-verification routine. It uses **strcmp( )** to check a user's input against a password.

```
#include <iostream>
#include <cstring>
#include <cstdio>
using namespace std;

bool password();

int main()
{
  if(password()) cout << "Logged on.\n";
  else cout << "Access denied.\n";

  return 0;
}

// Return true if password accepted; false otherwise.
bool password()
{
  char s[80];

  cout << "Enter password: ";
  gets(s);

  if(strcmp(s, "password")) {  // strings differ
    cout << "Invalid password.\n";
    return false;
  }
```

```
  // strings compared the same
  return true;
}
```

The key to using **strcmp( )** is to remember that it returns false when the strings match. Therefore, you will need to use the **!** (NOT) operator if you want something to occur when the strings are equal. For example, the following program continues to request input until the user types the word "quit":

```
#include <iostream>
#include <cstdio>
#include <cstring>
using namespace std;

int main()
{
  char s[80];

  for(;;) {
    cout << "Enter a string: ";
    gets(s);
    if(!strcmp("quit", s)) break;
  }

  return 0;
}
```

strlen

The general form of a call to **strlen( )** is

　　　　strlen(*s*);

where *s* is a string. The **strlen( )** function returns the length of the string pointed to by *s*.

The following program will print the length of a string entered from the keyboard:

```
#include <iostream>
#include <cstdio>
#include <cstring>
using namespace std;

int main()
{
  char str[80];

  cout << "Enter a string: ";

  gets(str);
```

5

```
  cout << "Length is: " <<  strlen(str);

  return 0;
}
```

If the user enters the string "Hi there", this program will display **8**. The null terminator is not counted by **strlen( )**.

When the following program is run, the string entered at the keyboard is printed in reverse. For example, "hello" will be displayed as **olleh**. Remember that strings are simply character arrays; thus each character can be referenced individually.

```
// Print a string backwards.
#include <iostream>
#include <cstdio>
#include <cstring>
using namespace std;

int main()
{
  char str[80];
  int i;

  cout << "Enter a string: ";
  gets(str);

  // Print the string in reverse.
  for(i=strlen(str)-1; i>=0; i--) cout << str[i];

  return 0;
}
```

As a final example, the following program illustrates the use of all four string functions:

```
#include <iostream>
#include <cstdio>
#include <cstring>
using namespace std;

int main()
{
  char s1[80], s2[80];

  cout << "Enter two strings: ";

  gets(s1); gets(s2);

  cout << "lengths: " << strlen(s1);
  cout << ' ' << strlen(s2) << '\n';
```

```
  if(!strcmp(s1, s2))
     cout << "The strings are equal\n";
  else cout << "not equal\n";

  strcat(s1, s2);
  cout << s1 << '\n';

  strcpy(s1, s2);
  cout << s1 << " and " << s2 << ' ';
  cout << "are now the same\n";

  return 0;
}
```

If this program is run and the strings "hello" and "there" are entered, then the output will be

```
lengths: 5 5
not equal
hellothere
there and there are now the same
```

One last reminder: Remember that **strcmp( )** returns false if the strings are equal. This is why you must use the **!** operator to reverse the condition, as shown in the preceding example, if you are testing for equality.

Using the Null Terminator

The fact that all strings are null-terminated can often be used to simplify various operations on strings. For example, look at how little code is required to uppercase every character in a string:

```cpp
// Convert a string to uppercase.
#include <iostream>
#include <cstring>
#include <cctype>
using namespace std;

int main()
{
  char str[80];
  int i;

  strcpy(str, "this is a test");

  for(i=0; str[i]; i++) str[i] = toupper(str[i]);

  cout << str;
```

5

```
  return 0;
}
```

This program will print **THIS IS A TEST**. It uses the library function **toupper( )**, which returns the uppercase equivalent of its character argument, to convert each character in the string. The **toupper( )** function uses the header **<cctype>**.

Notice that the test condition of the **for** loop is simply the array indexed by the control variable. This works because a true value is any non-zero value. Remember, all printable characters are represented by values that are non-zero, but the null terminating the string is zero. Therefore, the loop runs until it encounters the null terminator, which causes **str[i]** to become zero. Since the null terminator marks the end of the string, the loop stops precisely where it is supposed to. As you progress, you will see many examples that use the null terminator in a similar fashion.

T**IP:**   In addition to **toupper( )**, the C++ standard library contains several other character-manipulation functions. For example, the complement to **toupper( )** is **tolower( )**, which returns the lowercase equivalent of its character argument. Other character functions include **isalpha( )**, **isdigit( )**, **isspace( )**, and **ispunct( )**. These functions each take a character argument and determine if it belongs to that category. For example, **isalpha( )** returns true if its argument is a letter of the alphabet.

Two-Dimensional Arrays

C++ allows multidimensional arrays. The simplest form of the multidimensional array is the two-dimensional array. A two-dimensional array is, in essence, a list of one-dimensional arrays. To declare a two-dimensional integer array **twod** of size 10,20 you would write

```
int twod[10][20];
```

Pay careful attention to the declaration. Unlike some other computer languages, which use commas to separate the array dimensions, C++ places each dimension in its own set of brackets.

Similarly, to access point 3,5 of array **twod**, you would use **twod[3][5]**. In the next example, a two-dimensional array is loaded with the numbers 1 through 12.

```
#include <iostream>
using namespace std;

int main()
{
```

```
int t,i, num[3][4];

for(t=0; t<3; ++t) {
  for(i=0; i<4; ++i) {
    num[t][i] = (t*4)+i+1;
    cout << num[t][i] << ' ';
  }
  cout << '\n';
}

return 0;
}
```

In this example, **num[0][0]** will have the value 1, **num[0][1]** the value 2, **num[0][2]** the value 3, and so on. The value of **num[2][3]** will be 12. Conceptually, the array will look like that shown in Figure 5-1.

Two-dimensional arrays are stored in a row-column matrix, where the first index indicates the row and the second indicates the column. This means that when array elements are accessed in the order in which they are actually stored in memory, the right index changes faster than the left.

You should remember that storage for all array elements is determined at compile time. Also, the memory used to hold an array is required the entire time that the array is in existence. In the case of a two-dimensional array, you can use this formula to determine the number of bytes of memory that will be allocated:

bytes = row × column × number of bytes in type

Therefore, assuming two-byte integers, an integer array with dimensions 10,5 would have 10 × 5 × 2 (or 100) bytes allocated.

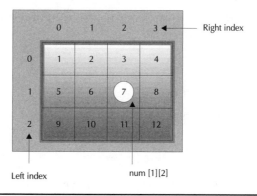

A conceptual view of the **num** array
Figure 5-1.

5

Multidimensional Arrays

C++ allows arrays with more than two dimensions. Here is the general form of a multidimensional array declaration:

   type name[size1][size2]...[sizeN];

For example, the following declaration creates a $4 \times 10 \times 3$ integer array:

```
int multidim[4][10][3];
```

Arrays of more than three dimensions are not often used, due to the amount of memory required to hold them. As stated before, storage for all array elements is allocated during the entire lifetime of an array. When multidimensional arrays are used, large amounts of memory can be consumed. For example, a four-dimensional character array with dimensions 10,6,9,4 would require $10 \times 6 \times 9 \times 4$ (or 2,160) bytes. If each array dimension is increased by a factor of 10 each (that is, $100 \times 60 \times 90 \times 40$), then the memory required for the array increases to 21,600,000 bytes! As you can see, large multidimensional arrays may cause a shortage of memory for other parts of your program. Thus, a program with arrays of more than two or three dimensions may find itself quickly out of memory!

Array Initialization

C++ allows the initialization of arrays. The general form of array initialization is similar to that of other variables, as shown here:

   type-specifier array_name[size] = {value-list};

The *value-list* is a comma-separated list of values that are type-compatible with the base type of the array. The first value will be placed in the first position of the array, the second value in the second position, and so on. Notice that a semicolon follows the }.

In the following example, a 10-element integer array is initialized with the numbers 1 through 10:

```
int i[10] = {1, 2, 3, 4, 5, 6, 7, 8, 9, 10};
```

This means that **i[0]** will have the value 1, and **i[9]** will have the value 10.

Character arrays that will hold strings allow a shorthand initialization that takes this form:

   char *array_name[size]* = "*string*";

For example, the following code fragment initializes **str** to the phrase "hello":

```
char str[6] = "hello";
```

This is the same as writing

```
char str[6] = { 'h', 'e', 'l', 'l', 'o', '\0' };
```

Because strings in C++ must end with a null, you must make sure that the array you declare is long enough to include it. This is why **str** is 6 characters long in these examples, even though "hello" is only 5. When a string literal is used, the compiler automatically supplies the null terminator.

Multidimensional arrays are initialized in the same way as one-dimensional arrays. For example, the following program initializes an array called **sqrs** with the numbers 1 through 10 and their squares:

```
int sqrs[10][2] = {
  1, 1,
  2, 4,
  3, 9,
  4, 16,
  5, 25,
  6, 36,
  7, 49,
  8, 64,
  9, 81,
  10, 100
};
```

5

Examine Figure 5-2 to see how the **sqrs** array appears in memory.

When initializing a multidimensional array, you may add braces around the initializers for each dimension. This is called *subaggregate grouping*. For example, here is another way to write the preceding declaration:

```
int sqrs[10][2] = {
  {1, 1},
  {2, 4},
  {3, 9},
  {4, 16},
  {5, 25},
  {6, 36},
  {7, 49},
  {8, 64},
  {9, 81},
  {10, 100}
};
```

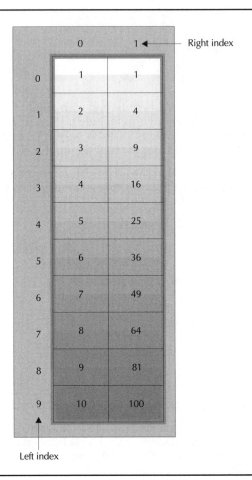

The initialized
sqrs array
Figure 5-2.

When using subaggregate grouping, if you don't supply enough initializers for a given group, the remaining members will be set to zero, automatically.

The following program uses the **sqrs** array to find the square of a number entered by the user. It first looks up the number in the array and then prints the corresponding square.

```
#include <iostream>
using namespace std;

int sqrs[10][2] = {
  {1, 1},
  {2, 4},
  {3, 9},
```

```
    {4, 16},
    {5, 25},
    {6, 36},
    {7, 49},
    {8, 64},
    {9, 81},
    {10, 100}
};

int main()
{
  int i, j;

  cout << "Enter a number between 1 and 10: ";
  cin >> i;

  // look up i
  for(j=0; j<10; j++)
    if(sqrs[j][0]==i) break;

  // display square
  cout << "The square of " << i << " is ";
  cout << sqrs[j][1];

  return 0;
}
```

Global arrays are initialized when the program begins. Local arrays are initialized each time the function that contains them is called, as shown here:

```
#include <iostream>
#include <cstring>
using namespace std;

void f1();

int main()
{
  f1();
  f1();

  return 0;
}

void f1()
{
  char s[80]="this is a test\n";

  cout << s;
  strcpy(s, "CHANGED\n"); // change s
  cout << s;
}
```

This program displays the following output:

```
this is a test
CHANGED
this is a test
CHANGED
```

In the program, the array **s** is initialized each time **f1( )** is called. The fact that **s** is changed in the function does not affect its reinitialization upon subsequent calls. This means that **f1( )** prints

```
this is a test
```

every time it is entered.

Unsized Array Initializations

Imagine that you are using array initialization to build a table of error messages, as shown here:

```
char e1[14] = "Divide by 0\n";
char e2[23] = "End-of-File\n";
char e3[21] = "Access Denied\n";
```

As you might guess, it is very tedious to manually count the characters in each message to determine the correct array dimension. It is possible to let C++ automatically dimension the arrays in this example through the use of *unsized arrays*. If an array-initialization statement does not specify the size of the array, then C++ will automatically create an array large enough to hold all the initializers present. When this approach is used, the message table becomes

```
char e1[] = "Divide by 0\n";
char e2[] = "End-of-File\n";
char e3[] = "Access Denied\n";
```

Besides being less tedious, the unsized array-initialization method allows you to change any of the messages without having to resize the array. This avoids errors caused by accidentally miscounting the number of characters in the message.

Unsized array initializations are not restricted to one-dimensional arrays. For a multidimensional array, you must specify all but the leftmost dimension so that C++ can index the array properly. Using unsized array initializations, you can build tables of varying lengths, with the compiler automatically allocating enough storage for them.

In the following example, **sqrs** is declared as an unsized array:

```
int sqrs[][2] = {
  1, 1,
  2, 4,
```

```
      3, 9,
      4, 16,
      5, 25,
      6, 36,
      7, 49,
      8, 64,
      9, 81,
      10, 100
};
```

The advantage to this declaration over the sized version is that the table may be lengthened or shortened without changing the array dimensions.

Arrays of Strings

A string array is a two-dimensional array of characters.

A special form of a two-dimensional array is an array of strings. It is not uncommon in programming to use an array of strings. The input processor to a database, for instance, may verify user commands against a string array of valid commands. To create an array of strings, a two-dimensional character array is used, with the size of the left index determining the number of strings, and the size of the right index specifying the maximum length of each string. For example, the following declares an array of 30 strings, each having a maximum length of 80 characters:

5

```
char str_array[30][80];
```

Accessing an individual string is quite easy: You simply specify only the left index. For example, the following statement calls **gets( )** with the third string in **str_array**:

```
gets(str_array[2]);
```

To better understand how string arrays work, study the next short program, which accepts lines of text entered at the keyboard and redisplays them after a blank line is entered.

```
// Enter and display strings.
#include <iostream>
#include <cstdio>
using namespace std;

int main()
{
  int t, i;
  char text[100][80];

  for(t=0; t<100; t++) {
    cout << t << ": ";
    gets(text[t]);
    if(!text[t][0]) break; // quit on blank line
  }

  // redisplay the strings
```

```
  for(i=0; i<t; i++)
    cout << text[i] << '\n';

  return 0;
}
```

Notice how the program checks for the entry of a blank line. The **gets( )** function returns a zero-length string if the only key you press is ENTER. This means that the first byte in that string will be the null character. A null value is always false, thus allowing the conditional expression to be true.

An Example Using String Arrays

Arrays of strings are commonly used for handling tables of information. One such application is an employee database that stores the name, telephone number, hours worked per pay period, and hourly wage of each employee. To create such a program for a staff of ten employees, you would define these four arrays (the first two of which are string arrays):

```
char name[10][80];   // this array holds employee names
char phone[10][20];  // their phone numbers
float hours[10];     // hours worked per week
float wage[10];      // wage
```

To enter information about each employee, you could use a function like **enter( )**, as shown here:

```
// Enter information.
void enter()
{
  int i;
  char temp[80];

  for(i=0; i<10; i++) {
    cout << "Enter last name: ";
    cin >> name[i];
    cout << "Enter phone number: ";
    cin >> phone[i];
    cout << "Enter number of hours worked: ";
    cin >> hours[i];
    cout << "Enter wage: ";
    cin >> wage[i];
  }
}
```

Once information has been entered, the database can report the data and calculate the amount of pay each employee is to receive, using the **report( )** function, as shown here:

```
// Display report.
void report()
{
  int i;

  for(i=0; i<10; i++) {
    cout << name[i] << ' ' << phone[i] << '\n';
    cout << "Pay for the week: " << wage[i] * hours[i];
    cout << '\n';
  }
}
```

The entire employee database program is shown next. Pay special attention to how each array is accessed. This version of the employee database program is not particularly useful, because the information is lost when the program is terminated. Later in this book, however, you will learn how to store information in a disk file.

5

```
// A simple employee database program.

#include <iostream>
using namespace std;

char name[10][80];  // this array holds employee names
char phone[10][20]; // their phone numbers
float hours[10];    // hours worked per week
float wage[10];     // wage

int menu();
void enter(), report();

int main()
{
  int choice;

  do {
    choice = menu(); // get selection
    switch(choice) {
      case 0: break;
      case 1: enter();
        break;
      case 2: report();
        break;
      default: cout << "Try again.\n\n";
    }
  } while(choice != 0);

  return 0;
}

// Return a user's selection.
```

```cpp
int menu()
{
  int choice;

  cout << "0. Quit\n";
  cout << "1. Enter information\n";
  cout << "2. Report information\n";
  cout << "\nChoose one: ";
  cin >> choice;

  return choice;
}

// Enter information.
void enter()
{
  int i;
  char temp[80];

  for(i=0; i<10; i++) {
    cout << "Enter last name: ";
    cin >> name[i];
    cout << "Enter phone number: ";
    cin >> phone[i];
    cout << "Enter number of hours worked: ";
    cin >> hours[i];
    cout << "Enter wage: ";
    cin >> wage[i];
  }
}

// Display report.
void report()
{
  int i;

  for(i=0; i<10; i++) {
    cout << name[i] << ' ' << phone[i] << '\n';
    cout << "Pay for the week: " << wage[i] * hours[i];
    cout << '\n';
  }
}
```

CHAPTER 6

Pointers

105

Pointers are without a doubt one of the most important—and troublesome—aspects of C++. In fact, a large measure of C++'s power is derived from pointers. For example, they allow C++ to support such things as linked lists and dynamic memory allocation. They also provide one means by which a function can alter the contents of an argument. However, these and other uses of pointers will be discussed in subsequent chapters. In this chapter, you will learn the basics about pointers, see how to manipulate them, and discover how to avoid some potential troubles.

In a few places in this chapter, it is necessary to refer to the size of several of C++'s basic data types. For the sake of discussion, assume that characters are one byte in length, integers are four bytes long, **float**s are four bytes long, and **double**s have a length of eight bytes. Thus, we will be assuming a typical 32-bit environment.

What Are Pointers?

A *pointer* is a variable that contains a memory address. Very often this address is the location of another variable. For example, if **x** contains the address of **y**, then **x** is said to "point to" **y**.

A pointer is a variable that contains the address of another object.

Pointer variables must be declared as such. The general form of a pointer variable declaration is

   type *var-name;

Here, *type* is the pointer's base type; it must be a valid C++ type. *var-name* is the name of the pointer variable. For example, to declare **p** to be a pointer to an integer, use this declaration:

```
int *p;
```

For a **float** pointer, use

```
float *p;
```

The base type of a pointer determines what type of data it will point to.

In general, in a declaration statement, preceding a variable name with an ***** causes that variable to become a pointer.

The type of data that a pointer will point to is determined by its *base type*. Here is an example:

```
int *ip; // pointer to integers

double *dp; // pointer to doubles
```

As the comments indicate, **ip** is a pointer to integers because its base type is **int**, and **dp** is a pointer to **double**s because its base type is **double**. As you will see, the base type is very important in pointer operations.

The Pointer Operators

There are two special operators that are used with pointers: * and &. The & is a unary operator that returns the memory address of its operand. (Recall that a unary operator requires only one operand.) For example,

```
balptr = &balance;
```

puts into **balptr** the memory address of the variable **balance**. This address is the location of the variable in the computer's internal memory. It has *nothing* to do with the *value* of **balance**. The operation of & can be remembered as returning "the address of" the variable it precedes. Therefore, the above assignment statement could be verbalized as "**balptr** receives the address of **balance**." To better understand this assignment, assume that the variable **balance** is located at address 100. Then, after the assignment takes place, **balptr** has the value 100.

The second operator is *, and it is the complement of &. It is a unary operator that returns the value of the variable located at the address specified by its operand. Continuing with the same example, if **balptr** contains the memory address of the variable **balance**, then

6

```
value = *balptr;
```

will place the value of **balance** into **value**. For example, if **balance** originally had the value 3,200, then **value** will have the value 3,200, because that is the value stored at location 100, the memory address that was assigned to **balptr**. The operation of * can be remembered as "at address." In this case, then, the statement could be read as "**value** receives the value at address **balptr**." Figure 6-1 depicts the actions of the two preceding statements.

The following program executes the sequence of operations shown in Figure 6-1:

```cpp
#include <iostream>
using namespace std;

int main()
{
  int balance;
  int *balptr;
  int value;

  balance = 3200;
  balptr = &balance;
  value = *balptr;
  cout << "balance is: " << value << '\n';

  return 0;
}
```

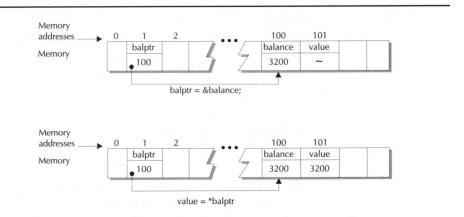

The * and
& pointer
operators
Figure 6-1.

The output is shown here.

```
balance is: 3200
```

*Indirection is the
process of using a
pointer to access
some object.*

It is unfortunate that the multiplication symbol and the "at address" symbol are the
same. This fact sometimes confuses newcomers to the C++ language. These operators
have no relationship to each other. Keep in mind that both **&** and ***** have a higher
precedence than any of the arithmetic operators except the unary minus, with which
they are equal.

The act of using a pointer is often called *indirection,* because you are accessing one
variable indirectly through another variable.

The Base Type Is Important

In the preceding discussion, you saw that it was possible to assign **value** the value
of **balance** indirectly through a pointer. At this point, you may have thought of
this important question: How does C++ know how many bytes to copy into **value**
from the address pointed to by **balptr**? Or, more generally, how does the compiler
transfer the proper number of bytes for any assignment using a pointer? The answer
is that the base type of the pointer determines the type of data that the compiler
assumes the pointer is pointing to. In this case, because **balptr** is an integer pointer,
C++ copies four bytes of information (assuming 32-bit integers) into **value** from the
address pointed to by **balptr**. However, if it had been a **double** pointer, for example,
then eight bytes would have been copied.

Your pointer variables must always point to the correct type of data. For example,
when you declare a pointer to be of type **int**, the compiler assumes that anything
it points to will be an integer value. Generally, you won't need to worry about this
because C++ will not allow you to assign one type of pointer to another unless the
two types of pointers are compatible (i.e., essentially, the same).

For example, the following fragment is incorrect:

```
int *p;
double f;
// ...
p = &f; // ERROR
```

This fragment is invalid because you cannot assign a **double** pointer to an integer pointer. That is, **&f** generates a pointer to a **double**, but **p** is a pointer to an **int**. These two types are not compatible. (In fact, the compiler would flag an error at this point and not compile your program.)

Although two pointers must have compatible types in order for one to be assigned to another, you can override this restriction (at your own risk) by using a cast. For example, the following fragment is now technically correct:

```
int *p ;
double f;
// ...
p = (int *) &f; // Now technically OK
```

The cast to **int *** causes the **double** pointer to be converted to an integer pointer. However, to use a cast for this purpose is questionable, because the base type of a pointer determines how the compiler treats the data it points to. In this case, even though **p** is actually pointing to a floating-point value, the compiler still "thinks" that **p** is pointing to an integer (because **p** is an integer pointer).

To better understand why using a cast to assign one type of pointer to another is not usually a good idea, consider the following short program:

```
// This program will not work right.
#include <iostream>
using namespace std;

int main()
{
  double x, y;
  int *p;

  x = 123.23;
  p = (int *) &x; // use cast to assign double * to int *

  y = *p; // What will this do?
  cout << y; // What will this print?

  return 0;
}
```

As you can see, **p** (which is an integer pointer) has been assigned the address of **x** (which is a **double**). Thus, when **y** is assigned the value pointed to by **p**, **y** receives only four bytes of data (and not the eight required for a **double** value), because **p** is an integer pointer. Therefore, the **cout** statement displays not 123.23, but a garbage value instead. (Try this program and observe the result.)

Assigning Values Through a Pointer

You can use a pointer on the left side of an assignment statement to assign a value to the location pointed to by the pointer. Assuming that **p** is an integer pointer, this assigns the value 101 to the location pointed to by **p**:

```
*p = 101;
```

You can verbalize this assignment like this: "at the location pointed to by **p**, assign the value 101." To increment or decrement the value at the location pointed to by a pointer, you can use a statement like this:

```
(*p)++;
```

The parentheses are necessary because the ***** operator has lower precedence than the **++** operator.

The following program demonstrates assignment using a pointer.

```
#include <iostream>
using namespace std;

int main()
{
  int *p, num;

  p = &num;

  *p = 100;
  cout << num << ' ';
  (*p)++;
  cout << num << ' ';
  (*p)--;
  cout << num << '\n';

  return 0;
}
```

The output from the program is shown here.

```
100 101 100
```

Pointer Expressions

Pointers can be used in most valid C++ expressions. However, some special rules apply. Remember also that you may need to surround some parts of a pointer expression with parentheses in order to ensure that the outcome is what you desire.

Pointer Arithmetic

There are only four arithmetic operators that can be used on pointers: **++, – –, +,** and
–. To understand what occurs in pointer arithmetic, let **p1** be an integer pointer with
a current value of 2,000 (that is, it contains the address 2,000). Assuming 32-bit integers,
after the expression

```
p1++;
```

the contents of **p1** will be 2,004, not 2,001! Each time **p1** is incremented, it will point
to the *next integer*. The same is true of decrements. For example,

```
p1--;
```

will cause **p1** to have the value 1,996, assuming that it previously was 2,000. Here is
why: Each time that a pointer is incremented, it will point to the memory location
of the next element of its base type. Each time it is decremented, it will point to the
location of the previous element of its base type.

6

In the case of character pointers, an increment or decrement will appear as "normal"
arithmetic because characters are one byte long. However, every other type of pointer
will increase or decrease by the length of its base type.

You are not limited to only increment and decrement operations. You can also add or
subtract integers to or from pointers. The expression

```
p1 = p1 + 9;
```

makes **p1** point to the ninth element of **p1**'s base type, beyond the one to which it is
currently pointing.

While you cannot add pointers, you can subtract one pointer from another (provided
they are both of the same base type). The remainder will be the number of elements
of the base type that separate the two pointers.

Other than addition and subtraction of a pointer and an integer, or the subtraction
of two pointers, no other arithmetic operations can be performed on pointers. For
example, you cannot add or subtract **float** or **double** values to or from pointers.

To see the effects of pointer arithmetic, execute the next short program. It prints the
actual physical addresses to which an integer pointer (**i**) and a floating-point pointer
(**f**) are pointing. Observe how each changes, relative to its base type, each time the loop
is repeated. (For most 32-bit compilers, **i** will increase by 4s and **f** will increase by 8s.)
Notice that when using a pointer in a **cout** statement, its address is automatically
displayed in the addressing format applicable to the current processor and environment.

```
// Demonstrate pointer arithmetic.
#include <iostream>
using namespace std;

int main()
```

```
{
  int *i, j[10];
  double *f, g[10];
  int x;

  i = j;
  f = g;

  for(x=0; x<10; x++)
    cout << i+x << ' ' << f+x << '\n';

  return 0;
}
```

Here is sample output. (The addresses you see when you run the program may differ from those shown here, but the net effect will be the same.)

```
0012FE5C 0012FE84
0012FE60 0012FE8C
0012FE64 0012FE94
0012FE68 0012FE9C
0012FE6C 0012FEA4
0012FE70 0012FEAC
0012FE74 0012FEB4
0012FE78 0012FEBC
0012FE7C 0012FEC4
0012FE80 0012FECC
```

REMEMBER: All pointer arithmetic is performed relative to the base type of the pointer.

Pointer Comparisons

Pointers may be compared by using relational operators, such as ==, <, and >. However, for the outcome of a pointer comparison to be meaningful, the two pointers normally must have some relationship to each other. For example, if **p1** and **p2** are pointers that point to two separate and unrelated variables, then any comparison between **p1** and **p2** is generally meaningless. However, if **p1** and **p2** point to variables that are related to each other, such as elements of the same array, then **p1** and **p2** can be meaningfully compared. Later in this chapter, you will see a sample program that does this.

Pointers and Arrays

In C++, there is a close relationship between pointers and arrays. In fact, frequently a pointer and an array are interchangeable. In this section, you will see how pointers and arrays relate.

To begin, consider this fragment:

```
char str[80];
char *p1;

p1 = str;
```

An array name without an index generates a pointer to the start of the array.

Here, **str** is an array of 80 characters and **p1** is a character pointer. However, it is the third line that is of interest. In this line, **p1** is assigned the address of the first element in the **str** array. (That is, after the assignment, **p1** will point to **str[0]**.) Here's why: In C++, using the name of an array without an index generates a pointer to the first element in the array. Thus the assignment **p1 = str** assigns the address of **str[0]** to **p1**. This is a crucial point to understand: When an unindexed array name is used in an expression, it yields a pointer to the first element in the array.

Since, after the assignment, **p1** points to the beginning of **str**, you may use **p1** to access elements in the array. For example, if you want to access the fifth element in **str**, you could use

```
str[4]
```

or

```
*(p1+4)
```

Both statements will return the fifth element. Remember, array indices start at zero, so when **str** is indexed, a 4 is used to access the fifth element. A 4 is also added to the pointer **p1** to get the fifth element, because **p1** currently points to the first element of **str**.

The parentheses surrounding **p1+4** are necessary because the * operation has a higher priority than the + operation. Without the parentheses, the expression would first find the value pointed to by **p1** (the first location in the array) and then add 4 to it.

TIP: Be sure to properly parenthesize a pointer expression. If you don't, the error will be hard to find later because your program will look correct. If in doubt about whether or not to add parentheses, add them; they will do no harm.

In effect, C++ allows two methods of accessing array elements: pointer arithmetic and array indexing. This is important because pointer arithmetic can sometimes be faster than array indexing—especially when you are accessing an array in strictly sequential order. Since speed is often a consideration in programming, the use of pointers to access array elements is very common in C++ programs. Also, you can sometimes write tighter code by using pointers rather than array indexing.

To get the flavor of the difference between using array indexing and pointer arithmetic, two versions of the same program will be shown next. The program extracts words, separated by spaces, from a string. For example, given "Hello Tom," the program would extract "Hello" and "Tom." Programmers typically refer to delineated character sequences as *tokens,* and the process of extracting tokens is generally called *tokenizing*. The program scans the input string, copying characters from the string into another array, called **token**, until a space is encountered. It then prints the token and repeats the process until the null at the end of the string is reached. For example, if you enter **This is a test.** the program displays the following:

```
This
is
a
test.
```

Here is the pointer version of the tokenizing program:

```cpp
// Tokenizing program: pointer version.
#include <iostream>
#include <cstdio>
using namespace std;

int main()
{
  char str[80];
  char token[80];
  char *p, *q;

  cout << "Enter a sentence: ";
  gets(str);

  p = str;

  // Read a token at a time from the string.
  while(*p) {
    q = token;  // set q pointing to start of token

    /* Read characters until either a space or the
       null terminator is encountered. */
    while(*p!=' ' && *p) {
      *q = *p;
      q++; p++;
    }
    if(*p) p++; // advance past the space
    *q = '\0'; // null terminate the token
    cout << token << '\n';
  }

  return 0;
}
```

Here is the array-indexing version:

```
// Tokenizing program: array-indexing version.
#include <iostream>
#include <cstdio>
using namespace std;

int main()
{
  char str[80];
  char token[80];
  int i, j;

  cout << "Enter a sentence: ";
  gets(str);

  // Read a token at a time from the string.
  for(i=0; ; i++) {
    /* Read characters until either a space or the
       null terminator is encountered. */
    for(j=0; str[i]!=' ' && str[i]; j++, i++)
      token[j] = str[i];

    token[j] = '\0'; // null terminate the token
    cout << token << '\n';
    if(!str[i]) break;
  }

  return 0;
}
```

Because of the way some C++ compilers generate code, these two programs may not
be equivalent in performance. Generally, it takes more machine instructions to index
an array than it does to perform arithmetic on a pointer. Consequently, in professionally
written C++ code, it is common to see the pointer version used more frequently.
However, as a beginning C++ programmer, feel free to use array indexing until you
are comfortable with pointers.

Indexing a Pointer

As you have just seen, it is possible to access an array by using pointer arithmetic.
What you might find surprising is that the reverse is also true. In C++, it is possible
to index a pointer as if it were an array. This further illustrates the close relationship
between pointers and arrays. Here is an example that indexes a pointer.

```
// Indexing a pointer like an array.
#include <iostream>
#include <cctype>
using namespace std;

int main()
{
  char str[20] = "hello tom";
  char *p;
```

```
  int i;

  p = str; // put address of str into p

  // now, index p like an array
  for(i=0; p[i]; i++) p[i] = toupper(p[i]);

  cout << p; // display the string

  return 0;
}
```

The program displays

```
HELLO TOM
```

Here is how it works. First the program loads the string **str** with "hello tom". It then assigns the address of the beginning of **str** to **p**. Next, using **toupper( )**, it converts each character in the string to uppercase by indexing **p**. Remember, the expression **p[i]** is functionally identical to ***(p+i)**.

Are Pointers and Arrays Interchangeable?

As the preceding few pages have shown, pointers and arrays are strongly related. In fact, pointers and arrays are interchangeable in many cases. For example, a pointer that points to the beginning of an array can access that array by using either pointer arithmetic or array-style indexing. However, pointers and arrays are not completely interchangeable. For example, consider this fragment:

```
int num[10];
int i;

for(i=0; i<10; i++) {
  *num = i; // this is OK
  num++; // ERROR -- cannot modify num
}
```

Here, **num** is an array of integers. As the comments describe, while it is perfectly acceptable to apply the ***** operator to **num** (which is a pointer operation), it is illegal to modify **num**'s value. The reason for this is that **num** is a constant that points to the beginning of an array. Thus, you cannot increment it. More generally, while an array name without an index does generate a pointer to the beginning of an array, it cannot be changed.

Although an array name generates a pointer constant, it can still take part in pointer-style expressions, as long as it is not modified. For example, the following is a valid statement that assigns **num[3]** the value 100:

```
*(num+3) = 100; // This is OK because num is not changed
```

Pointers and String Literals

You might be wondering how string literals, like the one in the fragment shown here, are handled by C++:

```
cout << strlen("C++ Compiler");
```

The answer is that when the compiler encounters a string literal, it stores it in the program's *string table* and generates a pointer to the string. Therefore, the following program is perfectly valid, and prints the phrase **Pointers are fun to use.**
on the screen:

```
#include <iostream>
using namespace std;

int main()
{
  char *s;

  s = "Pointers are fun to use.\n";

  cout << s;

  return 0;
}
```

In this program, the characters that make up a string literal are stored in the string table, and **s** is assigned a pointer to the string in that table.

The string table is a table generated by the compiler that holds the strings used by your program.

Since a pointer into your program's string table is generated automatically whenever a string literal is used, you might be tempted to use this fact to modify the contents of the string table. However, this is usually not a good idea because many C++ compilers create optimized tables in which one string literal may be used at two or more different places in your program. Thus, changing a string may cause undesired side effects. Furthermore, string literals are constants and some modern C++ compilers will not let you change their contents. Attempting to do so generates a run-time error.

A Comparison Example

Earlier you learned that it is legal to compare the value of one pointer to that of another. However, in order for a pointer comparison to be meaningful, the two pointers must have some relationship to each other. The most common way such a relationship is established is when both pointers point to elements of the same array. For example, given two pointers, A and B, that both point into the same array, if A is less than B then A points to an element at a smaller index than the element pointed to by B. Such comparisons are especially useful for determining boundary conditions.

The following program demonstrates a pointer comparison. The program creates two pointer variables. One, called **start**, initially points to the beginning of an array, and the other, called **end**, points to the end of the array. As the user enters numbers, the array is filled sequentially from the beginning to the end. Each time a number is entered into the array, **start** is incremented. To determine if the array is full, the program simply compares **start** with **end**. When **start** is greater than **end**, the array has been filled. Once the array is full, the contents of the array are displayed.

```cpp
// A pointer comparison example.
#include <iostream>
using namespace std;

int main()
{
  int num[10];
  int *start, *end;

  start = num;
  end = &num[9];

  // enter the values
  while(start <= end) {
    cout << "Enter a number: ";
    cin >> *start;
    start++;
  }

  start = num;  // reset the starting pointer

  // display the values
  while(start <= end) {
    cout << *start << ' ';
    start++;
  }

  return 0;
}
```

As this program illustrates, because **start** and **end** both point to a common object, in this case the array **num**, they can be meaningfully compared. This type of pointer comparison is used frequently in professionally written C++ code.

Arrays of Pointers

Pointers can be arrayed like any other data type. For example,

```cpp
int *ipa[10];
```

declares **ipa** as an array of 10 integer pointers. Thus, each element in **ipa** holds a pointer to an **int** value.

To assign the address of an **int** variable called **var** to the third element of **ipa**, you would write

```cpp
ipa[2] = &var;
```

Remember, **ipa** is an array of integer pointers. The only values that its array elements can hold are the addresses of integer variables. This is why **var** is preceded by the **&** operator.

Using the **ipa** array to assign the value of **var** to an **int** variable called **x**, you would write:

```
x = *ipa[2];
```

Because the address of **var** is stored at **ipa[2]**, applying the * operator to this index causes the value of **var** to be obtained.

Like other arrays, arrays of pointers can be initialized. A common use for initialized pointer arrays is to hold pointers to strings. For example, to create a function that will output a fortune, you can define a number of different messages in a pointer array, as shown here:

```
char *fortunes[] = {
  "Soon, you will come into some money.\n",
  "A new love will enter your life.\n",
  "You will live long and prosper.\n",
  "Now is a good time to invest for the future.\n",
  "A close friend will ask for a favor.\n"
};
```

Remember, C++ stores all string literals in the string table associated with your program, so the array need only store pointers to the strings. Thus, to print the second message, use a statement like this:

```
cout << fortunes[1];
```

An entire "fortune cookie" program is shown here. It uses **rand( )** to generate a random number. It then uses the modulus operator to obtain a number between 0 and 4, which it uses to index the array.

```
#include <iostream>
#include <cstdlib>
#include <conio.h>
using namespace std;

char *fortunes[] = {
  "Soon, you will come into some money.\n",
  "A new love will enter your life.\n",
  "You will live long and prosper.\n",
  "Now is a good time to invest for the future.\n",
  "A close friend will ask for a favor.\n"
};

int main()
{
  int chance;
```

6

```
  cout << "To see your fortune, press a key: ";

  // randomize the random number generator
  while(!kbhit()) rand();

  cout << '\n';

  chance = rand();
  chance = chance % 5;
  cout << fortunes[chance];

  return 0;
}
```

Notice the **while** loop in the program, which calls **rand( )** repeatedly until a key is pressed. Because the **rand( )** function always generates the same sequence of random numbers, it is important to have some way for the program to start using this sequence at a random point. (Otherwise, the same fortune will be given each time the program is run.) This is achieved by repeated calls to **rand( )**. When the user presses a key, the loop stops at a random point in the sequence, and the fortune is displayed on the screen. Remember, **kbhit( )** is a common extension provided by many compilers, but it is not defined by C++.

The next example uses a two-dimensional array of pointers to create the skeleton of a program that displays a syntax reminder for the C++ keywords. This program initializes a list of string pointers. The first dimension points to a C++ keyword, and the second dimension points to a short description of the keyword. The list is terminated by two null strings. These nulls are used to mark the end of the list. The user enters a keyword, and the program displays the description. As you can see, only a few keywords have been listed. The expansion of the list is left to you, as an exercise.

```
// A simple C++ keyword synopsis program.

#include <iostream>
#include <cstring>
using namespace std;

char *keyword[][2] = {
  "for", "for(initialization; condition; increment)",
  "if", "if(condition) ... else ...",
  "switch", "switch(value) { case-list }",
  "while", "while(condition) ...",
  // add the rest of the C++ keywords here
  "", ""   // terminate the list with nulls
};

int main()
{
  char str[80];
```

```
   int i;

   cout << "Enter keyword: ";
   cin >> str;

   // display syntax
   for(i=0; *keyword[i][0]; i++)
     if(!strcmp(keyword[i][0], str))
       cout << keyword[i][1];

   return 0;
}
```

Here is a sample run.

```
Enter keyword: for
for(initialization; condition; increment)
```

In the program, notice the expression controlling the **for** loop. It causes the loop to terminate when **keyword[i][0]** contains a pointer that points to a null, which is a false value. Thus, when the loop encounters the null strings at the end of the pointer array, the loop stops.

The Null Pointer Convention

After a pointer is declared, but before it has been assigned a value, it will contain an arbitrary value. Should you try to use the pointer prior to giving it a value, you will probably crash not only your program, but perhaps even the operating system of your computer (a very nasty type of error!). While there is no sure way to avoid using an uninitialized pointer, C++ programmers have adopted a procedure that helps prevent some errors. By convention, if a pointer contains the null (zero) value, it is assumed to point to nothing. Thus, if all unused pointers are given the null value and you avoid the use of a null pointer, you can avoid the accidental misuse of an uninitialized pointer. This is a good practice to follow.

Any type of pointer can be initialized to null when it is declared. For example, the following initializes **p** to null:

```
float *p = 0; // p is now a null pointer
```

To check for a null pointer, use an **if** statement, like one of these:

```
if(p) // succeeds if p is not null
```

```
if(!p) // succeeds if p is null
```

If you follow the null pointer convention, you will avoid many problems when using pointers.

6

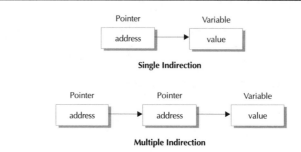

Multiple Indirection

A pointer to a pointer is a form of multiple indirection, or a chain of pointers. Consider Figure 6-2. As you can see, in the case of a normal pointer, the pointer contains the address of a value. In the case of a pointer to a pointer, the first pointer contains the address of the second pointer, which points to the location that contains the desired value.

IN DEPTH

Pointers and 16-bit Environments

Although the most common computing environment today is 32-bits, there are still 16-bit environments in use, and there is a lot of old 16-bit code still in existence. The most important 16-bit environment is DOS, followed by Windows 3.1. These operating systems were designed for the 8086 family of processors, which includes the 80286, 80386, 80486, and Pentium, when running in 8086-emulation mode. Although most new code is designed for a 32-bit environment, programs are still being written and maintained for the more compact 16-bit environments. Because there are some issues unique to the 16-bit environment that impact the way code is written, a brief discussion is in order for the benefit of those programmers working in one of these environments, adapting older code, or porting 16-bit code to 32 bits.

When writing 16-bit code for the 8086 family of processors you have up to six different ways to compile your program, each organizing the memory of the machine differently. You can compile your programs for the tiny, small, medium, compact, large, and huge *memory models*. Each of these models optimizes the space reserved for data, code, and stack in its own way. The reason for the different memory organizations is based on the 8086 family's use of a segmented architecture when running 16-bit code. In 16-bit segmented mode, the 8086 family divides memory into 64K segments.

The memory model can, in some cases, have an effect on how pointers behave and on what you can do with them. The main issue is what happens when a pointer is incremented beyond a segment boundary. It is beyond the scope of this book to discuss the behaviors and nuances of each 8086 16-bit memory model. Just be aware that if you are working in a 16-bit 8086 environment then you will need to consult your compiler's documentation about memory models and their effect on pointers.

One last thing: When writing for the modern, 32-bit environment, there is only one way to organize memory, which is called the *flat model*.

Multiple indirection can be carried on to whatever extent desired, but there are few cases where more than a pointer to a pointer is needed, or, indeed, is even wise to use. Excessive indirection is difficult to follow and prone to conceptual errors.

6

A variable that is a pointer to a pointer must be declared as such. This is done by placing an additional asterisk in front of its name. For example, this declaration tells the compiler that **balance** is a pointer to a pointer of type **int**:

```
int **balance;
```

It is important to understand that **balance** is not a pointer to an integer, but rather a pointer to an **int** pointer.

When a target value is indirectly pointed to by a pointer to a pointer, accessing that value requires that the asterisk operator be applied twice, as is shown in this short example:

```
// Demonstrate multiple indirection.
#include <iostream>
using namespace std;

int main()
{
  int x, *p, **q;

  x = 10;
  p = &x;
  q = &p;

  cout << **q; // prints the value of x

  return 0;
}
```

Here, **p** is declared as a pointer to an integer, and **q** as a pointer to a pointer to an integer. The **cout** statement will print the number 10 on the screen.

Problems with Pointers

Nothing will get you into more trouble than a "wild" pointer! Pointers are a mixed blessing. They give you tremendous power and are useful for a number of different operations. But, when a pointer accidentally contains the wrong value, it can be the most difficult bug to track down.

Bugs caused by bad pointers are hard to find because often the pointer itself does not exhibit the problem. Instead, the problem shows itself only indirectly, perhaps several steps after you have performed a pointer operation. For example, if a pointer accidentally points to the wrong data, then a pointer operation may alter this data, but the problem associated with this unintended alteration will not manifest itself until later in the program's execution. This may lead you to look for the bug in the wrong place. By the time the problem is evident, there may be little or no indication that the pointer was the original cause of the problem. For this reason, pointer bugs have caused programmers to lose sleep time and time again.

Since pointer problems are so troublesome, let's look at some ways they can happen, and how they can be avoided.

Uninitialized Pointers

The classic example of a pointer error is the *uninitialized pointer*. Consider this example:

```
// This program is wrong.
int main(){
  int x, *p;

  x = 10;
  *p = x; // where does p point?

  return 0;
}
```

Here, **p** contains an unknown address because it has never been defined. You will have no way of knowing where the value of **x** has been written. When your program is very small, as it is here, the odds are that **p** will contain an address that is not in your code or data area. Most of the time, your program will seem to work fine. However, as your program grows, the probability of **p** pointing into either your program's code or data area increases. Eventually your program stops working. The way to prevent this type of program is obvious: make sure that a pointer is pointing to something valid before using it!

Invalid Pointer Comparisons

Comparisons between pointers that do not access the same array are generally invalid, and often cause errors. You should not make assumptions about where your data will be placed in memory, whether it will always be in the same place, or whether every compiler or execution environment will treat it in the same way. Therefore, making any comparisons between pointers to two different objects may yield unexpected results. Here is an example:

```
char s[80];
char y[80];
char *p1, *p2;

p1 = s;
p2 = y;
if(p1 < p2) . . .
```

This code is based on an invalid concept since C++ makes no guarantees about the placement of variables in memory. You should write your applications in such a way that they work no matter where data is located.

A related error assumes that two back-to-back arrays can be indexed as one simply by incrementing a pointer across the array boundaries. For example:

```
int first[10];
int second[10];

int *p, t;

p = first;
for(t=0; t<20; ++t) {
  *p = t;
  p++;
}
```

6

The aim here is to initialize arrays **first** and **second** with the numbers 0 through 19, but the code is not reliable. Even though it may work with some compilers under certain circumstances, it assumes that both arrays will be placed back-to-back in memory with **first** first. However, C++ does not guarantee how variables will be located in memory.

Forgetting to Reset a Pointer

The following (incorrect) program inputs a string entered from the keyboard and then displays the ASCII code for each character in the string. (Notice that it uses a cast to cause the ASCII codes to be displayed.) However, this program has a serious bug.

```
// This program is wrong.

#include <iostream>
#include <cstdio>
#include <cstring>
using namespace std;

int main()
{
  char s[80];
  char *p1;

  p1 = s;

  do {
```

```
    cout << "Enter a string: ";
    gets(p1); // read a string
    // print the ASCII values of each character
    while(*p1) cout << (int) *p1++ << ' ';
    cout << '\n';
  } while(strcmp(s, "done"));

  return 0;
}
```

Can you find the error?

The pointer **p1** is assigned the address of **s** once. This assignment is made outside of the loop. The first time through the loop, **p1** does point to the first character in **s**. However, the second time through, it continues on from where it left off, because it has not been reset to the start of the array **s**. This will eventually cause **s** to be overrun.

The proper way to write this program is shown here:

```
// This program is correct.

#include <iostream>
#include <cstdio>
#include <cstring>
using namespace std;

int main()
{
  char s[80];
  char *p1;

  do {
    p1 = s; // reset p1 each time through the loop

    cout << "Enter a string: ";
    gets(p1); // read a string
    // print the ASCII values of each character
    while(*p1) cout << (int) *p1++ << ' ';
    cout << '\n';
  } while(strcmp(s, "done"));

  return 0;
}
```

Here, each time the loop iterates, **p1** is set to the beginning of the string.

REMEMBER: The key to the safe use of pointers is to know where your pointers are pointing at all times.

CHAPTER 7

Functions, Part One:
The Fundamentals

This chapter begins an in-depth discussion of the function. Functions are the building blocks of C++, and a firm understanding of them is fundamental to becoming a successful C++ programmer. Aside from their brief introduction in Chapter 2, you have been using functions more or less intuitively. In this chapter you will study them in detail. Topics include the scope rules of a function, recursive functions, some special properties of the **main( )** function, the **return** statement, and function prototypes.

Scope Rules of Functions

The scope rules define how an object may be accessed and determine its lifetime.

The *scope rules* of a language are the rules that govern how an object may be accessed by various parts of your program. In other words, the scope rules determine what code has access to a variable. The scope rules also determine the lifetime of a variable. As mentioned earlier, there are three types of variables: local variables, formal parameters, and global variables. Let's look more closely at the scope rules at this time, with emphasis on how they relate to functions.

Local Variables

As you know, variables that are declared inside a function are called *local variables*. However, C++ supports a more subtle concept of the local variable than you have previously seen. In C++, variables can be localized to a block. That is, a variable can be declared inside any block of code and is then local to it. (Remember, a block begins with an opening curly brace and ends with a closing curly brace.) In reality, variables local to a function are simply a special case of the more general concept.

A local variable can be used only by statements located within the block in which it is declared. Stated another way, a local variable is not known outside its own code block. Thus, statements outside a block cannot access an object defined within the block.

One of the most important things to understand about local variables is that they exist only while the block of code in which they are declared is executing. This means that a local variable is created upon entry into its block and destroyed upon exit. Because a local variable is destroyed upon exit from its block, its value is lost.

The most common code block is the function. In C++, each function defines a block of code that begins with the function's opening curly brace and ends with its closing curly brace. A function's code and data are private to that function, and cannot be accessed by any statement in any other function, except through a call to that function. (It is not possible, for instance, to use a **goto** statement to jump into the middle of another function.) The body of a function is hidden from the rest of the program and, unless it uses global variables, it can neither affect nor be affected by other parts of the program. Thus, the contents of one function are completely separate from the contents of another. Stated another way, the code and data that are defined within one function cannot interact with the code or data defined in another function, because the two functions have a different scope.

Because each function defines its own scope, the variables declared within one function have no effect on those declared in another—even if those variables share the same name. For example, consider the following program:

```
#include <iostream>
using namespace std;

void f1();

int main()
{
  char str[] = "this is str in main()";

  cout << str << '\n';
  f1();
  cout << str << '\n';

  return 0;
}

void f1()
{
  char str[80];

  cout << "Enter something: ";
  cin >> str;
  cout << str << '\n';
}
```

7

A character array called **str** is declared twice here, once in **main( )** and once in **f1( )**. The **str** in **main( )** has no bearing on, or relationship to, the one in **f1( )**. The reason for this is that each **str** is known only to the block in which it is declared. To confirm this, try running the program. As you will see, even though **str** receives a string entered by the user inside **f1( )**, the contents of **str** in **main( )** remain unchanged.

The C++ language contains the keyword **auto**, which can be used to declare local variables. However, since all non-global variables are, by default, assumed to be **auto**, it is virtually never used. Hence, you will not see it used in any of the examples in this book. However, if you choose to use it, place it immediately before the variable's type, as shown here:

```
auto char ch;
```

It is common practice to declare all variables needed within a function at the beginning of that function's code block. This is done mainly so that anyone reading the code can easily determine what variables are used. However, the beginning of the function's block is not the only place where local variables can be declared. A local variable can be declared anywhere, within any block of code. A variable declared within a block is local to that block. This means that the variable does not exist until the block is entered and is destroyed when the block is exited. Furthermore, no code outside that block—including other code in the function—can access that variable.

To understand this, try the following program:

```
/* This program illustrates how variables can be
   local to a block.
*/

#include <iostream>
#include <cstring>
using namespace std;

int main()
{
  int choice;

  cout << "(1) add numbers or ";
  cout << "(2) concatenate strings?: ";

  cin >> choice;
  if(choice == 1) {
    int a, b;   /* activate two integer vars */
    cout << "Enter two numbers: ";
    cin >> a >> b;
    cout << "Sum is " << a+b << '\n';
  }
  else {
    char s1[80], s2[80];   /* activate two strings */
    cout << "Enter two strings: ";
    cin >> s1;
    cin >> s2;
    strcat(s1, s2);
    cout << "Concatenation is " << s1 << '\n';
  }

  return 0;
}
```

This program either adds two numbers or concatenates two strings, depending on the user's choice. Notice the variable declarations for **a** and **b** in the **if** block and those for **s1** and **s2** in the **else** block. These variables will come into existence only when their respective blocks are entered, and they will cease to exist when their blocks are exited. If the user chooses to add numbers, then **a** and **b** are created. If the user wants to concatenate strings, **s1** and **s2** are created. Finally, none of these variables can be referenced from outside of its block—not even in other parts of the function. For example, if you try to compile the following (incorrect) version of the program, you will receive an error message:

```
/* This program is incorrect. */

#include <iostream>
#include <cstring>
using namespace std;

int main()
{
```

```
   int choice;

   cout << "(1) add numbers or ";
   cout << "(2) concatenate strings?: ";

   cin >> choice;
   if(choice == 1) {
     int a, b;   /* activate two integer vars */
     cout << "Enter two numbers: ";
     cin >> a >> b;
     cout << "Sum is " << a+b << '\n';
   }
   else {
     char s1[80], s2[80];   /* activate two strings */
     cout << "Enter two strings: ";
     cin >> s1;
     cin >> s2;
     strcat(s1, s2);
     cout << "Concatenation is " << s1 << '\n';
   }

   a = 10; // *** Error *** -- a not known here!

   return 0;
}
```

In this case, **a** is not known outside of the **else** block. Thus, it is an error to attempt to use it.

When a local variable declared in an inner block has the same name as a variable declared in an outer block, the variable declared in the inner block overrides the one in the outer block, within the scope of the inner block. For example:

```
#include <iostream>
using namespace std;

int main()
{
  int i, j;

  i = 10;
  j = 100;

  if(j > 0) {
    int i; // this i is separate from outer i

    i = j / 2;
    cout << "inner i: " << i << '\n';
  }

  cout << "outer i: " << i << '\n';

  return 0;
}
```

7

The output from this program is shown here:

```
inner i: 50
outer i: 10
```

The **i** declared within the **if** block overrides, or hides, the outer **i**. Changes that take place on the inner **i** have no effect on the outer **i**. Furthermore, outside of the **if** block, the inner **i** is unknown and the outer **i** comes back into view.

Because local variables are created and destroyed with each entry and exit from the blocks in which they are declared, a local variable will not hold its value between activations of its block. This is especially important to remember in terms of a function call. When a function is called, its local variables are created, and upon its return, they are destroyed. This means that local variables cannot retain their values between calls. (There is one way around this restriction, however, which will be explained later in this book.)

A local variable will not hold its value between activations.

Unless otherwise specified, storage for local variables is on the stack. The fact that the stack is a dynamic, changing region of memory explains why local variables cannot, in general, hold their values between function calls.

As mentioned earlier, although local variables are typically declared at the beginning of their block, they need not be. A local variable can be declared anywhere within a block, as long as it is declared before it is used. For example, this is a perfectly valid program:

```
#include <iostream>
using namespace std;

int main()
{
  cout << "Enter a number: ";
  int a; // declare one variable
  cin >> a;

  cout << "Enter a second number: ";
  int b; // declare another variable
  cin >> b;

  cout << "Product: " << a*b << '\n';

  return 0;
}
```

In this example, **a** and **b** are not declared until just before they are needed. Frankly, most programmers declare all local variables at the beginning of the block that uses them, but this is a stylistic issue.

Declaring Variables Within Iteration and Selection Statements

It is possible to declare a variable within the initialization portion of a **for** loop or the conditional expression of an **if**, **switch**, or **while**. A variable declared in one of these places has its scope limited to the block of code controlled by that statement.

For example, a variable declared within a **for** statement will be local to that loop, as the following example shows.

```
#include <iostream>
using namespace std;

int main()
{
  // i is local to for
  for(int i = 0; i<10; i++) {
    cout << i << " ";
    cout << "squared is " << i * i << "\n";
  }

  // i = 10; // *** Error *** -- i not known here!

  return 0;
}
```

Here, **i** is declared within the initialization portion of the **for** and is used to control the loop. Outside the loop, **i** is unknown.

In general, when the loop control variable of a **for** is not needed outside the loop, declaring it inside the **for** statement, as shown in the example, is a good idea because it localizes the variable to the loop and prevents its accidental misuse elsewhere. In professionally written C++ code, you will frequently find the loop control variable declared within the **for** statement. Of course, if the variable is required by code outside the loop, then it cannot be declared within the **for** statement.

7

T**IP:** Whether or not a variable declared within the initialization portion of a **for** loop is local to that loop has changed over time. Originally, the variable was available after the **for**. However, Standard C++ restricts the variable to the scope of the **for** loop. Compilers continue to differ on this point, though.

If your compiler fully complies with Standard C++, then you can also declare a variable within the conditional expression of the **if**, **switch,** or **while**. For example, this fragment

```
if(int x = 20) {
  cout << "This is x: ";
  cout << x;
}
```

declares **x** and assigns it the value 20. Since this is a true value, the **cout** statements execute. Variables declared within a conditional statement have their scope limited to the block of code controlled by that statement. Thus, in this case, **x** is not known outside the **if**. Frankly, not all programmers believe that declaring variables within conditional statements is good practice, and this technique will not be used in this book.

Formal Parameters

As you know, if a function uses arguments, then it must declare variables that will accept the values of those arguments. These variables are called the *formal parameters* of the function. Aside from receiving the arguments when a function is called, formal parameters behave like any other local variables inside the function. The scope of a parameter is local to its function.

You must make sure that the formal parameters you declare are of the same type as the arguments you will pass to the function. Also, even though these variables perform the special task of receiving the values of the arguments, they can be used like any other local variable. For example, you can assign a new value to a parameter within the function.

Global Variables

Global variables are, in many ways, the opposite of local variables. They are known throughout the entire program, can be used by any piece of code, and maintain their values during the entire execution of the program. Therefore, their scope extends to the entire program. You can create global variables by declaring them outside of any function. Because they are global, they can be accessed by any expression, regardless of the function in which the expression is located.

When a global and a local variable share the same name, the local variable has precedence. Put differently, a local variable will hide a global variable of the same name. Thus, even though global variables can be accessed by any code in your program, this will happen only when no local variable's name overrides the global variable.

The following program demonstrates the use of global variables. As you can see, the variables **count** and **num_right** have been declared outside of all functions; they are, therefore, global. Common practice dictates that it is best to declare global variables near the top of the program. However, technically, they simply have to be declared before they are first used. This program is a simple addition drill. It first asks you how many problems you want. For each problem, the program calls **drill( )**, which generates two random numbers in the range 0 through 99. It prompts for, and then checks, your answer. You get three tries per problem. At the end, the program displays the number of answers you've gotten right. Pay special attention to the global variables used in this program:

```
// A simple addition drill program.

#include <iostream>
#include <cstdlib>
using namespace std;

void drill();

int count;  // count and num_right are global
int num_right;

int main()
{
  cout << "How many practice problems: ";
  cin >> count;
```

```
      num_right = 0;
      do {
        drill();
        count--;
      } while(count);
      cout << "You got " << num_right << " right.\n";

      return 0;
    }

    void drill()
    {
      int count;   /* This count is local and unrelated to
                      the global one.
                   */
      int a, b, ans;

      // Generate two numbers between 0 and 99.
      a = rand() % 100;
      b = rand() % 100;

      // The user gets three tries to get it right.
      for(count=0; count<3; count++) {
        cout << "What is " << a << " + " << b << "? ";
        cin >> ans;
        if(ans==a+b) {
          cout << "Right\n";
          num_right++;
          return;
        }
      }
      cout << "You've used up all your tries.\n";
      cout << "The answer is " << a+b << '\n';
    }
```

7

Looking closely at this program, it should be clear that both **main( )** and **drill( )** access the global **num_right**. However, **count** is a little more complex. The reference to **count** in **main( )** is to the global **count**. However, **drill( )** has declared a local variable called **count**. When **drill( )** uses **count**, it is referring to its local variable, not the global one. Remember that if, within a function, a global variable and a local variable have the same name, all uses of that variable will refer to the local variable, not the global variable.

Storage for global variables is in a fixed region of memory set aside for this purpose by your program. Global variables are helpful when the same data is used by several functions in your program, or when a variable must hold its value throughout the duration of the program. You should avoid using unnecessary global variables, however, for three reasons:

◆ They take up memory the entire time your program is executing, not just when they are needed.

◆ Using a global variable where a local variable is sufficient makes a function less general, because it relies on something that must be defined outside itself.

♦ Using a large number of global variables can lead to program errors because of unknown, and unwanted, side effects. A major problem in developing large programs is the accidental modification of a variable's value due to its use elsewhere in a program. This can happen in C++ if you use too many global variables in your programs.

Passing Pointers and Arrays

Up to now, the examples in this book have only passed simple variables to functions. However, there will be times when you will want to use pointers and arrays as arguments. While passing these types of arguments is a straightforward process, some special issues need to be addressed.

Calling Functions with Pointers

C++ allows you to pass a pointer to a function. To do so, simply declare the parameter as a pointer type. Here is an example:

```
// Pass a pointer to a function.
#include <iostream>
using namespace std;

void f(int *j);

int main()
{
  int i;
  int *p;

  p = &i; // p now points to i

  f(p);

  cout << i;   // i is now 100

  return 0;
}

void f(int *j)
{
  *j = 100; // var pointed to by j is assigned 100
}
```

Study this program carefully. As you can see, **f( )** takes one parameter: an integer pointer. Inside **main( )**, **p** is assigned the address of **i**. Next, **f( )** is called with **p** as an argument. When the pointer parameter **j** receives **p**, it then also points to **i** within **main( )**. Thus, the assignment

```
*j = 100;
```

causes **i** to be given the value 100. Thus, the program displays **100**. For the general case, **f( )** assigns 100 to whatever address it is called with.

In the preceding example, it is not actually necessary to use the pointer variable **p**. Instead, you can simply precede **i** with an **&** when **f( )** is called. (This, of course, will cause the address of **i** to be generated.) The revised program is shown here:

```
// Pass a pointer to a function -- revised version.
#include <iostream>
using namespace std;

void f(int *j);

int main()
{
  int i;

  f(&i);

  cout << i;

  return 0;
}

void f(int *j)
{
  *j = 100; // var pointed to by j is assigned 100
}
```

7

It is crucial that you understand one important point about passing pointers to functions: When you perform an operation within the function that uses the pointer, you are operating on the variable that is pointed to by that pointer. Thus, the function will be able to change the value of the object pointed to by the parameter.

Calling Functions with Arrays

When an array is an argument to a function, only the address of the first element of the array is passed, not a copy of the entire array. (Remember, in C++, an array name without an index is a pointer to the first element in the array.) This means that the parameter declaration must be of a compatible type. There are three ways to declare a parameter that is to receive an array pointer. First, it can be declared as an array of the same type and size as that used to call the function, as shown here:

```
#include <iostream>
using namespace std;

void display(int num[10]);

int main()
{
  int t[10],i;

  for(i=0; i<10; ++i) t[i]=i;

  display(t); // pass array t to a function
```

```
    return 0;
}

// Print some numbers.
void display(int num[10])
{
  int i;

  for(i=0; i<10; i++) cout << num[i] << ' ';
}
```

Even though the parameter **num** is declared to be an integer array of 10 elements, the C++ compiler will automatically convert it to an integer pointer. This is necessary because no parameter can actually receive an entire array. Since only a pointer to the array will be passed, a pointer parameter must be there to receive it.

A second way to declare an array parameter is to specify it as an unsized array, as shown here:

```
void display(int num[])
{
  int i;

  for(i=0; i<10; i++) cout << num[i] << ' ';
}
```

Here, **num** is declared to be an integer array of unknown size. Since C++ provides no array boundary checks, the actual size of the array is irrelevant to the parameter (but not to the program, of course). This method of declaration is also automatically transformed into an integer pointer by the compiler.

The final way that **num** can be declared is as a pointer. This is the method most commonly used in professionally written C++ programs. Here is an example:

```
void display(int *num)
{
  int i;

  for(i=0; i<10; i++) cout << num[i] << ' ';
}
```

The reason it is possible to declare **num** as a pointer is that any pointer can be indexed using [ ], as if it were an array. Recognize that all three methods of declaring an array parameter yield the same result: a pointer.

On the other hand, an array *element* used as an argument is treated like any other simple variable. For example, the preceding program could also be written without passing the entire array, as shown here:

```
#include <iostream>
using namespace std;

void display(int num);
```

```
int main()
{
  int t[10],i;

  for(i=0; i<10; ++i) t[i]=i;
  for(i=0; i<10; i++) display(t[i]);

  return 0;
}

// Print some numbers.
void display(int num)
{
  cout << num << ' ';
}
```

As you can see, the parameter to **display( )** is of type **int**. It is not relevant that **display( )** is called using an array element, because only that one value of the array is passed.

It is important to remember that when an array is used as a function argument, its address is passed to a function. This means that the code inside the function will be operating on, and potentially altering, the actual contents of the array used to call the function. For example, in the following program, examine the function **cube( )**, which converts the value of each element in an array into its cube. To call **cube( )**, pass the address of the array as the first argument, and the size of the array as the second.

```
#include <iostream>
using namespace std;

void cube(int *n, int num);

int main()
{
  int i, nums[10];

  for(i=0; i<10; i++) nums[i] = i+1;
  cout << "Original contents: ";
  for(i=0; i<10; i++) cout << nums[i] << ' ';
  cout << '\n';

  cube(nums, 10); // compute cubes

  cout << "Altered contents: ";
  for(i=0; i<10; i++) cout << nums[i] << ' ';

  return 0;
}

void cube(int *n, int num)
{
  while(num) {
```

7

```
    *n = *n * *n * *n;
    num--;
    n++;
  }
}
```

Here is the output produced by this program:

```
Original contents: 1 2 3 4 5 6 7 8 9 10
Altered contents: 1 8 27 64 125 216 343 512 729 1000
```

As you can see, after the call to **cube( )**, the contents of array **nums** in **main( )** will be cubes of its original values. That is, the values of the elements of **nums** have been modified by the statements within **cube( )**, because **n** points to **nums**.

Passing Strings

As you know, strings are simply character arrays that are null-terminated. Thus, when you pass a string to a function, only a pointer to the beginning of the string is actually passed. This is a pointer of type **char ***. For example, consider the following program. It defines the function **stringupper( )**, which converts a string to uppercase.

```
// Pass a string to a function.
#include <iostream>
#include <cstring>
#include <cctype>
using namespace std;

void stringupper(char *str);

int main()
{
  char str[80];

  strcpy(str, "this is a test");

  stringupper(str);
  cout << str; // display uppercase string
  return 0;
}

void stringupper(char *str)
{
  while(*str) {
    *str = toupper(*str); // uppercase one char
    str++; // move on to next char
  }
}
```

The output from the program is shown here.

```
THIS IS A TEST
```

In the program, notice that the **str** parameter to **stringupper( )** is declared as **char ***. This enables it to receive a pointer to a character array that holds a string.

Here is another example of passing a string to a function. As you learned in Chapter 5, the standard library function **strlen( )** returns the length of a string. This program shows one way to implement this function.

```
// A custom version of strlen().
#include <iostream>
using namespace std;

int mystrlen(char *str);

int main()
{
  cout << "Length of Hello There is: ";
  cout << mystrlen("Hello There");

  return 0;
}

// A custom version of strlen().
int mystrlen(char *str)
{
  int i;

  for(i=0; str[i]; i++) ; // find the end of the string

  return i;
}
```

7

On your own, you might want to try implementing the other string functions, such as **strcpy( )** or **strcat( )**. Doing so is a good way to test your understanding of arrays, strings, and pointers.

argc and argv: Arguments to main( )

A command line argument is information specified on the command line after a program's name.

Sometimes you will want to pass information into a program when you run it. This generally is accomplished by passing *command line arguments* to **main( )**. A command line argument is the information that follows the program's name on the command line of the operating system. (In Windows, the Run command also uses a command line.) For example, you might compile C++ programs from the command line by typing something like this,

   cl *prog-name*

where *prog-name* is the program that you want compiled. The name of the program is passed into the C++ compiler as a command line argument.

C++ defines two built-in, but optional, parameters to **main( )**. They are **argc** and **argv**, and they receive the command line arguments. These are the only parameters defined by C++ for **main( )**. However, other arguments may be supported in your specific operating environment, so you will want to check your compiler's documentation. Let's now look at **argc** and **argv** more closely.

NOTE: Technically, the names of the command line parameters are arbitrary—you can use any names you like. However, **argc** and **argv** have been used by convention for several years, and it is best that you use these names so that anyone reading your program can quickly identify them as the command line parameters.

The **argc** parameter is an integer that holds the number of arguments on the command line. It will always be at least 1, because the name of the program is also counted.

The **argv** parameter is a pointer to an array of character pointers. Each pointer in the **argv** array points to a string containing a command line argument. The program's name is pointed to by **argv[0]**; **argv[1]** will point to the first argument, **argv[2]** to the second argument, and so on. All command line arguments are passed to the program as strings, so numeric arguments will have to be converted by your program into their proper internal format.

It is important that you declare **argv** properly. The most common method is

```
char *argv[];
```

You can access the individual arguments by indexing **argv**. The following program demonstrates how to access the command line arguments. It prints **Hello**, followed by your name, which must be the first command line argument.

```
#include <iostream>
using namespace std;

int main(int argc, char *argv[])
{
  if(argc!=2) {
    cout << "You forgot to type your name.\n";
    return 1;
  }
  cout << "Hello " << argv[1] << '\n';

  return 0;
}
```

If you titled this program **name** and your name was Tom, then to run the program, you would type **name Tom**. The output from the program would be **Hello Tom**. For example, if you were logged into drive A and using the command prompt, you would see:

```
A>name Tom
  Hello Tom
A>
```

C++ does not stipulate the exact nature of a command line argument because host environments (operating systems) vary considerably on this point. However, the most common convention is as follows: Each command line argument must be separated by spaces or tabs. Often, commas, semicolons, and the like are not valid argument separators. For example,

```
one, two, and three
```

is made up of four strings, while

```
one,two,and three
```

has two strings—the comma is not a legal separator.

If you need to pass a command line argument that does, in fact, contain spaces, then you must place it between quotes. For example, this will be treated as a single command line argument:

```
"this is one argument"
```

Keep in mind that the examples provided here apply to a wide variety of environments, but not necessarily to yours.

7

To access an individual character in one of the command strings, add a second index to **argv**. For example, the program below will display all the arguments it is called with, one character at a time.

```cpp
/* The program prints all command line arguments it is
   called with one character at a time. */
#include <iostream>
using namespace std;

int main(int argc, char *argv[])
{
  int t, i;

  for(t=0; t<argc; ++t) {
    i = 0;
    while(argv[t][i]) {
      cout << argv[t][i];
      ++i;
    }
    cout << ' ';
  }

  return 0;
}
```

As applied to **argv**, the first index accesses the string, and the second index accesses a character in the string.

Usually, you will use **argc** and **argv** to get initial options or values into your program. In C++, you can have as many command line arguments as the operating system will allow. You normally use these arguments to indicate a filename or an option. Using command line arguments will give your program a professional appearance and will facilitate the program's use in batch files.

Passing Numeric Command Line Arguments

As mentioned, when you pass numeric data as a command line argument to a program, that data will be received in string form. Your program will need to convert it into the proper internal format by using one of the standard library functions supported by C++. For example, the program shown next prints the sum of the two numbers that follow its name on the command line. The program uses the **atof( )** function to convert each argument into its internal representation. **atof( )** is another of C++'s standard library functions. It converts the string form of a number into a **double**.

```
/* This program displays the sum of the two numeric
   command line arguments.
*/

#include <iostream>
#include <cstdlib>
using namespace std;

int main(int argc, char *argv[])
{

  double a, b;

  if(argc!=3) {
    cout << "Usage: add num num\n";
    return 1;
  }

  a = atof(argv[1]);
  b = atof(argv[2]);

  cout << a + b;

  return 0;
}
```

To add two numbers, use this type of command line (assuming the program is called **add**):

```
C>add 100.2 231
```

IN DEPTH

Converting Numeric Strings to Numbers

The C++ standard library includes several functions that allow you to convert the string representation of a number into its internal format. These are **atoi( )**, **atol( )**, and **atof( )**, which convert a numeric string into an integer, long integer, and double floating-point value, respectively. These functions all require the header file **<cstdlib>**. The following program illustrates their use:

```cpp
// Demonstrate atoi(), atol(), and atof().
#include <iostream>
#include <cstdlib>
using namespace std;

int main()
{
  int i;
  long j;
  double k;

  i = atoi("100");
  j = atol("100000");
  k = atof("-0.123");

  cout << i << ' ' << j << ' ' << k;
  cout << '\n';

  return 0;
}
```

The output is shown here:

```
100 100000 -0.123
```

The string-conversion functions are especially useful when passing numeric data to a program through a command line argument. They are also useful in a variety of other programming situations.

7

The return Statement

You have been using the **return** statement without much explanation since Chapter 2. As you know, the **return** statement performs two important operations: First, it will cause a function to return immediately to its caller. Second, it can be used to return a value. This section of the chapter presents some important issues related to both of these processes.

Returning from a Function

As you already know, a function returns to its caller in one of two situations: either when the function's closing curly brace is encountered or when a **return** statement is executed. The **return** statement can be used with or without an associated value. However, functions that are declared as returning a value (i.e., that have a non-**void** return type) must return a value. Only functions declared as **void** can use **return** without a value.

For **void** functions, the **return** statement is mostly used as a program-control device. For example, the function shown next will print the outcome of one number raised to a positive integer power. If the exponent is negative, the **return** statement causes the function to terminate before any attempt is made to compute the exponent. In this capacity, it acts as a control statement designed to prevent part of the function from executing.

```
void power(int base, int exp)
{
  int i;

  if(exp<0) return; /* Can't do negative exponents,
                       so return to calling routine
                       and bypass the rest of the
                       function. */

  i = 1;

  for( ; exp; exp--) i = base * i;
  cout << "The answer is: " << i;
}
```

A function may contain several **return** statements. As soon as one is encountered, the function returns. For example, this fragment is perfectly valid:

```
void f()
{
  // ...

  switch(c) {
    case 'a': return;
    case 'b': // ...
    case 'c': return;
  }
  if(count<100) return;
  // ...
}
```

Be aware, however, that having too many **return**s can muddy the operation of a algorithm and confuse its meaning. It is best to use multiple **return**s only when they help clarify a function.

Returning Values

Every function, unless it is of type **void**, returns a value. This value is explicitly specified by the **return** statement. This means that as long as a function is not declared to be **void**, it can be used as an operand in an expression. Therefore, each of the following expressions is valid in C++:

```
x = power(y);

if(max(x, y)) > 100) cout << "greater";

switch(abs(x)) {
```

Although all non-**void** functions return values, you don't necessarily have to use the values for anything. A very common question regarding function return values is, "Don't I have to assign this value to some variable, since a value is being returned?" The answer is no. If there is no assignment specified, then the return value is simply discarded.

Examine the following program, which uses the standard library function **abs( )**:

```
#include <iostream>
#include <cstdlib>
using namespace std;

int main()
{
  int i;

  i = abs(-10);       // line 1
  cout << abs(-23);   // line 2
  abs(100);           // line 3

  return 0;
}
```

7

The **abs( )** function returns the absolute value of its integer argument. It uses the **<cstdlib>** header. In line 1, the return value of **abs( )** is assigned to **i**. In line 2, the return value is not actually assigned, but it is used by the **cout** statement. Finally, in line 3, the return value is lost because it is neither assigned to another variable nor used as part of an expression.

If a non-**void** function returns because its closing curly brace is encountered, an undefined (i.e., unknown) value is returned. Because of a quirk in the formal C++ syntax, a non-**void** function need not actually execute a **return** statement. This can happen if the end of the function is reached prior to a **return** statement being encountered. However, because the function is declared as returning a value, a value will still be returned—even though it is just a garbage value. Generally, any non-**void** function that you create should return a value via an explicit **return** statement.

Just as a **void** function may have more than one **return** statement, so too may a function that returns a value. For example, the **find_substr( )** function shown in the next program uses two **return** statements to simplify its operation. The function searches a string for a substring. It returns the index of the first matching substring, or if no match is found, it returns –1. For example, if the string is "I like C++" and the substring is "like", then the function returns 2 (which is the index of the "l" in like).

```cpp
#include <iostream>
using namespace std;

int find_substr(char *sub, char *str);

int main()
{
  int index;

  index = find_substr("three", "one two three four");

  cout << "Index of three is " << index; // index is 8

  return 0;
}

// Return index of substring or -1 if not found.
int find_substr(char *sub, char *str)
{
  int t;
  char *p, *p2;

  for(t=0; str[t]; t++) {
    p = &str[t]; // reset pointers
    p2 = sub;
    while(*p2 && *p2==*p) { // check for substring
      p++;
      p2++;
    }

    /* If at end of p2 (i.e., substring), then
       a match has been found. */
    if(!*p2) return t; // return index of match
  }
  return -1; // no match found
}
```

The output from the program is shown here.

```
Index of three is 8
```

Since the string being sought is found, the first **return** statement executes. On your own, try searching for a word that is not part of the string. In this case, **find_substr( )** returns –1 via the second **return** statement.

A function can be declared to return any valid C++ data type (except that a function cannot return an array.) The method of declaration is similar to that used with variables: The type specifier precedes the function name. The type specifier tells the compiler what type of data will be returned by the function. This return type must be compatible with the type of data used in the **return** statement. If it isn't, a compile-time error will result.

void Functions

As you have seen, functions that don't return values are declared **void**. This prevents their use in an expression and helps head off accidental misuse. In the following example, the function **print_vertical( )** prints its string argument vertically down the side of the screen. Since it returns no value, it is declared as **void**.

```
#include <iostream>
using namespace std;

void print_vertical(char *str);

int main(int argc, char *argv[])
{
  if(argc==2) print_vertical(argv[1]);

  return 0;
}

void print_vertical(char *str)
{
  while(*str)
    cout << *str++ << '\n';
}
```

Since **print_vertical( )** is declared as **void**, it cannot be used in an expression. For example, the following statement is wrong, and will not compile:

```
x = print_vertical("hello"); // Error
```

T**IP:** Early versions of the C language did not have the **void** return type. Thus, in old C programs, functions that did not return values were simply allowed to default to type **int**. You may still encounter functions of this sort when updating older C programs to C++. If you do, simply convert them to **void** functions.

Functions That Return Pointers

Functions can return pointers. Pointers are returned like any other data type, and they pose no special problem. However, because the pointer is one of C++'s more confusing features, a short discussion of pointer return types is warranted.

7

In order to return a pointer, a function must declare its return type to be a pointer. For example, here the return type of **f( )** is declared to be an integer pointer:

```
int *f();
```

If a function's return type is a pointer, then the value used in its **return** statement must also be a pointer. (As with all functions, the return value must be compatible with the return type.)

The following program demonstrates the use of a pointer return type. It reworks the **find_substr( )** function, shown earlier, so that it returns a pointer to the substring, rather than the index of the substring. If no match is found, a null pointer is returned.

```cpp
// Rework find_substr() to return a pointer.
#include <iostream>
using namespace std;

char *find_substr(char *sub, char *str);

int main()
{
  char *substr;

  substr = find_substr("three", "one two three four");

  cout << "substring found: " << substr;

  return 0;
}

// Return pointer to substring or null if not found.
char *find_substr(char *sub, char *str)
{
  int t;
  char *p, *p2, *start;

  for(t=0; str[t]; t++) {
    p = &str[t]; // reset pointers
    start = p;
    p2 = sub;
    while(*p2 && *p2==*p) { // check for substring
      p++;
      p2++;
    }

    /* If at end of p2 (i.e., substring), then
       a match has been found. */
    if(!*p2)
      return start; // return pointer to beginning of substring
  }
  return 0; // no match found
}
```

The output from this version of the program is shown here.

```
substring found: three four
```

In this case, when "three" is found within "one two three four", a pointer to the beginning of the matching "three" is returned and assigned to **substr** inside **main( )**. Thus, when **substr** is output, the remainder of the string, "three four", is displayed.

Many of the string-related library functions supported by C++ return character pointers. For example, the **strcpy( )** function returns a pointer to the first argument. Check your compiler's library reference for other examples.

Function Prototypes

A prototype declares a function prior to its first use.

Until this point, prototypes have been used without explanation in the sample programs. Now it is time to explain them formally. In C++, all functions must be declared before they are used. Typically, this is accomplished by use of a function prototype. Prototypes specify three things about a function:

◆   Its return type

◆   The type of its parameters

◆   The number of its parameters

Prototypes allow the compiler to perform three important operations:

◆   They tell the compiler what type of code to generate when a function is called. Different return and parameter types must be handled differently by the compiler.

◆   They allow C++ to find and report any illegal type conversions between the type of arguments used to call a function and the type definition of its parameters.

◆   They allow the compiler to detect differences between the number of arguments used to call a function and the number of parameters in the function.

The general form of a function prototype is as follows. It is the same as a function definition, except that no body is present.

> *type func-name(type parm_name1, type parm_name2,...,*
> *type parm_nameN);*

The use of parameter names in a prototype is optional. However, their use does let the compiler identify any type mismatches by name when an error occurs, so it is a good idea to include them.

To better understand the usefulness of function prototypes, consider the following program. If you try to compile it, an error message will be issued because the program attempts to call **sqr_it( )** with an integer argument instead of the integer pointer required. (It is illegal to transform an integer into a pointer.)

7

```
/* This program uses a function prototype to
   enforce strong type checking.
*/

void sqr_it(int *i); // prototype

int main()
{
  int x;

  x = 10;
  sqr_it(x); // *** Error *** -- type mismatch!

  return 0;
}

void sqr_it(int *i)
{
  *i = *i * *i;
}
```

TIP: Although the C language accepts prototypes, it does not currently require them. This is because early versions of C did not accept full prototypes. If you are porting older C code to C++, you may need to fully prototype all functions before the program will compile.

Headers: A Closer Look

Earlier in this book, you were introduced to the standard C++ headers. You have learned that these headers contain information needed by your programs. While this partial explanation is true, it does not tell the whole story. C++'s headers contain the prototypes for the functions in the standard library. (They also contain various values and definitions used by those functions.) Like functions that you write, the standard library functions must be prototyped before they are used. For this reason, any program that uses a library function must also include the header containing the prototype of that function.

To find out which header a library function requires, look in your compiler's library reference. Along with a description of each function, you will find the name of the header that must be included in order to use that function.

IN DEPTH

Old-Style versus Modern Function Parameter Declarations

If you have ever examined older C code, you may have noticed that the function parameter declarations look different. When C was first invented, it used a fundamentally different parameter declaration method. This old-style method, sometimes called the *classic form*, is outdated but still found in older code. The declaration approach used by C++ (and newer C code) is called the *modern form*. Because you may need to work on older C programs, especially if you are updating them to C++, it is useful to understand the old-style parameter declaration form.

The old-style function parameter declaration consists of two parts: A parameter list, which goes inside the parentheses that follow the function name; and the actual parameter declarations, which go between the closing parenthesis and the function's opening curly brace. For example, this modern declaration:

```
float f(int a, int b, char ch)
{ ...
```

will look like this in its old-style form

```
float f(a, b, ch)
int a, b;
char ch;
{ ...
```

Notice that in classic form, more than one parameter can be in a list after the type name. This isn't allowed in the modern form.

In general, to convert the old-style form into the modern (C++ style) form, simply move the parameter declarations inside the function's parentheses. Remember, each parameter must be declared separately, each with its own type specifier.

Recursion

A recursive function is a function that calls itself.

The last topic that we will examine in this chapter is *recursion*. Sometimes called *circular definition*, recursion is the process of defining something in terms of itself. As it relates to programming, recursion is the process of a function calling itself. A function that calls itself is said to be *recursive*.

The classic example of recursion is the function **factr( )**, which computes the factorial of an integer. The factorial of a number *N* is the product of all the whole numbers between 1 and *N*. For example, 3 factorial is 1×2×3, or 6. Both **factr( )** and its iterative equivalent are shown here:

```
#include <iostream>
using namespace std;

int factr(int n);
int fact(int n);

int main()
{
  // use recursive version
  cout << "4 factorial is " << factr(4);
  cout << '\n';

  // use iterative version
  cout << "4 factorial is " << fact(4);
  cout << '\n';

  return 0;
}

// Recursive version.
int factr(int n)
{
  int answer;

  if(n==1) return(1);
  answer = factr(n-1)*n;
  return(answer);
}

// Iterative version.
int fact(int n)
{
  int t, answer;

  answer = 1;
  for(t=1; t<=n; t++) answer = answer*(t);
  return(answer);
}
```

The operation of the nonrecursive version of **fact( )** should be clear. It uses a loop starting at 1 and progressively multiplies each number by the moving product.

The operation of the recursive **factr( )** is a little more complex. When **factr( )** is called with an argument of 1, the function returns 1; otherwise it returns the product of **factr(n–1)*n**. To evaluate this expression, **factr( )** is called with **n–1**. This happens until **n** equals 1 and the calls to the function begin returning. For example, when the factorial of 2 is calculated, the first call to **factr( )** will cause a second call to be made with the argument of 1. This call will return 1, which is then multiplied by 2 (the original **n** value). The answer is then 2. You might find it interesting to insert **cout** statements into **factr( )** that will show at what level each call is, and what the intermediate answers are.

When a function calls itself, new local variables and parameters are allocated storage on the stack, and the function code is executed with these new variables from the start. A recursive call does not make a new copy of the function; only the values are new. As each recursive call returns, the old local variables and parameters are removed from the stack, and execution resumes at the point of the function call inside the function. Recursive functions could be said to "telescope" out and back.

Keep in mind that most recursive routines do not significantly reduce code size. Also, the recursive versions of most routines may execute a bit more slowly than their iterative equivalents, due to the added overhead of the additional function calls. Too many recursive calls to a function may cause a stack overrun. Because storage for function parameters and local variables is on the stack, and each new call creates a new copy of these variables, it is possible that the stack will be exhausted. If this occurs, other data may be destroyed as well. However, you probably will not have to worry about any of this unless a recursive function runs wild.

The main advantage of recursive functions is that they can be used to create clearer and simpler versions of several algorithms than those produced with their iterative relatives. For example, the Quicksort sorting algorithm is quite difficult to implement in an iterative way. Also, some problems, especially those related to artificial intelligence, seem to lend themselves to recursive solutions. Finally, some people find it easier to think recursively rather than iteratively.

7

When writing a recursive function, you must include a conditional statement, such as an **if**, to force the function to return without execution of the recursive call. If you don't provide the conditional statement, then once you call the function, it will never return. This is a very common error. When developing programs with recursive functions, use **cout** statements liberally so that you can watch what is going on, and abort execution if you see that you have made a mistake.

Here is another example of a recursive function, called **reverse( )**. It prints its string argument backwards on the screen.

```
// Print a string backwards using recursion.
#include <iostream>
using namespace std;

void reverse(char *s);

int main()
{
  char str[] = "this is a test";

  reverse(str);

  return 0;
}
```

```
// Print string backwards.
void reverse(char *s)
{
  if(*s)
    reverse(s+1);
  else
    return;

  cout << *s;
}
```

The **reverse( )** function first checks to see if it has been passed a pointer to the null terminating the string. If not, then **reverse( )** calls itself with a pointer to the next character in the string. When the null terminator is finally found, the calls begin unraveling, and the characters are displayed in reverse order.

Creating recursive functions is often difficult for beginners. Over time, however, you will grow more accustomed to using them.

CHAPTER 8

Functions, Part Two: References, Overloading, and Default Arguments

This chapter continues our examination of the function. Specifically, it discusses three of C++'s most important function-related topics: references, function overloading, and default arguments. These three features vastly expand the capabilities of a function. As you will see, a reference is an implicit pointer. Function overloading is the quality that allows one function to be implemented two or more different ways, each performing a separate task. Function overloading is one way that C++ supports polymorphism. Using a default argument, it is possible to specify a value for a parameter that will be automatically used when no corresponding argument is specified.

Since references are frequently applied to function parameters (it is the main reason for their existence), this chapter begins with a brief discussion of how arguments can be passed to functions.

Two Approaches to Argument Passing

Call-by-value passes the value of an argument to a function.

To understand the genesis of the reference, you must understand the theory behind argument passing. In general, there are two ways that a computer language can pass an argument to a subroutine. The first is called *call-by-value*. This method copies the *value* of an argument into the formal parameter of the subroutine. Therefore, changes made to the parameters of the subroutine will not affect the arguments used to call it.

Call-by-reference passes the address of an argument to a function.

Call-by-reference is the second way a subroutine can be passed arguments. This method copies the *address* of an argument (not its value) into the parameter. Inside the subroutine, this address is used to access the actual argument specified in the call. This means that changes made to the parameter will affect the argument used to call the subroutine.

How C++ Passes Arguments

By default, C++ uses the *call-by-value* method for passing arguments. This means that, in general, code inside a function cannot alter the arguments used to call the function. In this book, all of the programs up to this point have used the call-by-value method.

Consider this function:

```
#include <iostream>
using namespace std;

int sqr_it(int x);
int main()
{
  int t=10;

  cout << sqr_it(t) << ' ' << t;

  return 0;
}

int sqr_it(int x)
{
  x = x*x;
  return x;
}
```

In this example, the value of the argument to **sqr_it( )**, 10, is copied into the parameter **x**. When the assignment **x = x*x** takes place, the only thing modified is the local variable **x**. The variable **t**, used to call **sqr_it( )**, will still have the value 10 and is unaffected by the operations inside the function. Hence, the output will be **100 10**.

REMEMBER: By default, a copy of an argument is passed into a function. What occurs inside the function will not affect the variable used in the call.

Using a Pointer to Create a Call-by-Reference

Even though C++'s default parameter-passing convention is call-by-value, it is possible to manually create a call-by-reference by passing the address of an argument (i.e., a pointer to the argument) to a function. It will then be possible for code inside the function to change the value of the argument outside of the function. You saw an example of this in the preceding chapter when the passing of pointers was discussed. As you know, pointers are passed to functions just like any other values. Of course, it is necessary to declare the parameters as pointer types.

To see how passing a pointer allows you to manually create a call-by-reference, examine this version of **swap( )**. It exchanges the values of the two variables pointed to by its arguments.

```
void swap(int *x, int *y)
{
  int temp;

  temp = *x; // save the value at address x
  *x = *y;   // put y into x
  *y = temp; // put x into y
}
```

The ***x** and the ***y** refer to the variables pointed to by **x** and **y**, which are the addresses of the arguments used to call the function. Consequently, the contents of the variables used to call the function will be swapped.

Since **swap( )** expects to receive two pointers, you must remember to call **swap( )** with the *addresses* of the variables you wish to exchange. The correct method is shown in this program:

```
#include <iostream>
using namespace std;

// Declare swap() using pointers.
void swap(int *x, int *y);

int main()
{
```

8

```
    int i, j;

    i = 10;
    j = 20;

    cout << "Initial values of i and j: ";
    cout << i << ' ' << j << '\n';
    swap(&j, &i); // call swap() with addresses of i and j
    cout << "Swapped values of i and j: ";
    cout << i << ' ' << j << '\n';

    return 0;
}

// Exchange arguments.
void swap(int *x, int *y)
{
    int temp;

    temp = *x; // save the value at address x
    *x = *y;   // put y into x
    *y = temp; // put x into y
}
```

The output from the program is shown here:

```
Initial values of i and j: 10 20
Swapped values of i and j: 20 10
```

In this example, the variable **i** is assigned the value 10, and **j** the value 20. Then **swap( )** is called with the addresses of **i** and **j**. The unary operator **&** is used to produce the addresses of the variables. Therefore, the addresses of **i** and **j**, not their values, are passed into the function **swap( )**. When **swap( )** returns, **i** and **j** will have their values exchanged.

Reference Parameters

While it is possible to achieve a call-by-reference manually by using the pointer operators, this approach is rather clumsy. First, it compels you to perform all operations through pointers. Second, it requires that you remember to pass the addresses (rather than the values) of the arguments when calling the function. Fortunately, in C++, it is possible to tell the compiler to automatically use call-by-reference rather than call-by-value for one or more parameters of a particular function. You can accomplish this with a *reference parameter*. When you use a reference parameter, the address (not the value) of an argument is automatically passed to the function. Within the function, operations on the reference parameter are automatically de-referenced, so there is no need to use the pointer operators.

A reference parameter automatically receives the address of its corresponding argument.

A reference parameter is declared by preceding the parameter name in the function's declaration with an **&**. Operations performed on a reference parameter affect the argument used to call the function, not the reference parameter itself.

To understand reference parameters, let's begin with a simple example. In the following, the function **f( )** takes one reference parameter of type **int**:

```
// Using a reference parameter.
#include <iostream>
using namespace std;

void f(int &i);

int main()
{
  int val = 1;

  cout << "Old value for val: " << val << '\n';

  f(val); // pass address of val to f()

  cout << "New value for val: " << val << '\n';

  return 0;
}

void f(int &i)
{
  i = 10; // this modifies calling argument
}
```

8

This program displays the following output:

```
Old value for val: 1
New value for val: 10
```

Pay special attention to the definition of **f( )**, shown here:

```
void f(int &i)
{
  i = 10; // this modifies calling argument
}
```

Notice the declaration of **i**. It is preceded by an **&**, which causes it to become a reference parameter. (This declaration is also used in the function's prototype.) Inside the function, the following statement

```
i = 10;
```

does *not* cause **i** to be given the value 10. Instead, it causes the variable *referenced* by **i** (in this case, **val**) to be assigned the value 10. Notice that this statement does not use the ***** pointer operator. When you use a reference parameter, the C++ compiler automatically knows that it is an address (i.e., a pointer) and de-references it for you. In fact, using the ***** would be an error.

Since **i** has been declared as a reference parameter, the compiler will automatically pass **f( )** the *address* of any argument it is called with. Thus, in **main( )**, the statement

```
f(val); // pass address of val to f()
```

passes the address of **val** (not its value) to **f( )**. There is no need to precede **val** with the **&** operator. (Doing so would be an error.) Since **f( )** receives the address of **val** in the form of a reference, it may modify the value of **val**.

To illustrate reference parameters in actual use—and to fully demonstrate their benefits—the **swap( )** function is rewritten using references in the following program. Look carefully at how **swap( )** is declared and called.

```cpp
#include <iostream>
using namespace std;

// Declare swap() using reference parameters.
void swap(int &x, int &y);

int main()
{
  int i, j;

  i = 10;
  j = 20;

  cout << "Initial values of i and j: ";
  cout << i << ' ' << j << '\n';
  swap(j, i);
  cout << "Swapped values of i and j: ";
  cout << i << ' ' << j << '\n';

  return 0;
}

/* Here, swap() is defined as using call-by-reference,
   not call-by-value. Thus, it can exchange the two
   arguments it is called with.
*/
void swap(int &x, int &y)
{
  int temp;

  temp = x; // save the value at address x
  x = y;    // put y into x
  y = temp; // put x into y
}
```

Notice again that by making **x** and **y** reference parameters, there is no need to use the ***** operator when exchanging values. As explained, it would be an error to do so.

Remember, the compiler automatically generates the addresses of the arguments used to call **swap( )**, and automatically de-references **x** and **y**.

Let's review. When you create a reference parameter, that parameter automatically refers to (i.e., implicitly points to) the argument used to call the function. Further, there is no need to apply the **&** operator to an argument. Also, inside the function, the reference parameter is used directly; the ***** operator is not necessary or, in fact, correct. All operations involving the reference parameter automatically refer to the argument used in the call to the function.

REMEMBER: When you assign a value to a reference, you are actually assigning that value to the variable that the reference is pointing to. In the case of function parameters, this will be the variable used in the call to the function.

IN DEPTH

Declaring Reference Parameters

8

When Bjarne Stroustrup wrote *The C++ Programming Language* (in which he first described C++) in 1986, he introduced a style of declaring reference parameters, which some other programmers have adopted. In this approach, the **&** is associated with the type name rather than the variable name. For example, here is another way to write the prototype to **swap( )**:

```
void swap(int& x, int& y);
```

As you can see, the **&** is immediately adjacent to **int** and not to **x**.

Further, some programmers also specify pointers by associating the ***** with the type rather than the variable, as shown here:

```
float* p;
```

These types of declarations reflect the desire by some programmers for C++ to contain a separate reference or pointer type. However, the trouble with associating the **&** or ***** with the type rather than the variable is that, according to the formal C++ syntax, neither the **&** nor the ***** is distributive over a list of variables, and this can lead to confusing declarations. For example, the following declaration creates one, *not two*, integer pointers.

```
int* a, b;
```

IN DEPTH

CONTINUED

Here, **b** is declared as an integer (not an integer pointer) because, as specified by the C++ syntax, when used in a declaration, an ***** or an **&** is linked to the individual variable that it precedes, not to the type that it follows.

It is important to understand that, as far as the C++ compiler is concerned, it doesn't matter whether you write **int *p** or **int* p**. Thus, if you prefer to associate the ***** or **&** with the type rather than the variable, feel free to do so. However, to avoid confusion, this book will continue to associate the ***** and the **&** with the variable name that each modifies, rather than the type name.

TIP: The C language does not support references. Thus, the only way to create a call-by-reference in C is to use pointers, as shown earlier in the first version of **swap( )**. When converting C code to C++, you will want to convert these types of parameters to references, where feasible.

Returning References

A function can return a reference. In C++ programming, there are several uses for reference return values. You will see some of these later in this book when you learn about operator overloading. However, reference return values have other important applications that you can use now.

When a function returns a reference, it returns an implicit pointer to its return value. This gives rise to a rather startling possibility: The function can be used on the left side of an assignment statement! For example, consider this simple program:

```
// Returning a reference.
#include <iostream>
using namespace std;

double &f();

double val = 100.0;

int main()
{
  double newval;

  cout << f() << '\n'; // display val's value

  newval = f(); // assign value of val to newval
  cout << newval << '\n'; // display newval's value
```

```
   f() = 99.1; // change val's value
   cout << f() << '\n'; // display val's new value

   return 0;
}

double &f()
{
   return val; // return reference to val
}
```

The output of this program is shown here:

```
100
100
99.1
```

Let's examine this program closely. At the beginning, **f( )** is declared as returning a reference to a **double**, and the global variable **val** is initialized to 100. Next, the following statement displays the original value of **val**:

```
cout << f() << '\n'; // display val's value
```

When **f( )** is called, it returns a reference to **val**. Because **f( )** is declared as returning a reference, the line

```
return val; // return reference to val
```

automatically returns a reference to **val**. This reference is then used by the **cout** statement to display **val**'s value.

In the line

```
newval = f(); // assign value of val to newval
```

the reference to **val** returned by **f( )** is used to assign the value of **val** to **newval**.

The most interesting line in the program is shown here:

```
f() = 99.1; // change val's value
```

This statement causes the value of **val** to be changed to 99.1. Here is why: Since **f( )** returns a reference to **val**, this reference becomes the target of the assignment statement. Thus, the value of 99.1 is assigned to **val** indirectly, through the reference to it returned by **f( )**.

Finally, in this line

```
cout << f() << '\n'; // display val's new value
```

8

the new value of **val** is displayed when a reference to **val** is returned by the call to **f( )** inside the **cout** statement.

Here is another sample program that uses a reference return type:

```
#include <iostream>
using namespace std;

double &change_it(int i); // return a reference

double vals[] = {1.1, 2.2, 3.3, 4.4, 5.5};

int main()
{
  int i;

  cout << "Here are the original values: ";
  for(i=0; i<5; i++)
    cout << vals[i] << ' ';
  cout << '\n';

  change_it(1) = 5298.23; // change 2nd element
  change_it(3) = -98.8; // change 4th element

  cout << "Here are the changed values: ";
  for(i=0; i<5; i++)
    cout << vals[i] << ' ';
  cout << '\n';

  return 0;
}

double &change_it(int i)
{
  return vals[i]; // return a reference to the ith element
}
```

This program changes the values of the second and fourth elements in the **vals** array. The program displays the following output:

```
Here are the original values: 1.1 2.2 3.3 4.4 5.5
Here are the changed values: 1.1 5298.23 3.3 -98.8 5.5
```

Let's see how this is accomplished. The **change_it( )** function is declared as returning a reference to a **double**. Specifically, it returns a reference to the element of **vals** that is specified by its parameter **i**. Thus, inside **main( )**, when this statement executes

```
change_it(1) = 5298.23; // change 2nd element
```

change_it( ) returns a reference to **vals[1]**. Through this reference, **vals[1]** is then assigned the value 5298.23. A similar process occurs when this statement executes.

```
change_it(3) = -98.8; // change 4th element
```

Because **change_it( )** returns a reference to a specific element of the **vals** array, it can be used on the left side of an assignment statement to assign a new value to that array element.

When returning a reference, be careful that the object being referred to does not go out of scope. For example, consider this function:

```
// Error, cannot return reference to local var.
int &f()
{
  int i=10;
  return i;
}
```

In **f( )**, the local variable **i** will go out of scope when the function returns. Therefore, the reference to **i** returned by **f( )** will be undefined. Actually, some compilers will not compile **f( )** as written, precisely for this reason. However, this type of problem can be created indirectly, so be careful which object you return a reference to.

Creating a Bounded Array

One good use for a reference return type is to create a bounded array. As you know, in C++, there is no run-time boundary checking on array indexing. This means that arrays can be overrun. That is, an array index may be specified that exceeds the size of the array. However, it is possible to prevent array overruns by creating a *bounded* or *safe array*. When a bounded array is created, any out-of-bounds index is prevented from indexing the array.

8

The following program illustrates one way to create a bounded array:

```
// A simple safe array.
#include <iostream>
using namespace std;

int &put(int i); // put value into the array
int get(int i); // obtain a value from the array

int vals[10];
int error = -1;

int main()
{
  put(0) = 10; // put values into the array
  put(1) = 20;
  put(9) = 30;

  cout << get(0) << ' ';
  cout << get(1) << ' ';
  cout << get(9) << ' ';
```

```
  // now, intentionally generate an error
  put(12) = 1; // Out of Bounds

  return 0;
}

// Put a value into the array.
int &put(int i)
{
  if(i>=0 && i<10)
    return vals[i]; // return a reference to the ith element
  else {
    cout << "Bounds Error!\n";
    return error; // return a reference to error
  }
}

// Get a value from the array.
int get(int i)
{
  if(i>=0 && i<10)
    return vals[i]; // return the value of the ith element
  else {
    cout << "Bounds Error!\n";
    return error; // return an error
  }
}
```

The output produced by this program is shown here:

```
10 20 30 Bounds Error!
```

This program creates a safe array of ten integers. To put a value into the array, use the **put( )** function. To retrieve a value, call **get( )**. For both functions, the index of the desired element is specified as an argument. As the program shows, both **get( )** and **put( )** prevent an array overrun. Notice that **put( )** returns a reference to the specified element and is thus used on the left side of an assignment statement.

While the approach to implementing a bounded array shown in this example is correct, an even better implementation is possible. As you will see when you learn about operator overloading later in this book, it is possible to create your own custom, bounded arrays that also use standard array notation.

Independent References

Even though the reference is included in C++ primarily for supporting call-by-reference parameter passing and for use as a function return type, it is possible to declare a stand-alone reference variable. This is called an *independent reference*. It must be stated at the outset, however, that independent reference variables are seldom used, because they tend to confuse and destructure your program. With these reservations in mind, we will take a short look at them here.

An independent reference is simply another name for some other variable.

An independent reference must point to some object. Thus, an independent reference must be initialized when it is declared. Generally, this means that it will be assigned the address of a previously declared variable. Once this is done, the name of the reference variable can be used anywhere that the variable it refers to can be used. In fact, there is virtually no distinction between the two. For example, consider the program shown here:

```cpp
#include <iostream>
using namespace std;

int main()
{
  int j, k;
  int &i = j; // independent reference

  j = 10;

  cout << j << " " << i; // outputs 10 10

  k = 121;
  i = k; // copies k's value into j
         // not k's address

  cout << "\n" << j;  // outputs 121

  return 0;
}
```

This program displays the following output:

```
10 10
121
```

The address pointed to by a reference variable is fixed; it cannot be changed. Thus, when the statement **i = k** is evaluated, it is **k**'s value that is copied into **j** (pointed to by **i**), not its address. For another example, **i++** does *not* cause **i** to point to a new address. Instead, **j** is increased by 1.

As stated earlier, it is generally not a good idea to use independent references, because they are not necessary and they tend to garble your code. Having two names for the same variable is an inherently confusing situation.

A Few Restrictions When Using References

There are some restrictions that apply to reference variables:

◆   You cannot reference a reference variable.

◆   You cannot create arrays of references.

◆   You cannot create a pointer to a reference. That is, you cannot apply the **&** operator to a reference.

◆   References are not allowed on bit-fields. (Bit-fields are discussed later in this book.)

8

Function Overloading

In this section, you will learn about one of C++'s most exciting features: function overloading. In C++, two or more functions can share the same name, as long as their parameter declarations are different. In this situation, the functions that share the same name are said to be *overloaded,* and the process is referred to as *function overloading.* Function overloading is one way that C++ achieves polymorphism.

Let's begin with a short sample program:

```cpp
// Overload a function three times.
#include <iostream>
using namespace std;

void f(int i);        // integer parameter
void f(int i, int j); // two integer parameters
void f(double k);     // one double parameter

int main()
{
  f(10);     // call f(int)

  f(10, 20); // call f(int, int)

  f(12.23);  // call f(double)

  return 0;
}

void f(int i)
{
  cout << "In f(int), i is " << i << '\n';
}

void f(int i, int j)
{
  cout << "In f(int, int), i is " << i;
  cout << ", j is " << j << '\n';
}

void f(double k)
{
  cout << "In f(double), k is " << k << '\n';
}
```

This program produces the following output:

```
In f(int), i is 10
In f(int, int), i is 10, j is 20
In f(double), k is 12.23
```

As you can see, **f( )** is overloaded three times. The first version takes one integer parameter, the second version requires two integer parameters, and the third version has one **double** parameter. Because the parameter list for each version is different, the compiler is able to call the correct version of each function. In general, to overload a function, you simply declare different versions of it.

The compiler uses the type and/or number of arguments as its guide to determining which version of an overloaded function to call. Thus, overloaded functions must differ in the type and/or number of their parameters. While overloaded functions may have different return types, the return type alone is not sufficient to distinguish two versions of a function. (Return types do not provide sufficient information in all cases for the compiler to correctly decide which function to use.)

To better understand the benefit of function overloading, consider these three functions, which are located in the standard library: **abs( )**, **labs( )**, and **fabs( )**. These functions were first defined by the C language and, for compatibility, are also included in C++. The **abs( )** function returns the absolute value of an integer, **labs( )** returns the absolute value of a **long**, and **fabs( )** returns the absolute value of a **double**. In C (which does not support function overloading), three slightly different names must be used to represent these essentially similar tasks. This makes the situation more complex, conceptually, than it actually is. Even though the underlying concept of each function is the same, the programmer has three names to remember, not just one. However, in C++ it is possible to use just one name for all three functions, as illustrated in this example:

8

```
// Create an overloaded version of abs() called myabs().
#include <iostream>
using namespace std;

// myabs() is overloaded three ways.
int myabs(int i);
double myabs(double d);
long myabs(long l);

int main()
{
  cout << myabs(-10) << "\n";

  cout << myabs(-11.0) << "\n";

  cout << myabs(-9L) << "\n";

  return 0;
}

int myabs(int i)
{
  cout << "Using integer myabs(): ";
```

```
  if(i<0) return -i;
  else return i;
}

double myabs(double d)
{
  cout << "Using double myabs(): ";

  if(d<0.0) return -d;
  else return d;
}

long myabs(long l)
{
  cout << "Using long myabs(): ";

  if(l<0) return -l;
  else return l;
}
```

Here is the output produced by the program.

```
Using integer myabs(): 10
Using double myabs(): 11
Using long myabs(): 9
```

This program creates three similar but different functions called **myabs**, each of which returns the absolute value of its argument. The compiler knows which function to use in each given situation because of the type of the argument. The value of overloading is that it allows related sets of functions to be accessed using a common name. Thus, the name **myabs** represents the *general action* that is being performed. It is left to the compiler to choose the correct *specific* version for a particular circumstance. Therefore, through the application of polymorphism, three things to remember have been reduced to one. Although this example is fairly simple, if you expand the concept, you can see how overloading can help you manage greater complexity.

When you overload a function, each version of that function can perform any activity you desire. That is, there is no rule stating that overloaded functions must relate to one another. However, from a stylistic point of view, function overloading implies a relationship. Thus, while you can use the same name to overload unrelated functions, you should not. For example, you could use the name **sqr** to create functions that return the *square* of an **int** and the *square root* of a **double**. These two operations are fundamentally different, however, and applying function overloading in this manner defeats its original purpose. (In fact, programming in this manner is considered to be extremely bad style!) In practice, you should overload only closely related operations.

IN DEPTH

The overload Anachronism

When C++ was created, overloaded functions had to be explicitly declared as such by using the **overload** keyword. The **overload** keyword is no longer required or supported by C++. In fact, it is not even defined as a keyword by Standard C++. However, you may still encounter **overload** from time to time—especially in older books and articles.

The general form of **overload** is shown here:

overload *func-name*;

where *func-name* is the name of the function being overloaded. This statement must precede the overloaded declarations. (Generally, it is found near the top of the program.) For example, if the function **Counter( )** is being overloaded, then this line will be included in the program:

```
overload Counter;
```

If you encounter **overload** declarations when working with older programs, you can simply remove them; they are no longer needed. Because **overload** is an anachronism, you should not use it in new C++ programs. In fact, most compilers will not accept it.

8

Default Function Arguments

The next function-related feature discussed in this chapter is the *default argument*. In C++, you can give a parameter a default value that is automatically used when no argument corresponding to that parameter is specified in a call to a function. Default arguments can be used to simplify calls to complex functions. Also, they can sometimes be used as a "shorthand" form of function overloading.

A default argument is specified in a manner syntactically similar to a variable initialization. Consider the following example, which declares **myfunc( )** as taking one **double** argument with a default value of 0.0, and one character argument with a default value of 'X':

```
void myfunc(double num = 0.0, char ch = 'X')
{
    .
    .
    .
}
```

Now, **myfunc( )** can be called by one of the three methods shown here:

```
myfunc(198.234, 'A');  // pass explicit values

myfunc(10.1); // pass num a value, let ch default

myfunc();    // let both num and ch default
```

The first call passes the value 198.234 to **num** and 'A' to **ch**. The second call automatically gives **num** the value 10.1 and allows **ch** to default to 'X'. Finally, the third call causes both **num** and **ch** to default.

One reason that default arguments are included in C++ is that they enable the programmer to manage greater complexity. In order to handle the widest variety of situations, quite frequently a function will contain more parameters than are required for its most common usage. Thus, when the default arguments apply, you need remember and specify only the arguments that are meaningful to the exact situation, not all those needed for the most general case.

A default argument is a value that will automatically be passed to a function when no explicit argument is specified.

A simple illustration of how useful a default function argument can be is shown by the **clrscr( )** function in the following program. The **clrscr( )** function clears the screen by outputting a series of linefeeds (not the most efficient way, but sufficient for this example!). Since a very common video mode displays 25 lines of text, the default argument of 25 is provided. However, since some video modes can display more or less than 25 lines, you can override the default argument by specifying another one explicitly.

```
#include <iostream>
using namespace std;

void clrscr(int size=25);

int main()
{
  int i;

  for(i=0; i<30; i++ ) cout << i << '\n';
  clrscr(); // clears 25 lines

  for(i=0; i<30; i++ ) cout << i << '\n';
  clrscr(10); // clears 10 lines

  return 0;
}

void clrscr(int size)
{
    for(; size; size--) cout << '\n';
}
```

As this program illustrates, when the default value is appropriate to the situation, no argument need be specified when calling **clrscr( )**. However, it is still possible to override the default and give **size** a different value.

There are two important points to remember about creating a function that has default argument values: The default values must be specified only once, and this specification must happen the first time the function is declared within the file. In the preceding example, the default argument was specified in **clrscr( )**'s prototype. If you try to specify new (or even the same) default values in **clrscr( )**'s definition, the compiler will display an error message and will not compile your program.

Even though default arguments must be specified only once, you can specify different default arguments for each version of an overloaded function. Thus, different versions of an overloaded function can have different default arguments.

It is important to understand that all parameters that take default values must appear to the right of those that do not. For example, the following prototype is invalid:

```
// wrong!
void f(int a = 1, int b);
```

Once you've begun defining parameters that take default values, you cannot specify a non-defaulting parameter. That is, a declaration like the following is also wrong and will not compile:

```
int myfunc(float f, char *str, int i=10, int j);
```

8

Since **i** has been given a default value, **j** must be given one too.

Default Arguments versus Overloading

As mentioned at the beginning of this section, one application of default arguments is as a shorthand form of function overloading. To see why this is the case, imagine that you want to create two customized versions of the standard **strcat( )** function. One version will operate like **strcat( )** and concatenate the entire contents of one string to the end of another. The other version will take a third argument that specifies the number of characters to concatenate. That is, this version will concatenate only a specified number of characters from one string to the end of another.

Assuming that you call your customized functions **mystrcat( )**, they will have the following prototypes:

```
void mystrcat(char *s1, char *s2, int len);
void mystrcat(char *s1, char *s2);
```

The first version will copy **len** characters from **s2** to the end of **s1**. The second version will copy the entire string pointed to by **s2** onto the end of the string pointed to by **s1** and will operate like **strcat( )**.

While it would not be wrong to implement two versions of **mystrcat( )** to create the two versions that you want, there is an easier way. Using a default argument, you can create only one version of **mystrcat( )** that performs both functions. The following program demonstrates this:

```
// A customized version of strcat().
#include <iostream>
#include <cstring>
using namespace std;

void mystrcat(char *s1, char *s2, int len = -1);

int main()
{
  char str1[80] = "This is a test";
  char str2[80] = "0123456789";

  mystrcat(str1, str2, 5); // concatenate 5 chars
  cout << str1 << '\n';

  strcpy(str1, "this is a test"); // reset str1

  mystrcat(str1, str2); // concatenate entire string
  cout << str1 << '\n';

  return 0;
}

// A custom version of strcat().
void mystrcat(char *s1, char *s2, int len)
{
  // find end of s1
  while(*s1) s1++;

  if(len == -1) len = strlen(s2);

  while(*s2 && len) {
    *s1 = *s2; // copy chars
    s1++;
    s2++;
    len--;
  }

  *s1 = '\0'; // null terminate s1
}
```

Here, **mystrcat( )** concatenates up to **len** characters from the string pointed to by **s2** onto the end of the string pointed to by **s1**. However, if **len** is –1, as it will be when it is allowed to default, **mystrcat( )** concatenates the entire string pointed to by **s2** onto **s1**. (Thus, when **len** is –1, the function operates like the standard **strcat( )** function.) By using a default argument for **len**, it is possible to combine both operations into one function. As this example illustrates, default arguments sometimes provide a shorthand form of function overloading.

Using Default Arguments Correctly

Although default arguments can be a very powerful tool when used correctly, they can also be misused. The point of default arguments is to allow a function to perform its job in an efficient, easy-to-use manner, while still allowing considerable flexibility. Towards this end, all default arguments should reflect the way a function is generally used, or a reasonable alternate usage. When there is no single value that is normally associated with a parameter, then there is no reason to declare a default argument. In fact, declaring default arguments when there is insufficient basis for doing so destructures your code, because they are liable to mislead and confuse anyone reading your program. Finally, a default argument should cause no harm. That is, the accidental use of a default argument should not have irreversible, negative consequences. For example, forgetting to specify an argument should not cause an important data file to be erased!

Function Overloading and Ambiguity

Ambiguity results when the compiler cannot resolve the difference between two overloaded functions.

Before concluding this chapter, we must examine a type of error unique to C++: *ambiguity*. It is possible to create a situation in which the compiler is unable to choose between two (or more) correctly overloaded functions. When this happens, the situation is said to be *ambiguous*. Ambiguous statements are errors, and programs containing ambiguity will not compile.

By far the main cause of ambiguity involves C++'s automatic type conversions. C++ automatically attempts to convert the type of the arguments used to call a function into the type of the parameters defined by the function. Here is an example:

8

```
int myfunc(double d);
.
.
.
cout << myfunc('c');  // not an error, conversion applied
```

As the comment indicates, this is not an error, because C++ automatically converts the character **c** into its **double** equivalent. Actually, in C++, very few type conversions of this sort are disallowed. While automatic type conversions are convenient, they are also a prime cause of ambiguity. Consider the following program:

```
// Overloading ambiguity.
#include <iostream>
using namespace std;

float myfunc(float i);
double myfunc(double i);

int main()
{
  // unambiguous, calls myfunc(double)
  cout << myfunc(10.1) << " ";

  // ambiguous
  cout << myfunc(10);
```

```
  return 0;
}

float myfunc(float i)
{
  return i;
}

double myfunc(double i)
{
  return -i;
}
```

Here, **myfunc( )** is overloaded so that it can take arguments of either type **float** or type **double**. In the unambiguous line, **myfunc(double)** is called because, unless explicitly specified otherwise, all floating-point literals in C++ are automatically of type **double**. However, when **myfunc( )** is called using the integer 10, ambiguity is introduced, because the compiler has no way of knowing whether it should be converted to a **float** or to a **double**. Both are valid conversions. This confusion causes an error message to be displayed and prevents the program from compiling.

The central issue illustrated by the preceding example is that it is not the overloading of **myfunc( )** relative to **double** and **float** that causes the ambiguity. Rather, the confusion is caused by the specific call to **myfunc( )** using an indeterminate type of argument. Put differently, it is not the overloading of **myfunc( )** that is in error, but the specific invocation.

Here is another example of ambiguity caused by the automatic type conversions in C++:

```
// Another ambiguity error.
#include <iostream>
using namespace std;

char myfunc(unsigned char ch);
char myfunc(char ch);

int main()
{
  cout << myfunc('c');  // this calls myfunc(char)
  cout << myfunc(88) << " "; // ambiguous

  return 0;
}

char myfunc(unsigned char ch)
{
  return ch-1;
}
```

```
char myfunc(char ch)
{
  return ch+1;
}
```

In C++, **unsigned char** and **char** are *not* inherently ambiguous. (They are different types.) However, when **myfunc( )** is called with the integer 88, the compiler does not know which function to call. That is, should 88 be converted into a **char** or **unsigned char**? Both are valid conversions.

Another way you can cause ambiguity is by using default arguments in overloaded functions. To see how, examine this program:

```
// More ambiguity.
#include <iostream>
using namespace std;

int myfunc(int i);
int myfunc(int i, int j=1);

int main()
{
  cout << myfunc(4, 5) << " "; // unambiguous
  cout << myfunc(10); // ambiguous

  return 0;
}

int myfunc(int i)
{
  return i;
}

int myfunc(int i, int j)
{
  return i*j;
}
```

8

Here, in the first call to **myfunc( )** two arguments are specified; therefore, no ambiguity is introduced, and **myfunc(int i, int j)** is called. However, the second call to **myfunc( )** results in ambiguity, because the compiler does not know whether to call the version of **myfunc( )** that takes one argument, or to apply the default to the version that takes two arguments.

As you continue to write your own C++ programs, be prepared to encounter ambiguity errors. Unfortunately, until you become more experienced, you will find that they are fairly easy to create.

CHAPTER 9

More Data Types
and Operators

B efore we move on to the more advanced features of C++, now is a good time to return to data types and operators. In addition to the data types that you have been using so far, C++ supports several others. Some of these consist of modifiers added to the types you already know about. Other data types include enumerations and **typedef**s. C++ also provides several additional operators that greatly expand its scope and facilitate its application to various programming tasks. These include the bitwise, shift, **?**, and **sizeof** operators. Also, two special operators, **new** and **delete**, are discussed in this chapter. These operators support C++'s dynamic memory allocation system.

The const and volatile Qualifiers

The cv-qualifiers control how a variable can be accessed.

C++ has two type qualifiers that affect the ways in which variables can be accessed or modified: **const** and **volatile**. Formally called the *cv-qualifiers*, they precede the base type when a variable is declared.

const

Variables declared with the **const** qualifier cannot have their values changed during the execution of your program. You may give a variable declared as **const** an initial value, however. For example,

```
const double version =  3.2;
```

creates a **double** variable called **version** that contains the value 3.2 and that value cannot be changed by your program. The variable can, however, be used in other types of expressions. A **const** variable will receive its value either from an explicit initialization or by some hardware-dependent means. Applying the **const** qualifier to a variable's declaration ensures that the variable will not be modified by other parts of your program.

*The **const** qualifier prevents a variable from being modified by your program.*

The **const** qualifier has several important uses. Perhaps the most common is to create **const** pointer parameters. A **const** pointer parameter prevents the object pointed to by the parameter from being modified by a function. That is, when a pointer parameter is preceded by **const**, no statement in the function can modify the variable pointed to by that parameter. For example, the **code( )** function in this short program shifts each letter in a message by one (so that an **A** becomes a **B**, and so forth), thus displaying the message in code. The use of **const** in the parameter declaration prevents the code inside the function from modifying the object pointed to by the parameter.

```
#include <iostream>
using namespace std;

void code(const char *str);

int main()
{
  code("this is a test");

  return 0;
```

```
  }

/* Use of const ensures str cannot modify the
   argument to which it points. */
void code(const char *str)
{
  while(*str) {
    cout << (char) (*str+1);
    str++;
  }
}
```

Since **str** is declared as being a **const** pointer, the function can make no changes to the string pointed to by **str**. However, if you attempted to write **code( )** as shown in the next example, an error would result, and the program would not compile:

```
// This is wrong.
void code(const char *str)
{
  while(*str) {
    *str = *str + 1; // Error, can't modify the argument
    cout << (char) *str;
    str++;
  }
}
```

Because **str** is **const**, it can't be used to modify the object to which it points.

The **const** qualifier can also be used on reference parameters to prevent functions from modifying the variables that they reference. For example, the following program is incorrect because **f( )** attempts to modify the variable referred to by **i**:

9

```
// const references cannot be modified.
#include <iostream>
using namespace std;

void f(const int &i);

int main()
{
  int k = 10;

  f(k);
  return 0;
}

// Use a const reference parameter.
void f(const int &i)
{
  i = 100; // Error, can't modify a const reference.
  cout <<  i;
}
```

Another use for **const** is to provide verification that your program does not, in fact, alter a variable. Recall that a variable of type **const** can be modified by something outside your program. For example, a hardware device may set its value. By declaring a variable as **const**, you can prove that any changes to that variable occur because of external events.

Finally, **const** is used to create named constants. Often, programs will require the same value for many different purposes. For example, several different arrays may be declared that must all be the same size. When such a "magic number" is needed, one good way to implement it is as a **const** variable. Then you can use the name of the variable instead of the value, and if that value needs to be changed, you will need to change it in only one place in your program. The following example gives you the flavor of this application of **const**:

```
#include <iostream>
using namespace std;

const int size = 10;

int main()
{
  int A1[size], A2[size], A3[size];

  // ...
}
```

In this example, if you need to use a new size for the arrays, you need only change the declaration of **size** and recompile your program. All three arrays will be automatically resized.

volatile

The **volatile** qualifier tells the compiler that a variable's value may be changed in ways not explicitly specified by the program. For example, the address of a global variable may be passed to an interrupt-driven clock routine that updates the variable with each tick of the clock. In this situation, the contents of the variable are altered without the use of any explicit assignment statements in the program. The reason the external alteration of a variable may be important is that a C++ compiler is permitted to optimize certain expressions on the assumption that the content of a variable is unchanged if it does not occur on the left side of an assignment statement. However, if factors external to the program change the value of a variable, then problems can occur.

For example, in the following fragment, assume that **clock** is being updated every millisecond by the computer's clock mechanism. However, since **clock** is not declared as **volatile**, the fragment may not always work properly. (Pay special attention to the lines labeled A and B.)

```
int clock, timer;
// ...
```

```
timer = clock;                              // line A
// ... do something
cout << "Elapsed time is " << clock-timer; // line B
```

In this fragment, the value of **clock** is obtained when it is assigned to **timer** in line A. However, because **clock** is not declared as **volatile**, the compiler is free to optimize the code in such a way that the value of **clock** is not reexamined in the **cout** statement in line B if there has been no intervening assignment to **clock** between lines A and B. (That is, in line B the compiler could simply reuse the value for **clock** that it obtained in line A.) However, if a clock tick occurs between lines A and B, then the value of **clock** will have changed, and line B will not produce the correct output.

To solve this problem, you must declare **clock** to be **volatile**, as shown here:

```
volatile int clock;
```

Now, **clock**'s value will be obtained each time it is used.

Although it seems strange at first thought, it is possible to use **const** and **volatile** together. For example, the following declaration is perfectly valid. It creates a **const** pointer to a **volatile** object.

```
const volatile unsigned char *port = (const volatile char *) 0x2112;
```

In this example, the cast is needed in order to transform the integer literal 0x2112 into a **const volatile** character pointer.

Storage Class Specifiers

9

There are five storage class specifiers supported by C++. They are:

auto
extern
register
static
mutable

The storage class specifiers determine how a variable is stored.

These tell the compiler how a variable should be stored. The storage specifier precedes the rest of the variable declaration.

The **mutable** specifier applies only to **class** objects, which are discussed later in this book. Each of the other specifiers is examined here.

auto

*The seldom used **auto** specifier declares a local variable.*

The **auto** specifier declares a local variable. However, it is rarely (if ever) used, because local variables are **auto** by default. It is extremely unusual to see this keyword used in a program.

extern

All the programs that you have worked with so far have been quite small. However, in reality, computer programs tend to be much larger. As a program file grows, the compilation time eventually becomes long enough to be annoying. When this happens, you should break your program into two or more separate files. Once you divide your program this way, small changes to one file will not require that the entire program be recompiled. The multiple file approach can yield a substantial time savings with large projects. The **extern** keyword helps support this approach. Let's see how.

In programs that consist of two or more files, each file must know the names and types of the global variables used by the program. However, you cannot simply declare copies of the global variables in each file. The reason for this is that in C++, your program can include only one copy of each global variable. Therefore, if you try to declare the global variables needed by your program in each file, you will have trouble. When the linker tries to link together the files, it will find the duplicated global variables, and will not link your program. The solution to this dilemma is to declare all of the global variables in one file and use **extern** declarations in the others, as shown in Figure 9-1.

The ***extern*** specifier declares a variable, but does not allocate storage for it.

File One declares and defines **x**, **y**, and **ch**. In File Two, the global variable list is copied from File One, and the **extern** specifier is added to the declarations. The **extern** specifier allows a variable to be made known to a module, but does not actually create that variable. In other words, **extern** lets the compiler know what the types and names are for these global variables, without actually creating storage for them again. When the linker links the two modules together, all references to the external variables are resolved.

While we haven't yet worried about the distinction between the declaration and the definition of a variable, it is important here. A *declaration* declares the name and type of a variable. A *definition* causes storage to be allocated for the variable. In most cases, variable declarations are also definitions. By preceding a variable name with the **extern** specifier, you can declare a variable without defining it.

There is another use of **extern** which does not involve multi-file projects. Although most of the time you will declare global variables at the top of your program, this is

Using global variables in separately compiled modules

Figure 9-1.

File One	File Two
```int x, y;``` ```char ch;```	```extern int x,y;``` ```extern char ch;```

```int main()```
```{```
`    // ...`
```}```
	```void func22()```
	```{```
	`    x = y/10`
	```}```

```void func1()```
```{```
`    x = 123`
```}```
	```void func23()```
	```{```
	`    y = 10;`
	```}```

not technically necessary. If a function uses a global variable that is defined later in the file, the global variable can be declared as **extern** inside the function. Later, when the variable's definition is encountered, references to the variable are resolved. Consider the following example. Notice that the global variables **first** and **last** are declared *after* **main( )**.

```
#include <iostream>
using namespace std;

int main()
{
  extern int first, last; // use global vars

  cout << first << " " << last << "\n";

  return 0;
}

// global definition of first and last
int first = 10, last = 20;
```

This programs outputs **10 20** because the global variables **first** and **last** used by the **cout** statement are initialized to these values. Because the **extern** declaration inside **main( )** tells the compiler that **first** and **last** are declared elsewhere (in this case, later in the same file), the program can be compiled without error even though **first** and **last** are used prior to their definition.

It is important to understand that the **extern** variable declarations as shown in the preceding program are necessary only because **first** and **last** had not yet been defined prior to their use in **main( )**. Had their definitions occurred prior to **main( )**, then there would have been no need for the **extern** statement. Remember, if the compiler finds a variable that has not been declared within the current block, it checks if the variable matches any of the variables declared within enclosing blocks. If it does not, the compiler then checks the previously defined global variables. If a match is found, the compiler assumes that it is the variable being referenced. The **extern** specifier is needed only when you want to use a variable that is declared later in the file, or in another file.

One other point: Although an **extern** statement declares but does not define a variable, there is one exception to this rule. If, in an **extern** declaration, you initialize the variable, then the **extern** declaration becomes a definition. This is important because an object can have multiple declarations, but only one definition.

static Variables

Variables of type **static** are permanent variables within their own function or file. They differ from global variables because they are not known outside their function or file. Because **static** affects local variables differently than it does global ones, local and global variables will be examined separately here.

9

static Local Variables

When the **static** modifier is applied to a local variable, permanent storage for the variable is allocated in much the same way that it is for a global variable. This allows a **static** variable to maintain its value between function calls. (That is, its value is not lost when the function returns, unlike the value of a normal local variable.) The key difference between a **static** local variable and a global variable is that the **static** local variable is known only to the block in which it is declared. Thus, a **static** local variable is, more or less, a global variable that has restricted scope.

To declare a **static** variable, precede its type with the word **static**. For example, this statement declares **count** as a static variable:

```
static int count;
```

A **static** variable may be given an initial value. For example, this statement gives **count** an initial value of 200:

```
static int count = 200;
```

Local **static** variables are initialized only once, when program execution begins, not each time the function in which they are declared is entered.

It is important to the creation of stand-alone functions that **static** local variables are available, because there are several types of routines that must preserve a value between calls. If **static** variables were not allowed, then global variables would have to be used—opening the door to possible side effects.

Here is an example of a **static** variable. It keeps a running average of the numbers entered by the user.

```
/* Compute a running average of numbers entered by
   the user.
*/
#include <iostream>
using namespace std;

int r_avg(int i);

int main()
{
  int num;

  do {
    cout << "Enter numbers (-1 to quit): ";
    cin >> num;
    if(num != -1)
      cout << "Running average is: " << r_avg(num);
    cout << '\n';
  } while(num > -1);

  return 0;
```

```
   }

// Compute a running average.
int r_avg(int i)
{
  static int sum=0, count=0;

  sum = sum + i;

  count++;

  return sum / count;
}
```

Here, the local variables **sum** and **count** are both declared as **static** and initialized to 0. Remember, for **static** variables, the initialization occurs only once—not each time the function is entered. The program uses **r_avg( )** to compute and report the current average of the numbers entered by the user. Because both **sum** and **count** are **static**, they will maintain their values between calls, causing the program to work properly. To prove to yourself that the **static** modifier is necessary, try removing it and running the program. As you can see, the program no longer works correctly, because the running total is lost each time **r_avg( )** returns.

static Global Variables

A **static** global variable is known only to the file in which the variable is declared.

When the **static** specifier is applied to a global variable, it tells the compiler to create a global variable that is known only to the file in which the **static** global variable is declared. This means that even though the variable is global, other functions in other files have no knowledge of it and cannot alter its contents. Thus, it is not subject to unauthorized changes. Therefore, for the few situations where a local **static** cannot do the job, you can create a small file that contains only the functions that need the global **static** variable, separately compile that file, and use it without fear of side effects.

Here is an example that reworks the running-average program shown in the previous section. It consists of two files and uses global **static** variables to hold the running average and the count.

```
// --------------------- First File ---------------------

#include <iostream>
using namespace std;

int r_avg(int i);
void reset();

int main()
{
  int num;

  do {
    cout << "Enter numbers (-1 to quit, -2 to reset): ";
```

9

```
    cin >> num;
    if(num==-2) {
      reset();
      continue;
    }
    if(num != -1)
      cout << "Running average is: " << r_avg(num);
    cout << '\n';
  } while(num != -1);

  return 0;
}

// --------------------- Second File ---------------------

static int sum=0, count=0;

int r_avg(int i)
{
  sum = sum + i;

  count++;

  return sum / count;
}

void reset()
{
  sum = 0;
  count = 0;
}
```

In this version of the program, the variables **sum** and **count** are global **static**s that are restricted to the second file. Thus, they may be accessed by both **r_avg( )** and **reset( )**, both in the second file. This allows them to be reset so that a second set of numbers can be averaged. However, no functions outside the second file can access those variables. When you run this program, you can reset the average by entering –2. This causes a call to **reset( )**. You should try this now. You might also try to access either **sum** or **count** from the first file. (You will receive an error message.)

To review: The name of a local **static** variable is known only to the function or block of code in which it is declared, and the name of a global **static** variable is known only to the file in which it resides. In essence, the **static** modifier allows variables to exist that are known only to the functions that need them, thereby controlling and limiting the possibility of side effects. Variables of type **static** enable you, the programmer, to hide portions of your program from other portions. This can be a tremendous advantage when you are trying to manage a very large and complex program.

TIP: Although global **static** variables are still valid and widely used in C++ code, Standard C++ deprecates their use. Instead, it recommends another method of controlling access to global variables that involves the use of namespaces. This technique is described later in this book.

Register Variables

Perhaps the most frequently used storage class specifier is **register**. The **register** modifier tells the compiler to store a variable in such a way that it can be accessed as quickly as possible. Typically, this means storing the variable either in a register of the CPU or in cache memory. As you probably know, accessing the registers of the CPU (or cache memory) is fundamentally faster than is accessing the main memory of the computer. Thus, a variable stored in a register will be accessed much more quickly than if that variable had been stored in RAM, for example. Because the speed by which variables can be accessed has a profound effect on the overall speed of your programs, the careful use of **register** is an important programming technique.

The **register** *specifier requests that a variable be optimized for access speed.*

Technically, **register** is only a request to the compiler, which the compiler is free to ignore. The reason for this is easy to understand: There is a finite number of registers (or fast-access memory), and these may differ from environment to environment. Thus, if the compiler runs out of fast access memory, it simply stores the variable normally. Generally, this causes no harm, but of course the **register** advantage is lost.

Since only a limited number of variables can actually be granted the fastest access, it is important to choose carefully those to which you apply the **register** modifier. (Only by choosing the right variables can you gain the greatest increase in performance.) In general, the more often a variable is accessed, the more benefit there will be to optimizing it as a **register** variable. For this reason, variables that control or are accessed within loops are good variables to declare as **register**. The following example uses a **register** variable of type **int** to control a loop. This function computes the result of m^e for integers, while preserving the sign. Thus, –2 squared is –4.

9

```
int signed_pwr(register int m, register int e)
{
  register int temp;
  int sign;

  if(m < 0) sign = -1;
  else sign = 1;

  temp = 1;
  for( ;e ;e--) temp = temp * m;

  return temp * sign;
}
```

In this example, **m**, **e** and **temp** are all declared as **register** because they are all used within the loop and are accessed frequently. However, **sign** is not specified as **register** because it is not part of the loop and is accessed less frequently.

The Origins of the register Modifier

The **register** modifier was first defined by the C language. It originally applied only to variables of type **int** and **char**, or to pointers. It caused variables of these types to be held in a register of the CPU rather than in memory, where normal variables are stored. This meant that operations on **register** variables could occur much faster than on variables stored in memory, because no memory access was required to determine or modify their values.

When C was standardized, a decision was made to expand the definition of **register**. According to the ANSI C standard, the **register** modifier may be applied to any type of data. It simply tells the compiler to make access to a **register** type as fast as possible. For situations involving characters and integers, this still usually means putting them into a CPU register, so the traditional definition still holds. Since C++ is built upon ANSI standard C, it has also adopted the expanded definition of **register.**

As stated, the exact number of **register** variables that will actually be optimized within any one function is determined by both the processor type and the specific implementation of C++ that you are using. You can generally count on at least two. You don't have to worry about declaring too many **register** variables, though, because C++ will automatically make register variables into non-register variables when the limit is reached. (This is done to ensure portability of C++ code across a broad line of processors.)

To show the difference that register variables can make, the following program measures the execution time of two **for** loops that differ only in the type of variable that controls them. This program uses the **clock( )** function found in C++'s standard library. The **clock( )** function returns the number of system clock ticks that have elapsed since the program began running. It requires the header **<ctime>**.

```
/* This program shows the difference a register variable
   can make to the speed of program execution.
*/

#include <iostream>
#include <ctime>
using namespace std;

unsigned int i; // non-register
unsigned int delay;

int main()
{
  register unsigned int j;
```

```
long start, end;

start = clock();
for(delay=0; delay<50; delay++)
  for(i=0; i < 64000000; i++);
end = clock();
cout << "Number of clock ticks for non-register loop: ";
cout << end-start << '\n';

start = clock();
for(delay=0; delay<50; delay++)
  for(j=0; j < 64000000; j++) ;
end = clock();
cout << "Number of clock ticks for register loop: ";
cout << end-start << '\n';

  return 0;
}
```

When you run this program, you will find that the register-controlled loop executes in about half the time of the non-register-controlled loop. If you don't see the expected difference, it probably means that your compiler is simply optimizing all of the variables for speed. Just play with the program a bit until the difference becomes apparent.

NOTE: At the time of this writing, Visual C++ ignores the **register** keyword. Instead, Visual C++ applies optimizations as it sees fit. Thus, you won't see any optimization caused by **register** in the preceding program. However, the **register** keyword is still accepted by the compiler without error. It just doesn't have any effect.

9

Enumerations

In C++, you can define a list of named integer constants. Such a list is called an *enumeration*. These constants can then be used anywhere that an integer can. Enumerations are defined using the keyword **enum**, and this general format:

   enum *type-name* { *enumeration list* } *variable-list*;

The enumeration list is a comma-separated list of names that represent the values of the enumeration. The variable list is optional because variables may be declared later by using the enumeration type name. The following example defines an enumeration called **apple**, and two variables of type **apple** called **red** and **yellow**.

```
enum apple {Jonathan, Golden_Del, Red_Del, Winesap,
        Cortland, McIntosh} red, yellow;
```

Once you have defined an enumeration, you can declare additional variables of its type by using its name. For example, this statement declares one variable, called **fruit**, of enumeration **apple**:

```
apple fruit;
```

The statement can also be written like this:

```
enum apple fruit;
```

*The **enum** keyword declares an enumeration.*

However, the use of **enum** here is redundant. In C (which also supports enumerations), this second form was required, so you may see it used in some programs.

Assuming the preceding declarations, the following types of statements are perfectly valid:

```
fruit = Winesap;
if(fruit==Red_Del) cout << "Red Delicious\n";
```

The key point to understand about an enumeration is that each of the symbols stands for an integer value. As such, they can be used in any integer expression. Unless initialized otherwise, the value of the first enumeration symbol is 0, the value of the second symbol is 1, and so forth. Therefore,

```
cout << Jonathan << ' ' << Cortland;
```

displays **0 4** on the screen.

Although enumerated constants are automatically converted to integers, integers are not automatically converted into enumerated constants. For example, the following statement is incorrect:

```
fruit = 1; // Error
```

This statement causes a compile-time error because there is no automatic conversion from integer to **apple**. However, you could fix the preceding statement by using a cast, as shown here:

```
fruit = (apple) 1; // now OK, but probably poor style
```

This causes **fruit** to contain the value **Golden_Del**, because it is the **apple** constant associated with the value 1. As the comment suggests, while this statement is now correct, it would be considered poor style, except in unusual circumstances.

It is possible to specify the value of one or more of the enumerated constants by using an initializer. This is done by following the symbol with an equal sign and an integer value. Whenever an initializer is used, the symbol that appears after it is assigned a value 1 greater than the preceding initialization value. For example, the following statement assigns the value of 10 to **Winesap**:

```
enum apple {Jonathan, Golden_Del, Red_Del, Winesap=10,
              Cortland, McIntosh};
```

Now, the values of these symbols are as follows:

Jonathan	0
Golden_Del	1
Red_Del	2
Winesap	10
Cortland	11
McIntosh	12

One common, but erroneous, assumption sometimes made about enumerations is that the symbols can be input and output as a string. This is not the case. For example, the following code fragment will not perform as desired:

```
// This will not print "McIntosh" on the screen.
fruit = McIntosh;
cout << fruit;
```

Remember, the symbol **McIntosh** is simply a name for an integer; it is not a string. Thus, the preceding code will display the numeric value of **McIntosh**, not the string "McIntosh". Actually, to create code that inputs and outputs enumeration symbols as strings is quite tedious. For example, the following code is needed in order to display, in words, the kind of apple that **fruit** contains:

9

```
switch(fruit) {
  case Jonathan: cout << "Jonathan";
    break;
  case Golden_Del: cout << "Golden Delicious";
    break;
  case Red_Del: cout << "Red Delicious";
    break;
  case Winesap: cout << "Winesap";
    break;
  case Cortland: cout << "Cortland";
    break;
  case McIntosh: cout << "McIntosh";
    break;
}
```

Sometimes it is possible to declare an array of strings and use the enumeration value as an index in order to translate an enumeration value into its corresponding string. For example, the following program prints the names of three apples:

```
#include <iostream>
using namespace std;
```

```
enum  apple {Jonathan, Golden_Del, Red_Del, Winesap,
             Cortland, McIntosh};

// Array of strings that correspond to the apple enumeration.
char name[][20] = {
  "Jonathan",
  "Golden Delicious",
  "Red Delicious",
  "Winesap",
  "Cortland",
  "McIntosh"
};

int main()
{
  apple fruit;

  fruit = Jonathan;
  cout << name[fruit] << '\n';

  fruit = Winesap;
  cout << name[fruit] << '\n';

  fruit = McIntosh;
  cout << name[fruit] << '\n';

  return 0;
}
```

The output is shown here.

```
Jonathan
Winesap
McIntosh
```

The approach this program uses to convert an enumeration value into a string can be applied to any type of enumeration, as long as that enumeration does not contain initializers. To properly index the array of strings, the enumerated constants must begin at zero, be in strictly ascending order, and each be precisely one greater than the previous.

Given the fact that enumeration values must be converted manually to their human-readable string values, they find their greatest use in routines that do not make such conversions. It is common to see an enumeration used to define a compiler's symbol table, for example.

typedef

C++ allows you to define new data type names with the **typedef** keyword. When you use **typedef**, you actually are not creating a new data type, but rather are defining a new name for an existing type. This process can help make machine-dependent programs more portable; only the **typedef** statements have to be changed. It also can help you self-document your code by allowing descriptive names for the standard data types. The general form of the **typedef** statement is

typedef *type new-name*;

where *type* is any valid data type, and *new-name* is the new name for this type. The new name you define is in addition to, not a replacement for, the existing type name.

For example, you could create a new name for **float** using

```
typedef float balance;
```

This statement would tell the compiler to recognize **balance** as another name for **float**. Next, you could create a **float** variable using **balance**:

```
balance over_due;
```

Here, **over_due** is a floating-point variable of type **balance**, which is another name for **float**.

typedef lets you create a new name for an existing data type.

More Operators

9

Earlier in this book, you learned about the more commonplace C++ operators. Unlike many computer languages, C++ provides several special operators that greatly increase its power and flexibility. These operators are the subject of the remainder of this chapter.

Bitwise Operators

The bitwise operators operate upon individual bits.

Since C++ is designed to allow full access to the computer's hardware, it is important that it have the ability to operate directly upon the bits within a byte or word. Towards this end, C++ contains the bitwise operators. *Bitwise operations* refer to the testing, setting, or shifting of the actual bits in a byte or word, which correspond to C++'s character and integer types. Bitwise operations may not be used on **bool**, **float**, **double**, **long double**, **void**, or other more complex data types. Bitwise operations are important in a wide variety of systems-level programming in which status information from a device must be interrogated or constructed. Table 9-1 lists the bitwise operators. Let's now look at each operator in turn.

Operator	Action
&	AND
|	OR
^	exclusive OR (XOR)
~	one's complement (NOT)
>>	shift right
<<	shift left

The Bitwise
Operators
Table 9-1.

AND, OR, XOR, and NOT

The bitwise AND, OR, and one's complement (NOT) are governed by the same truth table as their logical equivalents, except that they work on a bit-by-bit level. The exclusive OR (XOR) operates according to the following truth table:

p	q	p ^ q
0	0	0
1	0	1
1	1	0
0	1	1

As the table indicates, the outcome of an XOR is true only if exactly one of the operands is true; it is false otherwise.

In terms of its most common usage, you can think of the bitwise AND as a way to turn bits off. That is, any bit that is 0 in either operand will cause the corresponding bit in the outcome to be set to 0. For example:

```
    1101 0011
&   1010 1010
    ---------
    1000 0010
```

The following program reads characters from the keyboard, and turns any lowercase letter into uppercase by resetting the sixth bit to 0. As the ASCII character set is defined, the lowercase letters are the same as the uppercase ones, except that they are greater in value by exactly 32. Therefore, to uppercase a lowercase letter, you need to turn off the sixth bit, as this program illustrates:

```
// Uppercase letters.
#include <iostream>
using namespace std;
```

```
int main()
{
  char ch;

  do {
    cin >> ch;

    // This statement turns off the 6th bit.
    ch = ch & 223; // ch is now uppercase

    cout << ch;
  } while(ch!='Q');

  return 0;
}
```

The value 223 used in the AND statement is the decimal representation of 1101 1111. Hence, the AND operation leaves all bits in **ch** unchanged, except for the sixth one, which is set to zero.

The AND operator is also useful when you want to determine whether a bit is on or off. For example, this statement checks to see if bit 4 in **status** is set:

```
if(status & 8) cout << "bit 4 is on";
```

To understand why 8 is used to determine if bit 4 is set, recall that, in binary, 8 is represented as 0000 1000. Thus, the number 8 has only the fourth bit set. Therefore, the **if** statement can succeed only when bit 4 of **status** is also on. An interesting use of this technique is the **disp_binary( )** function, shown next. It displays, in binary format, the bit pattern of its argument. You will use **disp_binary( )** later in this chapter to examine the effects of other bitwise operations.

9

```
// Display the bits within a byte.
void disp_binary(unsigned u)
{
  register int t;

  for(t=128; t>0; t = t/2)
    if(u & t) cout << "1 ";
    else cout << "0 ";
  cout << "\n";
}
```

The **disp_binary( )** function works by successively testing each bit in the low-order byte of **u**, using the bitwise AND, to determine if it is on or off. If the bit is on, the digit **1** is displayed; otherwise **0** is displayed. For fun, try expanding this function so that it displays all of the bits in **u**, not just its low-order byte.

The bitwise OR, as the reverse of AND, can be used to turn bits on. A bit that is set to 1 in either operand will cause the corresponding bit in the result to be set to 1. For example:

```
  1 1 0 1  0 0 1 1
| 1 0 1 0  1 0 1 0
  ---------------
  1 1 1 1  1 0 1 1
```

You can make use of the OR to change the uppercasing program, used earlier, into a lowercasing program, as shown here:

```cpp
// Lowercase letters.
#include <iostream>
using namespace std;

int main()
{
  char ch;

  do {
    cin >> ch;

    /* This lowercases the letter by turning
       on bit 6.
    */
    ch = ch | 32;

    cout << ch;
  } while(ch != 'q');

  return 0;
}
```

Setting the sixth bit causes an uppercase letter to be transformed into its lowercase equivalent.

An exclusive OR, usually abbreviated XOR, will set a bit if and only if the bits being compared are different, as illustrated here:

```
  0 1 1 1 1 1 1 1
^ 1 0 1 1 1 0 0 1
  ---------------
  1 1 0 0 0 1 1 0
```

The 1's complement (NOT) unary operator reverses the state of all the bits of its operand. For example, if some integer called **A** has the bit pattern 1001 0110, then ~**A** produces a result with the bit pattern 0110 1001.

The following program demonstrates the NOT operator by displaying a number and its complement in binary, using the **disp_binary( )** function shown earlier:

```
#include <iostream>
using namespace std;

void disp_binary(unsigned u);

int main()
{
  unsigned u;

  cout << "Enter a number between 0 and 255: ";
  cin >> u;

  cout << "Here's the number in binary: ";
  disp_binary(u);

  cout << "Here's the complement of the number: ";
  disp_binary(~u);

  return 0;
}

// Display the bits within a byte.
void disp_binary(unsigned u)
{
  register int t;

  for(t=128; t>0; t = t/2)
    if(u & t) cout << "1 ";
    else cout << "0 ";
  cout << "\n";
}
```

9

Here is a sample run produced by the program:

```
Enter a number between 0 and 255: 99
Here's the number in binary: 0 1 1 0 0 0 1 1
Here's the complement of the number: 1 0 0 1 1 1 0 0
```

One last point: Be careful not to confuse the logical and bitwise operators. They perform different functions. The **&**, |, and ~ apply their operations directly to each bit in the value individually. The equivalent logical operators work on true/false (zero/nonzero) values. For this reason, the bitwise operators cannot be used to replace their logical equivalents in conditional statements. For example, if *x* equals 7, then *x* && 8 evaluates to true, whereas *x* & 8 evaluates to false.

REMEMBER: A relational or logical operator always produces a result that is either true or false, whereas the similar bitwise operator produces a value in accordance with the specific operation.

The Shift Operators

The shift operators, >> and <<, move all bits in a value to the right or left. The general form of the right-shift operator is

> *value >> num-bits*

and the left-shift operator is

> *value << num-bits*

The shift operators shift the bits within an integral value.

The value of *num-bits* determines how many bit places the bits are shifted. Each left-shift causes all bits within the specified value to shift left one position, and it brings in a zero bit on the right. Each right-shift shifts all bits to the right one position, and brings in a zero on the left. However, if the value is a signed integer containing a negative value, then each right-shift brings in a 1 on the left, which preserves the sign bit. Remember, a shift is not a rotation. That is, the bits shifted off of one end do not come back around to the other.

The shift operators work only with integral types, such as characters, integers, and long integers. They cannot be applied to floating-point values, for example.

Bit shift operations can be very useful for decoding external device input, like D/A converters, and processing status information. The bitwise shift operators can also be used to perform very fast multiplication and division of integers. A shift left will effectively multiply a number by 2, and a shift right will divide it by 2.

The following program illustrates the effects of the shift operators:

```cpp
// Demonstrate bitshifting.
#include <iostream>
using namespace std;

void disp_binary(unsigned u);

int main()
{
  int i=1, t;

  for(t=0; t<8; t++) {
    disp_binary(i);
    i = i << 1;
  }

  cout << "\n";

  for(t=0; t<8; t++) {
    i = i >> 1;
    disp_binary(i);
  }

  return 0;
}

// Display the bits within a byte.
```

```
void disp_binary(unsigned u)
{
  register int t;

  for(t=128; t>0; t=t/2)
    if(u & t) cout << "1 ";
    else cout << "0 ";
  cout << "\n";
}
```

This program produces the following output:

```
0 0 0 0 0 0 0 1
0 0 0 0 0 0 1 0
0 0 0 0 0 1 0 0
0 0 0 0 1 0 0 0
0 0 0 1 0 0 0 0
0 0 1 0 0 0 0 0
0 1 0 0 0 0 0 0
1 0 0 0 0 0 0 0

1 0 0 0 0 0 0 0
0 1 0 0 0 0 0 0
0 0 1 0 0 0 0 0
0 0 0 1 0 0 0 0
0 0 0 0 1 0 0 0
0 0 0 0 0 1 0 0
0 0 0 0 0 0 1 0
0 0 0 0 0 0 0 1
```

9

The ? Operator

One of C++'s most fascinating operators is the **?**. The **?** operator can be used to replace **if-else** statements of this general form:

> if (*condition*)
>   *var* = *expression1*;
> else
>   *var* = *expression2*;

Here, the value assigned to *var* depends upon the outcome of the condition controlling the **if**.

The **?** is called a *ternary operator* because it requires three operands. It takes the general form

> *Exp1* **?** *Exp2* : *Exp3*;

where *Exp1*, *Exp2*, and *Exp3* are expressions. Notice the use and placement of the colon.

The value of a **?** expression is determined like this: *Exp1* is evaluated. If it is true, then *Exp2* is evaluated and becomes the value of the entire **?** expression. If *Exp1* is false, then *Exp3* is evaluated and its value becomes the value of the expression. Consider this example:

```
while(something) {
  x = count > 0 ? 0 : 1;
  // ...
}
```

Here, **x** will be assigned the value 0 until **count** is less than or equal to 0. The same code written using an **if-else** statement would look like this:

```
while(something) {
  if(count > 0) x = 0;
  else x = 1;
  // ...
}
```

Here's an example of the **?** operator in action. This program divides two numbers, but will not allow a division by zero.

```
/* This program uses the ? operator to prevent
   a division by zero. */

#include <iostream>
using namespace std;

int div_zero();

int main()
{
  int i, j, result;

  cout << "Enter dividend and divisor: ";
  cin >> i >> j;

  // This statement prevents a divide by zero error.
  result = j ? i/j : div_zero();

  cout << "Result: " << result;

  return 0;
}

int div_zero()
{
  cout << "Cannot divide by zero.\n";
  return 0;
}
```

Here, if **j** is non-zero, then **i** is divided by **j**, and the outcome is assigned to **result**. Otherwise, the **div_zero( )** error handler is called and zero is assigned to **result**.

Compound Assignment

C++ has a special shorthand called *compound assignment* that combines assignment with another operation. For example,

```
x = x + 10;
```

can be written using a compound assignment as

```
x += 10;
```

The operator pair **+=** tells the compiler to assign to **x** the value of **x** plus 10. As this example illustrates, compound assignment simplifies the coding of a certain type of assignment statement. Depending upon the compiler, it may also produce more efficient code.

Compound assignment operators exist for all of the binary operators in C++ (that is, those that require two operands). Thus, for the binary operators, any assignment that has this general form

   var = var op expression;

can be rewritten as

   var op = expression;

Here is another example:

```
x = x - 100;
```

is the same as

```
x -= 100;
```

You will see compound assignment used widely in professionally written C++ programs, so you should become familiar with it.

The Comma Operator

Another interesting C++ operator is the comma. You have seen some examples of the comma operator in the **for** loop, where it has been used to allow multiple initialization or incrementation statements. However, the comma can be used as a part of any expression. Its purpose is to string together several expressions. The value of a comma-separated list of expressions is the value of the right-most expression. The values of the other expressions will be discarded. This means that the expression on the right side will become the value of the entire comma-separated expression. For example,

```
var = (count=19, incr=10, count+1);
```

first assigns **count** the value 19, assigns **incr** the value 10, then adds 1 to **count**, and finally, assigns **var** the value of the rightmost expression, **count+1**, which is 20. The

9

parentheses are necessary because the comma operator has a lower precedence than the assignment operator.

To see the effects of the comma operator, try running the following program:

```
#include <iostream>
using namespace std;

int main()
{
  int i, j;

  j = 10;

  i = (j++, j+100, 999+j);

  cout << i;

  return 0;
}
```

This program prints 1010 on the screen. Here is why: **j** starts with the value 10. **j** is then incremented to 11. Next, **j** is added to 100. Finally, **j** (still containing 11) is added to 999, which yields the result 1010.

Essentially, the comma's effect is to cause a sequence of operations to be performed. When it is used on the right side of an assignment statement, the value assigned is the value of the last expression in the comma-separated list. You can, in some ways, think of the comma operator as having the same meaning that the word "and" has in English when used in the phrase "do this and this and this."

Multiple Assignments

C++ allows a very convenient method of assigning many variables the same value: using multiple assignments in a single statement. For example, this fragment assigns **count**, **incr**, and **index** the value 10:

```
count = incr = index = 10;
```

In professionally written programs, you will often see variables assigned a common value using this format.

Using sizeof

Sometimes it is helpful to know the size, in bytes, of a type of data. Since the sizes of C++'s built-in types can differ between computing environments, knowing the size of a variable in all situations can be difficult. To solve this problem, C++ includes the **sizeof** compile-time operator, which has these general forms:

sizeof (*type*)
sizeof *value*

sizeof is a
compile-time
operator that
obtains the size
of a type or value.

The first version returns the size of the specified data type, and the second returns the size of the specified value. As you can see, if you want to know the size of a data type, such as **int**, you must enclose the type name in parentheses. If you want to know the size of a value, no parentheses are needed, although you can use them if you want.

To see how **sizeof** works, try the following short program. For many 32-bit environments, it displays the values 1, 4, 4, and 8.

```
// Demonstrate sizeof.
#include <iostream>
using namespace std;

int main()
{
  char ch;
  int i;

  cout << sizeof ch << ' '; // size of char
  cout << sizeof i << ' ';  // size of int
  cout << sizeof (float) << ' '; // size of float
  cout << sizeof (double) << ' '; // size of double

  return 0;
}
```

As mentioned earlier, **sizeof** is a compile-time operator. All information necessary for computing the size of a variable or data type is known during compilation.

You may apply **sizeof** to any data type. For example, when it is applied to an array, it returns the number of bytes used by the array. Consider this fragment:

9

```
int nums[4];

cout << sizeof nums; // displays 16
```

Assuming 4-byte integers, this fragment displays the value 16 (i.e., 4 bytes times 4 elements).

sizeof primarily helps you write code that depends upon the size of the C++ data types. Remember, since the sizes of types in C++ are defined by the implementation, it is bad style to make assumptions about their sizes in code that you write.

Dynamic Allocation Using new and delete

There are two primary ways in which a C++ program can store information in the main memory of the computer. The first is through the use of variables. The storage provided by variables is fixed at compile time, and cannot be altered during the execution of a program. The second way information can be stored is through the use of C++'s dynamic allocation system. In this method, storage for data is allocated as needed from the free memory area that lies between your program (and its permanent storage area) and the stack. This region is called the *heap*. (Figure 9-2 shows conceptually how a C++ program appears in memory.)

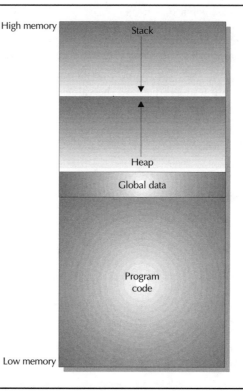

High memory

Stack

Heap

Global data

Program
code

Low memory

A conceptual
view of memory
usage in a C++
program
Figure 9-2.

*Dynamic
allocation is the
means by which a
program can
obtain memory
during its
execution.*

Dynamically allocated storage is obtained at run time. Thus, dynamic allocation makes it possible for your program to create variables during its execution, and it can create as many or as few variables as required, depending upon the situation. This makes dynamic allocation especially valuable for data structures such as linked lists and binary trees, which change size as they are used. Dynamic allocation for one purpose or another is an important part of nearly all real-world programs.

Memory to satisfy a dynamic allocation request is taken from the heap. As you might guess, it is possible, under fairly extreme cases, for free memory to become exhausted. Therefore, while dynamic allocation offers greater flexibility, it, too, is finite.

*new allocates
dynamic memory.*

C++ contains two operators, **new** and **delete**, that perform the functions of allocating and freeing memory. Their general forms are shown here:

*delete frees
previously
allocated dynamic
memory.*

> *pointer-var* = new *var-type*;
> delete *pointer-var*;

Here, *pointer-var* is a pointer of type *var-type*. The **new** operator allocates sufficient memory to hold a value of type *var-type* and returns a pointer to it. Any valid data type can be allocated using **new**. The **delete** operator frees the memory pointed to by *pointer-var*. Once freed, this memory can be reallocated to different purposes by a subsequent **new** allocation request.

Since the heap is finite, it can become exhausted. If there is insufficient available memory to fill an allocation request, then **new** will fail and an exception will be generated. An *exception* is a run-time error and C++ has a complete subsystem dedicated to handling such errors. (Exceptions are described in Chapter 17.) In general, your program should handle this exception and take appropriate action, if possible. If this exception is not handled by your program, then your program will be terminated.

The actions of **new** on failure as just described are specified by Standard C++. This is also the way that all modern compilers work, including the latest versions of Visual C++ and C++ Builder. The trouble is that some older compilers will implement **new** in a different way. When C++ was first invented, **new** returned a null pointer on failure. Later, this was changed so that **new** throws an exception on failure, as just described. Because this book teaches Standard C++, the examples in this book assume that **new** generates an exception on failure. If you are using an older compiler, check your compiler's documentation to see precisely how it implements **new**, making changes to the examples, if necessary.

Because exceptions will not be examined until later in this book, after classes and objects have been described, we won't be handling any exceptions caused by a **new** failure at this time. Also, none of the examples in this and subsequent chapters will cause **new** to fail, since only a handful of bytes are being allocated by any single program. However, should an allocation failure occur, it will simply cause your program to terminate. In Chapter 17, which discusses exception handling, you will learn how to handle the exception generated by a **new** failure.

Here is a simple example illustrating the use of **new** and **delete**:

```
#include <iostream>
using namespace std;

int main()
{
  int *p;

  p = new int; // allocate memory for int

  *p = 20; // assign that memory the value 20
  cout << *p; // prove that it works by displaying value

  delete p; // free the memory

  return 0;
}
```

9

This program assigns to **p** an address in the heap that is large enough to hold an integer. It then assigns that memory the value 20, and displays the contents of the memory on the screen. Finally, it frees the dynamically allocated memory.

Because of the way dynamic allocation is managed, you must only use **delete** with a pointer to memory that has been allocated using **new**. Using **delete** with any other type of address will cause serious problems.

Initializing Dynamically Allocated Memory

You can initialize dynamically allocated memory by using the **new** operator. To do this, specify the initial value, inside parentheses, after the type name. For example, the following program uses initialization to give the memory pointed to by **p** the value 99:

```
#include <iostream>
using namespace std;

int main()
{
  int *p;

  p = new int (99);  // initialize with 99

  cout << *p; // displays 99

  delete p;

  return 0;
}
```

Allocating Arrays

You can allocate arrays by using **new**. This is the general form used to allocate a singly dimensioned array:

pointer-var = new *type* [*size*];

Here, *size* specifies the number of elements in the array.

To free a dynamically allocated array, use this form of **delete**:

delete [ ] *pointer-var*;

Here, *pointer-var* is the address obtained when the array was allocated. The square brackets tell C++ that a dynamically allocated array is being deleted, and it automatically frees all the memory allocated to the array.

 T IP: Older C++ compilers may require that you specify the size of the array being deleted, because early versions of C++ required this form of **delete** for freeing an array:

delete [*size*] *pointer-var*;

Here, *size* is the number of elements in the array. Standard C++ no longer requires that the size of the array be specified.

The following program allocates space for a 10-element array of **double**s, assigns the array the values 100 to 109, and displays the contents of the array on the screen:

```
#include <iostream>
using namespace std;

int main()
{
  double *p;
  int i;

  p = new double [10]; // get a 10-element array

  // assign the values 100 through 109
  for(i=0; i<10; i++) p[i] = 100.00 + i;

  // display the contents of the array
  for(i=0; i<10; i++)  cout << p[i] << " ";

  delete [] p; // delete the entire array

  return 0;
}
```

There is one important point to remember about allocating an array: You cannot initialize it.

IN DEPTH

9

C's Approach to Dynamic Allocation: malloc( ) and free( )

The C language does not contain the **new** or the **delete** operators. Instead, C uses library functions to allocate and free memory. For compatibility, C++ still provides support for C's dynamic allocation system, and it is still quite common to find the C-like dynamic allocation system used in C++ programs. The following discussion explains how it works.

At the core of C's allocation system are the functions **malloc( )** and **free( )**. The **malloc( )** function allocates memory, and the **free( )** function releases it. That is, each time a **malloc( )** memory request is made, a portion of the remaining free memory is allocated. Each time **free( )** is called, memory is returned to the system. Any program that uses these functions must include the header **<cstdlib>.**

The **malloc( )** function has this prototype:

> void *malloc(size_t *num_bytes*);

Here, *num_bytes* is the number of bytes of memory you want to allocate. (**size_t** is a defined type that is some type of unsigned integer). The **malloc( )** function returns a pointer of type **void**, which signifies a generic pointer. You must use a cast to convert this pointer into the type of pointer needed by your program. After a successful call, **malloc( )** will return a pointer to the first byte of the region of memory allocated from the heap. If there is not enough memory to satisfy the request, an allocation failure occurs, and **malloc( )** returns a null.

The **free( )** function is the opposite of **malloc( )** in that it returns previously allocated memory to the system. Once the memory has been released, it may be reused by a subsequent call to **malloc( )**. The function **free( )** has this prototype:

> void free(void *ptr*);

Here, *ptr* is a pointer to memory previously allocated using **malloc( )**. You must never call **free( )** with an invalid argument; this would cause the free list to be destroyed.

The following program illustrates **malloc( )** and **free( )**:

```
// Demonstrate malloc() and free().
#include <iostream>
#include <cstdlib>
using namespace std;

int main()
{
  int *i;
  double *j;

  i = (int *) malloc(sizeof(int));
  if(!i) {
    cout << "Allocation Failure.\n";
    return 1;
  }

  j = (double *) malloc(sizeof(double));
  if(!j) {
    cout << "Allocation Failure.\n";
    return 1;
  }

  *i= 10;
```

```
*j = 100.123;

cout << *i << ' ' << *j;

// free the memory
free(i);
free(j);

return 0;
}
```

While **malloc( )** and **free( )** are fully capable dynamic allocation functions, there are several reasons why C++ defines its own approach to dynamic allocation. First, **new** automatically computes the size of the type being allocated. You don't have to make use of the **sizeof** operator, so you save some effort. More importantly, automatic computation prevents the wrong amount of memory from being allocated. The second advantage to the C++ approach is that **new** automatically returns the correct pointer type—you don't need to use a type cast. Third, by using **new**, you can initialize the object being allocated. Finally, as you will see later in this book, you can create your own, customized versions of **new** and **delete**.

One last point: Because of possible incompatibilities, you should not mix **malloc( )** and **free( )** with **new** and **delete** in the same program.

9

Precedence Summary

Table 9-2 lists the precedence, from highest to lowest, of all C++ operators. Most operators associate from left to right. The unary operators, the assignment operators, and the **?** operator associate from right to left. Note that the table includes a few operators that you have not yet learned about; most of these are used in object-oriented programming.

Precedence of the C++ Operators
Table 9-2.

Precedence	Operators
Highest	() [] -> :: .
	! ~ ++ -- - * & sizeof new delete typeid *type-casts*
	.* ->*
	* / %
	+ -

Precedence	Operators
	<< >>
	< <= > >=
	== !=
	&
	^
	|
	&&
	||
	?:
	= += −= *= /= %= >>= <<= &= ^= |=
Lowest	,

Precedence of
the C++
Operators
(continued)
Table 9-2.

CHAPTER 10

Structures and Unions

C++ defines several compound data types. These are data types that are comprised of two or more elements. You have already learned about one compound type: the array. Three more are the structure, the union, and the class. This chapter discusses the structure and the union. A discussion of the class is deferred until Chapter 11. Although they fill different needs, both the structure and the union provide a convenient means of managing groups of related variables. Another important aspect of structures and unions is that when you create one, you are also creating a new, programmer-defined data type. The ability to create your own data types is a powerful feature of C++.

In C++, structures and unions have both object-oriented and non-object-oriented attributes. This chapter discusses only their non-object-oriented features. Their object-oriented qualities are discussed in the following chapter, after classes and objects have been introduced.

Structures

A structure is a group of related variables.

In C++, a *structure* is a collection of variables that are referenced under one name, providing a convenient means of keeping related information together. Structures are called *aggregate data types* because they consist of several different, yet logically connected, variables. You will also see structures referred to as *compound* or *conglomerate* data types, for the same reason.

Before a structure object can be created, the form of the structure must be defined. This is accomplished by means of a structure declaration. The structure declaration determines what type of variables the structure contains. The variables that comprise the structure are called *members* of the structure. Structure members are also commonly referred to as *elements* or *fields*.

A structure member is a variable that is part of a structure.

Generally, all members of the structure will be logically related to each other. For example, structures are typically used to hold information such as mailing addresses, compiler symbol tables, library card catalog entries, and the like. Of course, the relationship between the members of a structure is purely subjective, and thus determined by you. The compiler doesn't know (or care).

Let's begin our examination of structures with an example. We will define a structure that can hold the information relating to a company's inventory. An inventory record typically consists of several pieces of information, such as the item name, cost, and number on hand, so a structure is a good way to manage this information. The following code fragment declares a structure that defines the item name, cost and retail price, number on hand, and resupply time for maintaining an inventory. The keyword **struct** tells the compiler that a structure declaration is beginning.

```
struct inv_type {
  char item[40]; // name of item
  double cost;   // cost
  double retail; // retail price
  int on_hand;   // amount on hand
  int lead_time; // number of days before resupply
};
```

Notice that the declaration is terminated by a semicolon. This is because a structure declaration is a statement. The type name of the structure is **inv_type**. As such, **inv_type** identifies this particular data structure and is its type specifier.

In the preceding declaration, no variable has actually been created. Only the form of the data has been defined. To declare an actual variable (i.e., a physical object) with this structure, you would write something like this:

```
inv_type inv_var;
```

This declares a structure variable of type **inv_type** called **inv_var**. Remember, when you define a structure, you are defining a new data type. It is not until you declare a variable of that type that one actually exists.

C++ will automatically allocate sufficient memory to accommodate all the members of a structure. Figure 10-1 shows how **inv_var** would appear in memory (assuming 8-byte **double**s and 4-byte **int**s).

You can also declare one or more variables at the same time that you define a structure, as shown here:

```
struct inv_type {
  char item[40]; // name of item
  double cost;   // cost
  double retail; // retail price
  int on_hand;   // amount on hand
  int lead_time; // number of days before resupply
} inv_varA, inv_varB, inv_varC;
```

This defines a structure type called **inv_type** and declares variables **inv_varA**, **inv_varB**, and **inv_varC** of that type. It is important to understand that each structure variable contains its own copies of the structure's members. For example, the **cost** field of **inv_varA** is separate from the **cost** field of **inv_varB**. Thus, changes to one do not affect the other.

10

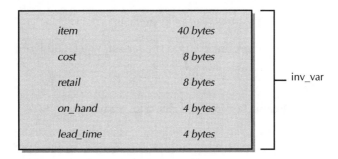

The **inv_var** structure as it appears in memory
Figure 10-1.

If you need only one structure variable, then it is not necessary to include the name of the structure type. Consider this example:

```
struct {
  char item[40]; // name of item
  double cost;    // cost
  double retail; // retail price
  int on_hand;    // amount on hand
  int lead_time; // number of days before resupply
} temp;
```

struct is the keyword that begins a structure declaration.

This fragment declares one variable named **temp**, as defined by the structure preceding it.

The general form of a structure declaration is shown here:

```
struct struct-type-name {
    type element_name1;
    type element_name2;
    type element_name3;
       .
       .
       .
    type element_nameN;
} structure-variables;
```

Accessing Structure Members

Individual structure members are accessed through the use of a period (generally called the "dot" operator). For example, the following code will assign the value 10.39 to the **cost** field of the structure variable **inv_var**, declared earlier.

```
inv_var.cost = 10.39;
```

The structure variable name, followed by a period and the member name, refers to that member. All structure elements are accessed in the same way. The general form is

structure-varname.member-name

The dot operator (.) accesses a member of a structure.

Therefore, to print **cost** on the screen, you could write

```
cout << inv_var.cost;
```

In the same fashion, the character array **inv_var.item** can be used to call **gets( )**, as shown here:

```
gets(inv_var.item);
```

This will pass a character pointer to the beginning of the element **item**.

If you want to access the individual elements of the array **inv_var.item**, you can index **item**. For example, you can print the contents of **inv_var.item** one character at a time by using this code:

```
int t;

for(t=0; inv_var.item[t]; t++)
  cout << inv_var.item[t];
```

Arrays of Structures

Structures may be arrayed. In fact, structure arrays are quite common. To declare an array of structures, you must first define a structure, then declare an array of its type. For example, to declare a 100-element array of structures of type **inv_type** (defined earlier), you would write

```
inv_type invtry[100];
```

To access a specific structure within an array of structures, you must index the structure name. For example, to display the **on_hand** member of the third structure, you would write

```
cout << invtry[2].on_hand;
```

Like all array variables, arrays of structures begin their indexing at zero.

A Simple Inventory Example

To illustrate the value of structures, a simple inventory-management program will be developed that uses an array of structures of type **inv_type** to hold the inventory information. The functions in this program interact with structures and their elements in various ways.

The inventory will be held in structures of type **inv_type**, organized into an array called **invtry**, as shown here:

```
const int SIZE = 100;

struct inv_type {
  char item[40]; // name of item
  double cost;    // cost
  double retail; // retail price
  int on_hand;    // amount on hand
  int lead_time; // number of days before resupply
} invtry[SIZE];
```

10

The size of the array is arbitrary. Feel free to change it if you desire. Notice that the array dimension is specified using a **const** variable. Since the size of the array will be used at several places in the full program, using a **const** variable for this value is a good idea. To change the size of the array, simply change the value of **SIZE** and then recompile. Using a **const** variable to define a "magic number" that is used frequently within a program is common practice in professionally written C++ code.

The program will provide these three options:

◆   Enter inventory information

◆   Display the inventory

◆   Modifiy a specific item

The first function needed for the program is **main( )**, which is shown here:

```
int main()
{
  char choice;

  init_list();

  for(;;) {
    choice = menu();
    switch(choice) {
      case 'e': enter();
        break;
      case 'd': display();
        break;
      case 'u': update();
        break;
      case 'q': return 0;
    }
  }
}
```

The **main( )** function begins by calling **init_list( )**, which initializes the structure array. It then enters a loop that displays the menu and processes the user's selection.

The **init_list( )** function is shown here:

```
// Initialize the array.
void init_list()
{
  int t;

  // a zero length name signifies empty
  for(t=0; t<SIZE; t++) *invtry[t].item = '\0';
}
```

The **init_list( )** function prepares the structure array for use by putting a null character into the first byte of the **item** field. The program assumes that a structure is not in use if the **item** field is empty.

The **menu_select( )** function, shown next, displays the options and returns the user's selection:

```cpp
// Get a menu selection.
int menu()
{
  char ch;

  cout << '\n';
  do {
    cout << "(E)nter\n";
    cout << "(D)isplay\n";
    cout << "(U)pdate\n";
    cout << "(Q)uit\n\n";
    cout << "choose one: ";
    cin >> ch;
  } while(!strchr("eduq", tolower(ch)));
  return tolower(ch);
}
```

The user selects an option by entering the specified letter. For example, to display the inventory list, press **D**.

The **menu( )** function makes use of another of C++'s library functions, **strchr( )**, which has this prototype:

char *strchr(const char *str, int ch);

This function searches the string pointed to by *str* for an occurrence of the character in the low-order byte of *ch*. If the character is found, a pointer to that character is returned. This is by definition a true value. However, if no match is found, a null is returned, which is by definition false. It is used in this program to see whether the user entered a valid menu selection.

10

The **enter( )** function sets up the call to **input( )**, which prompts the user for information. Both functions are shown here:

```cpp
// Enter items into the list.
void enter()
{
  int i;

  // find the first free structure
  for(i=0; i<SIZE; i++)
    if(!*invtry[i].item) break;

  // i will equal SIZE if the list is full
  if(i==SIZE) {
    cout << "List full.\n";
    return;
  }

  input(i);
```

```
}

// Input the information.
void input(int i)
{
  // enter the information
  cout << "Item: ";
  cin >> invtry[i].item;

  cout << "Cost: ";
  cin >> invtry[i].cost;

  cout << "Retail price: ";
  cin >> invtry[i].retail;

  cout << "On hand: ";
  cin >> invtry[i].on_hand;

  cout << "Lead time to resupply (in days): ";
  cin >> invtry[i].lead_time;
}
```

The **enter( )** function first finds an empty structure. To do this, **enter( )** starts with the first element in **invtry** and advances through the array, checking the **item** field. If it finds an **item** field that is null, it assumes that structure is unused. If no free structure is found before the end of the array is reached, the loop control variable **i** will be equal to the size of the array. This condition indicates that the array is full and no further information can be added. If an open array element is found, then **input( )** will be called to obtain the inventory information entered by the user. The reason the input code is not part of **enter( )** is that **input( )** is also used by the **update( )** function, which you will see next.

Because inventory information changes, the inventory program lets you change the information about the individual items. This is accomplished with a call to the **update( )** function, shown here:

```
// Modify an existing item.
void update()
{
  int i;
  char name[80];

  cout << "Enter item: ";
  cin >> name;

  for(i=0; i<SIZE; i++)
    if(!strcmp(name, invtry[i].item)) break;

  if(i==SIZE) {
    cout << "Item not found.\n";
    return;
  }
```

```
    cout << "Enter new information.\n";
    input(i);
}
```

This function prompts the user for the name of the item to be changed. It then looks in the list to see if the item is there. If it is, **input( )** is called, and the new information can be entered.

The final function used by the program is **display( )**. It displays the entire inventory list on the screen. The **display( )** function is shown here:

```
// Display the list.
void display()
{
  int t;

  for(t=0; t<SIZE; t++) {
    if(*invtry[t].item) {
      cout << invtry[t].item << '\n';
      cout << "Cost: $" << invtry[t].cost;
      cout << "\nRetail: $";
      cout << invtry[t].retail << '\n';
      cout << "On hand: " << invtry[t].on_hand;
      cout << "\nResupply time: ";
      cout << invtry[t].lead_time << " days\n\n";
    }
  }
}
```

The complete inventory program is shown next. You should enter this program into your computer and study its execution. Make some changes and watch the effects they have. You should also try to expand the program by adding functions that search the list for a specific inventory item, remove an item from the list, or reset the inventory list.

```
/* A simple inventory program that uses an array
   of structures. */

#include <iostream>
#include <cctype>
#include <cstring>
#include <cstdlib>
using namespace std;

const int SIZE = 100;

struct inv_type {
  char item[40]; // name of item
  double cost;   // cost
  double retail; // retail price
  int on_hand;   // amount on hand
```

```
    int lead_time; // number of days before resupply
}  invtry[SIZE];

void enter(), init_list(), display();
void update(), input(int i);
int menu();

int main()
{
  char choice;

  init_list();

  for(;;) {
    choice = menu();
    switch(choice) {
      case 'e': enter();
        break;
      case 'd': display();
        break;
      case 'u': update();
        break;
      case 'q': return 0;
    }
  }
}

// Initialize the array.
void init_list()
{
  int t;

  // a zero length name signifies empty
  for(t=0; t<SIZE; t++) *invtry[t].item = '\0';
}

// Get a menu selection.
int menu()
{
  char ch;

  cout << '\n';
  do {
    cout << "(E)nter\n";
    cout << "(D)isplay\n";
    cout << "(U)pdate\n";
    cout << "(Q)uit\n\n";
    cout << "choose one: ";
    cin >> ch;
  } while(!strchr("eduq", tolower(ch)));
  return tolower(ch);
}

// Enter items into the list.
```

```
void enter()
{
  int i;

  // find the first free structure
  for(i=0; i<SIZE; i++)
    if(!*invtry[i].item) break;

  // i will equal SIZE if the list is full
  if(i==SIZE) {
    cout << "List full.\n";
    return;
  }

  input(i);
}

// Input the information.
void input(int i)
{
  // enter the information
  cout << "Item: ";
  cin >> invtry[i].item;

  cout << "Cost: ";
  cin >> invtry[i].cost;

  cout << "Retail price: ";
  cin >> invtry[i].retail;

  cout << "On hand: ";
  cin >> invtry[i].on_hand;

  cout << "Lead time to resupply (in days): ";
  cin >> invtry[i].lead_time;
}

// Modify an existing item.
void update()
{
  int i;
  char name[80];

  cout << "Enter item: ";
  cin >> name;

  for(i=0; i<SIZE; i++)
    if(!strcmp(name, invtry[i].item)) break;

  if(i==SIZE) {
    cout << "Item not found.\n";
    return;
  }
```

10

```
    cout << "Enter new information.\n";
    input(i);
}

// Display the list.
void display()
{
  int t;

  for(t=0; t<SIZE; t++) {
    if(*invtry[t].item) {
      cout << invtry[t].item << '\n';
      cout << "Cost: $" << invtry[t].cost;
      cout << "\nRetail: $";
      cout << invtry[t].retail << '\n';
      cout << "On hand: " << invtry[t].on_hand;
      cout << "\nResupply time: ";
      cout << invtry[t].lead_time << " days\n\n";
    }
  }
}
```

Passing Structures to Functions

When a structure is used as an argument to a function, the entire structure is passed by using the standard call-by-value parameter passing mechanism. This, of course, means that any changes made to the contents of the structure inside the function to which it is passed do not affect the structure used as an argument. However, be aware that passing large structures can incur significant overhead. (As a general rule, the more data passed to a function, the longer it takes.)

When using a structure as a parameter, remember that the type of the argument must match the type of the parameter. For example, the following program declares a structure called **sample**, and then a function called **f1( )** that takes a parameter of type **sample**.

```
// Pass a structure to a function.
#include <iostream>
using namespace std;

// define a structure type
struct sample {
  int a;
  char ch;
} ;

void f1(sample parm);

int main()
{
  struct sample arg; // declare arg
```

```
  arg.a = 1000;
  arg.ch = 'X';

  f1(arg);

  return 0;
}

void f1(sample parm)
{
  cout << parm.a << " " << parm.ch << "\n";
}
```

Here, both **arg** in **main( )** and **parm** in **f1( )** are of the same type. Thus, **arg** can be passed to **f1( )**. If the structure types had differed, a compile-time error would have resulted.

Assigning Structures

You can assign the contents of one structure to another as long as both structures are of the same type. For example, the following program assigns the value of **svar1** to **svar2**:

```
// Demonstrate structure assignments.
#include <iostream>
using namespace std;

struct stype {
  int a, b;
};

int main()
{
  stype svar1, svar2;

  svar1.a = svar1.b = 10;
  svar2.a = svar2.b = 20;

  cout << "Structures before assignment.\n";
  cout << "svar1: " << svar1.a << ' ' << svar1.b;
  cout << '\n';
  cout << "svar2: " << svar2.a << ' ' << svar2.b;
  cout << "\n\n";

  svar2 = svar1; // assign structures

  cout << "Structures after assignment.\n";
  cout << "svar1: " << svar1.a << ' ' << svar1.b;
  cout << '\n';
  cout << "svar2: " << svar2.a << ' ' << svar2.b;
```

10

```
    return 0;
}
```

This program displays the following output:

```
Structures before assignment.
svar1: 10 10
svar2: 20 20

Structures after assignment.
svar1: 10 10
svar2: 10 10
```

In C++, each new structure declaration defines a new type. Therefore, even if two structures are physically the same, if they have different type names, they will be considered different by the compiler and, thus, cannot be assigned to one another. Consider the following fragment, which is not valid, and will not compile.

```
struct stype1 {
  int a, b;
};

struct stype2 {
  int a, b;
};

stype1 svar1;
stype2 svar2;

svar2 = svar1; // Error - type mismatch
```

Even though **stype1** and **stype2** are physically the same, they are separate types as far as the compiler is concerned.

REMEMBER: One structure can be assigned to another only if both are of the same type.

Pointers to Structures and the Arrow Operator

C++ allows pointers to structures in the same way that it allows pointers to any other type of variable. However, there are some special aspects to using structure pointers that you must be aware of.

You declare a structure pointer as you would any other pointer variable, by putting an * in front of a structure variable's name. For example, assuming the previously defined structure **inv_type**, the following statement declares **inv_pointer** to be a pointer to data of that type:

```
inv_type *inv_pointer;
```

To find the address of a structure variable, you must place the **&** operator before the structure variable's name. For example, given the following fragment,

```
struct bal {
  float balance;
  char name[80];
} person;

bal *p; // declare a structure pointer
```

then

```
p = &person;
```

puts the address of **person** into the pointer **p**.

The members of a structure can be accessed through a pointer to the structure. However, you do not use the dot operator for this purpose. Instead, you must use the **->** operator. For example, this fragment accesses **balance** through **p**:

```
p->balance
```

The **->** is called the *arrow* operator. It is formed by using the minus sign followed by a greater than sign.

The arrow operator (->) accesses the members of a structure through a pointer.

One important use of a structure pointer is as a function parameter. Because of the overhead that occurs when a large structure is passed to a function, many times only a pointer to a structure is passed. (Passing a pointer is always faster than passing a large structure.)

10

REMEMBER: To access members of a structure, use the dot operator. To access members of a structure through a pointer, use the arrow operator.

An Example Using Structure Pointers

An interesting use of structure pointers can be found in C++'s time and date functions. These functions obtain the current system time and date. The time and date functions require the header **<ctime>**. This header supplies two data types needed by the time and date functions. The first type is **time_t**. It is capable of representing the system time and date as a long integer. This is referred to as the *calendar time*. The second type is a structure called **tm**, which holds the individual elements of the date and time. This is called the *broken-down time*. The **tm** structure is defined as shown here:

```
struct tm {
  int tm_sec;   // seconds, 0-61
  int tm_min;   // minutes, 0-59
  int tm_hour;  // hours, 0-23
  int tm_mday;  // day of the month, 1-31
  int tm_mon;   // months since Jan, 0-11
  int tm_year;  // years from 1900
  int tm_wday;  // days since Sunday, 0-6
  int tm_yday;  // days since Jan 1, 0-365
  int tm_isdst; // Daylight Saving Time indicator
};
```

The value of **tm_isdst** will be positive if daylight saving time is in effect, 0 if it is not in effect, and negative if there is no information available.

The foundation for C++'s time and date functions is **time( )**, which has this prototype:

> time_t time(time_t *curtime);

The **time( )** function returns the current calendar time. It can be called either with a null pointer or with a pointer to a variable of type **time_t**. If the latter is used, then the variable pointed to by *curtime* will also be assigned the current calendar time.

To convert the calendar time into broken-down time, use **localtime( )**, which has this prototype:

> struct tm *localtime(const time_t *curtime);

The **localtime( )** function returns a pointer to the broken-down form of *curtime*, in the form of a **tm** structure. The time is represented in local time. The *curtime* value is generally obtained through a call to **time( )**.

The structure used by **localtime( )** to hold the broken-down time is internally allocated by the **localtime( )** function and is overwritten each time the function is called. If you want to save the contents of the structure, you must copy it elsewhere.

The following program demonstrates the use of **time( )** and **localtime( )** by displaying the current system time:

```
// This program displays the current system time.
#include <iostream>
#include <ctime>
using namespace std;

int main()
{
  struct tm *ptr;
  time_t lt;
```

```
lt = time('\0');

ptr = localtime(&lt);

cout << ptr->tm_hour << ':' << ptr->tm_min;
cout << ':' << ptr->tm_sec;

return 0;
}
```

Here is sample output from the program:

```
4:15:46
```

Although your programs can use the broken-down form of the time and date (as illustrated in the preceding example), the easiest way to generate a time and date string is to use **asctime( )**, whose prototype is shown here:

char *asctime(const struct tm *ptr);

The **asctime( )** function returns a pointer to a string, which is the conversion of the information stored in the structure pointed to by *ptr*. This string has the following form:

day month date hours:minutes:seconds year\n\0

Often the structure pointer passed to **asctime( )** is the one obtained from **localtime( )**.

The memory used by **asctime( )** to hold the formatted output string is an internally allocated character array, and is overwritten each time the function is called. If you want to save the contents of the string, you must copy it elsewhere.

The following program uses **asctime( )** to display the system time and date.

10

```
// This program displays the current system time.
#include <iostream>
#include <ctime>
using namespace std;

int main()
{
  struct tm *ptr;
  time_t lt;

  lt = time('\0');

  ptr = localtime(&lt);
  cout << asctime(ptr);

  return 0;
}
```

Here is sample output.

```
Fri Feb 28 12:27:54 2003
```

C++ contains several other time and date functions; to learn about these, check your compiler's documentation.

References to Structures

You can create a reference to a structure. A structure reference is frequently used as a function parameter, or as a function return type. When accessing members through a structure reference, use the dot operator. The arrow operator is explicitly reserved for accessing members through a pointer.

The following program shows how a structure can be used as a reference parameter:

```
// Demonstrate a reference to a structure.
#include <iostream>
using namespace std;

struct mystruct {
  int a;
  int b;
};

mystruct &f(mystruct &var);

int main()
{
  mystruct x, y;
  x.a = 10; x.b = 20;

  cout << "Original x.a and x.b: ";
  cout << x.a << ' ' << x.b << '\n';

  y = f(x);

  cout << "Modified x.a and x.b: ";
  cout << x.a << ' ' << x.b << '\n';
  cout << "Modified y.a and y.b: ";
  cout << y.a << ' ' << y.b << '\n';

  return 0;
}

// Receive and return a reference to a structure.
mystruct &f(mystruct &var)
{
  var.a = var.a * var.a;
  var.b = var.b / var.b;
  return var;
}
```

Here is the output produced by this program:

```
Original x.a and x.b: 10 20
Modified x.a and x.b: 100 1
Modified y.a and y.b: 100 1
```

Since there is significant overhead incurred when passing a structure to a function, or when returning a structure, many C++ programmers use references when performing these tasks.

Arrays and Structures Within Structures

A structure member can be of any valid data type, including other aggregate types such as arrays and other structures. Because this is an area that often causes confusion, a close examination is warranted.

A structure member that is an array is treated as you might expect from the earlier examples. Consider this structure:

```
struct stype {
  int nums[10][10]; // 10 x 10 array of ints
  float b;
} var;
```

To refer to integer 3,7 in **nums** of **var** of structure **stype**, you would write

```
var.nums[3][7]
```

As this example shows, when an array is a member of a structure, it is the array name that is indexed—not the structure name.

When a structure is a member of another structure, it is called a *nested* structure. In the following example, the structure **addr** is nested inside **emp**:

10

```
struct addr {
  char name[40];
  char street[40];
  char city[40];
  char zip[10];
}

struct emp {
  addr address;
  float wage;
} worker;
```

Here, structure **emp** has been defined as having two members. The first member is the structure of type **addr** that will contain an employee's address. The second is **wage**, which holds the employee's wage. The following code fragment will assign the ZIP code 98765 to the **zip** field of **address** of **worker**:

```
worker.address.zip = 98765;
```

As you can see, the members of each structure are specified left to right, from the outermost to the innermost.

A structure may also contain a pointer to a structure as a member. In fact, it is perfectly valid for a structure to contain a member that is a pointer to itself. For example, in the following structure, **sptr** is declared as a pointer to a structure of type **mystruct**, which is the structure being declared.

```
struct mystruct {
  int a;
  char str[80];
  mystruct *sptr; // pointer to mystruct objects
};
```

Structures containing pointers to themselves are quite common when various data structures, such as linked lists, are created. As you progress in C++, you will frequently see applications that make use of this feature.

IN DEPTH

C Structure Versus C++ Structures

C++ structures are derived from C structures. Thus, any C structure is also a valid C++ structure. There are two important differences, however. First, as you will see in the next chapter, C++ structures have some unique attributes that allow them to support object-oriented programming. Second, in C a structure *does not* actually define a new data type. A C++ structure does. As you know, when you define a structure in C++, you are defining a new type, which is the name of the structure. This new type can be used to declare variables, function return types, and the like. However, in C, the name of a structure is called its *tag*. The tag, by itself, is not a type name.

To understand the difference, consider the following C code fragment:

```
struct C_struct {
 int a;
 int b;
}

// declare a C_struct variable
struct C_struct svar:
```

Notice that the structure definition is exactly the same as it is in C++. However, look closely at the declaration of the structure variable **svar**. Its declaration also starts with the keyword **struct**. In C, after you have defined a structure, you must still use the keyword **struct** in conjunction with the structure's tag (in this case, **C_struct**) to specify a complete data type.

If you will be converting older C programs to C++, you won't need to worry about the differences between C and C++ structures, because C++ still accepts the C-like declarations. The preceding code fragment, for instance, will compile correctly as part of a C++ program. It is just that the redundant use of **struct** in the declaration of **svar** is unnecessary in C++.

Bit-Fields

A bit-field is a bit-based structure member.

Unlike many other computer languages, C++ has a built-in method for accessing a single bit within a byte. Bit access is achieved through the use of a *bit-field*. Bit-fields can be useful for a number of reasons. Here are three examples. First, if storage is limited, you can store several Boolean values in one byte; second, certain device interfaces transmit information encoded into bits within one byte; and third, certain encryption routines need to access the bits within a byte. All of these functions can be performed using the bitwise operators, as you saw in the previous chapter; however, a bit-field can add more transparency and readability to your program. It might also make your code more portable.

The method that C++ uses to access bits is based on the structure. A bit-field is really just a special type of structure member that defines its length in bits. The general form of a bit-field definition is

```
struct struct-type-name {
  type name1 : length;
  type name2 : length;
  .
  .
  .
  type nameN : length;
};
```

Here, *type* is the type of the bit-field and *length* is the number of bits in the field. A bit-field must be declared as an integral or enumeration type. Bit-fields of length 1 should be declared as **unsigned**, because a single bit cannot have a sign.

Bit-fields are commonly used for analyzing the input from a hardware device. For example, the status port of a serial communications adapter might return a status byte organized like this:

Bit	Meaning When Set
0	Change in clear-to-send line
1	Change in data-set-ready
2	Trailing edge detected

10

Bit	Meaning When Set
3	Change in receive line
4	Clear-to-send
5	Data-set-ready
6	Telephone ringing
7	Received signal

You can use the following bit-field to represent the information in a status byte:

```
struct status_type {
  unsigned delta_cts: 1;
  unsigned delta_dsr: 1;
  unsigned tr_edge:   1;
  unsigned delta_rec: 1;
  unsigned cts:       1;
  unsigned dsr:       1;
  unsigned ring:      1;
  unsigned rec_line:  1;
} status;
```

You might use code similar to that shown next to determine when you can send or receive data:

```
status = get_port_status ();
if(status.cts) cout << "clear to send";
if(status.dsr) cout << "data ready";
```

To assign a value to a bit-field, simply use the same form that you would use for any other type of structure element. For example, the following statement clears the **ring** field:

```
status.ring = 0;
```

As you can see from these examples, each bit-field is accessed by using the dot operator. However, if the structure is accessed through a pointer, you must use the –> operator.

You do not have to name each bit-field. This makes it easy to reach the bit you want, passing up those that are unused. For example, if you care only about the **cts** and **dsr** bits, you could declare the **status_type** structure like this:

```
struct status_type {
  unsigned : 4;
  unsigned cts: 1;
  unsigned dsr: 1;
} status;
```

Notice here that the bits after **dsr** do not need to be mentioned at all.

It is valid to mix normal structure members with bit-field elements. Here is an example:

```
struct emp {
  struct addr address;
  float pay;
  unsigned lay_off: 1; // lay off or active
  unsigned hourly: 1: // hourly pay or wage
  unsigned deductions: 3: // tax deductions
};
```

This structure defines an employee record that uses only one byte to hold three pieces of information: the employee's status, whether or not the employee is salaried, and the number of deductions. Without the use of the bit-field, this information would require three bytes.

Bit-fields have certain restrictions. You cannot take the address of a bit-field, or reference a bit-field. Bit-fields cannot be arrayed. They cannot be declared as **static**. You cannot know, from machine to machine, whether the fields will run from right to left or from left to right; this implies that any code using bit-fields may have some machine dependencies. Other restrictions may be imposed by various specific implementations of C++, so check your compiler's documentation.

The next section presents a program that uses a bit-field to display the ASCII character codes in binary.

Unions

A union is comprised of two or more variables that share the same memory location.

A *union* is comprised of two or more variables that share the same memory location. Thus, a union provides a way of interpreting the same bit pattern in two or more different ways. A union declaration is similar to that of a structure, as shown in this example:

10

```
union utype {
  short int i;
  char ch;
} ;
```

The **union** keyword begins a union declaration.

This declares a union in which a **short int** and a **char** both share the same location. Be clear on one point: It is not possible to have this union hold *both* an integer and a character *at the same time*, because **i** and **ch** overlay each other. Instead, your program can treat the information in the union as an integer or a character at any time. Thus, a union gives two or more ways to view the same piece of data. As the example shows, a union is declared by using the **union** keyword.

As with structures, a union declaration does not define any variables. You may declare a variable either by placing its name at the end of the declaration, or by using a separate declaration statement. To declare a union variable called **u_var** of type **utype** you would write

```
utype u_var;
```

In **u_var**, both the short integer **i** and the character **ch** share the same memory location. (Of course, **i** occupies two bytes and **ch** uses only one.) Figure 10-2 illustrates how **i** and **ch** share the same address.

When a union is declared, the compiler will automatically allocate enough storage to hold the largest variable type in the union.

To access a union element, use the same syntax that you would use for structures: the dot and arrow operators. If you are operating on the union directly (or through a reference), use the dot operator. If the union variable is accessed through a pointer, use the arrow operator. For example, to assign the letter 'A' to element **ch** of **u_var**, you would write the following:

```
u_var.ch = 'A';
```

In the next example, a pointer to **u_var** is passed to a function. Inside the function, **i** is assigned the value 10 through the pointer:

```
  // ...
  func1(&u_var); // pass func1() a pointer to u_var
  // ...
}
void func1(utype *un)
{
  un->i = 10; /* Assign 10 to u_var using
                 a pointer. */
}
```

Because unions allow your program to interpret data in more than one way, they are often used when an unusual type conversion is needed. For example, the following program uses a union to exchange the two bytes that comprise a short integer. It uses

i and **ch** both utilize the union **u_var**

Figure 10-2.

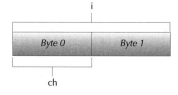

the **disp_binary( )** function, developed in Chapter 9, to display the contents of the integer. (This program assumes that short integers are two bytes.)

```cpp
// Use a union to exchange the bytes within a short integer.
#include <iostream>
using namespace std;

void disp_binary(unsigned u);

union swap_bytes {
  short int num;
  char ch[2];
};

int main()
{
  swap_bytes sb;
  char temp;

  sb.num = 15;   // binary: 0000 0000 0000 1111


  cout << "Original bytes:   ";
  disp_binary(sb.ch[1]);
  cout << "   ";
  disp_binary(sb.ch[0]);
  cout << "\n\n";


  // exchange the bytes
  temp = sb.ch[0];
  sb.ch[0] = sb.ch[1];
  sb.ch[1] = temp;

  cout << "Exchanged bytes: ";
  disp_binary(sb.ch[1]);
  cout << "   ";
  disp_binary(sb.ch[0]);
  cout << "\n\n";

  return 0;
}

// Display the bits within a byte.
void disp_binary(unsigned u)
{
  register int t;

  for(t=128; t>0; t=t/2)
    if(u & t) cout << "1 ";
    else cout << "0 ";
}
```

10

The output from this program is shown here:

```
Original bytes:  0 0 0 0 0 0 0 0   0 0 0 0 1 1 1 1
Exchanged bytes: 0 0 0 0 1 1 1 1   0 0 0 0 0 0 0 0
```

In the program, 15 is assigned to the integer variable **sb.num**. The two bytes that form that integer are exchanged by swapping the two characters that comprise the array in **ch**. This causes the high- and low-order bytes of **num** to be swapped. The fact that both **num** and **ch** share the same memory location makes this operation possible.

Another use for a union is shown in the following program, which combines unions with bit-fields to display, in binary, the ASCII code generated when you press a key. This program also shows an alternative method for displaying the individual bits that make up a byte. The union allows the value of the key to be assigned to a character variable, while the bit-field is used to display the individual bits.

```cpp
// Display the ASCII code in binary for characters.

#include <iostream>
#include <conio.h>
using namespace std;

// a bit field that will be decoded
struct byte {
  unsigned a : 1;
  unsigned b : 1;
  unsigned c : 1;
  unsigned d : 1;
  unsigned e : 1;
  unsigned f : 1;
  unsigned g : 1;
  unsigned h : 1;
};

union bits {
  char ch;
  struct byte bit;
} ascii ;

void disp_bits(bits b);

int main()
{
  do {
    cin >> ascii.ch;
    cout << ": ";
    disp_bits(ascii);
  } while(ascii.ch!='q'); // quit if q typed

  return 0;
}
```

```
// Display the bit pattern for each character.
void disp_bits(bits b)
{
  if(b.bit.h) cout << "1 ";
    else cout << "0 ";
  if(b.bit.g) cout << "1 ";
    else cout << "0 ";
  if(b.bit.f) cout << "1 ";
    else cout << "0 ";
  if(b.bit.e) cout << "1 ";
    else cout << "0 ";
  if(b.bit.d) cout << "1 ";
    else cout << "0 ";
  if(b.bit.c) cout << "1 ";
    else cout << "0 ";
  if(b.bit.b) cout << "1 ";
    else cout << "0 ";
  if(b.bit.a) cout << "1 ";
    else cout << "0 ";
  cout << "\n";
}
```

A sample run of the program is shown here:

```
a: 0 1 1 0 0 0 0 1
b: 0 1 1 0 0 0 1 0
c: 0 1 1 0 0 0 1 1
d: 0 1 1 0 0 1 0 0
e: 0 1 1 0 0 1 0 1
f: 0 1 1 0 0 1 1 0
g: 0 1 1 0 0 1 1 1
h: 0 1 1 0 1 0 0 0
i: 0 1 1 0 1 0 0 1
j: 0 1 1 0 1 0 1 0
k: 0 1 1 0 1 0 1 1
l: 0 1 1 0 1 1 0 0
m: 0 1 1 0 1 1 0 1
n: 0 1 1 0 1 1 1 0
o: 0 1 1 0 1 1 1 1
p: 0 1 1 1 0 0 0 0
q: 0 1 1 1 0 0 0 1
```

10

TIP: Because a union causes two or more variables to share the same memory location, unions provide a good way for your program to store and access information that may contain differing data types, depending upon the situation. If you think about it, unions provide low-level support for the principle of polymorphism. That is, a union provides a single interface to several different types of data, thus embodying the concept of "one interface, multiple methods" in its simplest form.

Anonymous Unions

There is a special type of union in C++ called an *anonymous union*. An anonymous union does not have a type name, and you can declare no objects of an anonymous union. Instead, an anonymous union tells the compiler that its members will share the same memory location. However, the variables themselves are referred to directly, without the normal dot operator syntax.

Consider this example:

```
// Demonstrate an anonymous union.
#include <iostream>
using namespace std;

int main()
{
  // this is an anonymous union
  union {
    short int count;
    char ch[2];
  };

  // Here, refer to union members directly
  ch[0] = 'X';
  ch[1] = 'Y';
  cout << "union as chars: " << ch[0] << ch[1] << '\n';
  cout << "union as integer: " << count << '\n';

  return 0;
}
```

This program displays the following output. 22872 is the integer produced by putting the characters X and Y into the low- and high-order bytes, respectively, of **count**.

```
union as chars: XY
union as integer: 22872
```

As you can see, both **count** and **ch** are accessed as if they were normal variables, and not part of a union. Even though they are declared as being part of an anonymous union, their names are at the same scope level as any other local variable declared at the same point. Thus, a member of an anonymous union cannot have the same name as any other variable declared within the same scope.

The anonymous union provides a way for you to tell the compiler that you want two or more variables to share the same memory location. Aside from this special attribute, members of an anonymous union behave like other variables.

Using sizeof to Ensure Portability

You have seen that structures and unions create objects of varying sizes, depending upon the sizes and number of their members. Furthermore, sizes of the built-in types, such as **int**, can change from machine to machine. Also, sometimes the compiler will pad a structure or union so that it aligns on an even word or on a paragraph boundary. (A paragraph is 16 bytes.) Therefore, when you need to determine the size, in bytes, of a structure or union, use the **sizeof** operator. Do not try to manually add up the sizes of the individual members. Because of padding, or other machine dependencies, the size of a structure or union may be larger than the sum of the sizes of its individual members.

One other point: A union will always be large enough to hold its largest member. Consider this example:

```
union x {
  char ch;
  int i;
  double f;
} u_var;
```

Here, the **sizeof u_var** will be 8 (assuming eight-byte **double**s). At run time, it does not matter what **u_var** is *actually* holding; all that matters is the size of the largest variable it can hold, because the union must be as large as its largest element.

Moving On to Object-Oriented Programming

10

This is the last chapter that describes those attributes of C++ that are not explicitly object-oriented. Beginning with the next chapter, features that support OOP will be examined. To understand and apply the object-oriented features of C++ requires a thorough understanding of the material in this and the preceding nine chapters. For this reason, you might want to take some time to quickly review. Specifically, make sure that you are comfortable with pointers, structures, functions, and function overloading.

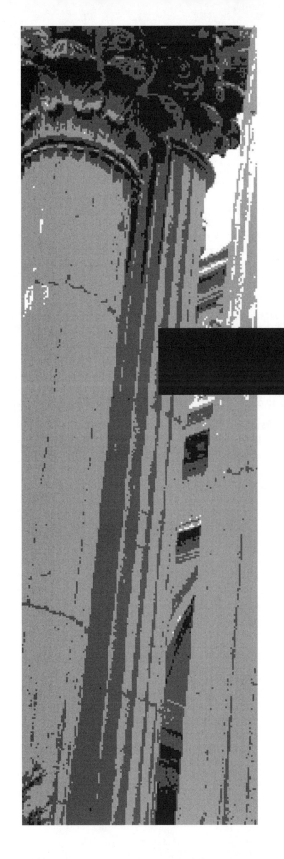

CHAPTER 11

Introducing
the Class

This chapter introduces the *class*. The class is the foundation of C++'s support for object-oriented programming, and is at the core of many of its more advanced features. The class is C++'s basic unit of encapsulation and it provides the mechanism by which objects are created.

Class Fundamentals

The class forms the foundation for object-oriented programming.

Let's begin by defining the terms class and object. A *class* defines a new data type that specifies the form of an *object*. A class includes both data and the code that will operate on that data. Thus, a class *links data with code*. C++ uses a class specification to construct objects. Objects are *instances* of a class. Therefore, a class is essentially a set of plans that specify how to build an object. It is important to be clear on one issue: A class is a logical abstraction. It is not until an object of that class has been created that a physical representation of that class exists in memory.

When you define a class, you declare the data that it contains and the code that operates on that data. Although very simple classes might contain only code or only data, most real-world classes contain both. Within a class, data is contained in variables and code is contained in functions. Collectively, the functions and variables that constitute a class are called *members* of the class. Thus, a variable declared within a class is called a *member variable*, and a function declared within a class is called a *member function*. Sometimes the term *instance variable* is used in place of member variable.

class *is the keyword that begins a class declaration.*

A class is created by using the keyword **class**. A class declaration is syntactically similar to a structure. Here is an example. The following class defines a type called **queue**, which will be used to implement a queue. (A queue is a first-in, first-out list.)

```
// This creates the class queue.
class queue {
  int q[100];
  int sloc, rloc;
public:
  void init();
  void qput(int i);
  int qget();
};
```

Let's look closely at this class declaration.

By default, members of a class are private.

All members of **queue** are declared within its **class** statement. The member variables of **queue** are **q**, **sloc**, and **rloc**. The member functions are **init( )**, **qput( )**, and **qget( )**.

A class can contain private as well as public members. By default, all items defined in a class are private. For example, the variables **q**, **sloc**, and **rloc** are private. This means that they can be accessed only by other members of the **queue** class, and not by any other part of your program. This is one way encapsulation is achieved—you can tightly control access to certain items of data by keeping them private. Although there are none in this example, you can also define private functions, which can be called only by other members of the class.

The **public** keyword is used to declare the public members of a class.

To make parts of a class public (i.e., accessible to other parts of your program), you must declare them after the **public** keyword. All variables or functions defined after the **public** specifier are accessible by all other functions in your program. Therefore, in **queue**, the functions **init( )**, **qput( )**, and **qget( )** are public. Typically, your program will access the private members of a class through its public functions. Notice that the **public** keyword is followed by a colon.

Keep in mind that an object forms a bond between code and data. Thus, a member function has access to the private elements of its class. This means that **init( )**, **qput( )**, and **qget( )** have access to **q**, **sloc**, and **rloc**. To add a member function to a class, specify its prototype within the class declaration.

Once you have defined a class, you can create an object of that type by using the class name. A class name becomes a new type specifier. For example, the following statement creates two objects called **Q1** and **Q2** of type **queue**:

```
queue Q1, Q2;
```

When an object of a class is created, it will have its own copy of the member variables that comprise the class. This means that **Q1** and **Q2** will each have their own, separate copies of **q**, **sloc**, and **rloc**. Thus, the data associated with **Q1** is distinct and separate from the data associated with **Q2**.

To access a public member of a class through an object of that class, use the dot operator, just the way you do when operating on a structure. For example, to output **Q1**'s value of **sloc**, use the following statement.

```
cout << Q1.sloc;
```

Let's review: In C++, a **class** creates a new data type that can be used to create objects. Specifically, a class creates a logical framework that defines a relationship between its members. When you declare a variable of a class, you are creating an object. An object has physical existence, and is a specific instance of a class. (That is, an object occupies memory space, but a type definition does not.) Further, each object of a class has its own copy of the data defined within that class.

11

Inside the declaration of **queue**, prototypes for the member functions are specified. Because the member functions are prototyped within the class definition, they need not be prototyped elsewhere.

To implement a function that is a member of a class, you must tell the compiler to which class the function belongs by qualifying the function name with the class name. For example, here is one way to code the **qput( )** function:

```
void queue::qput(int i)
{
  if(sloc==100) {
    cout << "Queue is full.\n";
    return;
```

```
  }
  sloc++;
  q[sloc] = i;
}
```

The **::** is called the *scope resolution operator*. Essentially, it tells the compiler that this version of **qput( )** belongs to the **queue** class. Or, put differently, **::** states that this **qput( )** is in **queue**'s scope. Several different classes can use the same function names. The compiler knows which function belongs to which class because of the scope resolution operator and the class name.

Member functions can only be invoked relative to a specific object. To call a member function from a part of your program that is outside the class, you must use the object's name and the dot operator. For example, this calls **init( )** on object **ob1**:

```
queue ob1, ob2;

ob1.init();
```

The invocation **ob1.init( )** causes **init( )** to operate on **ob1**'s copy of the data. Keep in mind that **ob1** and **ob2** are two separate objects. This means, for example, that initializing **ob1** does not cause **ob2** to also be initialized. The only relationship **ob1** has with **ob2** is that it is an object of the same type.

When one member function calls another member function of the same class, it can do so directly, without using an object and the dot operator. In this case, the compiler already knows which object is being operated upon. It is only when a member function is called by code that is outside the class that the object name and the dot operator must be used. By the same reasoning, a member function can refer directly to a member variable, but code outside the class must refer to the variable through an object and the dot operator.

The program shown here puts together all the pieces and missing details, and illustrates the **queue** class:

```
#include <iostream>
using namespace std;

// This creates the class queue.
class queue {
  int q[100];
  int sloc, rloc;
public:
  void init();
  void qput(int i);
  int qget();
};

// Initialize the queue.
void queue::init()
{
```

```
    rloc = sloc = 0;
}

// Put an integer into the queue.
void queue::qput(int i)
{
  if(sloc==100) {
    cout << "Queue is full.\n";
    return;
  }
  sloc++;
  q[sloc] = i;
}

// Get an integer from the queue.
int queue::qget()
{
  if(rloc == sloc) {
    cout << "Queue underflow.\n";
    return 0;
  }
  rloc++;
  return q[rloc];
}

int main()
{
  queue a, b;  // create two queue objects

  a.init();
  b.init();

  a.qput(10);
  b.qput(19);

  a.qput(20);
  b.qput(1);

  cout << "Contents of queue a: ";
  cout << a.qget() << " ";
  cout << a.qget() << "\n";

  cout << "Contents of queue b: ";
  cout << b.qget() << " ";
  cout << b.qget() << "\n";

  return 0;
}
```

11

This program displays the following output:

```
Contents of queue a: 10 20
Contents of queue b: 19 1
```

Keep in mind that the private members of a class are accessible only by functions that are members of that class. For example, a statement like

```
a.rloc = 0;
```

could not be included in the **main( )** function of the program.

The General Form of a class

All classes are declared in a fashion similar to the **queue** class just described. The general form of a **class** declaration is shown here.

```
class class-name {
    private data and functions
public:
    public data and functions
} object-list;
```

Here *class-name* specifies the name of the class. This name becomes a new type name that can be used to create objects of the class. You can also create objects of the class by specifying them immediately after the class declaration in *object-list*, but this is optional. Once a class has been declared, objects can be created where needed.

A Closer Look at Class Member Access

How to access class members is the cause of considerable confusion for beginners. For this reason, we will take a closer look at it here. Consider the following simple class:

```
// Demonstrate class member access.
#include <iostream>
using namespace std;

class myclass {
  int a; // private data
public:
  int b; // public data
  void setab(int i); // public functions
  int geta();
  void reset();
};

void myclass::setab(int i)
{
  a = i; // refer directly to a
  b = i*i; // refer directly to b
}

int myclass::geta()
{
  return a; // refer directly to a
}
```

```
void myclass::reset()
{
  // call setab() directly
  setab(0); // the object is already known
}

int main()
{
  myclass ob;

  ob.setab(5); // set ob.a and ob.b
  cout << "ob after setab(5): ";
  cout << ob.geta() << ' ';
  cout << ob.b; // can access b because it is public
  cout << '\n';

  ob.b = 20; // can access b because it is public
  cout << "ob after ob.b=20: ";
  cout << ob.geta() << ' ';
  cout << ob.b;
  cout << '\n';

  ob.reset();
  cout << "ob after ob.reset(): ";
  cout << ob.geta() << ' ';
  cout << ob.b;
  cout << '\n';

  return 0;
}
```

This program produces the following output:

```
ob after setab(5): 5 25
ob after ob.b=20: 5 20
ob after ob.reset(): 0 0
```

11

Let's look carefully at how the members of **myclass** are accessed. First, notice the way that **setab( )** assigns values to the member variables **a** and **b** using the lines of code shown here.

```
a = i; // refer directly to a
b = i*i; // refer directly to b
```

Because it is a member function, **setab( )** can refer to **a** and **b** directly, without explicit reference to an object, and without the use of the dot operator. As explained earlier, a member function is always invoked relative to an object. Once this invocation has occurred, the object is known. Thus, within a member function, there is no need to specify the object a second time. Therefore, references to **a** and **b** will apply to the invoking object's copy of these variables.

Next, notice that **b** is a public member of **myclass**. This means that **b** can be accessed by code outside of **myclass**. This is demonstrated when **b** is assigned the value 20 inside **main( )** using this line of code.

```
ob.b = 20; // can access b because it is public
```

Because this statement is outside of **myclass**, **b** must be accessed through an object (in this case, **ob**) and by use of the dot operator.

Now, notice how **reset( )** is called from within **main( )**, as shown here.

```
ob.reset();
```

Because **reset( )** is a public member function, it too can be called from code outside of **myclass**, through an object (in this case, **ob**).

Finally, examine the code inside **reset( )**. Since **reset( )** is a member function, it can directly refer to other members of the class, without use of the dot operator or object. In this case, it calls **setab( )**. Again, because the object is already known (because it was used to call **reset( )**), there is no need to specify it again.

The key point to understand is this: When a member of a class is referred to outside of its class, it must be qualified with an object. However, code inside a member function can refer to other members of the class directly.

NOTE: Don't worry if you are still a little unsure about how class members are accessed. A bit of uneasiness about this issue is common at first. As you read on and study more examples, member access will become clear.

Constructors and Destructors

A constructor is a function that is called when an object is created.

It is very common for some part of an object to require initialization before it can be used. For example, consider the **queue** class, shown earlier in this chapter. Before the queue could be used, the variables **rloc** and **sloc** had to be set to zero. This was performed using the function **init( )**. Because the requirement for initialization is so common, C++ allows objects to initialize themselves when they are created. This automatic initialization is performed through the use of a *constructor*.

A constructor is a special function that is a member of a class and that has the same name as the class. For example, here is how the **queue** class looks when it is converted to use a constructor for initialization:

```
// This creates the class queue.
class queue {
  int q[100];
  int sloc, rloc;
```

```
public:
  queue();  // constructor
  void qput(int i);
  int qget();
};
```

Notice that the constructor **queue( )** has no return type. In C++, constructors do not return values and, therefore, have no return type. (Not even **void** may be specified.)

The **queue( )** function is coded as follows:

```
// This is the constructor.
queue::queue()
{
  sloc = rloc = 0;
  cout << "Queue Initialized.\n";
}
```

Here, the message **Queue Initialized** is output as a way to illustrate the constructor. In actual practice, most constructors do not print a message.

An object's constructor is called when the object is created. This means that it is called when the object's declaration is executed. For global objects, the constructor is called when the program begins execution, prior to the call to **main( )**. For local objects, the constructor is called each time the object declaration is encountered.

A destructor is the function that is called when an object is destroyed.

The complement of the constructor is the *destructor*. In many circumstances, an object will need to perform some action or series of actions when it is destroyed. Local objects are created when their block is entered, and destroyed when the block is left. Global objects are destroyed when the program terminates. There are many reasons why a destructor may be needed. For example, an object may need to deallocate memory that it had previously allocated. In C++, it is the destructor that handles deactivation. The destructor has the same name as the constructor, but the destructor's name is preceded by a ~. Like constructors, destructors do not have return types.

Here is the **queue** class that contains a constructor and destructor. (Keep in mind that the **queue** class does not require a destructor, so the one shown here is just for illustration.)

11

```
// This creates the class queue.
class queue {
  int q[100];
  int sloc, rloc;
public:
  queue();  // constructor
  ~queue(); // destructor
  void qput(int i);
  int qget();
};
```

```
// This is the constructor.
queue::queue()
{
  sloc = rloc = 0;
  cout << "Queue initialized.\n";
}

// This is the destructor.
queue::~queue()
{
  cout << "Queue destroyed.\n";
}
```

Here is a new version of the queue program that demonstrates the constructor and destructor:

```
// Demonstrate a constructor and a destructor.
#include <iostream>
using namespace std;

// This creates the class queue.
class queue {
  int q[100];
  int sloc, rloc;
public:
  queue();   // constructor
  ~queue(); // destructor
  void qput(int i);
  int qget();
};

// This is the constructor.
queue::queue()
{
  sloc = rloc = 0;
  cout << "Queue initialized.\n";
}

// This is the destructor.
queue::~queue()
{
  cout << "Queue destroyed.\n";
}

// Put an integer into the queue.
void queue::qput(int i)
{
  if(sloc==100) {
    cout << "Queue is full.\n";
    return;
  }
  sloc++;
```

```
  q[sloc] = i;
}

// Get an integer from the queue.
int queue::qget()
{
  if(rloc == sloc) {
    cout << "Queue Underflow.\n";
    return 0;
  }
  rloc++;
  return q[rloc];
}

int main()
{
  queue a, b;  // create two queue objects

  a.qput(10);
  b.qput(19);

  a.qput(20);
  b.qput(1);

  cout << a.qget() << " ";
  cout << a.qget() << " ";
  cout << b.qget() << " ";
  cout << b.qget() << "\n";

  return 0;
}
```

This program displays the following output:

```
Queue initialized.
Queue initialized.
10 20 19 1
Queue destroyed.
Queue destroyed.
```

11

Parameterized Constructors

A constructor can have parameters. This allows you to give member variables program-defined initial values when an object is created. You do this by passing arguments to an object's constructor. The next example will enhance the **queue** class to accept an argument that will act as the queue's ID number. First, **queue** is changed to look like this:

```
// This creates the class queue.
class queue {
  int q[100];
```

```
    int sloc, rloc;
    int who; // holds the queue's ID number
public:
    queue(int id);  // parameterized constructor
    ~queue(); // destructor
    void qput(int i);
    int qget();
};
```

The variable **who** is used to hold an ID number that will identify the queue. Its actual value will be determined by what is passed to the constructor in **id** when a variable of type **queue** is created. The **queue( )** constructor looks like this:

```
// This is the constructor.
queue::queue(int id)
{
    sloc = rloc = 0;
    who = id;
    cout << "Queue " << who << " initialized.\n";
}
```

To pass an argument to the constructor, you must associate the argument with an object when the object is declared. C++ supports two ways to accomplish this. The first method is illustrated here:

```
queue a = queue(101);
```

This declaration creates a queue called **a** and passes the value 101 to it. However, this form is seldom used (in this context), because the second method is shorter and more to the point. In the second method, the argument must follow the object's name and must be enclosed between parentheses. For example, this statement accomplishes the same thing as the previous declaration:

```
queue a(101);
```

This is the most common way that parameterized objects are declared. Using this method, the general form of passing arguments to constructors is

>   *class-type var(arg-list);*

Here, *arg-list* is a comma-separated list of arguments that are passed to the constructor.

NOTE: Technically, there is a small difference between the two initialization forms, which you will learn about later in this book. However, this difference does not affect the programs in this chapter, or most programs that you will write.

The following version of the queue program demonstrates a parameterized constructor:

```cpp
// Use a parameterized constructor.
#include <iostream>
using namespace std;

// This creates the class queue.
class queue {
  int q[100];
  int sloc, rloc;
  int who; // holds the queue's ID number
public:
  queue(int id);  // parameterized constructor
  ~queue(); // destructor
  void qput(int i);
  int qget();
};

// This is the constructor.
queue::queue(int id)
{
  sloc = rloc = 0;
  who = id;
  cout << "Queue " << who << " initialized.\n";
}

// This is the destructor.
queue::~queue()
{
  cout << "Queue " << who << " destroyed.\n";
}

// Put an integer into the queue.
void queue::qput(int i)
{
  if(sloc==100) {
    cout << "Queue is full.\n";
    return;
  }
  sloc++;
  q[sloc] = i;
}

// Get an integer from the queue.
int queue::qget()
{
  if(rloc == sloc) {
    cout << "Queue underflow.\n";
    return 0;
  }
  rloc++;
```

11

```
  return q[rloc];
}

int main()
{
  queue a(1), b(2);   // create two queue objects

  a.qput(10);
  b.qput(19);

  a.qput(20);
  b.qput(1);

  cout << a.qget() << " ";
  cout << a.qget() << " ";
  cout << b.qget() << " ";
  cout << b.qget() << "\n";

  return 0;
}
```

This program produces the following output:

```
Queue 1 initialized.
Queue 2 initialized.
10 20 19 1
Queue 2 destroyed.
Queue 1 destroyed.
```

As you can see by looking at **main( )**, the queue associated with **a** is given the ID number 1, and the queue associated with **b** is given the number 2.

Although the **queue** example passes only a single argument when an object is created, it is possible to pass two or more. In the following example, objects of type **widget** are passed two values:

```
#include <iostream>
using namespace std;

class widget {
  int i;
  int j;
public:
  widget(int a, int b);
  void put_widget();
} ;

// Pass 2 arguments to widget().
widget::widget(int a, int b)
{
  i = a;
```

```
    j = b;
}

void widget::put_widget()
{
  cout << i << " " << j << "\n";
}

int main()
{
  widget x(10, 20), y(0, 0);

  x.put_widget();
  y.put_widget();

  return 0;
}
```

This program displays

```
10 20
0 0
```

T IP: Unlike constructors, destructors cannot have parameters. The reason for this is easy to understand: There is no means by which to pass arguments to an object that is being destroyed. Although the situation is rare, if your object needs access to some run-time-defined data when its destructor is called, you will need to create a specific variable for this purpose. Then, just prior to the object's destruction, set that variable to the desired value.

An Initialization Alternative

If a constructor takes only one parameter, then you can use an alternative method to initialize it. Consider the following program:

11

```
#include <iostream>
using namespace std;

class myclass {
  int a;
public:
  myclass(int x);
  int get_a();
};

myclass::myclass(int x)
{
  a = x;
```

```
}

int myclass::get_a()
{
  return a;
}

int main()
{
  myclass ob = 4; // calls myclass(4)

  cout << ob.get_a();

  return 0;
}
```

Here, the constructor for **myclass** takes one parameter. Pay special attention to how **ob** is declared in **main( )**. It uses this declaration:

```
myclass ob = 4;
```

In this form of initialization, 4 is automatically passed to the **x** parameter in the **myclass( )** constructor. That is, the declaration statement is handled by the compiler as if it were written like this:

```
myclass ob = myclass(4);
```

In general, any time that you have a constructor that requires only one argument, you can use either *ob(x)* or *ob = x* to initialize an object. The reason for this is that whenever you create a constructor that takes one argument, you are also implicitly creating a conversion from the type of that argument to the type of the class.

Remember that the alternative shown here applies only to constructors that have exactly one parameter.

Classes and Structures Are Related

As mentioned in the preceding chapter, in C++ the structure also has object-oriented capabilities. In fact, classes and structures are closely related. With one exception, they are interchangeable because the structure can also include data, and the code that manipulates that data, in just the same way that a class can. The only difference between a C++ structure and a class is that, by default, the members of a class are private, while the members of a structure are public. Aside from this distinction, structures and classes serve the same purpose. In fact, according to the formal C++ syntax, a structure declaration actually creates a class type.

Here is an example of a structure that uses its class-like features:

```
// Use struct to create a class.
#include <iostream>
```

```
using namespace std;

struct cl {
  int get_i();         // these are public
  void put_i(int j); // by default
private:
  int i;
};

int cl::get_i()
{
  return i;
}

void cl::put_i(int j)
{
  i = j;
}

int main()
{
  cl s;

  s.put_i(10);
  cout << s.get_i();

  return 0;
}
```

This program defines a structure type called **cl**, in which **get_i( )** and **put_i( )** are public and **i** is private. Notice that **struct**s use the keyword **private** to introduce the private elements of the structure.

The **private** keyword is used to declare the private members of a class.

The following program shows an equivalent program that uses a **class** rather than a **struct**:

11

```
// Now, use class, instead.
#include <iostream>
using namespace std;

class cl {
  int i; // private by default
public:
  int get_i();
  void put_i(int j);
};

int cl::get_i()
{
  return i;
}

void cl::put_i(int j)
```

```
{
  i = j;
}

int main()
{
  cl s;

  s.put_i(10);
  cout << s.get_i();

  return 0;
}
```

C++ programmers sometimes use the term POD-struct when referring to structures that do not contain member functions.

For the most part, C++ programmers will use a **class** to define the form of an object that contains member functions, and use a **struct** in its more traditional role to create objects that contain only data members. Sometimes the acronym POD is used to describe a structure that does not contain member functions. It stands for Plain Old Data.

IN DEPTH

Structures versus Classes

On the surface, the fact that both structures and classes have virtually identical capabilities seems redundant. Many newcomers to C++ wonder why this apparent duplication exists. It is not uncommon to hear the suggestion that either the keyword **class** or **struct** is unnecessary.

The answer to this line of reasoning is rooted in C++'s derivation from C, and the desire to keep C++ upwardly compatible with C. As C++ is currently defined, a standard C structure is also a completely valid C++ structure. In C, which does not contain the **public** or **private** keywords, all structure members are public. This is why members of C++ structures are public (rather than private) by default. Since the **class** construct is expressly designed to support encapsulation, it makes sense that its members are private by default. Thus, to avoid incompatibility with C on this issue, the structure default could not be altered, so a new keyword was added. However, in the long term, there is a more important reason for the separation of structures and classes. Because **class** is an entity syntactically separate from **struct**, the definition of a class is free to evolve in ways that may not be syntactically compatible with C-like structures. Since the two are separated, the future direction of C++ is not encumbered by concerns of compatibility with C structures.

Before leaving this topic, one important point must be emphasized: A structure defines a class type. Thus a structure *is* a class. This was intentional on the part of Bjarne Stroustrup. He believed that if structures and classes were made more or less equivalent, the transition from C to C++ would be eased. History has proven him correct!

Unions and Classes Are Related

The fact that structures and classes are related is not too surprising; however, you might be surprised to learn that unions are also related to classes. As far as C++ is concerned, a union is essentially a class in which all data members are stored in the same location. (Thus, a union, too, defines a class type.) A union can contain a constructor and destructor, as well as member functions. Of course, members of a union are public, not private, by default.

Here is a program that uses a union to display the characters that comprise the low and high order bytes of a short integer (assuming short integers are two bytes):

```
// Create union-based class.
#include <iostream>
using namespace std;

union u_type {
  u_type(short int a);  // public by default
  void showchars();
  short int i;
  char ch[2];
};

// constructor
u_type::u_type(short int a)
{
  i = a;
}

// Show the characters that comprise a short int.
void u_type::showchars()
{
  cout << ch[0] << " ";
  cout << ch[1] << "\n";
}

int main()
{
  u_type u(1000);

  u.showchars();

  return 0;
}
```

11

Like the structure, the C++ union is derived from its C forerunner. However, in C++ it has the expanded capabilities of the class. But just because C++ gives unions greater power and flexibility does not mean that you have to use it. When you simply need a traditional-style union, you are free to use one in that manner. However, in cases where you can encapsulate a union along with the functions that manipulate it, doing so will add considerable clarity to your program.

Inline Functions

Before we continue exploring the class, a small, but important digression is in order. Although it does not pertain specifically to object-oriented programming, one very useful feature of C++, called an *inline function*, is frequently used in class definitions. An inline function is a function whose code is expanded in line at the point at which it is invoked, rather than being called. There are two ways to create an inline function. The first is to use the **inline** modifier. For example, to create an inline function called **f** that returns an **int** and takes no parameters, you declare it like this:

```
inline int f()
{
  // ...
}
```

The **inline** modifier precedes all other aspects of a function's declaration.

An inline function is a small function whose code is expanded in line rather than called.

The reason for inline functions is efficiency. Every time a function is called, a series of instructions must be executed, both to set up the function call, including pushing arguments onto the stack, and to return from the function. In some cases, many CPU cycles are used to perform these actions. However, when a function is expanded in line, no such overhead exists, and the overall speed of your program will increase. Even so, in cases where the inline function is large, the overall size of your program will also increase. For this reason, the best inline functions are those that are very small. Larger functions are usually left as normal functions.

The following program demonstrates **inline**.

```
#include <iostream>
using namespace std;

class cl {
  int i; // private by default
public:
  int get_i();
  void put_i(int j);
} ;

inline int cl::get_i()
{
  return i;
}

inline void cl::put_i(int j)
{
  i = j;
}

int main()
{
```

```
    cl s;

    s.put_i(10);
    cout << s.get_i();

    return 0;
}
```

Here, the code for **get_i( )** and **put_i( )** is expanded in line rather than being called. Thus, in **main( )**, the line

```
s.put_i(10);
```

is functionally equivalent to this assigment statement:

```
s.i = 10;
```

Of course, because **i** is private to **cl**, this line could not actually be used in **main( )**, but by in-lining **put_i( )**, the same effect is produced and the function call is avoided.

It is important to understand that technically, **inline** is a *request*, not a *command*, that the compiler generate inline code. There are various situations that might prevent the compiler from complying with the request. Here are some examples:

◆   Some compilers will not generate inline code if a function contains a loop, a **switch**, or a **goto**.

◆   Often, you cannot have inline recursive functions.

◆   Inline functions that contain **static** variables are frequently disallowed.

REMEMBER: Inline restrictions are implementation-dependent, so you must check your compiler's documentation to learn the restrictions that apply to your situation.

11

Creating Inline Functions Inside a Class

There is another way to create an inline function. This is accomplished by defining the code to a member function *inside* a class declaration. Any function that is defined inside a class declaration is automatically made into an inline function. It is not necessary to precede its declaration with the keyword **inline**. For example, the preceding program can be rewritten as shown here:

```
#include <iostream>
using namespace std;

class cl {
```

```
    int i; // private by default
public:
  // automatic inline functions
  int get_i() { return i; }
  void put_i(int j) { i = j; }
} ;

int main()
{
  cl s;

  s.put_i(10);
  cout << s.get_i();

  return 0;
}
```

Here, **get_i( )** and **put_i( )** are defined inside **cl** and are automatically inline.

Notice the way the function code is arranged inside **cl**. For very short functions, this arrangement reflects common C++ style. However, there is no reason that you could not format the functions as shown here:

```
class cl {
  int i; // private by default
public:
  // inline functions
  int get_i()
  {
    return i;
  }

  void put_i(int j)
  {
    i = j;
  }
};
```

Generally, short functions like those illustrated in this example are defined inside the class declaration. This convention will be followed by the rest of the examples in this book.

T IP: Defining short member functions inside their class declaration is very common in C++ programming. The reason for this is not necessarily because of the automatic inlining feature, but because it is very convenient. In fact, it is quite rare to see short member functions defined outside their class in professionally written code.

Arrays of Objects

You can create arrays of objects in the same way that you create arrays of any other data type. For example, the following program establishes a class called **display** that holds the resolution of a video display mode. Inside **main( )**, an array of three **display** objects is created, and the objects that comprise the elements of the array are accessed by using the normal array-indexing procedure.

```cpp
// An example of arrays of objects
#include <iostream>
using namespace std;

enum resolution {low, medium, high};

class display {
  int width;
  int height;
  resolution res;
public:
  void set_dim(int w, int h) {width = w; height = h;}
  void get_dim(int &w, int &h) {w = width; h = height;}
  void set_res(resolution r) {res = r;}
  resolution get_res() {return res;}
};

char names[3][7] = {
  "low",
  "medium",
  "high",
} ;

int main()
{
  display display_mode[3];
  int i, w, h;

  display_mode[0].set_res(low);
  display_mode[0].set_dim(640, 480);

  display_mode[1].set_res(medium);
  display_mode[1].set_dim(800, 600);

  display_mode[2].set_res(high);
  display_mode[2].set_dim(1600, 1200);

  cout << "Available display modes:\n\n";

  for(i=0; i<3; i++) {
    cout << names[display_mode[i].get_res()] << ": ";
    display_mode[i].get_dim(w, h);
```

11

```
    cout << w << " by " << h << "\n";
  }

  return 0;
}
```

This program produces the following output:

```
Available display modes:

low: 640 by 480
medium: 800 by 600
high: 1600 by 1200
```

Notice how the two-dimensional character array **names** is used to convert between an enumerated value and its equivalent character string. In all enumerations that do not contain explicit initializations, the first constant has the value 0, the second 1, and so on. Therefore, the value returned by **get_res( )** can be used to index the **names** array, causing the appropriate name to be printed.

Multidimensional arrays of objects are indexed in precisely the same way as arrays of other types of data.

Initializing Object Arrays

If the class includes a parameterized constructor, an array of objects can be initialized. For example, in the following program, **samp** is a parameterized class and **sampArray** is an initialized array of objects of that class:

```
// Initialize an array of objects.
#include <iostream>
using namespace std;

class samp {
  int a;
public:
  samp(int n) { a = n; }
  int get_a() { return a; }
};

int main()
{
  samp sampArray[4] = { -1, -2, -3, -4 };
  int i;

  for(i=0; i<4; i++) cout << sampArray[i].get_a() << ' ';

  cout << "\n";

  return 0;
}
```

This program displays the following:

```
-1 -2 -3 -4
```

As the output confirms, the values –1 through –4 are passed to the **samp** constructor. Actually, the syntax shown in the initialization list is shorthand for this longer form:

```
samp sampArray[4] = { samp(-1), samp(-2), samp(-3), samp(-4) };
```

However, the form used in the program is more common, although this form will work only with arrays whose constructors take only one argument. When initializing an array of objects whose constructor takes more than one argument, you must use the longer form of initialization. For example:

```cpp
#include <iostream>
using namespace std;

class samp {
  int a, b;
public:
  samp(int n, int m) { a = n; b = m; }
  int get_a() { return a; }
  int get_b() { return b; }
};

int main()
{
  samp sampArray[4][2] = {
    samp(1, 2), samp(3, 4),
    samp(5, 6), samp(7, 8),
    samp(9, 10), samp(11, 12),
    samp(13, 14), samp(15, 16)
  };

  int i;

  for(i=0; i<4; i++) {
    cout << sampArray[i][0].get_a() << ' ';
    cout << sampArray[i][0].get_b() << "\n";
    cout << sampArray[i][1].get_a() << ' ';
    cout << sampArray[i][1].get_b() << "\n";
  }

  cout << "\n";

  return 0;
}
```

11

In this example, **samp**'s constructor takes two arguments. Here, the array **sampArray** is declared and initialized in **main( )** by using direct calls to **samp**'s constructor. When initalizing arrays, you can always use the long form of initialization, even if the object takes only one argument. It's just that the short form is more convenient when only one argument is required. The program displays

```
1  2
3  4
5  6
7  8
9  10
11  12
13  14
15  16
```

Pointers to Objects

As you saw in the previous chapter, you can access a structure directly, or through a pointer to the structure. In like fashion, you can access an object either directly (as has been the case in all preceding examples), or by using a pointer to the object. To access an element of an object when using the actual object itself, use the dot operator. To access a specific element of an object when using a pointer to the object, you must use the arrow operator. (The use of the dot and arrow operators for objects parallels their use for structures and unions.)

To declare an object pointer, you use the same declaration syntax that you would use for any other pointer type. The next program creates a simple class called **P_example**, defines an object of that class, called **ob**, and defines a pointer to an object of type **P_example**, called **p**. It then illustrates how to access **ob** directly, and how to use a pointer to access it indirectly.

```cpp
// A simple example using an object pointer.
#include <iostream>
using namespace std;

class P_example {
  int num;
public:
  void set_num(int val) {num = val;}
  void show_num();
};

void P_example::show_num()
{
  cout << num << "\n";
}

int main()
{
  P_example ob, *p; // declare an object and pointer to it

  ob.set_num(1); // access ob directly
```

```
  ob.show_num();

  p = &ob; // assign p the address of ob
  p->show_num(); // access ob using pointer

  return 0;
}
```

Notice that the address of **ob** is obtained by using the **&** (address of) operator in the same way that the address is obtained for any type of variable.

As you know, when a pointer is incremented or decremented, it is increased or decreased in such a way that it will always point to the next element of its base type. The same thing occurs when a pointer to an object is incremented or decremented: the next object is pointed to. To illustrate this, the preceding program has been modified here so that **ob** is a two-element array of type **P_example**. Notice how **p** is incremented and decremented to access the two elements in the array.

```
// Incrementing and decrementing an object pointer.
#include <iostream>
using namespace std;

class P_example {
  int num;
public:
  void set_num(int val) {num = val;}
  void show_num();
};

void P_example::show_num()
{
  cout << num << "\n";
}

int main()
{
  P_example ob[2], *p;

  ob[0].set_num(10);   // access objects directly
  ob[1].set_num(20);

  p = &ob[0];  // obtain pointer to first element
  p->show_num(); // show value of ob[0] using pointer

  p++;   // advance to next object
  p->show_num(); // show value of ob[1] using pointer

  p--;   // retreat to previous object
  p->show_num(); // again show value of ob[0]

  return 0;
}
```

11

The output from this program is

```
10
20
10
```

As you will see later in this book, object pointers play an important role in one of C++'s most important concepts: polymorphism.

Object References

Objects can be referenced in the same way as any other data type. There are no special restrictions or instructions that apply. However, as you will see in the next chapter, the use of object references does help to solve some special problems that you may encounter when using classes.

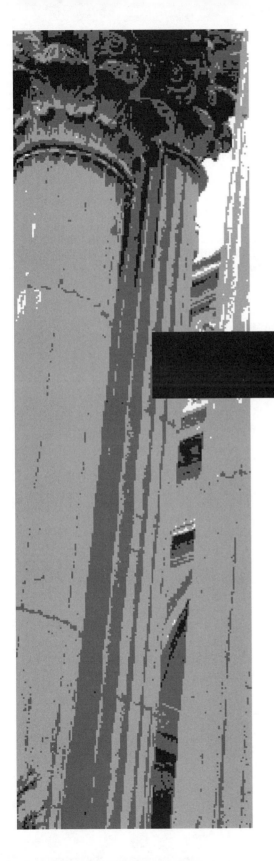

CHAPTER 12

A Closer Look
at Classes

273

This chapter continues the discussion of the class begun in Chapter 11. It discusses friend functions, overloading constructors, passing objects to functions, and returning objects. It also examines a special type of constructor, called the copy constructor, which is used when a copy of an object is needed. The chapter concludes with a description of the **this** keyword.

Friend Functions

It is possible to allow a non-member function access to the private members of a class by declaring it a *friend* of the class. To make a function a friend of a class, include its prototype in the **public** section of the class declaration and precede it with the **friend** keyword. For example, in this fragment **frnd( )** is declared to be a friend of the class **cl**:

```
class cl {
  // ...
public:
  friend void frnd(cl ob);
  // ...
};
```

The **friend** keyword gives a non-member function access to the private members of a class.

As you can see, the keyword **friend** precedes the rest of the prototype. A function may be a friend of more than one class.

Here is a short example that uses a friend function to access the private members of **myclass**:

```
// Demonstrate a friend function.
#include <iostream>
using namespace std;

class myclass {
  int a, b;
public:
  myclass(int i, int j) { a=i; b=j; }
  friend int sum(myclass x); // sum() is a friend of myclass
};

// Note: sum() is not a member function of any class.
int sum(myclass x)
{
  /* Because sum() is a friend of myclass, it can
     directly access a and b. */

  return x.a + x.b;
}

int main()
{
  myclass n(3, 4);

  cout << sum(n);
```

```
   return 0;
}
```

In this example, the **sum( )** function is not a member of **myclass**. However, it still has full access to the private members of **myclass**. Specifically, it can access **x.a** and **x.b**. Notice also that **sum( )** is called normally—not in conjunction with an object and the dot operator. Since it is not a member function, it does not need to be qualified with an object's name. (In fact, it *cannot* be qualified with an object.) Typically, a friend function is passed one or more objects of the class for which it is a friend, as is the case with **sum( )**.

While there is nothing gained by making **sum( )** a friend rather than a member function of **myclass**, there are some circumstances in which friend functions are quite valuable. First, friends can be useful for overloading certain types of operators. Second, friend functions simplify the creation of some types of I/O functions. Both of these uses are discussed later in this book.

The third reason that friend functions may be desirable is that, in some cases, two or more classes may contain members that are interrelated relative to other parts of your program. For example, imagine two different classes that each display a pop-up message on the screen when some sort of event occurs. Other parts of your program that are designed to write to the screen will need to know whether the pop-up message is active, so that no message is accidentally overwritten. It is possible to create a member function in each class that returns a value indicating whether a message is active or not; however, checking this condition involves additional overhead (i.e., two function calls, not just one). If the status of the pop-up message needs to be checked frequently, the additional overhead may not be acceptable. However, by using a friend function, it is possible to directly check the status of each object by calling only one function that has access to both classes. In situations like this, a friend function helps you write more efficient code. The following program illustrates this concept.

```
// Use a friend function.
#include <iostream>
using namespace std;

const int IDLE=0;
const int INUSE=1;

class C2;  // forward declaration

class C1 {
  int status;  // IDLE if off, INUSE if on screen
  // ...
public:
  void set_status(int state);
  friend int idle(C1 a, C2 b);
};

class C2 {
  int status; // IDLE if off, INUSE if on screen
  // ...
```

12

```
public:
  void set_status(int state);
  friend int idle(C1 a, C2 b);
};

void C1::set_status(int state)
{
  status = state;
}

void C2::set_status(int state)
{
  status = state;
}

// idle( ) is a friend of C1 and C2.
int idle(C1 a, C2 b)
{
  if(a.status || b.status) return 0;
  else return 1;
}

int main()
{
  C1 x;
  C2 y;

  x.set_status(IDLE);
  y.set_status(IDLE);

  if(idle(x, y)) cout << "Screen Can Be Used.\n";
  else cout << "Pop-up In Use.\n";

  x.set_status(INUSE);

  if(idle(x, y)) cout << "Screen Can Be Used.\n";
  else cout << "Pop-up In Use.\n";

  return 0;
}
```

The output produced by this program is shown here:

```
Screen Can Be Used.
Pop-up In Use.
```

Because **idle( )** is a friend of both **C1** and **C2** it has access to the private **status** member defined by both classes. Thus, a single call to **idle( )** can simultaneously check the status of an object of each class.

A forward
declaration
declares a class
type-name prior
to the definition
of the class.

Notice that this program uses a *forward declaration* (also called a *forward reference*) for the class **C2**. This is necessary because the declaration of **idle( )** inside **C1** refers to **C2** before it is declared. To create a forward declaration to a class, simply use the form shown in this program.

A friend of one class can be a member of another. For example, here is the preceding program rewritten so that **idle( )** is a member of **C1**. Notice the use of the scope resolution operator when declaring **idle( )** to be a friend of **C2**.

```
/* A function can be a member of one class and
   a friend of another. */
#include <iostream>
using namespace std;

const int IDLE=0;
const int INUSE=1;

class C2;  // forward declaration

class C1 {
  int status;  // IDLE if off, INUSE if on screen
  // ...
public:
  void set_status(int state);
  int idle(C2 b);  // now a member of C1
};

class C2 {
  int status;  // IDLE if off, INUSE if on screen
  // ...
public:
  void set_status(int state);
  friend int C1::idle(C2 b); // a friend, here
};

void C1::set_status(int state)
{
  status = state;
}

void C2::set_status(int state)
{
  status = state;
}

// idle() is member of C1, but friend of C2.
int C1::idle(C2 b)
{
  if(status || b.status) return 0;
  else return 1;
}
```

12

```
int main()
{
  C1 x;
  C2 y;

  x.set_status(IDLE);
  y.set_status(IDLE);

  if(x.idle(y)) cout << "Screen Can Be Used.\n";
  else cout << "Pop-up In Use.\n";

  x.set_status(INUSE);

  if(x.idle(y)) cout << "Screen Can Be Used.\n";
  else cout << "Pop-up In Use.\n";

  return 0;
}
```

Since **idle( )** is a member of **C1**, it can access the **status** variable of objects of type **C1** directly. Thus, only objects of type **C2** need be passed to **idle( )**.

Overloading Constructors

Although they perform a unique service, constructors are not much different from other types of functions, and they too can be overloaded. To overload a class's constructor, simply declare the various forms it will take and define each action relative to these forms. For example, the following program declares a class called **timer**, which acts as a countdown timer (such as a darkroom timer). When an object of type **timer** is created, it is given an initial time value. When the **run( )** function is called, the timer counts down to zero and then rings the bell. In this example, the constructor has been overloaded to allow the time to be specified in seconds as either an integer or a string, or in minutes and seconds by specifying two integers. This program makes use of the standard library function **clock( )**, which returns the number of system clock ticks since the program began running. Its prototype is shown here:

   clock_t clock( );

The type **clock_t** is a defined type that is some form of long integer. Dividing the return value of **clock( )** by **CLOCKS_PER_SEC** converts the return value into seconds. Both the prototype for **clock( )** and the definition of **CLOCKS_PER_SEC** are found in the header **<ctime>**.

```
// Use overloaded constructors.
#include <iostream>
#include <cstdlib>
#include <ctime>
using namespace std;
```

```
class timer{
  int seconds;
public:
  // seconds specified as a string
  timer(char *t) { seconds = atoi(t); }

  // seconds specified as integer
  timer(int t) { seconds = t; }

  // time specified in minutes and seconds
  timer(int min, int sec) { seconds = min*60 + sec; }

  void run();
} ;

void timer::run()
{
  clock_t t1;

  t1 = clock();

  while((clock()/CLOCKS_PER_SEC - t1/CLOCKS_PER_SEC) < seconds);

  cout << "\a"; // ring the bell
}

int main()
{
  timer a(10), b("20"), c(1, 10);

  a.run(); // count 10 seconds
  b.run(); // count 20 seconds
  c.run(); // count 1 minute, 10 seconds

  return 0;
}
```

When **a**, **b**, and **c** are created inside **main( )**, they are given initial values using the three different methods supported by the overloaded constructor functions. Each approach causes the appropriate constructor to be utilized, thus properly initializing all three variables.

In the preceding program, you may see little value in overloading a constructor function, because it is not difficult to simply decide on a single way of specifying the time. However, if you were creating a library of classes for someone else to use, then you might want to supply constructors for the most common forms of initialization, thereby allowing the programmer to utilize the most appropriate form for his or her program. Also, as you will see shortly, there is one C++ attribute that makes overloaded constructors quite valuable.

12

Dynamic Initialization

In C++, both local and global variables can be initialized at run time. This process is sometimes referred to as *dynamic initialization*. So far, most initializations that you have seen in this book have used constants. However, under dynamic initialization, a variable can be initialized at run time using any C++ expression valid at the time the variable is declared. This means that you can initialize a variable by using other variables and/or function calls, so long as the overall expression has meaning when the declaration is encountered. For example, the following are all perfectly valid variable initializations in C++:

```
int n = strlen(str);

double arc = sin(theta);

float d = 1.02 * count / deltax;
```

Applying Dynamic Initialization to Constructors

Like simple variables, objects can be initialized dynamically when they are created. This feature allows you to create exactly the type of object you need, using information that is known only at run time. To illustrate how dynamic initialization works, let's rework the timer program from the previous section.

Recall that in the first example of the timer program, there is little to be gained by overloading the **timer( )** constructor, because all objects of its type are initialized using constants provided at compile time. However, in cases where an object will be initialized at run time, there may be significant advantages to providing a variety of initialization formats. This allows you, the programmer, the flexibility of using the constructor that most closely matches the format of the data available at the moment.

For example, in the following version of the timer program, dynamic initialization is used to construct two objects, **b** and **c**, at run time:

```
// Demonstrate dynamic initialization.
#include <iostream>
#include <cstdlib>
#include <ctime>
using namespace std;

class timer{
  int seconds;
public:
  // seconds specified as a string
  timer(char *t) { seconds = atoi(t); }

  // seconds specified as integer
  timer(int t) { seconds = t; }

  // time specified in minutes and seconds
  timer(int min, int sec) { seconds = min*60 + sec; }
```

```
  void run();
} ;

void timer::run()
{
  clock_t t1;

  t1 = clock();

  while((clock()/CLOCKS_PER_SEC - t1/CLOCKS_PER_SEC) < seconds);

  cout << "\a"; // ring the bell
}

int main()
{
  timer a(10);

  a.run();

  cout << "Enter number of seconds: ";
  char str[80];
  cin >> str;
  timer b(str);  // initialize at run time
  b.run();

  cout << "Enter minutes and seconds: ";
  int min, sec;
  cin >> min >> sec;
  timer c(min, sec);  // initialize at run time
  c.run();

  return 0;
}
```

As you can see, object **a** is constructed using an integer constant. However, objects **b** and **c** are constructed using information entered by the user. For **b**, since the user enters a string, it makes sense that **timer( )** is overloaded to accept it. In similar fashion, object **c** is also constructed at run time from user input. In this case, since the time is entered as minutes and seconds, it is logical to use this format for constructing object **c**. As the example shows, having a variety of initialization formats keeps you from having to perform conversions when initializing an object.

12

The point of overloading constructors is to help programmers handle greater complexity by allowing objects to be constructed in the most natural manner relative to their specific use. Since there are three common methods of passing timing values to an object, it makes sense that **timer( )** be overloaded to accept each method. However, overloading **timer( )** to accept days or nanoseconds is probably not a good idea. Littering your code with constructors to handle seldom-used contingencies has a destabilizing influence on your program.

Assigning Objects

If both objects are of the same type (that is, both are objects of the same class), then one object may be assigned to another. It is not sufficient for the two classes to simply be physically similar—their type names must be the same. By default, when one object is assigned to another, a bitwise copy of the first object's data is copied to the second. The following program demonstrates object assignment:

```
// Demonstrate object assignment.
#include <iostream>
using namespace std;

class myclass {
  int a, b;
public:
  void setab(int i, int j) { a = i, b = j; }
  void showab();
};

void myclass::showab()
{
  cout << "a is " << a << '\n';
  cout << "b is " << b << '\n';
}

int main()
{
  myclass ob1, ob2;

  ob1.setab(10, 20);
  ob2.setab(0, 0);
  cout << "ob1 before assignment: \n";
  ob1.showab();
  cout << "ob2 before assignment: \n";
  ob2.showab();
  cout << '\n';

  ob2 = ob1; // assign ob1 to ob2

  cout << "ob1 after assignment: \n";
  ob1.showab();
  cout << "ob2 after assignment: \n";
  ob2.showab();

  return 0;
}
```

This program displays the following output:

```
ob1 before assignment:
a is 10
b is 20
ob2 before assignment:
a is 0
b is 0
ob1 after assignment:
a is 10
b is 20
ob2 after assignment:
a is 10
b is 20
```

By default, all data from one object is assigned to the other using a bit-by-bit copy. (That is, an exact duplicate is created.) However, as you will see later, it is possible to overload the assignment operator so that customized assignment operations can be defined.

Remember: Assignment of one object to another simply makes the data in those objects identical. The two objects are still completely separate. Thus, a subsequent modification of one object's data has no effect on that of the other.

Passing Objects to Functions

An object can be passed to a function in the same way as any other data type. Objects are passed to functions by using the normal C++ call-by-value parameter-passing convention. This means that a *copy* of the object, not the actual object itself, is passed to the function. Therefore, changes made to the object inside the function do not affect the object used as the argument to the function. The following program illustrates this point:

```
#include <iostream>
using namespace std;

class OBJ {
  int i;
public:
  void set_i(int x) { i = x; }
  void out_i() { cout << i << " "; }
};

void f(OBJ x)
{
  x.out_i();   // outputs 10
  x.set_i(100);   // this affects only local copy
  x.out_i();   // outputs 100
}
```

12

```
int main()
{
  OBJ o;

  o.set_i(10);
  f(o);
  o.out_i();   // still outputs 10, value of i unchanged

  return 0;
}
```

The output from the program is shown here.

```
10 100 10
```

As the output shows, the modification of **x** within **f( )** has no effect on object **o** inside **main( )**.

Constructors, Destructors, and Passing Objects

Although passing simple objects as arguments to functions is a straightforward procedure, some rather unexpected events occur that relate to constructors and destructors. To understand why, consider this short program:

```
// Constructors, destructors, and passing objects.
#include <iostream>
using namespace std;

class myclass {
  int val;
public:
  myclass(int i) { val = i; cout << "Constructing\n"; }
  ~myclass() { cout << "Destructing\n"; }
  int getval() { return val; }
};

void display(myclass ob)
{
  cout << ob.getval() << '\n';
}

int main()
{
  myclass a(10);

  display(a);

  return 0;
}
```

This program produces the following, unexpected output:

```
Constructing
10
Destructing
Destructing
```

As you can see, there is one call to the constructor function (which occurs when **a** is created), but there are *two* calls to the destructor. Let's see why this is the case.

When an object is passed to a function, a copy of that object is made (and this copy becomes the parameter in the function). This means that a new object comes into existence. When the function terminates, the copy of the argument (i.e., the parameter) is destroyed. This raises two fundamental questions: First, is the object's constructor called when the copy is made? Second, is the object's destructor called when the copy is destroyed? The answers may, at first, surprise you.

When a copy of an argument is made during a function call, the normal constructor is *not* called. Instead, the object's *copy constructor* is called. A copy constructor defines how a copy of an object is made. (Later in this chapter you will see how to create a copy constructor.) However, if a class does not explicitly define a copy constructor, then C++ provides one by default. The default copy constructor creates a bitwise (that is, identical) copy of the object. The reason a bitwise copy is made is easy to understand if you think about it. Since a normal constructor is used to initialize some aspect of an object, it must not be called to make a copy of an already existing object. Such a call would alter the contents of the object. When passing an object to a function, you want to use the current state of the object, not its initial state.

However, when the function terminates and the copy of the object used as an argument is destroyed, the destructor *is* called. This is necessary because the object has gone out of scope. This is why the preceding program had two calls to the destructor. The first was when the parameter to **display( )** went out of scope. The second is when **a** inside **main( )** was destroyed when the program ended.

To summarize: When a copy of an object is created to be used as an argument to a function, the normal constructor is not called. Instead, the default copy constructor makes a bit-by-bit identical copy. However, when the copy is destroyed (usually by going out of scope when the function returns), the destructor is called.

12

A Potential Problem When Passing Objects

Even though objects are passed to functions by means of the normal call-by-value parameter-passing mechanism, which, in theory, protects and insulates the calling argument, it is still possible for a side effect to occur that may affect, or even damage, the object used as an argument. For example, if an object used as an argument allocates dynamic memory and frees that memory when it is destroyed, then its local copy inside the function will free the same memory when its destructor is called. This is a problem because the original object is still using the memory. This situation will leave the original object damaged and effectively useless. Consider this sample program:

```
// Demonstrate a problem when passing objects.
#include <iostream>
#include <cstdlib>
using namespace std;

class myclass {
  int *p;
public:
  myclass(int i);
  ~myclass();
  int getval() { return *p; }
};

myclass::myclass(int i)
{
  cout << "Allocating p\n";
  p = new int;
  *p = i;
}

myclass::~myclass()
{
  cout << "Freeing p\n";
  delete p;
}

// This will cause a problem.
void display(myclass ob)
{
  cout << ob.getval() << '\n';
}

int main()
{
  myclass a(10);

  display(a);

  return 0;
}
```

This program displays the following output:

```
Allocating p
10
Freeing p
Freeing p
```

This program contains a fundamental error. Here is why: When **a** is constructed within **main( )**, memory is allocated and assigned to **a.p**. When **a** is passed to **display( )**,

a is copied into the parameter **ob**. This means that both **a** and **ob** will have the same value for **p**. That is, both objects will have their copies of **p** pointing to the same dynamically allocated memory. When **display( )** terminates, **ob** is destroyed, and its destructor is called. This causes **ob.p** to be freed. However, the memory freed by **ob.p** is the same memory that is still in use by **a.p**! This is, in itself, a serious bug.

However, things get even worse. When the program ends, **a** is destroyed, and its dynamically allocated memory is freed a second time. The problem is that freeing the same piece of dynamically allocated memory a second time is an undefined operation which could, depending upon how the dynamic allocation system is implemented, cause a fatal error.

As you might guess, one way around the problem of a parameter's destructor destroying data needed by the calling argument is to pass either a pointer or a reference, instead of the object itself. When either a pointer to an object or a reference to an object is passed, no copy is made; thus, no destructor is called when the function returns. For example, here is one way to correct the preceding program:

```
// One solution to the problem of passing objects.
#include <iostream>
#include <cstdlib>
using namespace std;

class myclass {
  int *p;
public:
  myclass(int i);
  ~myclass();
  int getval() { return *p; }
};

myclass::myclass(int i)
{
  cout << "Allocating p\n";
  p = new int;
  *p = i;
}

myclass::~myclass()
{
  cout << "Freeing p\n";
  delete p;
}

/* This will NOT cause a problem.

   Because ob is now passed by reference, no
   copy of the calling argument is made and thus,
   no object goes out-of-scope when display()
   terminates.
*/
void display(myclass &ob)
{
```

12

```
  cout << ob.getval() << '\n';
}

int main()
{
  myclass a(10);

  display(a);

  return 0;
}
```

The output from this version of the program is shown here.

```
Allocating p
10
Freeing p
```

As you can see, only one call to the destructor occurs. This is because no copy of **a** is made when it is passed by reference to **display( )**.

Passing an object by reference is an excellent approach when the situation allows it, but it may not be applicable to all cases. Fortunately, a more general solution is available: you can create your own version of the copy constructor. Doing so lets you define precisely how a copy of an object is made, allowing you to avoid the type of problems just described. Before discussing the copy constructor, let's look at another, related situation that can also benefit from a copy constructor.

Returning Objects

Just as objects can be passed to functions, so functions can return objects. To return an object, first declare the function as returning a class type. Second, return an object of that type by using the normal **return** statement. Here is an example of a function that returns an object:

```
// Returning an object.
#include <iostream>
#include <cstring>
using namespace std;

class sample {
  char s[80];
public:
  void show() { cout << s << "\n"; }
  void set(char *str) { strcpy(s, str); }
};

// Return an object of type sample.
sample input()
{
  char instr[80];
```

```
  sample str;

  cout << "Enter a string: ";
  cin >> instr;

  str.set(instr);

  return str;
}

int main()
{
  sample ob;


  // assign returned object to ob
  ob = input();
  ob.show();

  return 0;
}
```

In this example, **input( )** creates a local object called **str** and then reads a string from the keyboard. This string is copied into **str.s**, and then **str** is returned by the function. This object is then assigned to **ob** inside **main( )** after it is returned by **input( )**.

A Potential Problem When Returning Objects

There is one important point to understand about returning objects from functions: When an object is returned by a function, a temporary object is automatically created, which holds the return value. It is this object that is actually returned by the function. After the value has been returned, this object is destroyed. The destruction of this temporary object may cause unexpected side effects in some situations. For example, if the object returned by the function has a destructor that frees dynamically allocated memory, that memory will be freed even though the object that receives the return value is still using it. Consider the following incorrect version of the preceding program:

```
// An error generated by returning an object.
#include <iostream>
#include <cstring>
#include <cstdlib>
using namespace std;

class sample {
  char *s;
public:
  sample() { s = 0; }
  ~sample() { if(s) delete [] s; cout << "Freeing s\n"; }
  void show() { cout << s << "\n"; }
  void set(char *str);
};
```

12

```
// Load a string.
void sample::set(char *str)
{
  s = new char[strlen(str)+1];
  strcpy(s, str);
}

// Return an object of type sample.
sample input()
{
  char instr[80];
  sample str;

  cout << "Enter a string: ";
  cin >> instr;

  str.set(instr);
  return str;
}

int main()
{
  sample ob;

  // assign returned object to ob
  ob = input();  // This causes an error!!!!
  ob.show(); // displays garbage

  return 0;
}
```

The output from this program is shown here:

```
Enter a string: Hello
Freeing s
Freeing s
garbage here
Freeing s
```

Notice that **sample**'s destructor is called three times! First, it is called when the local object **str** goes out of scope upon the return of **input( )**. The second time ~**sample( )** is called is when the temporary object returned by **input( )** is destroyed. When an object is returned from a function, an invisible (to you) temporary object is automatically generated, which holds the return value. In this case, the object is simply a bitwise copy of **str**, which is the return value of the function. Therefore, after the function has returned, the temporary object's destructor is executed. Because the memory holding the string entered by the user has already been freed (twice!), garbage is displayed when **show( )** is called. (Depending upon how your compiler implements dynamic allocation, you may not see garbage output, but the error is still present.) Finally, the destructor for object **ob**, inside **main( )**, is called when the program terminates. The trouble is that, in this situation, the first time the destructor executes, the memory allocated to hold the string obtained by **input( )** is freed. Thus, not only do the other two calls to **sample**'s destructor try to free an already released piece of dynamic memory, but they may also damage the dynamic allocation system in the process.

The key point to understand from this example is that when an object is returned from a function, the temporary object holding the return value will have its destructor called. Thus, you should avoid returning objects in which this situation can be harmful. One solution is to return either a pointer or a reference. However, this is not always feasible. Another way to solve this problem involves the use of a copy constructor, which is described next.

Creating and Using a Copy Constructor

One of the more important forms of an overloaded constructor is the copy constructor. As earlier examples have shown, problems can occur when an object is passed to, or returned from, a function. As you will learn in this section, one way to avoid these problems is to define a *copy constructor*, which is a special type of overloaded constructor.

To begin, let's restate the problems that a copy constructor is designed to solve. When an object is passed to a function, a bitwise (i.e., exact) copy of that object is made and given to the function parameter that receives the object. However, there are cases in which this identical copy is not desirable. For example, if the object contains a pointer to allocated memory, then the copy will point to the *same* memory as does the original object. Therefore, if the copy makes a change to the contents of this memory, it will be changed for the original object, too! Furthermore, when the function terminates, the copy will be destroyed, thus causing its destructor to be called. This may also have undesired effects on the original object.

A similar situation occurs when an object is returned by a function. The compiler will generate a temporary object that holds a copy of the value returned by the function. (This is done automatically, and is beyond your control.) This temporary object goes out of scope once the value is returned to the calling routine, causing the temporary object's destructor to be called. However, if the destructor destroys something needed by the calling routine, trouble will follow.

A copy constructor allows you to control precisely what occurs when a copy of an object is made.

At the core of these problems is the creation of a bitwise copy of the object. To prevent them, you need to define precisely what occurs when a copy of an object is made so that you can avoid undesired side effects. The way you accomplish this is by creating a copy constructor.

12

Before we explore the use of the copy constructor, it is important for you to understand that C++ defines two distinct types of situations in which the value of one object is given to another. The first situation is assignment. The second situation is initialization, which can occur three ways:

◆ When one object explicitly initializes another, such as in a declaration

◆ When a copy of an object is passed as a parameter to a function

◆ When a temporary object is generated (most commonly, as a return value)

The copy constructor applies only to initializations. It does not apply to assignments.

The copy constructor is called when one object initializes another.

The most common form of copy constructor is shown here:

> *classname* (const *classname* &*obj*) {
>   // body of constructor
>   }

Here, *obj* is a reference to an object that is being used to initialize another object. For example, assuming a class called **myclass**, and **y** as an object of type **myclass**, then the following statements would invoke the **myclass** copy constructor:

```
myclass x = y; // y explicitly initializing x
func1(y);      // y passed as a parameter
y = func2();   // y receiving a returned object
```

In the first two cases, a reference to **y** would be passed to the copy constructor. In the third, a reference to the object returned by **func2( )** would be passed to the copy constructor.

To fully explore the value of copy constructors, let's see how they impact each of the three situations to which they apply.

Copy Constructors and Parameters

When an object is passed to a function as an argument, a copy of that object is made. If a copy constructor exists, the copy constructor is called to make the copy. Here is a program that uses a copy constructor to properly handle objects of type **myclass** when they are passed to a function. (This is a corrected version of the incorrect program shown earlier in this chapter.)

```
// Use a copy constructor to construct a parameter.
#include <iostream>
#include <cstdlib>
using namespace std;

class myclass {
  int *p;
public:
  myclass(int i); // normal constructor
  myclass(const myclass &ob); // copy constructor
  ~myclass();
  int getval() { return *p; }
};

// Copy constructor.
```

```
myclass::myclass(const myclass &obj)
{
  p = new int;
  *p = *obj.p; // copy value
  cout << "Copy constructor called.\n";
}

// Normal Constructor.
myclass::myclass(int i)
{
  cout << "Allocating p\n";
  p = new int;
  *p = i;
}

myclass::~myclass()
{
  cout << "Freeing p\n";
  delete p;
}

// This function takes one object parameter.
void display(myclass ob)
{
  cout << ob.getval() << '\n';
}

int main()
{
  myclass a(10);

  display(a);

  return 0;
}
```

This program displays the following output:

```
Allocating p
Copy constructor called.
10
Freeing p
Freeing p
```

12

Here is what occurs when the program is run: When **a** is created inside **main( )**, the normal constructor allocates memory and assigns the address of that memory to **a.p**. Next, **a** is passed to **ob** of **display( )**. When this occurs, the copy constructor is called, and a copy of **a** is created. The copy constructor allocates memory for the copy, and a pointer to that memory is assigned to the copy's **p** member. Next, the value stored at the original object's **p** is assigned to the memory pointed to by the copy's **p**. Thus, the areas of memory pointed to by **a.p** and **ob.p** are separate and distinct, but the values that they point to are the same. If the copy constructor had not been created, then the default bitwise copy would have caused **a.p** and **ob.p** to point to the same memory.

When **display( )** returns, **ob** goes out of scope. This causes its destructor to be called, which frees the memory pointed to by **ob.p**. Finally, when **main( )** returns, **a** goes out of scope, causing its destructor to free **a.p**. As you can see, the use of the copy constructor has eliminated the destructive side effects associated with passing an object to a function.

Copy Constructors and Initializations

The copy constructor is also invoked when one object is used to initialize another. Examine this sample program:

```cpp
// The copy constructor is called for initialization.
#include <iostream>
#include <cstdlib>
using namespace std;

class myclass {
  int *p;
public:
  myclass(int i); // normal constructor
  myclass(const myclass &ob); // copy constructor
  ~myclass();
  int getval() { return *p; }
};

// Copy constructor.
myclass::myclass(const myclass &ob)
{
  p = new int;
  *p = *ob.p; // copy value
  cout << "Copy constructor allocating p.\n";
}

// Normal constructor.
myclass::myclass(int i)
{
  cout << "Normal constructor allocating p.\n";
  p = new int;
  *p = i;
}

myclass::~myclass()
{
  cout << "Freeing p\n";
  delete p;
}

int main()
{
  myclass a(10); // calls normal constructor
```

```
    myclass b = a; // calls copy constructor

    return 0;
}
```

This program displays the following output:

```
Normal constructor allocating p.
Copy constructor allocating p.
Freeing p
Freeing p
```

As the output confirms, the normal constructor is called for object **a**. However, when **a** is used to initialize **b**, the copy constructor is invoked. The use of the copy constructor ensures that **b** will allocate its own memory. Without the copy constructor, **b** would simply be an exact copy of **a**, and **a.p** would point to the same memory as **b.p**.

Keep in mind that the copy constructor is called only for initializations. For example, the following sequence does *not* call the copy constructor defined in the preceding program:

```
myclass a(2), b(3);
// ...
b = a;
```

In this case, **b = a** performs the assignment operation, not a copy operation.

Using Copy Constructors When an Object Is Returned
The copy constructor is also invoked when a temporary object is created as the result of a function returning an object. Consider this short program:

```
/* Copy constructor is called when a temporary object
   is created as a function return value.
*/
#include <iostream>
using namespace std;

class myclass {
public:
  myclass() { cout << "Normal constructor.\n"; }
  myclass(const myclass &obj) { cout << "Copy constructor.\n"; }
};

myclass f()
{
  myclass ob; // invoke normal constructor

  return ob; // implicitly invoke copy constructor
}

int main()
{
  myclass a; // invoke normal constructor
```

12

```
a = f(); // invoke copy constructor

return 0;
}
```

This program displays the following output:

```
Normal constructor.
Normal constructor.
Copy constructor.
```

Here, the normal constructor is called twice: once when **a** is created inside **main( )**, and once when **ob** is created inside **f( )**. The copy constructor is called when the temporary object is generated as a return value from **f( )**.

Although copy constructors may seem a bit esoteric at this point, virtually every real-world class will require one, due to the side effects that often result from the default bitwise copy.

IN DEPTH

Copy Constructors—Is There a Simpler Way?

As has been stated several times in this book, C++ is a very powerful language. It is also a very large, and at times, complex language. Copy constructors are a feature that many programmers point to as a prime example of this complexity because it is a non-intuitive feature. Newcomers often do not immediately understand why the copy constructor is important, nor is it always obvious to the novice when a copy constructor is needed and when one isn't. This situation often gives rise to the question "Isn't there a better way?" The answer is both Yes and No!

Languages such as Java and C# do not have copy constructors because neither language makes bitwise copies of an object. This is because both Java and C# dynamically allocate all objects and you operate on those objects exclusively through references. Thus, no copies of an object are made when passing one as a parameter or returning one from a function.

The fact that neither Java nor C# require copy constructors streamlines those languages, but it comes at a price. Operating on objects exclusively through references, rather directly as you can in C++, imposes limitations on the type of operations you can perform. Furthermore, because of their exclusive use of object references, in Java and C# you cannot precisely specify when an object will be destroyed. In C++, an object is always destroyed when it goes out of scope.

Because C++ gives you, the programmer, complete control, it is a bit more complicated language than are Java and C#. This is the price of programming power.

The this Keyword

Each time a member function is invoked, it is automatically passed a pointer, called **this**, to the object on which it is called. The **this** pointer is an *implicit* parameter to all member functions. Therefore, inside a member function, **this** may be used to refer to the invoking object.

As you know, a member function can directly access the private data of its class. For example, given this class,

```
class cl {
  int i;
  void f() { ... };
  // ...
};
```

inside **f( )**, the following statement can be used to assign **i** the value 10:

```
i = 10;
```

In actuality, the preceding statement is shorthand for this one:

```
this->i = 10;
```

To see how the **this** pointer works, examine the following short program:

```
#include <iostream>
using namespace std;

class cl {
  int i;
public:
  void load_i(int val) { this->i = val; } // same as i = val
  int get_i() { return this->i; } // same as return i
} ;

int main()
{
  cl o;

  o.load_i(100);
  cout << o.get_i();

  return 0;
}
```

This program displays the number **100**.

12

Of course, the preceding example is trivial—no one would actually use the **this** pointer in this way. Soon, however, you will see why the **this** pointer is important to C++ programming.

TIP: Friend functions do not have a **this** pointer, because friends are not members of a class. Only member functions have a **this** pointer.

CHAPTER 13

Operator
Overloading

In C++, operators can be overloaded relative to class types that you define. The principal advantage to overloading operators is that it allows you to seamlessly integrate new data types into your programming environment.

Operator overloading allows you to define the meaning of an operator for a particular class. For example, a class that defines a linked list might use the + operator to add an object to the list. A class that implements a stack might use the + to push an object onto the stack. Another class might use the + operator in an entirely different way. When an operator is overloaded, none of its original meaning is lost. It is simply that a new operation, relative to a specific class, is defined. Therefore, overloading the + to handle a linked list, for example, does not cause its meaning relative to integers (i.e., addition) to change.

Operator overloading is closely related to function overloading. To overload an operator, you must define what the operation means relative to the class to which it is applied. To do this, you create an **operator** function, which defines the action of the operator. The general form of an **operator** function is

> *type classname*::operator#(*arg-list*)
> {
>   *operation relative to the class*
> }

Here, the operator that you are overloading is substituted for the #, and *type* is the type of value returned by the specified operation. Although it can be of any type you choose, the return value is often of the same type as the class for which the operator is being overloaded. This correlation facilitates the use of the overloaded operator in compound expressions. The specific nature of *arg-list* is determined by several factors, as you will soon see.

Operator functions can be either members or nonmembers of a class. Nonmember operator functions are often friend functions of the class, however. Although similar, there are some differences between the way a member operator function is overloaded and the way a nonmember operator function is overloaded. Each approach is described here.

Operator Overloading Using Member Functions

To begin our examination of operator overloading using member fuctions, we will start with a simple example. The following program creates a class called **three_d**, which maintains the coordinates of an object in three-dimensional space. This program overloads the + and the = operators relative to the **three_d** class. Examine it closely:

```cpp
// Overload operators using member functions.
#include <iostream>
using namespace std;

class three_d {
  int x, y, z; // 3-D coordinates
public:
  three_d() { x = y = z = 0; }
  three_d(int i, int j, int k) {x = i; y = j; z = k; }
```

```
    three_d operator+(three_d op2); // op1 is implied
    three_d operator=(three_d op2); // op1 is implied

  void show() ;
};

// Overload +.
three_d three_d::operator+(three_d op2)
{
  three_d temp;

  temp.x = x + op2.x; // These are integer additions
  temp.y = y + op2.y; // and the + retains its original
  temp.z = z + op2.z; // meaning relative to them.
  return temp;
}

// Overload assignment.
three_d three_d::operator=(three_d op2)
{
  x = op2.x; // These are integer assignments
  y = op2.y; // and the = retains its original
  z = op2.z; // meaning relative to them.
  return *this;
}

// Show X, Y, Z coordinates.
void three_d::show()
{
  cout << x << ", ";
  cout << y << ", ";
  cout << z << "\n";
}

int main()
{
  three_d a(1, 2, 3), b(10, 10, 10), c;

  a.show();
  b.show();

  c = a + b; // add a and b together
  c.show();

  c = a + b + c; // add a, b and c together
  c.show();

  c = b = a; // demonstrate multiple assignment
  c.show();
  b.show();

  return 0;
}
```

13

This program produces the following output:

```
1, 2, 3
10, 10, 10
11, 12, 13
22, 24, 26
1, 2, 3
1, 2, 3
```

As you examined the program, you may have been surprised to see that both operator functions have only one parameter each, even though they overload binary operations. The reason for this apparent contradiction is that when a binary operator is overloaded using a member function, only one argument is explicitly passed to it. The other argument is implicitly passed using the **this** pointer. Thus, in the line

```
temp.x = x + op2.x;
```

the **x** refers to **this–>x**, which is the **x** associated with the object that invokes the operator function. In all cases, it is the object on the left side of an operation that causes the call to the operator function. The object on the right side is passed to the function.

In general, when you use a member function, no parameters are used when overloading a unary operator, and only one parameter is required when overloading a binary operator. (You cannot overload the ternary **?** operator.) In either case, the object that invokes the operator function is implicitly passed via the **this** pointer.

To understand how operator overloading works, let's examine the preceding program carefully, beginning with the overloaded operator **+**. When two objects of type **three_d** are operated on by the **+** operator, the magnitudes of their respective coordinates are added together, as shown in **operator+( )**. Notice, however, that this function does not modify the value of either operand. Instead, an object of type **three_d**, which contains the result of the operation, is returned by the function. To understand why the **+** operation does not change the contents of either object, think about the standard arithmetic **+** operation, as applied like this: 10 + 12. The outcome of this operation is 22, but neither 10 nor 12 is changed by it. Although there is no rule that prevents an overloaded operator from altering the value of one of its operands, it is best for the actions of an overloaded operator to be consistent with its original meaning.

Notice that **operator+( )** returns an object of type **three_d**. Although the function could have returned any valid C++ type, the fact that it returns a **three_d** object allows the **+** operator to be used in compound expressions, such as **a+b+c**. Here, **a+b** generates a result that is of type **three_d**. This value can then be added to **c**. Had any other type of value been generated by **a+b**, such an expression would not work.

In contrast with the **+** operator, the assignment operator does, indeed, cause one of its arguments to be modified. (This is, after all, the very essence of assignment.) Since the **operator=( )** function is called by the object that occurs on the left side of the assignment, it is this object that is modified by the assignment operation. Most often, the return value of an overloaded assignment operator is the object on the left, after the assignment has been made. (This is in keeping with the traditional action of the **=** operator.) For example, to allow statements like

```
a = b = c = d;
```

it is necessary for **operator=( )** to return the object pointed to by **this**, which will be the object that occurs on the left side of the assignment statement. This allows a string of assignments to be made. The assignment operation is one of the most important uses of the **this** pointer.

REMEMBER: When a member function is used for overloading a binary operator, the object on the left side of the operator invokes the operator function, and is passed to it implicitly through **this**. The object on the right is passed as a parameter to the operator function.

Using Member Functions to Overload Unary Operators

You may also overload unary operators, such as **++**, **– –**, or the unary **–** or **+**. As stated earlier, when a unary operator is overloaded by means of a member function, no object is explicitly passed to the operator function. Instead, the operation is performed on the object that generates the call to the function through the implicitly passed **this** pointer. For example, here is an expanded version of the previous example program. This version defines the increment operation for objects of type **three_d**.

```
// Overload a unary operator.
#include <iostream>
using namespace std;

class three_d {
  int x, y, z; // 3-D coordinates
public:
  three_d() { x = y = z = 0; }
  three_d(int i, int j, int k) {x = i; y = j; z = k; }

  three_d operator+(three_d op2); // op1 is implied
  three_d operator=(three_d op2); // op1 is implied
  three_d operator++(); // prefix version of ++

  void show() ;
} ;

// Overload +.
three_d three_d::operator+(three_d op2)
{
  three_d temp;

  temp.x = x + op2.x; // These are integer additions
  temp.y = y + op2.y; // and the + retains its original
  temp.z = z + op2.z; // meaning relative to them.
  return temp;
}

// Overload assignment.
```

13

```
three_d three_d::operator=(three_d op2)
{
  x = op2.x; // These are integer assignments
  y = op2.y; // and the = retains its original
  z = op2.z; // meaning relative to them.
  return *this;
}

// Overload the prefix version of ++.
three_d three_d::operator++()
{
  x++; // increment x, y, and z
  y++;
  z++;
  return *this;
}

// Show X, Y, Z coordinates.
void three_d::show()
{
  cout << x << ", ";
  cout << y << ", ";
  cout << z << "\n";
}

int main()
{
  three_d a(1, 2, 3), b(10, 10, 10), c;
  a.show();
  b.show();

  c = a + b; // add a and b together
  c.show();

  c = a + b + c; // add a, b and c together
  c.show();

  c = b = a; // demonstrate multiple assignment
  c.show();
  b.show();

  ++c;  // increment c
  c.show();

  return 0;
}
```

The output from the program is shown here.

```
1, 2, 3
10, 10, 10
11, 12, 13
```

```
22, 24, 26
1, 2, 3
1, 2, 3
2, 3, 4
```

As the last line of the output shows, **operator++( )** increments each coordinate in the object and returns the modified object. Again, this is in keeping with the traditional meaning of the **++** operator.

As you know, the **++** and **– –** have both a prefix and a postfix form. For example, both

```
++O;
```

and

```
O++;
```

are valid uses of the increment operator. As the comments in the preceding program state, the **operator++( )** function defines the prefix form of **++** relative to the **three_d** class. However, it is possible to overload the postfix form as well. The prototype for the postfix form of the **++** operator, relative to the **three_d** class, is shown here:

```
three_d three_d::operator++(int notused);
```

The increment and decrement operators have both a prefix and postfix form.

The parameter **notused** is not used by the function, and should be ignored. This parameter is simply a way for the compiler to distinguish between the prefix and postfix forms of the increment operator. (The postfix decrement uses the same approach.)

Here is one way to implement a postfix version of **++** relative to the **three_d** class:

```
// Overload the postfix version of ++.
three_d three_d::operator++(int notused)
{
  three_d temp = *this; // save original value

  x++;  // increment x, y, and z
  y++;
  z++;
  return temp; // return original value
}
```

13

Notice that this function saves the current state of the operand by using the statement

```
three_d temp = *this;
```

and then returns **temp**. Keep in mind that the traditional meaning of a postfix increment is to first obtain the value of the operand, and then to increment the operand. Therefore, it is necessary to save the current state of the operand and return its original value, before it is incremented, rather than its modified value.

The following version of the original program implements both forms of the **++** operator:

```cpp
// Demonstrate prefix and postfix ++.
#include <iostream>
using namespace std;

class three_d {
  int x, y, z; // 3-D coordinates
public:
  three_d() { x = y = z = 0; }
  three_d(int i, int j, int k) {x = i; y = j; z = k; }

  three_d operator+(three_d op2); // op1 is implied
  three_d operator=(three_d op2); // op1 is implied
  three_d operator++(); // prefix version of ++
  three_d operator++(int notused); // postfix version of ++

  void show() ;
};

// Overload +.
three_d three_d::operator+(three_d op2)
{
  three_d temp;

  temp.x = x + op2.x; // These are integer additions
  temp.y = y + op2.y; // and the + retains its original
  temp.z = z + op2.z; // meaning relative to them.
  return temp;
}

// Overload assignment.
three_d three_d::operator=(three_d op2)
{
  x = op2.x; // These are integer assignments
  y = op2.y; // and the = retains its original
  z = op2.z; // meaning relative to them.
  return *this;
}

// Overload the prefix version of ++.
three_d three_d::operator++()
{
  x++;  // increment x, y, and z
  y++;
  z++;
  return *this; // return altered value
}

// Overload the postfix version of ++.
```

```
three_d three_d::operator++(int notused)
{
  three_d temp = *this; // save original value

  x++; // increment x, y, and z
  y++;
  z++;
  return temp; // return original value
}

// Show X, Y, Z coordinates.
void three_d::show( )
{
  cout << x << ", ";
  cout << y << ", ";
  cout << z << "\n";
}

int main()
{
  three_d a(1, 2, 3), b(10, 10, 10), c;
  a.show();
  b.show();

  c = a + b; // add a and b together
  c.show();

  c = a + b + c; // add a, b and c together
  c.show();

  c = b = a; // demonstrate multiple assignment
  c.show();
  b.show();

  ++c; // prefix increment
  c.show();

  c++; // postfix increment
  c.show();

  a = ++c; // a receives c's value after increment
  a.show(); // a and c
  c.show(); // are the same

  a = c++; // a receives c's value prior to increment
  a.show(); // a and c
  c.show(); // now differ

  return 0;
}
```

13

The output is shown here.

```
1, 2, 3
10, 10, 10
11, 12, 13
22, 24, 26
1, 2, 3
1, 2, 3
2, 3, 4
3, 4, 5
4, 5, 6
4, 5, 6
4, 5, 6
5, 6, 7
```

As the last four lines show, the prefix increment increases the value of **c** before its value is assigned to **a**, and the postfix increment increases **c** after its value is assigned to **a**.

Remember that if the **++** precedes its operand, the **operator++( )** is called. If it follows its operand, the **operator++(int notused)** function is called. This same approach is also used to overload the prefix and postfix decrement operator relative to any class. You might want to try defining the decrement operator relative to **three_d** as an exercise.

TIP: Early versions of C++ did not distinguish between the prefix and postfix forms of the increment or decrement operators. For these old versions, the prefix form of the operator function was called for both uses of the operator. When working on older C++ code, be aware of this possibility.

Operator Overloading Tips and Restrictions

The action of an overloaded operator, as applied to the class for which it is defined, need not bear any relationship to that operator's default usage, as applied to C++'s built-in types. For example, the **<<** and **>>** operators, as applied to **cout** and **cin**, have little in common with the same operators applied to integer types. However, to maintain the transparency and readability of your code, an overloaded operator should reflect, when possible, the spirit of the operator's original use. For example, the **+** relative to **three_d** is conceptually similar to the **+** relative to integer types. There would be little benefit in defining the **+** operator relative to some class in such a way that it acts more the way you would expect the **||** operator, for instance, to perform. The central concept here is that, while you can give an overloaded operator any meaning you like, for clarity, it is best when its new meaning is related to its original meaning.

There are some restrictions to overloading operators. First, you cannot alter the precedence of any operator. Second, you cannot alter the number of operands required by the operator, although your operator function could choose to ignore an operand. Finally, except for the function call operator (discussed later), operator functions cannot have default arguments.

The only operators that you cannot overload are shown here:

. :: .* ?

The **.*** is a special-purpose operator, discussed later in this book.

Nonmember Operator Functions

Nonmember binary operator functions have two parameters. Nonmember unary operator functions have one parameter.

You can overload an operator for a class by using a nonmember function, which is often a friend of the class. As you learned earlier, nonmember functions, including friend functions, do not have a **this** pointer. Therefore, when a friend is used to overload an operator, both operands are passed explicitly when a binary operator is overloaded, and a single operand is passed when a unary operator is overloaded. The only operators that cannot be overloaded using nonmember functions are =, ( ), [ ], and –>.

IN DEPTH

Order Matters

When overloading binary operators, remember that in many cases, the order of the operands does make a difference. For example, while A + B is commutative, A – B is not. (That is, A – B is not the same as B – A!) Therefore, when implementing overloaded versions of the non-commutative operators, you must remember which operand is on the left and which is on the right. For example, in this fragment, subtraction is overloaded relative to the **three_d** class:

```
// Overload subtraction.
three_d three_d::operator-(three_d op2)
{
  three_d temp;

  temp.x = x - op2.x;
  temp.y = y - op2.y;
  temp.z = z - op2.z;
  return temp;
}
```

Remember, it is the operand on the left that invokes the operator function. The operand on the right is passed explicitly. This is why **x – op2.x** is the proper order for the subtraction.

13

For example, in the following program, a friend is used instead of a member function to overload the **+** operation:

```
// Overload + using a friend.
#include <iostream>
using namespace std;

class three_d {
  int x, y, z; // 3-D coordinates
public:
  three_d() { x = y = z = 0; }
  three_d(int i, int j, int k) { x = i; y = j; z = k;}

  friend three_d operator+(three_d op1, three_d op2);
  three_d operator=(three_d op2); // op2 is implied

  void show() ;
} ;

// This is now a friend function.
three_d operator+(three_d op1, three_d op2)
{
  three_d temp;

  temp.x = op1.x + op2.x;
  temp.y = op1.y + op2.y;
  temp.z = op1.z+ op2.z;
  return temp;
}

// Overload assignment.
three_d three_d::operator=(three_d op2)
{
  x = op2.x;
  y = op2.y;
  z = op2.z;
  return *this;
}

// Show X, Y, Z coordinates.
void three_d::show()
{
  cout << x << ", ";
  cout << y << ", ";
  cout << z << "\n";
}

int main()
{
  three_d a(1, 2, 3), b(10, 10, 10), c;

  a.show();
  b.show();
```

```
c = a + b;  // add a and b together
c.show();

c = a + b + c;  // add a, b and c together
c.show();

c = b = a;   // demonstrate multiple assignment
c.show();
b.show();

return 0;
}
```

As you can see by looking at **operator+( )**, now both operands are passed to it. The left operand is passed in **op1**, and the right operand in **op2**.

In many cases, there is no benefit to using a friend function rather than a member function when overloading an operator. However, there is one situation in which a friend function is quite useful: when you want an object of a built-in type to occur on the left side of a binary operator. To understand why, consider the following. As you know, a pointer to the object that invokes a member operator function is passed in **this**. In the case of a binary operator, it is the object on the left that invokes the function. This is fine, provided that the object on the left defines the specified operation. For example, assuming some object called **Ob**, which has integer addition defined for it, then the following is a perfectly valid expression:

```
Ob + 10; // will work
```

Because the object **Ob** is on the left side of the + operator, it invokes its overloaded operator function, which (presumably) is capable of adding an integer value to some element of **Ob**. However, this statement won't work:

```
10 + Ob; // won't work
```

The problem with this statement is that the object on the left of the + operator is an integer, a built-in type for which no operation involving an integer and an object of **Ob**'s type is defined.

The solution to the preceding problem is to overload the + using two friend functions. In this case, the operator function is explicitly passed both arguments, and it is invoked like any other overloaded function, based upon the types of its arguments. One version of the + operator function handles *object + integer*, and the other handles *integer + object*. Overloading the + (or any other binary operator) using friend functions allows a built-in type to occur on the left or right side of the operator. The following sample program shows you how to accomplish this:

```
#include <iostream>
using namespace std;

class CL {
```

13

```
public:
  int count;
  CL operator=(CL obj);
  friend CL operator+(CL ob, int i);
  friend CL operator+(int i, CL ob);
};

CL CL::operator=(CL obj)
{
  count = obj.count;
  return *this;
}

// This handles ob + int.
CL operator+(CL ob, int i)
{
  CL temp;

  temp.count = ob.count + i;
  return temp;
}

// This handles int + ob.
CL operator+(int i, CL ob)
{
  CL temp;

  temp.count = ob.count + i;
  return temp;
}

int main()
{
  CL O;

  O.count = 10;
  cout << O.count << " "; // outputs 10

  O = 10 + O; // add object to integer
  cout << O.count << " "; // outputs 20

  O = O + 12; // add integer to object
  cout << O.count;        // outputs 32

  return 0;
}
```

As you can see, the **operator+( )** function is overloaded twice, to accommodate the two ways in which an integer and an object of type **CL** can occur in the addition operation.

Using a Friend to Overload a Unary Operator

You can also overload a unary operator by using a friend function. However, doing so requires a little extra effort. To begin, think back to the original version of the overloaded **++** operator relative to the **three_d** class that was implemented as a member function. It is shown here for your convenience:

```
// Overload the prefix form of ++.
three_d three_d::operator++()
{
  x++;
  y++;
  z++;
  return *this;
}
```

As you know, every member function receives as an implicit argument **this**, which is a pointer to the object that invokes the function. When a unary operator is overloaded by use of a member function, no argument is explicitly declared. The only argument needed in this situation is the implicit pointer to the invoking object. Any changes made to the object's data will affect the object on which the operator function is called. Therefore, in the preceding function, **x++** increments the **x** member of the invoking object.

Unlike member functions, a nonmember function, including a friend, does not receive a **this** pointer, and therefore cannot access the object on which it was called. Instead, a friend operator function is passed its operand explicitly. For this reason, trying to create a friend **operator++( )** function, as shown here, will not work:

```
// THIS WILL NOT WORK
three_d operator++(three_d op1)
{
  op1.x++;
  op1.y++;
  op1.z++;
  return op1;
}
```

This function will not work because only a *copy* of the object that activated the call to **operator++( )** is passed to the function in parameter **op1**. Thus, the changes inside **operator++( )** will not affect the calling object, only the local parameter.

If you want to use a friend function to overload the increment or decrement operators, you must pass the object to the function as a reference parameter. Since a reference parameter is an implicit pointer to the argument, changes to the parameter *will* affect the argument. Using a reference parameter allows the function to increment or decrement the object used as an operand.

When a friend is used for overloading the increment or decrement operators, the prefix form takes one parameter (which is the operand). The postfix form takes two parameters. The second is an integer, which is not used.

13

Here is the entire **three_d** program, which uses a friend **operator++( )** function. Notice that both the prefix and postfix forms are overloaded.

```cpp
// This program uses friend operator++() functions.
#include <iostream>
using namespace std;

class three_d {
  int x, y, z; // 3-D coordinates
public:
  three_d() { x = y = z = 0; }
  three_d(int i, int j, int k) {x = i; y = j; z = k; }

  friend three_d operator+(three_d op1, three_d op2);
  three_d operator=(three_d op2);

  // use a reference to overload the ++
  friend three_d operator++(three_d &op1);
  friend three_d operator++(three_d &op1, int notused);

  void show() ;
} ;

// This is now a friend function.
three_d operator+(three_d op1, three_d op2)
{
  three_d temp;

  temp.x = op1.x + op2.x;
  temp.y = op1.y + op2.y;
  temp.z = op1.z + op2.z;
  return temp;
}

// Overload the =.
three_d three_d::operator=(three_d op2)
{
  x = op2.x;
  y = op2.y;
  z = op2.z;
  return *this;
}

/* Overload prefix ++ using a friend function.
   This requires the use of a reference parameter. */
three_d operator++(three_d &op1)
{
  op1.x++;
  op1.y++;
  op1.z++;
  return op1;
}
```

```
/* Overload postfix ++ using a friend function.
   This requires the use of a reference parameter. */
three_d operator++(three_d &op1, int notused)
{
  three_d temp = op1;

  op1.x++;
  op1.y++;
  op1.z++;
  return temp;


}

// Show X, Y, Z coordinates.
void three_d::show()
{
  cout << x << ", ";
  cout << y << ", ";
  cout << z << "\n";
}

int main()
{
  three_d a(1, 2, 3), b(10, 10, 10), c;

  a.show();
  b.show();

  c = a + b; // add a and b together
  c.show();

  c = a + b + c; // add a, b and c together
  c.show();

  c = b = a; // demonstrate multiple assignment
  c.show();
  b.show();

  ++c; // prefix increment
  c.show();

  c++; // postfix increment
  c.show();

  a = ++c; // a receives c's value after increment
  a.show( ); // a and c
  c.show( ); // are the same
```

13

```
a = c++; // a receives c's value prior to increment
a.show( ); // a and c
c.show( ); // now differ

return 0;
}
```

REMEMBER: In general, you should use member functions to implement overloaded operators. Friend functions are used in C++ mostly to handle certain special-case situations.

IN DEPTH

Overloading the Relational and Logical Operators

Overloading a relational or logical operator, such as ==, <, or && is a straightforward process. However, there is one small distinction. As you know, an overloaded operator function usually returns an object of the class for which it is overloaded. However, an overloaded relational or logical operator typically returns a true or false value. This is in keeping with the normal usage of these operators, and allows them to be used in conditional expression.

Here is an example that overloads the = = relative to the **three_d** class:

```
//overload ==.
bool three_d::operator==(three_d op2)
{
  if((x == op2.x) && (y == op2.y) && (z == op2.z))
    return true;
  else
    return false;
}
```

Once **operator==( )** has been implemented, the following fragment is perfectly valid:

```
three_d a, b;

// ...

if(a == b) cout << "a equals b\n";
else cout << "a does not equal b\n";
```

Because == returns a **bool** result, its outcome can be used to control an **if** statement. As an exercise, try implementing several of the relational and logical operators relative to the **three_d** class.

A Closer Look at the Assignment Operator

The preceding chapter discussed a potential problem associated with passing objects to functions, and with returning objects from functions. In both cases, the problem was caused by a copy of an object being made by use of the default copy constructor, which makes a bit-by-bit copy of an object. Recall that the solution to these problems was the creation of your own copy constructor, which could define precisely how a copy of an object was made. A similar type of problem can occur when one object is assigned to another. By default, the object on the left side of an assignment statement receives a bitwise copy of the object on the right. This can lead to trouble in cases in which an object allocates a resource, such as memory, when it is created and later alters or releases the resource. If, after an assignment, one object alters or releases that resource, the second object is also affected because it is still using that resource. The solution to this type of problem is to provide an overloaded assignment operator.

To fully understand the type of problem that the default, bitwise assignment operation can cause, examine the following (incorrect) program:

```
// An error generated by returning an object.
#include <iostream>
#include <cstring>
#include <cstdlib>
using namespace std;

class sample {
  char *s;
public:
  sample() { s = 0; }
  sample(const sample &ob); // copy constructor
  ~sample( ) { if(s) delete [] s; cout << "Freeing s\n"; }
  void show() { cout << s << "\n"; }
  void set(char *str);
};

// Copy constructor.
sample::sample(const sample &ob)
{
  s = new char[strlen(ob.s)+1];

  strcpy(s, ob.s);
}

// Load a string.
void sample::set(char *str)
{
  s = new char[strlen(str)+1];

  strcpy(s, str);
}

// Return an object of type sample.
sample input()
```

13

```
{
  char instr[80];
  sample str;

  cout << "Enter a string: ";
  cin >> instr;

  str.set(instr);
  return str;
}

int main()
{
  sample ob;

  // assign returned object to ob
  ob = input();  // This causes an error!!!!
  ob.show();

  return 0;
}
```

Sample output from this program is shown here:

```
Enter a string: Hello
Freeing s
Freeing s
garbage here
Freeing s
```

Depending upon your compiler, you may or may not see garbled output. The program might also generate a run-time error. In any event, an error will still have occurred. Here's why.

In this program, the copy constructor correctly handles the return of an object by **input( )**. Recall that when a function returns an object, it does so by creating a temporary object to hold the return value. Because the copy constructor allocates new memory when a copy is made, the **s** in the original object and the **s** in the copy point to different regions of memory, and are therefore independent.

However, an error still occurs when the return object is assigned to **ob** because the default assignment performs a bitwise copy. In this case, the temporary object returned by **input( )** is copied into **ob**. This causes **ob.s** to point to the same memory that the temporary object's **s** points to. However, after the assignment, this memory is released when the temporary object is destroyed. Thus, **ob.s** is pointing to freed memory! Further, when the program ends, **ob.s** is again released, causing the memory to be freed a second time. To prevent this problem, you must overload the assignment operator in such a way that the object on the left side of an assignment allocates its own memory.

The following corrected program shows how such a solution can be accomplished:

```
// This program is now fixed.
#include <iostream>
#include <cstring>
```

```
#include <cstdlib>
using namespace std;

class sample {
  char *s;
public:
  sample(); // normal constructor
  sample(const sample &ob); // copy constructor
  ~sample( ) { if(s) delete [] s; cout << "Freeing s\n"; }
  void show() { cout << s << "\n"; }
  void set(char *str);
  sample operator=(sample &ob); // overload assignment
};

// Normal constructor.
sample::sample()
{
  s = new char('\0'); // s points to a null string.
}

// Copy constructor.
sample::sample(const sample &ob)
{
  s = new char[strlen(ob.s)+1];

  strcpy(s, ob.s);
}

// Load a string.
void sample::set(char *str)
{
  s = new char[strlen(str)+1];

  strcpy(s, str);
}

// Overload assignment operator.
sample sample::operator=(sample &ob)
{
  /* If the target memory is not large enough
     then allocate new memory. */
  if(strlen(ob.s) > strlen(s)) {
    delete [] s;
    s = new char[strlen(ob.s)+1];
  }
  strcpy(s, ob.s);
  return *this;
}

// Return an object of type sample.
sample input()
{
  char instr[80];
  sample str;
```

13

```
  cout << "Enter a string: ";
  cin >> instr;

  str.set(instr);
  return str;
}

int main()
{
  sample ob;

  // assign returned object to ob
  ob = input();  // This is now OK
  ob.show();

  return 0;
}
```

This program now displays the following output (assuming that you enter "Hello" when prompted):

```
Enter a string: Hello
Freeing s
Freeing s
Freeing s
Hello
Freeing s
```

As you can see, the program now runs properly. You should be able to understand why each **Freeing s** message is printed. (Hint: One of them is caused by the **delete** statement inside the **operator=( )** function.)

Overloading [ ]

In addition to the more traditional operators, C++ also lets you overload several of the more exotic ones. One of the most useful is the **[ ]** array subscripting operator. In C++, the **[ ]** is considered a binary operator for the purposes of overloading. The **[ ]** can only be overloaded relative to a class, and only by a member function. Therefore, the general form of a member **operator[ ]( )** function is

```
type class-name::operator[ ](int index)
{
  // ...
}
```

The **[ ]** is
overloaded as a
binary operator.

Technically, the parameter does not have to be of type **int**, but **operator[ ]( )** functions are typically used to provide array subscripting, so an integer value is generally used.

Given an object called **Ob**, the expression

```
Ob[3]
```

translates into the following call to the **operator[ ]( )** function:

```
Ob.operator[](3)
```

That is, the value of the expression within the subscripting operator is passed to the **operator[ ]( )** function in its explicit parameter. The **this** pointer will point to **Ob**, the object that generated the call.

In the following program, **atype** declares an array of three integers. Its constructor initializes each member of the array. The overloaded **operator[ ]( )** function returns the value of the element specified by its parameter.

```cpp
// Overload [].
#include <iostream>
using namespace std;

const int SIZE = 3;

class atype {
  int a[SIZE];
public:
  atype() {
    register int i;

    for(i=0; i<SIZE; i++) a[i] = i;
  }
  int operator[](int i) {return a[i];}
};

int main()
{
  atype ob;

  cout << ob[2];   // displays 2

  return 0;
}
```

13

Here, **operator[ ]( )** returns the value of the **i**th element of **a**. Thus, **ob[2]** returns 2, which is displayed by the **cout** statement. The initialization of the array **a** by the constructor in this program, and in the following programs, is for the sake of illustration only. It is not required.

It is possible to design the **operator[ ]( )** function in such a way that the **[ ]** can be used on both the left and right sides of an assignment statement. To do this, simply specify that the return value of **operator[ ]( )** be a reference. This change is illustrated in the following program:

```
// Return a reference from [].
#include <iostream>
using namespace std;

const int SIZE = 3;

class atype {
  int a[SIZE];
public:
  atype() {
    register int i;

    for(i=0; i<SIZE; i++) a[i] = i;
  }
  int &operator[](int i) {return a[i];}
};

int main()
{
  atype ob;

  cout << ob[2];   // displays 2
  cout << " ";

  ob[2] = 25;   // [] on left of =

  cout << ob[2];   // now displays 25

  return 0;
}
```

The program generates the following output.

```
2 25
```

Because **operator[ ]( )** now returns a reference to the array element indexed by **i**, it can now be used on the left side of an assignment statement to modify an element of the array. (Of course, it can still be used on the right side as well.)

One advantage of being able to overload the **[ ]** operator is that it provides a means of implementing safe array indexing. As you know, in C++, it is possible to overrun (or underrun) an array boundary at run time without generating a run-time error message. However, if you create a class that contains the array, and allow access to that array only through the overloaded **[ ]** subscripting operator, then you can intercept an out-of-range index. For example, the program shown next adds a range check to the preceding program, and proves that it works:

```
// A safe array example.
#include <iostream>
#include <cstdlib>
```

```
using namespace std;

const int SIZE = 3;

class atype {
  int a[SIZE];
public:
  atype() {
    register int i;

    for(i=0; i<SIZE; i++) a[i] = i;
  }
  int &operator[](int i);
};

// Provide range checking for atype.
int &atype::operator[](int i)
{
  if(i<0 || i> SIZE-1) {
    cout << "\nIndex value of ";
    cout << i << " is out-of-bounds.\n";
    exit(1);
  }
  return a[i];
}

int main()
{
  atype ob;

  cout << ob[2];  // displays 2
  cout << " ";

  ob[2] = 25;  // [] appears on left

  cout << ob[2];  // displays 25

  ob[3] = 44; // generates runtime error, 3 out-of-range
  return 0;
}
```

The program displays the following output.

```
2 25
Index value of 3 is out-of-bounds.
```

When the statement

```
ob[3] = 44;
```

executes, the boundary error is intercepted by **operator[ ]( )**, and the program is terminated before any damage can be done.

13

Overloading ( )

Perhaps the most intriguing operator that you can overload is **( )**, the function call operator. When you overload **( )**, you are not creating a new way to call a function. Rather, you are creating an **operator** function that can be passed an arbitrary number of parameters. Let's begin with an example. Given the overloaded **operator** function declaration

```
int operator()(float f, char *p);
```

and an object **Ob** of its **class**, then the statement

```
Ob(99.57, "overloading");
```

translates into this call to the **operator( )** function:

```
operator()(99.57, "overloading");
```

In general, when you overload the **( )** operator, you define the parameters that you want to pass to that function. When you use the **( )** operator in your program, the arguments you specify are copied to those parameters. As always, the object that generates the call (**Ob** in this example) is pointed to by the **this** pointer.

Here is an example of overloading **( )** relative to the **three_d** class. It creates a new **three_d** object whose coordinates are the sums of the calling object's coordinates and the values passed as arguments.

```
// Overload ().
#include <iostream>
using namespace std;

class three_d {
  int x, y, z; // 3-D coordinates
public:
  three_d() { x = y = z = 0; }
  three_d(int i, int j, int k) {x = i; y = j; z = k; }
  three_d operator()(int a, int b, int c);
  void show() ;
};

// Overload ().
three_d three_d::operator()(int a, int b, int c)
{
  three_d temp;

  temp.x = x + a;
  temp.y = y + b;
  temp.z = z + c;

  return temp;
}
```

```
// Show X, Y, Z coordinates.
void three_d::show()
{
  cout << x << ", ";
  cout << y << ", ";
  cout << z << "\n";
}

int main()
{
  three_d ob1(1, 2, 3), ob2;

  ob2 = ob1(10, 11, 12); // invoke operator()

  cout << "ob1: ";
  ob1.show();

  cout << "ob2: ";
  ob2.show();

  return 0;
}
```

The output produced by this program is shown here:

```
ob1: 1, 2, 3
ob2: 11, 13, 15
```

Remember, when overloading **( )**, you can use any type of parameters and return any type of value. These types will be dictated by the demands of your programs.

Overloading Other Operators

Except for **new**, **delete**, **–>**, **–>***, and the comma operators, the other C++ operators are overloaded in the same way as those shown in the preceding examples. Overloading **new** and **delete** requires special techniques, a complete description of which is found in Chapter 17, where exception handling is discussed. The **–>**, **–>***, and comma are specialty operators that are beyond the scope of this book. The interested reader is directed to my book, *C++: The Complete Reference* (McGraw-Hill/Osborne), for additional examples of operator overloading.

Another Example of Operator Overloading

13

To close this chapter, we will develop what is often considered to be the quintessential example of operator overloading: a string class. Even though C++'s approach to strings—implemented as null-terminated character arrays rather than as a type unto themselves—is both efficient and flexible, to beginners it can still lack the conceptual clarity of the way strings are implemented in languages such as BASIC. Of course, this situation is easily addressed because it is possible to define a string class that implements strings in a manner somewhat like that provided by other computer languages. In fact, in the early days of C++, implementing a string class was a common pastime for programmers. Although Standard C++ now defines a string class, which is described later in this book, it is still fun to implement a simple one on your own. Doing so illustrates the power of operator overloading.

To begin, the following class declares the type **str_type**:

```
#include <iostream>
#include <cstring>
using namespace std;

class str_type {
  char string[80];
public:
  str_type(char *str = "") { strcpy(string, str); }

  str_type operator+(str_type str); // concatenate
  str_type operator=(str_type str); // assign

  // output the string
  void show_str() { cout << string; }
};
```

As you can see, **str_type** declares a private character array called **string**, which will be used to hold the string. For the sake of this example, no string can be longer than 79 bytes. A real-world string class would allocate strings dynamically, and would not have this restriction. Also, to keep the logic of this example clear, no checking for boundary errors is provided by this class, or by any of the subsequent functions. Of course, full error checking would be required by any real-world implementation.

The class has one constructor, which can be used to initialize the array **string** with a specific value or to assign it a null string in the absence of any initializer. The class also declares two overloaded operators, which perform concatenation and assignment. Finally, it declares the function **show_str( )**, which outputs **string** to the screen.

The overloaded operator functions are shown here:

```
// Concatenate two strings.
str_type str_type::operator+(str_type str) {
  str_type temp;

  strcpy(temp.string, string);
  strcat(temp.string, str.string);
  return temp;
}

// Assign one string to another.
str_type str_type::operator=(str_type str) {
  strcpy(string, str.string);
  return *this;
}
```

Given these definitions, the following **main( )** illustrates their use:

```
int main()
{
  str_type a("Hello "), b("There"), c;

  c = a + b;

  c.show_str();

  return 0;
}
```

This program outputs **Hello There** on the screen. It first concatenates **a** with **b**, and then assigns the resulting value to **c**.

Keep in mind that both the **=** and the **+** are defined only for objects of type **str_type**. For example, the following statement is invalid because it tries to assign object **a** a null-terminated string:

```
a = "this is currently wrong";
```

However, the **str_type** class can be enhanced to allow such a statement, as you will see next.

To expand the types of operations supported by the **str_type** class so that you can assign null-terminated strings to **str_type** objects, or concatenate a null-terminated string with a **str_type** object, you will need to overload the **+** and **=** operations a second time. First, the class declaration must be changed, as shown here:

```
class str_type {
  char string[80];
public:
  str_type(char *str = "") { strcpy(string, str); }

  str_type operator+(str_type str); // concatenate str_type objects
  str_type operator+(char *str); /* concatenate str_type object
                                    with a null-terminated string */

  str_type operator=(str_type str); /* assign one str_type object
                                        to another */
  char *operator=(char *str); /* assign null-terminated string
                                 to str_type object */

  void show_str() { cout << string; }
};
```

Next, the overloaded **operator+( )** and **operator=( )** are implemented, as shown here:

```
// Assign a null-terminated string to an str_type object.
str_type str_type::operator=(char *str)
{
  str_type temp;
```

13

```
  strcpy(string, str);
  strcpy(temp.string, string);
  return temp;
}

// Add a null-terminated string to an str_type object.
str_type str_type::operator+(char *str)
{
  str_type temp;

  strcpy(temp.string, string);
  strcat(temp.string, str);
  return temp;
}
```

Look carefully at these functions. Notice that the right-side argument is not an object of type **str_type**, but simply a pointer to a null-terminated character array—that is, a normal C++ string. However, both functions return an object of type **str_type**. Although the functions could, in theory, return some other type, it makes the most sense to return a **str_type** object, since the targets of these operations are also **str_type** objects. The advantage to defining a string operation that accepts a null-terminated string as the right-side operand is that it allows you to write certain statements in a natural way. For example, these are now valid statements:

```
str_type a, b, c;
a = "hi there"; // assign a null-terminated string to an object

c = a + " George"; /* concatenate an object with a
                       null-terminated string */
```

The following program incorporates the additional meanings of the **+** and **=** operators:

```
// Expanding the string type.
#include <iostream>
#include <cstring>
using namespace std;

class str_type {
  char string[80];
public:
  str_type(char *str = "") { strcpy(string, str); }

  str_type operator+(str_type str);
  str_type operator+(char *str);

  str_type operator=(str_type str);
  str_type operator=(char *str);

  void show_str() { cout << string; }
} ;
```

```
str_type str_type::operator+(str_type str) {
  str_type temp;

  strcpy(temp.string, string);
  strcat(temp.string, str.string);
  return temp;
}

str_type str_type::operator=(str_type str) {
  strcpy(string, str.string);
  return *this;
}

str_type str_type::operator=(char *str)
{
  str_type temp;

  strcpy(string, str);
  strcpy(temp.string, string);
  return temp;
}

str_type str_type::operator+(char *str)
{
  str_type temp;

  strcpy(temp.string, string);
  strcat(temp.string, str);
  return temp;
}

int main()
{
  str_type a("Hello "), b("There"), c;

  c = a + b;

  c.show_str();
  cout << "\n";

  a = "to program in because";
  a.show_str();
  cout << "\n";

  b = c = "C++ is fun";

  c = c+" "+a+" "+b;
  c.show_str();

  return 0;
}
```

This program displays this on the screen:

```
Hello There
to program in because
C++ is fun to program in because C++ is fun
```

Before continuing, you should make sure that you understand how this output is created. On your own, try creating other string operations. For example, you might try defining the – so that it performs a substring deletion. For example, if object **A**'s string is "This is a test" and object **B**'s string is "is", then **A–B** yields "th a test". In this case, all occurrences of the substring are removed from the original string. Also, define a friend function that allows a null-terminated string to appear on the left side of the + operator. Finally, add all necessary error checking.

T IP: You will want to experiment with operator overloading relative to classes that you create. As the examples in this chapter have shown, you can use operator overloading to add new data types to your programming environment. This is one of C++'s most powerful features.

CHAPTER 14

Inheritance

Inheritance is one of the cornerstones of OOP because it allows the creation of hierarchical classifications. With inheritance, it is possible to create a general class that defines traits common to a set of related items. This class may then be inherited by other, more specific classes, each adding only those things that are unique to the inheriting class.

In standard C++ terminology, a class that is inherited is referred to as a *base class*. The class that does the inheriting is called the *derived class*. Further, a derived class can be used as a base class for another derived class. In this way, a multilayered class hierarchy can be achieved.

Introducing Inheritance

A base class is inherited by a derived class.

C++ supports inheritance by allowing one class to incorporate another class into its declaration. Before discussing the theory and details, let's begin with an example of inheritance. The following class, called **road_vehicle**, very broadly defines vehicles that travel on the road. It stores the number of wheels a vehicle has and the number of passengers it can carry.

```
class road_vehicle {
  int wheels;
  int passengers;
public:
  void set_wheels(int num) { wheels = num; }
  int get_wheels() { return wheels; }
  void set_pass(int num) { passengers = num; }
  int get_pass() { return passengers; }
};
```

You can use this broad definition of a road vehicle to help define specific types of vehicles. For example, the fragment shown here inherits **road_vehicle** to create a class called **truck**.

```
class truck : public road_vehicle {
  int cargo;
public:
  void set_cargo(int size) { cargo = size; }
  int get_cargo() { return cargo; }
  void show();
};
```

Because **truck** inherits **road_vehicle**, **truck** includes all of **road_vehicle**. It then adds **cargo** to it, along with the supporting member functions.

Notice how **road_vehicle** is inherited. The general form for inheritance is shown here:

```
class derived-class : access base-class {
  body of new class
}
```

Here, *access* is optional. However, if present, it must be either **public**, **private**, or **protected**. You will learn more about these options later in this chapter. For now, all inherited classes will use **public**. Using **public** means that all the public members of the base class will also be public members of the derived class. Therefore, in the preceding example, members of **truck** have access to the public member functions of **road_vehicle**, just as if they had been declared inside **truck**. However, **truck** *does not* have access to the private members of **road_vehicle**. For example, **truck** does not have access to **wheels**.

Here is a program that uses inheritance to create two subclasses of **road_vehicle**. One is **truck** and the other is **automobile**.

```cpp
// Demonstrate inheritance.
#include <iostream>
using namespace std;

// Define a base class for vehicles.
class road_vehicle {
  int wheels;
  int passengers;
public:
  void set_wheels(int num) { wheels = num; }
  int get_wheels() { return wheels; }
  void set_pass(int num) { passengers = num; }
  int get_pass() { return passengers; }
};

// Define a truck.
class truck : public road_vehicle {
  int cargo;
public:
  void set_cargo(int size) { cargo = size; }
  int get_cargo() { return cargo; }
  void show();
};

enum type {car, van, wagon};

// Define an automoble.
class automobile : public road_vehicle {
  enum type car_type;
public:
  void set_type(type t) { car_type = t; }
  enum type get_type() { return car_type; }
  void show();
};

void truck::show()
{
  cout << "wheels: " << get_wheels() << "\n";
  cout << "passengers: " << get_pass() << "\n";
  cout << "cargo capacity in cubic feet: " << cargo << "\n";
}
```

14

```
void automobile::show()
{
  cout << "wheels: " << get_wheels() << "\n";
  cout << "passengers: " << get_pass() << "\n";
  cout << "type: ";
  switch(get_type()) {
    case van: cout << "van\n";
      break;
    case car: cout << "car\n";
      break;
    case wagon: cout << "wagon\n";
  }
}

int main()
{
  truck t1, t2;
  automobile c;

  t1.set_wheels(18);
  t1.set_pass(2);
  t1.set_cargo(3200);

  t2.set_wheels(6);
  t2.set_pass(3);
  t2.set_cargo(1200);

  t1.show();
  cout << "\n";
  t2.show();
  cout << "\n";

  c.set_wheels(4);
  c.set_pass(6);
  c.set_type(van);

  c.show();

  return 0;
}
```

The output from this program is shown here:

```
wheels: 18
passengers: 2
cargo capacity in cubic feet: 3200

wheels: 6
passengers: 3
cargo capacity in cubic feet: 1200

wheels: 4
passengers: 6
type: van
```

As this program shows, the major advantage of inheritance is that it lets you create a base class that can be incorporated into more specific classes. In this way, each derived class can be precisely tailored to its own needs while still being part of a general classification.

One other point: Notice that both **truck** and **automobile** include a member function called **show( )**, which displays information about each object. This illustrates another aspect of polymorphism. Since each **show( )** is linked with its own class, the compiler can easily tell which one to call for any given object.

Now that you have seen the basic procedure by which one class inherits another, let's examine inheritance in detail.

Base Class Access Control

When one class inherits another, the members of the base class become members of the derived class. The access status of the base class members inside the derived class is determined by the access specifier used for inheriting the base class. The base class access specifier must be **public**, **private**, or **protected**. If the access specifier is not used, then it is **private** by default if the derived class is a **class**. If the derived class is a **struct**, then **public** is the default in the absence of an explicit access specifier. Let's examine the ramifications of using **public** or **private** access. (The **protected** specifier is described in the next section.)

When a base class is inherited as **public**, its public members become public members of the derived class.

When a base class is inherited as **public**, all public members of the base class become public members of the derived class. In all cases, the private elements of the base class remain private to that class, and are not accessible by members of the derived class. For example, in the following program, the public members of **base** become public members of **derived**. Thus, they are accessible by other parts of the program.

```
#include <iostream>
using namespace std;

class base {
  int i, j;
public:
  void set(int a, int b) { i = a; j = b; }
  void show() { cout << i << " " << j << "\n"; }
};

class derived : public base {
  int k;
public:
  derived(int x) { k = x; }
  void showk() { cout << k << "\n"; }
};

int main()
{
  derived ob(3);
```

14

```
  ob.set(1, 2); // access member of base
  ob.show();    // access member of base

  ob.showk();   // uses member of derived class

  return 0;
}
```

Since **set( )** and **show( )** are inherited as **public**, they can be called on an object of type **derived** from within **main( )**. Since **i** and **j** are specified as **private**, they remain private to **base**.

When a base class is inherited as **private**, its public members become private members of the derived class.

The opposite of public inheritance is private inheritance. When the base class is inherited as **private**, then all public members of the base class become private members of the derived class. For example, the program shown next will not compile, because both **set( )** and **show( )** are now private members of **derived**, and thus cannot be called from **main( )**.

```
// This program won't compile.
#include <iostream>
using namespace std;

class base {
  int i, j;
public:
  void set(int a, int b) { i = a; j = b; }
  void show() { cout << i << " " << j << "\n"; }
};

// Public elements of base are private in derived.
class derived : private base {
  int k;
public:
  derived(int x) { k = x; }
  void showk() { cout << k << "\n"; }
};

int main()
{
  derived ob(3);

  ob.set(1, 2); // Error, can't access set()
  ob.show();    // Error, can't access show()

  return 0;
}
```

The key point to remember is that when a base class is inherited as **private**, public members of the base class become private members of the derived class. This means that they are still accessible by members of the derived class, but cannot be accessed by other parts of your program.

Using protected Members

In addition to public and private, a class member can be declared as protected. Further, a base class can be inherited as protected. Both of these actions are accomplished by using the **protected** access specifier. The **protected** keyword is included in C++ to provide greater flexibility for the inheritance mechanism.

When a member of a class is declared as **protected**, that member is not accessible to other, non-member elements of the program. With one important exception, access to a protected member is the same as access to a private member; it can be accessed only by other members of the class of which it is a part. The sole exception to this rule is when a protected member is inherited. In this case, a protected member differs substantially from a private one.

The **protected** access specifier declares protected members or inherits a protected class.

As you know, a private member of a base class is not accessible by any other part of your program, including any derived class. However, protected members behave differently. When a base class is inherited as public, protected members in the base class become protected members of the derived class, and *are* accessible to the derived class. Therefore, by using **protected**, you can create class members that are private to their class, but that can still be inherited and accessed by a derived class.

Consider this sample program:

```
#include <iostream>
using namespace std;

class base {
protected:
  int i, j; // private to base, but accessible to derived
public:
  void set(int a, int b) { i = a; j = b; }
  void show() { cout << i << " " << j << "\n"; }
};

class derived : public base {
  int k;
public:
  // derived may access base's i and j
  void setk() { k = i*j; }

  void showk() { cout << k << "\n"; }
};

int main()
{
  derived ob;

  ob.set(2, 3); // OK, known to derived
  ob.show();    // OK, known to derived
```

14

```
  ob.setk();
  ob.showk();

  return 0;
}
```

Here, because **base** is inherited by **derived** as public, and because **i** and **j** are declared as protected, **derived**'s function **setk( )** may access them. If **i** and **j** were declared as private by **base**, then **derived** would not have access to them, and the program would not compile.

REMEMBER: The **protected** *specifier* allows you to create a class member that is accessible within a class hierarchy, but is otherwise private.

When a derived class is used as a base class for another derived class, then any protected member of the initial base class that is inherited (as public) by the first derived class can be inherited again, as a protected member, by a second derived class. For example, the following program is correct, and **derived2** does, indeed, have access to **i** and **j**:

```
#include <iostream>
using namespace std;

class base {
protected:
  int i, j;
public:
  void set(int a, int b) { i = a; j = b; }
  void show() { cout << i << " " << j << "\n"; }
};

// i and j inherited as protected.
class derived1 : public base {
  int k;
public:
  void setk() { k = i*j; } // legal
  void showk() { cout << k << "\n"; }
};

// i and j inherited indirectly through derived1.
class derived2 : public derived1 {
  int m;
public:
  void setm() { m = i-j; } // legal
  void showm() { cout << m << "\n"; }
};

int main()
{
```

```
    derived1 ob1;
    derived2 ob2;

    ob1.set(2, 3);
    ob1.show();
    ob1.setk();
    ob1.showk();

    ob2.set(3, 4);
    ob2.show();
    ob2.setk();
    ob2.setm();
    ob2.showk();
    ob2.showm();

    return 0;
}
```

When a base class is inherited as private, protected members of the base class become private members of the derived class. Therefore, in the preceding example, if **base** were inherited as private, then all members of **base** would become private members of **derived1**, meaning that they would not be accessible to **derived2**. (However, **i** and **j** would still be accessible to **derived1**.) This situation is illustrated by the following program, which is in error (and won't compile). The comments describe each error.

```
// This program won't compile.
#include <iostream>
using namespace std;

class base {
protected:
  int i, j;
public:
  void set(int a, int b) { i = a; j = b; }
  void show() { cout << i << " " << j << "\n"; }
};

// Now, all elements of base are private in derived1.
class derived1 : private base {
  int k;
public:
  // This is legal because i and j are private to derived1.
  void setk() { k = i*j; }   // OK
  void showk() { cout << k << "\n"; }
};

// Access to i, j, set(), and show() not inherited.
class derived2 : public derived1 {
  int m;
public:
  // Illegal because i and j are private to derived1.
```

14

```
  void setm() { m = i-j; }  // error
  void showm() { cout << m << "\n"; }
};

int main()
{
  derived1 ob1;
  derived2 ob2;

  ob1.set(1, 2); // Error, can't use set()
  ob1.show();    // Error, can't use show()

  ob2.set(3, 4); // Error, can't use set()
  ob2.show();    // Error, can't use show()

  return 0;
}
```

Even though **base** is inherited as private by **derived1**, **derived1** still has access to the public and protected elements of **base**. However, it cannot pass this privilege along. This is the reason that **protected** is part of the C++ language. It provides a means of protecting certain members from being modified by non-member functions, but allows them to be inherited.

The **protected** specifier can also be used with structures. It cannot be used with a union, however, because a union cannot inherit another class or be inherited. (Some compilers will accept its use in a union declaration, but because unions cannot participate in inheritance, **protected** is the same as **private** in this context.)

The **protected** access specifier may occur anywhere in a class declaration, although typically it occurs after the (default) private members are declared, and before the public members. Thus, the most common full form of a class declaration is

```
class class-name {
  private members
protected:
  protected members
public:
  public members
};
```

Of course, the protected category is optional.

Using protected for Inheritance of a Base Class

In addition to specifying protected status for members of a class, the keyword **protected** can also be used to inherit a base class. When a base class is inherited as protected, all public and protected members of the base class become protected members of the derived class. Here is an example:

```cpp
// Demonstrate inheriting a protected base class.
#include <iostream>
using namespace std;

class base {
  int i;
protected:
  int j;
public:
  int k;
  void seti(int a) { i = a; }
  int geti() { return i; }
};

// Inherit base as protected.
class derived : protected base {
public:
  void setj(int a) { j = a; } // j is protected here
  void setk(int a) { k = a; } // k is also protected
  int getj() { return j; }
  int getk() { return k; }
};

int main()
{
  derived ob;

  /* This next line is illegal because seti() is
     a protected member of derived, which makes it
     inaccessible outside of derived. */
//  ob.seti(10);

//  cout << ob.geti(); // illegal -- geti() is protected
//  ob.k = 10; // also illegal because k is protected

  // these next statements are OK
  ob.setk(10);
  cout << ob.getk() << ' ';
  ob.setj(12);
  cout << ob.getj() << ' ';

  return 0;
}
```

As you can see by reading the comments in this program, **k**, **j**, **seti( )**, and **geti( )** in **base** become **protected** members of **derived**. This means that they cannot be accessed by code outside of **derived**. Thus, inside **main( )**, references to these members through **ob** are illegal.

14

IN DEPTH

Reviewing public, protected, and private

Because the access rights as defined by **public**, **protected**, and **private** are fundamental to C++ programming, let's review their meanings.

When a class member is declared as **public**, it can be accessed by any other part of a program. When a member is declared as **private**, it can be accessed only by members of its class. Further, derived classes do not have access to private base class members. When a member is declared as **protected**, it can be accessed only by members of its class, or by derived classes. Thus, **protected** allows a member to be inherited, but to remain private within a class hierarchy.

When a base class is inherited by use of **public**, its public members become public members of the derived class, and its protected members become protected members of the derived class.

When a base class is inherited by use of **protected**, its public and protected members become protected members of the derived class.

When a base class is inherited by use of **private**, its public and protected members become private members of the derived class.

In all cases, private members of a base class remain private to the base class, and are not inherited.

As you become more familiar with C++, the meaning of **public**, **protected**, and **private** will become second nature. For now, if you are unsure what precise effect an access specifier has, write a short sample program as an experiment and observe the results.

Inheriting Multiple Base Classes

It is possible for a derived class to inherit two or more base classes. For example, in this short program, **derived** inherits both **base1** and **base2**:

```
// An example of multiple base classes.
#include <iostream>
using namespace std;

class base1 {
protected:
  int x;
public:
  void showx() { cout << x << "\n"; }
};
```

```
class base2 {
protected:
  int y;
public:
  void showy() { cout << y << "\n"; }
};

// Inherit multiple base classes.
class derived: public base1, public base2 {
public:
  void set(int i, int j) { x = i; y = j; }
};

int main()
{
  derived ob;

  ob.set(10, 20); // provided by derived
  ob.showx();     // from base1
  ob.showy();     // from base2

  return 0;
}
```

As this example illustrates, to cause more than one base class to be inherited, you must use a comma-separated list. Further, be sure to use an access specifier for each base class inherited.

Constructors, Destructors, and Inheritance

There are two important questions that arise relative to constructors and destructors when inheritance is involved. First, when are base class and derived class constructors and destructors called? Second, how can parameters be passed to a base class constructor? This section answers these questions.

When Constructors and Destructors Are Executed

It is possible for a base class, a derived class, or both, to contain a constructor and/or destructor. It is important to understand the order in which these are executed when an object of a derived class comes into existence and when it goes out of existence.

Examine this short program:

```
#include <iostream>
using namespace std;

class base {
public:
  base() { cout << "Constructing base\n"; }
  ~base() { cout << "Destructing base\n"; }
};
```

14

```
class derived: public base {
public:
  derived() { cout << "Constructing derived\n"; }
  ~derived() { cout << "Destructing derived\n"; }
};

int main()
{
  derived ob;

  // do nothing but construct and destruct ob

  return 0;
}
```

As the comment in **main( )** indicates, this program simply constructs and then destroys an object called **ob**, which is of class **derived**. When executed, this program displays:

```
Constructing base
Constructing derived
Destructing derived
Destructing base
```

As you can see, the constructor of **base** is executed, followed by the constructor of **derived**. Next (since **ob** is immediately destroyed in this program), the destructor of **derived** is called, followed by that of **base**.

Constructors are called in order of derivation. Destructors are called in reverse order.

The results of the foregoing experiment can be generalized as follows: When an object of a derived class is created, the base class constructor is called first, followed by the constructor for the derived class. When a derived object is destroyed, its destructor is called first, followed by the destructor for the base class. Put differently, constructors are executed in the order of their derivation. Destructors are executed in reverse order of derivation.

If you think about it, it makes sense that constructor functions are executed in the order of their derivation. Because a base class has no knowledge of any derived class, any initialization it needs to perform is separate from, and possibly prerequisite to, any initialization performed by the derived class. Therefore, it must be executed first.

Likewise, it is quite sensible that destructors be executed in reverse order of derivation. Since the base class underlies a derived class, the destruction of the base class implies the destruction of the derived class. Therefore, the derived destructor must be called before the object is fully destroyed.

In the case of a large class hierarchy (i.e., where a derived class becomes the base class for another derived class), the general rule applies: Constructors are called in order of derivation, destructors in reverse order. For example, this program

```
#include <iostream>
using namespace std;

class base {
public:
```

```
    base() { cout << "Constructing base\n"; }
    ~base() { cout << "Destructing base\n"; }
};

class derived1 : public base {
public:
    derived1() { cout << "Constructing derived1\n"; }
    ~derived1() { cout << "Destructing derived1\n"; }
};

class derived2: public derived1 {
public:
    derived2() { cout << "Constructing derived2\n"; }
    ~derived2() { cout << "Destructing derived2\n"; }
};

int main()
{
    derived2 ob;

    // construct and destruct ob

    return 0;
}
```

displays this output:

```
Constructing base
Constructing derived1
Constructing derived2
Destructing derived2
Destructing derived1
Destructing base
```

The same general rule applies in situations involving multiple base classes. For example, this program

```
#include <iostream>
using namespace std;

class base1 {
public:
    base1() { cout << "Constructing base1\n"; }
    ~base1() { cout << "Destructing base1\n"; }
};

class base2 {
public:
    base2() { cout << "Constructing base2\n"; }
    ~base2() { cout << "Destructing base2\n"; }
};
```

14

```
class derived: public base1, public base2 {
public:
  derived() { cout << "Constructing derived\n"; }
  ~derived() { cout << "Destructing derived\n"; }
};

int main()
{
  derived ob;

  // construct and destruct ob

  return 0;
}
```

produces this output:

```
Constructing base1
Constructing base2
Constructing derived
Destructing derived
Destructing base2
Destructing base1
```

As you can see, constructors are called in order of derivation, left to right, as specified in **derived**'s inheritance list. Destructors are called in reverse order, right to left. This means that if **base2** were specified before **base1** in **derived**'s list, as shown here:

```
class derived: public base2, public base1 {
```

then the output of the preceding program would look like this:

```
Constructing base2
Constructing base1
Constructing derived
Destructing derived
Destructing base1
Destructing base2
```

Passing Parameters to Base Class Constructors

So far, none of the preceding examples have included constructors requiring arguments. In cases where only the constructor of the derived class requires one or more arguments, you simply use the standard parameterized constructor syntax. But how do you pass arguments to a constructor in a base class? The answer is to use an expanded form of the derived class' constructor declaration, which passes arguments along to one or more base class constructors. The general form of this expanded declaration is shown here:

$$derived\text{-}constructor(arg\text{-}list) : base1(arg\text{-}list),$$
$$base2(arg\text{-}list), \ldots$$
$$baseN(arg\text{-}list);$$

```
{
    body of derived constructor
}
```

Here, *base1* through *baseN* are the names of the base classes inherited by the derived class. Notice that a colon separates the constructor declaration of the derived class from the base classes, and that the base classes are separated from each other by commas, in the case of multiple base classes.

Consider this sample program:

```
#include <iostream>
using namespace std;

class base {
protected:
  int i;
public:
  base(int x) { i = x; cout << "Constructing base\n"; }
  ~base() { cout << "Destructing base\n"; }
};

class derived: public base {
  int j;
public:
  // derived uses x; y is passed along to base.
  derived(int x, int y): base(y)
    { j = x; cout << "Constructing derived\n"; }

  ~derived() { cout << "Destructing derived\n"; }
  void show() { cout << i << " " << j << "\n"; }
};

int main()
{
  derived ob(3, 4);

  ob.show();  // displays 4 3

  return 0;
}
```

Here, **derived**'s constructor is declared as taking two parameters, **x** and **y**. However, **derived( )** uses only **x**; **y** is passed along to **base( )**. In general, the constructor of the derived class must declare the parameter(s) that its class requires, as well as any required by the base class. As the preceding example illustrates, any parameters required by the base class are passed to it in the base class' argument list, specified after the colon.

14

Here is a sample program that uses multiple base classes:

```
#include <iostream>
using namespace std;

class base1 {
protected:
  int i;
public:
  base1(int x) { i = x; cout << "Constructing base1\n"; }
  ~base1() { cout << "Destructing base1\n"; }
};

class base2 {
protected:
  int k;
public:
  base2(int x) { k = x; cout << "Constructing base2\n"; }
  ~base2() { cout << "Destructing base2\n"; }
};

class derived: public base1, public base2 {
  int j;
public:
  derived(int x, int y, int z): base1(y), base2(z)
    { j = x; cout << "Constructing derived\n"; }

  ~derived() { cout << "Destructing derived\n"; }
  void show() { cout << i << " " << j << " " << k << "\n"; }
};

int main()
{
  derived ob(3, 4, 5);

  ob.show();  // displays 4 3 5

  return 0;
}
```

It is important to understand that arguments to a base class constructor are passed via arguments to the derived class' constructor. Therefore, even if a derived class' constructor does not use any arguments, it still must declare one or more arguments if the base class takes one or more arguments. In this situation, the arguments passed to the derived class are simply passed along to the base. For example, in the following program, the constructor of **derived** takes no arguments, but **base1( )** and **base2( )** do:

```
#include <iostream>
using namespace std;

class base1 {
protected:
```

```
    int i;
public:
    base1(int x) { i=x; cout << "Constructing base1\n"; }
    ~base1() { cout << "Destructing base1\n"; }
};

class base2 {
protected:
    int k;
public:
    base2(int x) { k = x; cout << "Constructing base2\n"; }
    ~base2() { cout << "Destructing base2\n"; }
};

class derived: public base1, public base2 {
public:
    /* Derived constructor uses no parameters,
       but still must be declared as taking them to
       pass them along to base classes.
    */
    derived(int x, int y): base1(x), base2(y)
      { cout << "Constructing derived\n"; }

    ~derived() { cout << "Destructing derived\n"; }
    void show() { cout << i << " " << k << "\n"; }
};

int main()
{
    derived ob(3, 4);

    ob.show();  // displays 3 4

    return 0;
}
```

The constructor of a derived class is free to use any and all parameters that it is declared as taking, whether or not one or more are passed along to a base class. Put differently, just because an argument is passed along to a base class does not preclude its use by the derived class as well. For example, this fragment is perfectly valid:

```
class derived: public base {
    int j;
public:
    // derived uses both x and y, and also passes them to base.
    derived(int x, int y): base(x, y)
      { j = x*y; cout << "Constructing derived\n"; }
// ...
```

One final point to keep in mind when passing arguments to base class constructors: An argument being passed can consist of any expression valid at the time, including function calls and variables. This is in keeping with the fact that C++ allows dynamic initialization.

14

Granting Access

When a base class is inherited as private, all members of that class (public, protected, or private) become private members of the derived class. However, in certain circumstances, you may want to restore one or more inherited members to their original access specification. For example, you might want to grant certain public members of the base class public status in the derived class, even though the base class is inherited as private. You have two ways to accomplish this. First, you may use a **using** declaration within the derived class. This is the method recommended by Standard C++ for use in new code. However, a discussion of **using** is deferred until later in this book when namespaces are examined. (The primary reason for **using** is to provide support for namespaces.) The second way to adjust access to an inherited member is to employ an *access declaration*. Access declarations are still supported by Standard C++, but they have recently been deprecated, which means that they should not be used for new code. Since they are still used in existing code, a discussion of access declarations is presented here.

An access declaration takes this general form:

base-class::member;

The access declaration restores the access level of an inherited member to what it was in the base class.

The access declaration is put under the appropriate access heading in the derived class. Notice that no type declaration is required (or allowed) in an access declaration.

To see how an access declaration works, let's begin with this short fragment:

```
class base {
public:
  int j;  // public in base
};

// Inherit base as private.
class derived: private base {
public:

  // here is access declaration
  base::j; // make j public again
  // ...
};
```

Because **base** is inherited as private by **derived**, the public variable **j** is made a private variable of **derived**. However, the inclusion of this access declaration

```
base::j;
```

under **derived**'s public heading restores **j** to its public status.

You can use an access declaration to restore the access rights of public and protected members. However, you cannot use an access declaration to raise or lower a member's access status. For example, a member declared as private within a base class cannot be made public by a derived class. (Allowing this would destroy encapsulation!)

The following program illustrates the use of access declarations:

```cpp
#include <iostream>
using namespace std;

class base {
  int i;  // private to base
public:
  int j, k;
  void seti(int x) { i = x; }
  int geti() { return i; }
};

// Inherit base as private.
class derived: private base {
public:
  /* The next three statements override
     base's inheritance as private
     and restore j, seti() and geti() to
     public access. */
  base::j;    // make j public again - but not k
  base::seti; // make seti() public
  base::geti; // make geti() public

// base::i;   // illegal, you cannot elevate access

  int a; // public
};

int main()
{
  derived ob;

//ob.i = 10;   // illegal because i is private in derived

  ob.j = 20;   // legal because j is made public in derived
//ob.k = 30;   // illegal because k is private in derived

  ob.a = 40;   // legal because a is public in derived
  ob.seti(10);

  cout << ob.geti() << " " << ob.j << " " << ob.a;

  return 0;
}
```

Notice how this program uses access declarations to restore **j**, **seti( )**, and **geti( )** to public status. The comments describe various other access restrictions.

14

C++ provides the ability to adjust access to inherited members to accommodate those special situations in which most of an inherited class is intended to be made private, but a few members are to retain their public or protected status. It is best to use this feature sparingly.

Reading C++ Inheritance Graphs

Sometimes C++ class hierarchies are depicted graphically to make them easier to understand. However, due to a quirk in the way they are usually drawn by C++ programmers, class inheritance graphs are sometimes misleading to newcomers. For example, consider a situation in which class A is inherited by class B, which in turn is inherited by C. Using standard C++ graphic notation, this situation is drawn as shown here:

As you can see, the arrows point up, not down. While most people initially find the direction of the arrows to be counterintuitive, this is the style that most C++ programmers have adopted. In C++ style graphs, the arrow points to the base class. Thus, the arrow means "derived from," and not "deriving." Here is another example. Can you describe, in words what it means?

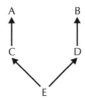

This graph states that class E is derived from both C and D. (That is, that E has multiple base classes, called C and D.) Further, C is derived from A, and D is derived from B.

While the direction of the arrows may be confusing at first, it is best that you become familiar with this style of graphic notation, since it is commonly used in books, magazines, and compiler documentation.

Virtual Base Classes

An element of ambiguity can be introduced into a C++ program when multiple base classes are inherited. Consider this incorrect program:

```
// This program contains an error and will not compile.
#include <iostream>
using namespace std;
```

```
class base {
public:
  int i;
};

// derived1 inherits base.
class derived1 :  public base {
public:
  int j;
};

// derived2 inherits base.
class derived2 : public base {
public:
  int k;
};

/* derived3 inherits both derived1 and derived2.
   This means that there are two copies of base
   in derived3! */
class derived3 : public derived1, public derived2 {
public:
  int sum;
};

int main()
{
  derived3 ob;

  ob.i = 10;   // this is ambiguous; which i???
  ob.j = 20;
  ob.k = 30;

  // i ambiguous here, too
  ob.sum = ob.i + ob.j + ob.k;

  // also ambiguous, which i?
  cout << ob.i << " ";

  cout << ob.j << " " << ob.k << " ";
  cout << ob.sum;

  return 0;
}
```

As the comments in this program indicate, both **derived1** and **derived2** inherit **base**. However, **derived3** inherits both **derived1** and **derived2**. As a result, there are two copies of **base** present in an object of type **derived3**, so that in an expression like

```
ob.i = 20;
```

which **i** is being referred to? The one in **derived1** or the one in **derived2**? Since there are two copies of **base** present in object **ob**, there are two **ob.i**s! As you can see, the statement is inherently ambiguous.

14

There are two ways to remedy the preceding program. The first is to apply the scope resolution operator to manually select one **i**. For example, the following version of the program will compile and run as expected:

```cpp
// This program uses explicit scope resolution to select i.
#include <iostream>
using namespace std;

class base {
public:
  int i;
};

// derived1 inherits base.
class derived1 :  public base {
public:
  int j;
};

// derived2 inherits base.
class derived2 : public base {
public:
  int k;
};

/* derived3 inherits both derived1 and derived2.
   This means that there are two copies of base
   in derived3! */
class derived3 : public derived1, public derived2 {
public:
  int sum;
};

int main()
{
  derived3 ob;

  ob.derived1::i = 10;  // scope resolved, use derived1's i
  ob.j = 20;
  ob.k = 30;

  // scope resolved
  ob.sum = ob.derived1::i + ob.j + ob.k;

  // also resolved here
  cout << ob.derived1::i << " ";

  cout << ob.j << " " << ob.k << " ";
  cout << ob.sum;

  return 0;
}
```

The inheritance of a base class as **virtual** ensures that only one copy of it will be present in any derived class.

By applying the **::**, the program manually selects **derived1**'s version of **base**. However, this solution raises a deeper issue: What if only one copy of **base** is actually required? Is there some way to prevent two copies from being included in **derived3**? The answer, as you probably have guessed, is yes. The solution is achieved with *virtual base classes*.

When two or more objects are derived from a common base class, you can prevent multiple copies of the base class from being present in an object derived from those classes, by declaring the base class as virtual when it is inherited. To do this, you precede the name of the base class with the keyword **virtual** when it is inherited.

To illustrate this process, here is another version of the sample program. This time, **derived3** contains only one copy of **base**.

```cpp
// This program uses virtual base classes.
#include <iostream>
using namespace std;

class base {
public:
  int i;
};

// derived1 inherits base as virtual.
class derived1 : virtual public base {
public:
  int j;
};

// derived2 inherits base as virtual.
class derived2 : virtual public base {
public:
  int k;
};

/* derived3 inherits both derived1 and derived2.
   This time, there is only one copy of base class. */
class derived3 : public derived1, public derived2 {
public:
  int sum;
};

int main()
{
  derived3 ob;

  ob.i = 10;  // now unambiguous
  ob.j = 20;
  ob.k = 30;

  // unambiguous
  ob.sum = ob.i + ob.j + ob.k;
```

14

```
  // unambiguous
  cout << ob.i << " ";

  cout << ob.j << " " << ob.k << " ";
  cout << ob.sum;

  return 0;
}
```

As you can see, the keyword **virtual** precedes the rest of the inherited class' specification. Now that both **derived1** and **derived2** have inherited **base** as virtual, any multiple inheritance involving them will cause only one copy of **base** to be present. Therefore, in **derived3** there is only one copy of **base**, and **ob.i = 10** is perfectly valid and unambiguous.

One further point to keep in mind: Even though both **derived1** and **derived2** specify **base** as virtual, **base** is still present in an object of either type. For example, the following sequence is perfectly valid:

```
// Define a class of type derived1.
derived1 myclass;

myclass.i = 88;
```

The difference between a normal base class and a virtual one becomes evident only when an object inherits the base class more than once. If the base class has been declared as virtual, then only one instance of it will be present in the inheriting object. Otherwise, multiple copies will be found.

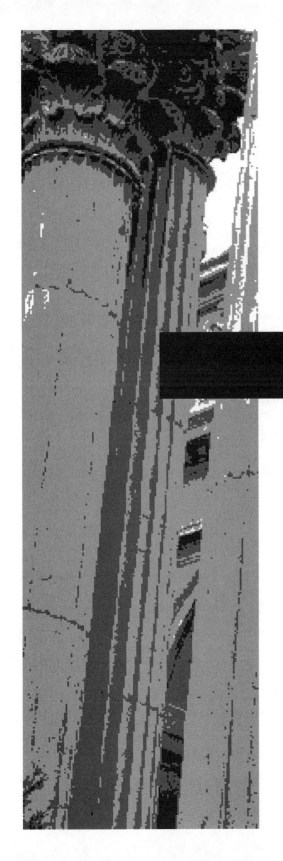

CHAPTER 15

Virtual Functions
and Polymorphism

One of the three major facets of object-oriented programming is polymorphism. As applied to C++, *polymorphism* is the term used to describe the process by which different implementations of a function can be accessed via the same name. For this reason, polymorphism is sometimes characterized by the phrase "one interface, multiple methods." This means that every member of a general class of operations can be accessed in the same fashion, even though the specific actions associated with each operation may differ.

In C++, polymorphism is supported both at run time and at compile time. Operator and function overloading are examples of compile-time polymorphism. As powerful as operator and function overloading are, they cannot perform all the tasks required by a true, object-oriented language. Therefore, C++ also allows run-time polymorphism through the use of derived classes and *virtual functions*, and these are the major topics of this chapter.

This chapter begins with a short discussion of pointers to derived types, because they provide support for run-time polymorphism.

Pointers to Derived Types

A base class pointer can point to any object derived from that base.

The foundation of run-time polymorphism is the base class pointer. Pointers to base classes and derived classes are related in ways that other types of pointers are not. As you learned earlier in this book, a pointer of one type generally cannot point to an object of another type. However, base class pointers and derived objects are the exceptions to this rule. In C++, a base class pointer may also be used to point to an object of any class derived from that base. For example, assume that you have a base class called **B_class** and a class called **D_class**, which is derived from **B_class**. In C++, any pointer declared as a pointer to **B_class** can also be a pointer to **D_class**. Therefore, given

```
B_class *p;    // pointer to object of type B_class
B_class B_ob;  // object of type B_class
D_class D_ob;  // object of type D_class
```

both of the following statements are perfectly valid:

```
p = &B_ob; // p points to object of type B_class
p = &D_ob; /* p points to object of type D_class,
              which is an object derived from B_class. */
```

In this example, **p** can be used to access all elements of **D_ob** inherited from **B_ob**. However, elements specific to **D_ob** cannot be referenced with **p**.

For a more concrete example, consider the following short program, which defines a base class called **B_class** and a derived class called **D_class**. This program uses a simple class hierarchy to store authors and titles.

```
// Using base pointers on derived class objects.
#include <iostream>
#include <cstring>
using namespace std;
```

```
class B_class {
  char author[80];
public:
  void put_author(char *s) { strcpy(author, s); }
  void show_author() { cout << author << "\n"; }
} ;

class D_class : public B_class {
  char title[80];
public:
  void put_title(char *num) {
    strcpy(title, num);
  }
  void show_title() {
    cout << "Title: ";
    cout <<  title << "\n";
  }
};

int main()
{
  B_class *p;
  B_class B_ob;

  D_class *dp;
  D_class D_ob;

  p = &B_ob;  // address of base

  // Access B_class via pointer.
  p->put_author("Tom Clancy");

  // Access D_class via base pointer.
  p = &D_ob;
  p->put_author("William Shakespeare");

  // Show that each author went into proper object.
  B_ob.show_author();
  D_ob.show_author();
  cout << "\n";

  /* Since put_title() and show_title() are not part
     of the base class, they are not accessible via
     the base pointer p and must be accessed either
     directly, or, as shown here, through a pointer to the
     derived type.
  */
  dp = &D_ob;
  dp->put_title("The Tempest");
  p->show_author(); // either p or dp can be used here.
  dp->show_title( );

  return 0;
}
```

15

This program displays the following:

```
Tom Clancy
William Shakespeare

William Shakespeare
Title: The Tempest
```

In this example, the pointer **p** is defined as a pointer to **B_class**. However, it can point to an object of the derived class **D_class** and can be used to access those elements of the derived class that are inherited from the base class. But remember, a base pointer cannot access those elements specific to the derived class. This is why **show_title( )** is accessed with the **dp** pointer, which is a pointer to the derived class.

If you want to access elements defined by a derived class by using a base class pointer, you must cast it into a pointer of the derived type. For example, this line of code will properly call the **show_title( )** function of **D_ob**:

```
((D_class *)p)->show_title();
```

The outer set of parentheses is necessary for associating the cast with **p** and not with the return type of **show_title( )**. While there is technically nothing wrong with casting a pointer in this manner, it is probably best avoided, because it simply adds confusion to your code. (Actually, most C++ programmers would consider this to be bad form.)

Another point to understand is that, while a base pointer can be used to point to any type of derived object, the reverse is not true. That is, you cannot access an object of the base type by using a pointer to a derived class.

A pointer is incremented and decremented relative to its base type. Therefore, when a base class pointer is pointing at a derived object, incrementing or decrementing it will *not* make it point to the next object of the derived class. Instead, it will point to (what it thinks is) the next object of the base class. Therefore, you should consider it invalid to increment or decrement a base class pointer when it is pointing to a derived object.

The fact that a pointer to a base type can be used to point to any object derived from that base is extremely important, and fundamental to C++. As you will soon learn, this flexibility is crucial to the way C++ implements run-time polymorphism.

References to Derived Types

Similar to the action of pointers just described, a base class reference can be used to refer to an object of a derived type. The most common application of this is found in function parameters. A base class reference parameter can receive objects of the base class as well as any other type derived from that base.

Virtual Functions

Run-time polymorphism is achieved through a combination of two features: inheritance and virtual functions. You learned about inheritance in the preceding chapter. Here, you will learn about the virtual function.

A *virtual function* is a function that is declared as **virtual** in a base class and redefined in one or more derived classes. Thus, each derived class can have its own version of a virtual function. What makes virtual functions interesting is what happens when one is called through a base class pointer (or reference). In this situation, C++ determines which version of the function to call based upon the *type* of the object *pointed to* by the pointer. And, this determination is made *at run time*. Thus, when different objects are pointed to, different versions of the virtual function are executed. In other words, it is the type of the object being pointed to (not the type of the pointer) that determines which version of the virtual function will be executed. Therefore, if a base class contains a virtual function, and if two or more different classes are derived from that base class, then when different types of objects are pointed to through a base class pointer, different versions of the virtual function are executed. The same thing occurs when using a base class reference.

You declare a function as virtual inside the base class by preceding its declaration with the keyword **virtual**. When a virtual function is redefined by a derived class, the keyword **virtual** need not be repeated (although it is not an error to do so).

A class that includes a virtual function is called a *polymorphic class*. This term also applies to a class that inherits a base class containing a virtual function.

Examine this short program, which demonstrates the use of virtual functions:

```
// A short example that uses virtual functions.
#include <iostream>
using namespace std;

class base {
public:
  virtual void who() { // specify a virtual
    cout << "Base\n";
  }
};

class first_d : public base {
public:
  void who() { // redefine who() relative to first_d
    cout << "First derivation\n";
  }
};

class second_d : public base {
public:
  void who() { // redefine who() relative to second_d
    cout << "Second derivation\n";
  }
};

int main()
{
  base base_obj;
  base *p;
```

15

```
    first_d first_obj;
    second_d second_obj;

    p = &base_obj;
    p->who();  // access base's who

    p = &first_obj;
    p->who(); // access first_d's who

    p = &second_obj;
    p->who();  // access second_d's who

    return 0;
}
```

This program produces the following output:

```
Base
First derivation
Second derivation
```

Let's examine the program in detail to understand how it works.

In **base**, the function **who( )** is declared as virtual. This means that the function can be redefined by a derived class. Inside both **first_d** and **second_d**, **who( )** is redefined relative to each class. Inside **main( )**, four variables are declared: **base_obj**, which is an object of type **base**; **p**, which is a pointer to **base** objects; and **first_obj** and **second_obj**, which are objects of the two derived classes. Next, **p** is assigned the address of **base_obj**, and the **who( )** function is called. Since **who( )** is declared as virtual, C++ determines, at run time, which version of **who( )** is referred to by the type of object pointed to by **p**. In this case, **p** points to an object of type **base**, so it is the version of **who( )** declared in **base** that is executed. Next, **p** is assigned the address of **first_obj**. Recall that a base class pointer can refer to an object of any derived class. Now, when **who( )** is called, C++ again checks to see what type of object is pointed to by **p** and, based on that type, determines which version of **who( )** to call. Since **p** points to an object of type **first_d**, that version of **who( )** is used. Likewise, when **p** is assigned the address of **second_obj**, the version of **who( )** declared inside **second_d** is executed.

REMEMBER: It is determined at run time which version of a virtual function actually gets called. Further, this determination is based solely upon the type of the object that is being pointed to by a base class pointer.

A virtual function can be called normally, with the standard object, dot-operator syntax. This means that in the preceding example, it would not be syntactically incorrect to access **who( )** by using this statement:

```
first_obj.who();
```

However, calling a virtual function in this manner ignores its polymorphic attributes. It is only when a virtual function is accessed through a base class pointer that run-time polymorphism is achieved.

When a virtual function is redefined in a derived class, it is said to be overridden.

At first, the redefinition of a virtual function in a derived class seems to be a special form of function overloading. However, this is not the case. In fact, the two processes are fundamentally different. First, an overloaded function must differ in its type and/or number of parameters, while a redefined virtual function must have exactly the same type and number of parameters. In fact, the prototypes for a virtual function and its redefinitions must be exactly the same. If the prototypes differ, then the function is simply considered to be overloaded, and its virtual nature is lost. Another restriction is that a virtual function must be a member, not a friend, of the class for which it is defined. However, a virtual function can be a friend of another class. Also, it is permissible for destructor functions to be virtual, but this is not so for constructors.

Because of the restrictions and differences between overloading normal functions and redefining virtual functions, the term *overriding* is used to describe the redefinition of a virtual function.

Virtual Functions Are Inherited

The virtual attribute is inherited.

Once a function is declared as virtual, it stays virtual no matter how many layers of derived classes it may pass through. For example, if **second_d** is derived from **first_d** instead of **base**, as shown in the next example, then **who( )** is still virtual and the proper version is still correctly selected:

```
// Derive from first_d, not base.
class second_d : public first_d {
public:
  void who() { // define who() relative to second_d
    cout << "Second derivation\n";
  }
};
```

When a derived class does not override a virtual function, then the function, as defined in the base class, is used. For example, try this version of the preceding program in which **second_d** doesn't override **who( )**.

```
#include <iostream>
using namespace std;

class base {
public:
  virtual void who() {
    cout << "Base\n";
  }
};

class first_d : public base {
public:
  void who() {
```

15

```
      cout << "First derivation\n";
  }
};

class second_d : public base {
// who() not defined
};

int main()
{
  base base_obj;
  base *p;
  first_d first_obj;
  second_d second_obj;

  p = &base_obj;
  p->who();  // access base's who()

  p = &first_obj;
  p->who(); // access first_d's who()

  p = &second_obj;
  p->who(); /* access base's who() because
               second_d does not redefine it */

  return 0;
}
```

The program now outputs the following:

```
Base
First derivation
Base
```

As the output confirms, because **who( )** is not overridden by **second_d**, when **p** points to **second_obj**, it is the version of **who( )** in **base** that is executed.

Keep in mind that inherited characteristics of **virtual** are hierarchical. Therefore, if the preceding example is changed such that **second_d** is derived from **first_d** instead of **base**, then when **who( )** is referenced relative to an object of type **second_d**, it is the version of **who( )** declared inside **first_d** that is called since it is the class closest to **second_d**, not the **who( )** inside **base**. The following program demonstrates this hierarchy.

```
#include <iostream>
using namespace std;

class base {
public:
  virtual void who() {
    cout << "Base\n";
  }
```

```
};

class first_d : public base {
public:
  void who() {
    cout << "First derivation\n";
  }
};

// second_d now inherited first_d -- not base.
class second_d : public first_d {
// who() not defined
};

int main()
{
  base base_obj;
  base *p;
  first_d first_obj;
  second_d second_obj;

  p = &base_obj;
  p->who();   // access base's who()

  p = &first_obj;
  p->who(); // access first_d's who()

  p = &second_obj;
  p->who(); /* access first_d's who() because
               second_d does not redefine it */

  return 0;
}
```

This program produces the following output:

```
Base
First derivation
First derivation
```

As you can see, **second_d** now uses **first_d**'s version of **who( )** because that version is closest in the inheritance chain.

Why Virtual Functions?

As stated at the beginning of this chapter, virtual functions in combination with derived types allow C++ to support run-time polymorphism. Polymorphism is essential to object-oriented programming for one reason: It allows a generalized class to specify those functions that will be common to all derivatives of that class, while allowing a derived class to define the specific implementation of some or all of those functions. Sometimes this idea is expressed as follows: The base class dictates the general *interface* that any object derived from that class will have, but lets the derived class define the

15

actual *method* used to implement that interface. This is why the phrase "one interface, multiple methods" is often used to describe polymorphism.

Part of the key to successfully applying polymorphism is understanding that the base and derived classes form a hierarchy, which moves from greater to lesser generalization (base to derived). When designed correctly, the base class provides all of the elements that a derived class can use directly. It also defines those functions that the derived class must implement on its own. This allows the derived class the flexibility to define its own methods, and yet still enforces a consistent interface. That is, since the form of the interface is defined by the base class, any derived class will share that common interface. Thus, the use of virtual functions makes it possible for the base class to define the generic interface that will be used by all derived classes.

At this point, you might be asking yourself why a consistent interface with multiple implementations is important. The answer, again, goes back to the central driving force behind object-oriented programming: It helps the programmer handle increasingly complex programs. For example, if you develop your program correctly, then you know that all objects you derive from a base class are accessed in the same general way, even if the specific actions vary from one derived class to the next. This means that you need to remember only one interface, rather than several. Also, your derived class is free to use any or all of the functionality provided by the base class. You need not reinvent those elements. Further, the separation of interface and implementation allows the creation of *class libraries,* which can be provided by a third party. If these libraries are implemented correctly, they will provide a common interface that you can use to derive classes of your own that meet your specific needs. For example, both the Microsoft Foundation Classes (MFC) and the newer .NET Framework Windows Forms class library support Windows programming. By using these classes, your program can inherit much of the functionality required by a Windows program. You need add only the features unique to your application. This is a major benefit when programming complex systems.

A Simple Application of Virtual Functions

To get an idea of the power of the "one interface, multiple methods" concept, examine the following short program. It creates a base class called **figure**. This class stores the dimensions of various two-dimensional objects and computes their areas. The function **set_dim( )** is a standard member function because this operation will be common to all derived classes. However, **show_area( )** is declared as virtual because the method of computing the area of each object will vary. The program uses **figure** to derive two specific classes called **rectangle** and **triangle**.

```
#include <iostream>
using namespace std;

class figure {
protected:
  double x, y;
public:
  void set_dim(double i, double j) {
    x = i;
    y = j;
  }
```

```
    virtual void show_area() {
      cout << "No area computation defined ";
      cout << "for this class.\n";
    }
} ;

class triangle : public figure {
  public:
    void show_area() {
      cout << "Triangle with height ";
      cout << x << " and base " << y;
      cout << " has an area of ";
      cout << x * 0.5 * y << ".\n";
    }
};

class rectangle : public figure {
  public:
    void show_area() {
      cout << "Rectangle with dimensions ";
      cout << x << " x " << y;
      cout << " has an area of ";
      cout << x *  y << ".\n";
    }
};

int main()
{
  figure *p; // create a pointer to base type

  triangle t; // create objects of derived types
  rectangle r;

  p = &t;
  p->set_dim(10.0, 5.0);
  p->show_area();

  p = &r;
  p->set_dim(10.0, 5.0);
  p->show_area();

  return 0;
}
```

The output is shown here.

```
Triangle with height 10 and base 5 has an area of 25.
Rectangle with dimensions 10 x 5 has an area of 50.
```

15

In the program, notice that the interface to both **rectangle** and **triangle** is the same, even though both provide their own methods for computing the area of each of their objects.

Given the declaration for **figure**, is it possible to derive a class called **circle** that will compute the area of a circle, given its radius? The answer is yes. All that you need to do is to create a new derived type that computes the area of a circle. The power of virtual functions is based in the fact that you can easily derive a new type that will still share a common interface with other related objects. For example, here is one way to do it:

```
class circle : public figure {
  public:
    void show_area() {
      cout << "Circle with radius ";
      cout << x;
      cout << " has an area of ";
      cout <<  3.14 * x * x;
    }
};
```

Before trying to use **circle**, look closely at the definition for **show_area( )**. Notice that it uses only the value of **x**, which is assumed to hold the radius. (Remember, the area of a circle is computed by using the formula πR^2.) However, the function **set_dim( )** as defined in **figure**, assumes that it will be passed two values, not just one. Since **circle** does not require this second value, what course of action can we take?

There are two ways to resolve this problem. First and worst, you could simply call **set_dim( )** using a dummy value as the second parameter when using a **circle** object. This has the disadvantage of being sloppy, along with requiring that you remember a special exception, which violates the "one interface, many methods" philosophy.

A better way to resolve the problem is to give the **y** parameter inside **set_dim( )** a default value. Then, when calling **set_dim( )** for a circle, you need specify only the radius. When calling **set_dim( )** for a triangle or a rectangle, you specify both values. The expanded program, which uses this method, is shown here:

```
#include <iostream>
using namespace std;

class figure {
protected:
  double x, y;
public:
  void set_dim(double i, double j=0) {
    x = i;
    y = j;
  }
  virtual void show_area() {
    cout << "No area computation defined ";
    cout << "for this class.\n";
  }
} ;
```

```
class triangle : public figure {
  public:
    void show_area() {
      cout << "Triangle with height ";
      cout << x << " and base " << y;
      cout << " has an area of ";
      cout << x * 0.5 * y << ".\n";
    }
};

class rectangle : public figure {
  public:
    void show_area() {
      cout << "Rectangle with dimensions ";
      cout << x << " x " << y;
      cout << " has an area of ";
      cout << x *  y << ".\n";
    }
};

class circle : public figure {
  public:
    void show_area() {
      cout << "Circle with radius ";
      cout << x;
      cout << " has an area of ";
      cout << 3.14 * x * x << ".\n";
    }
} ;

int main()
{
  figure *p; // create a pointer to base type

  triangle t; // create objects of derived types
  rectangle r;
  circle c;

  p = &t;
  p->set_dim(10.0, 5.0);
  p->show_area();

  p = &r;
  p->set_dim(10.0, 5.0);
  p->show_area();

  p = &c;
  p->set_dim(9.0);
  p->show_area();

  return 0;
}
```

15

This program produces the following output.

```
Triangle with height 10 and base 5 has an area of 25.
Rectangle with dimensions 10 x 5 has an area of 50.
Circle with radius 9 has an area of 254.34.
```

TIP: While virtual functions are syntactically easy to understand, their true power cannot be demonstrated in short examples. In general, polymorphism finds its greatest strength in large, complex systems. As you continue to use C++, opportunities to apply virtual functions will present themselves.

Pure Virtual Functions and Abstract Classes

As you have seen, when a virtual function that is not overridden in a derived class is called by an object of that derived class, the version of the function as defined in the base class is used. However, in many circumstances, there will be no meaningful definition of a virtual function inside the base class. For example, in the base class **figure** used in the preceding example, the definition of **show_area( )** is simply a place holder. It will not compute and display the area of any type of object. As you will see when you create your own class libraries, it is not uncommon for a virtual function to have no meaningful definition in the context of its base class.

A pure virtual function is a virtual function that has no definition in its base class.

When this situation occurs, there are two ways you can handle it. One way, as shown in the example, is to simply have the function report a warning message. While this approach can be useful in some situations, it will not be appropriate in most circumstances. For example, there may be virtual functions that simply must be defined by the derived class for the derived class to have any meaning. Consider the class **triangle**. It has no meaning if **show_area( )** is not defined. In this case, you want some method to ensure that a derived class does, indeed, define all necessary functions. In C++, the solution to this problem is the pure virtual function.

A *pure virtual function* is a function declared in a base class that has no definition relative to the base. As a result, any derived type must define its own version—it cannot simply use the version defined in the base. To declare a pure virtual function, use this general form:

virtual *type func-name(parameter-list)* = 0;

Here, *type* is the return type of the function, and *func-name* is the name of the function. It is the **= 0** that designates the virtual function as pure. For example, in the following version of **figure**, **show_area( )** is a pure virtual function:

```
class figure {
  double x, y;
public:
  void set_dim(double i, double j=0) {
    x = i;
    y = j;
  }
  virtual void show_area() = 0; // pure
};
```

By declaring a virtual function as pure, you force any derived class to define its own implementation. If a class fails to do so, the compiler will report an error. For example, try to compile this modified version of the figures program, in which the definition for **show_area( )** has been removed from the **circle** class:

```cpp
/*
   This program will not compile because the class
   circle does not override show_area().
*/
#include <iostream>
using namespace std;

class figure {
protected:
  double x, y;
public:
  void set_dim(double i, double j) {
    x = i;
    y = j;
  }
  virtual void show_area() = 0; // pure
} ;

class triangle : public figure {
  public:
    void show_area() {
      cout << "Triangle with height ";
      cout << x << " and base " << y;
      cout << " has an area of ";
      cout << x * 0.5 * y << ".\n";
    }
};

class rectangle : public figure {
  public:
    void show_area() {
      cout << "Rectangle with dimensions ";
      cout << x << "x" << y;
      cout << " has an area of ";
      cout << x *  y << ".\n";
    }
};

class circle : public figure {
// no definition of show_area() will cause an error
};

int main()
{
  figure *p; // create a pointer to base type

  triangle t; // create objects of derived types
```

15

```
      rectangle r;

      circle c; // Illegal -- can't create!

      p = &t;
      p->set_dim(10.0, 5.0);
      p->show_area();

      p = &r;
      p->set_dim(10.0, 5.0);
      p->show_area();

      return 0;
  }
```

A class that contains at least one pure virtual function is called an abstract class.

If a class has at least one pure virtual function, then that class is said to be *abstract*. An abstract class has one important feature: There can be no objects of that class. Instead, an abstract class must be used only as a base that other classes will inherit. The reason that an abstract class cannot be used to declare an object is, of course, that one or more of its functions have no definition. However, even if the base class is abstract, you still can use it to declare pointers or references, which are needed to support run-time polymorphism.

Early versus Late Binding

There are two terms that are commonly used when object-oriented programming languages are discussed: *early binding* and *late binding*. Relative to C++, these terms refer to events that occur at compile time and events that occur at run time, respectively.

Early binding resolves a function call at compile time. Late binding resolves a function call at run time.

Early binding means that a function call is resolved at compile time. That is, all information necessary to call a function is known when the program is compiled. Examples of early binding include standard function calls, overloaded function calls, and overloaded operator function calls. The principal advantage to early binding is efficiency—it is faster, and it often requires less memory. Its disadvantage is lack of flexibility.

Late binding means that a function call is resolved at run time. Thus, precisely which function to call is determined "on-the-fly" as the program executes. Late binding is achieved in C++ through the use of virtual functions and derived types. The advantage to late binding is that it allows greater flexibility. It can be used to support a common interface, while allowing various objects that utilize that interface to define their own implementations. Further, it can be used to help you create class libraries, which can be reused and extended. Its disadvantage, however, is a slight loss of execution speed.

IN DEPTH

Polymorphism and the Purist

Throughout this book, and in this chapter specifically, a distinction has been made between run-time and compile-time polymorphism. Compile-time polymorphic features are operator and function overloading. Run-time polymorphism is achieved with virtual functions. The most common definition of polymorphism is "one interface, multiple methods," and all of these features fit this meaning. However, some controversy does exist over the use of the term *polymorphism*.

Some OOP purists have insisted that the term be used to refer only to events that occur at run time. Thus, they would say that only virtual functions support polymorphism. Part of this view is founded in the fact that the earliest polymorphic computer languages were interpreters (in which all events occur at run time). The advent of compiled polymorphic languages expanded the concept of polymorphism. However, some still argue that the term *polymorphism* should refer only to run-time events. Most C++ programmers disagree with this view and hold that the term applies both to run-time and to compile-time features. However, don't be surprised if some day, someone strikes up an argument with you over the use of this term!

Whether your program uses early or late binding depends upon what the program is designed to do. (Actually, most large programs will use a combination of both.) Late binding is one of the most powerful features of C++. However, the price you pay for this power is that your program will run slightly slower. Therefore, it is best to use late binding only when it meaningfully adds to the structure and manageability of your program. (In essence, use—but don't abuse—the power.) Keep in mind, however, that the loss of performance caused by late binding is very slight, so when the situation calls for late binding, you should most definitely use it.

CHAPTER 16

Templates

375

The template is one of C++'s most sophisticated and high-powered features. Although not part of the original specification for C++, it was added several years ago and is now an integral part of C++ programming. Templates help you achieve one of the most elusive goals in programming: the creation of reusable code.

Using templates, it is possible to create generic functions and classes. In a generic function or class, the type of data upon which the function or class operates is specified as a parameter. Thus, you can use one function or class with several different types of data, without having to explicitly recode specific versions for each data type. Both generic functions and generic classes are discussed in this chapter.

Generic Functions

A generic function is capable of overloading itself.

A generic function defines a general set of operations that will be applied to various types of data. The type of data that the function will operate upon is passed to it as a parameter. Through a generic function, a single general procedure can be applied to a wide range of data. As you probably know, many algorithms are logically the same no matter what type of data is being operated upon. For example, the Quicksort sorting algorithm is the same whether it is applied to an array of integers or an array of **float**s. It is just that the type of data being sorted is different. By creating a generic function, you can define the nature of the algorithm, independent of any data. Once you have done this, the compiler will automatically generate the correct code for the type of data that is actually used when you execute the function. In essence, when you create a generic function, you are creating a function that can automatically overload itself.

A generic function is created by using the keyword **template**. The normal meaning of the word "template" accurately reflects its use in C++. It is used to create a template (or framework) that describes what a function will do, leaving it to the compiler to fill in the details, as needed. The general form of a template function definition is shown here:

```
template <class Ttype> ret-type func-name(parameter list)
{
    // body of function
}
```

template is the keyword that begins a generic function definition.

Here, *Ttype* is a placeholder name for a data type used by the function. This name can be used within the function definition. However, it is only a placeholder that the compiler will automatically replace with an actual data type when it creates a specific version of the function. Although the use of the keyword **class** to specify a generic type in a **template** declaration is traditional, you may also use the keyword **typename**.

The following example creates a generic function that swaps the values of the two variables with which it is called. Because the general process of exchanging two values is independent of the type of the variables, it is a good candidate for being made into a generic function.

```
// Function template example.
#include <iostream>
using namespace std;

// This is a function template.
```

16

```cpp
template <class X> void swapargs(X &a, X &b)
{
  X temp;

  temp = a;
  a = b;
  b = temp;
}

int main()
{
  int i=10, j=20;
  double x=10.1, y=23.3;
  char a='x', b='z';

  cout << "Original i, j: " << i << ' ' << j << '\n';
  cout << "Original x, y: " << x << ' ' << y << '\n';
  cout << "Original a, b: " << a << ' ' << b << '\n';

  swapargs(i, j); // swap integers
  swapargs(x, y); // swap floats
  swapargs(a, b); // swap chars

  cout << "Swapped i, j: " << i << ' ' << j << '\n';
  cout << "Swapped x, y: " << x << ' ' << y << '\n';
  cout << "Swapped a, b: " << a << ' ' << b << '\n';

  return 0;
}
```

The output is shown here.

```
Original i, j: 10 20
Original x, y: 10.1 23.3
Original a, b: x z
Swapped i, j: 20 10
Swapped x, y: 23.3 10.1
Swapped a, b: z x
```

Let's look closely at this program. The line

```cpp
template <class X> void swapargs(X &a, X &b)
```

tells the compiler two things: that a template is being created, and that a generic definition is beginning. Here, **X** is a generic type that is used as a placeholder. After the **template** portion, the function **swapargs( )** is declared, using **X** as the data type of the values that will be swapped. In **main( )**, the **swapargs( )** function is called using three different types of data: **int**s, **float**s, and **char**s. Because **swapargs( )** is a generic function, the compiler automatically creates three versions of **swapargs( )**: one that will exchange integer values, one that will exchange floating-point values, and one that will swap characters.

Here are some important terms related to templates. First, a generic function (that is, a function definition preceded by a **template** statement) is also called a *template function*. Both terms will be used interchangeably in this book. When the compiler creates a specific version of this function, it is said to have created a *specialization*. This is also called a *generated function*. The act of generating a function is referred to as *instantiating* it. Put differently, a generated function is a specific instance of a template function.

Since C++ does not recognize end-of-line as a statement terminator, the **template** portion of a generic function definition does not have to be on the same line as the function's name. The following example shows another common way to format the **swapargs( )** function:

```
template <class X>
void swapargs(X &a, X &b)
{
  X temp;

  temp = a;
  a = b;
  b = temp;
}
```

If you use this form, it is important to understand that no other statements can occur between the **template** statement and the start of the generic function definition. For example, the fragment shown next will not compile:

```
// This will not compile.
template <class X>
int i; // this is an error
void swapargs(X &a, X &b)
{
  X temp;

  temp = a;
  a = b;
  b = temp;
}
```

As the comments imply, the **template** specification must directly precede the function definition. You cannot put a variable declaration statement (or any other kind of statement) between the two.

A Function with Two Generic Types

You can define more than one generic data type in the **template** statement by using a comma-separated list. For example, this program creates a template function that has two generic types:

```
#include <iostream>
using namespace std;
```

```
template <class type1, class type2>
void myfunc(type1 x, type2 y)
{
  cout << x << ' ' << y << '\n';
}

int main()
{
  myfunc(10, "hi");

  myfunc(0.23, 10L);

  return 0;
}
```

In this example, the placeholder types **type1** and **type2** are replaced by the compiler with the data types **int** and **char ***, and **double** and **long**, respectively, when the compiler generates the specific instances of **myfunc( )** within **main( )**.

REMEMBER: When you create a template function, you are, in essence, allowing the compiler to generate as many different versions of that function as are necessary for handling the various ways that your program calls the function.

Explicitly Overloading a Generic Function

A manually overloaded version of a generic function is called an explicit specialization.

Even though a generic function overloads itself as needed, you can explicitly overload one, too. This is formally called *explicit specialization*. If you overload a generic function, then that overloaded function overrides (or "hides") the generic function relative to that specific version. For example, consider the following, revised version of the first example in this chapter:

```
// Overriding a template function.
#include <iostream>
using namespace std;

template <class X> void swapargs(X &a, X &b)
{
  X temp;

  temp = a;
  a = b;
  b = temp;
  cout << "Inside template swapargs.\n";
}

// This overrides the generic version of swapargs() for ints.
void swapargs(int &a, int &b)
{
```

```
   int temp;

   temp = a;
   a = b;
   b = temp;
   cout << "Inside swapargs int specialization.\n";
}

int main()
{
  int i=10, j=20;
  double x=10.1, y=23.3;
  char a='x', b='z';

  cout << "Original i, j: " << i << ' ' << j << '\n';
  cout << "Original x, y: " << x << ' ' << y << '\n';
  cout << "Original a, b: " << a << ' ' << b << '\n';

  swapargs(i, j); // calls explicitly overloaded swapargs()
  swapargs(x, y); // calls generic swapargs()
  swapargs(a, b); // calls generic swapargs()

  cout << "Swapped i, j: " << i << ' ' << j << '\n';
  cout << "Swapped x, y: " << x << ' ' << y << '\n';
  cout << "Swapped a, b: " << a << ' ' << b << '\n';

  return 0;
}
```

This program displays the following output:

```
Original i, j: 10 20
Original x, y: 10.1 23.3
Original a, b: x z
Inside swapargs int specialization.
Inside template swapargs.
Inside template swapargs.
Swapped i, j: 20 10
Swapped x, y: 23.3 10.1
Swapped a, b: z x
```

As the comments inside the program indicate, when **swapargs(i, j)** is called, it invokes the explicitly overloaded version of **swapargs( )** defined in the program. Thus, the compiler does not generate this version of the generic **swapargs( )** function, because the generic function is overridden by the explicit overloading.

There is a newer, alternative syntax that you can use to denote the explicit specialization of a function. This modern approach uses the **template** keyword. For example, using the new-style specialization syntax, the overloaded **swapargs( )** function from the preceding program looks like this:

```
// Use the newer-style specialization syntax.
template<> void swapargs<int>(int &a, int &b)
```

16

```
{
  int temp;

  temp = a;
  a = b;
  b = temp;
  cout << "Inside swapargs int specialization.\n";
}
```

As you can see, the new-style syntax uses the **template<>** construct to indicate specialization. The type of data for which the specialization is being created is placed inside the angle brackets following the function name. This same syntax is used to specialize any type of generic function. While there is no advantage to using one specialization syntax over the other at this point in time, the new-style is probably a better approach for the long term.

Explicit specialization of a template allows you to tailor a version of a generic function to accommodate a unique situation—perhaps to take advantage of some performance boost that applies to only one type of data, for example. However, as a general rule, if you need to have different versions of a function for different data types, you should use overloaded functions rather than templates.

Overloading a Function Template

In addition to creating explicit, overloaded versions of a generic function, you can also overload the **template** specification, itself. To do so, simply create another version of the template that differs from any others in its parameter list. For example:

```
// Overload a function template declaration.
#include <iostream>
using namespace std;

// First version of f() template.
template <class X> void f(X a)
{
  cout << "Inside f(X a)\n";
}

// Second version of f() template.
template <class X, class Y> void f(X a, Y b)
{
  cout << "Inside f(X a, Y b)\n";
}

int main()
{
  f(10);      // calls f(X)
  f(10, 20); // calls f(X, Y)

  return 0;
}
```

Here, the template for **f( )** is overloaded to accept either one or two parameters.

Using Standard Parameters with Template Functions

You can mix standard parameters with generic type parameters in a template function. These non-generic parameters work just like they do with any other function. For example:

```cpp
// Using standard parameters in a template function.
#include <iostream>
using namespace std;

// Display data specified number of times.
template<class X> void repeat(X data, int times)
{
  do {
    cout << data << "\n";
    times--;
  } while(times);
}

int main()
{
  repeat("This is a test", 3);
  repeat(100, 5);
  repeat(99.0/2, 4);

  return 0;
}
```

Here is the output produced by this program:

```
This is a test
This is a test
This is a test
100
100
100
100
100
49.5
49.5
49.5
49.5
```

In the program, the function **repeat( )** displays its first argument the number of times requested by its second argument. Since the first argument is a generic type, **repeat( )** can be used to display any type of data. The **times** parameter is a standard, call-by-value parameter. The mixing of generic and non-generic parameters causes no trouble and, indeed, is common.

Generic Function Restrictions

Generic functions are similar to overloaded functions, except that they are more restrictive. When functions are overloaded, you may have different actions performed within the body of each function. But a generic function must perform the same general action for all versions—only the type of data can differ. Consider the overloaded functions in the following example. These functions could *not* be replaced by a generic function, because they do not do the same thing.

16

```
void outdata(int i)
{
  cout << i;
}

void outdata(double d)
{
  cout << d * 3.1416;
}
```

IN DEPTH

Creating a Generic abs( ) Function

Let's return to the **abs( )** function one last time. Recall that in Chapter 8, the standard library functions **abs( )**, **labs( )**, and **fabs( )** were consolidated into three overloaded functions called **myabs( )**. Each of the overloaded versions of **myabs( )** were designed to return the absolute value of a different type of data. While the manual overloading of **abs( )** in Chapter 8 was an improvement over the use of three different library functions (each having different names), it is still not the best way to create an absolute value function. Since the procedure that returns the absolute value of a number is the same for all types of numeric values, **abs( )** is an excellent choice for a template function. Once a generic version of **abs( )** exists, the compiler can automatically create whatever version of the function it needs. You, the programmer, do not need to anticipate each application. (You also won't be cluttering your source code with multiple, manually overloaded versions.)

The following program contains the generic version of **myabs( )**. You might want to compare it to the overloaded versions in Chapter 8. As you will see, the generic version has shorter source code and is more flexible.

```
// A generic version of myabs().
#include <iostream>
using namespace std;
```

```
template <class X> X myabs(X val)
{
  return val < 0 ? -val : val;
}

int main()
{
  cout << myabs(-10) << '\n';    // integer abs

  cout << myabs(-10.0) << '\n';  // double abs

  cout << myabs(-10L) << '\n';    // long abs

  cout << myabs(-10.0F) << '\n'; // float abs

  return 0;
}
```

On your own, you should try to find other library functions that are good candidates for being made into generic functions. Remember, the key is that the same algorithm be applicable to a wide range of data.

Generic Classes

In addition to generic functions, you can also define a generic class. When you do this, you create a class that defines all the algorithms used by that class; however, the actual type of the data being manipulated will be specified as a parameter when objects of that class are created.

Generic classes are useful when a class uses logic that can be generalized. For example, the same algorithms that maintain a queue of integers will also work for a queue of characters, and the same mechanism that maintains a linked list of mailing addresses will also maintain a linked list of auto part information. When you create a generic class, it can perform the operation you define, such as maintaining a queue or a linked list, for any type of data. The compiler will automatically generate the correct type of object, based upon the type you specify when the object is created.

The general form of a generic class declaration is shown here:

```
template <class Ttype> class class-name {
    .
    .
    .
}
```

Here, *Ttype* is the placeholder type name, which will be specified when a class is instantiated. If necessary, you can define more than one generic data type by using a comma-separated list.

Once you have created a generic class, you create a specific instance of that class by using the following general form:

   class-name <type> ob;

Here, *type* is the type name of the data that the class will be operating upon. Member functions of a generic class are, themselves, automatically generic. You don't need to use **template** to explicitly specify them as such.

In the following program, the **queue** class (first introduced in Chapter 11) is reworked into a generic class. Thus, it can be used to queue objects of any type. In this example, a character queue and a floating-point queue are created, but any data type can be used.

```
// Demonstrate a generic queue class.
#include <iostream>
using namespace std;

const int SIZE=100;

// This creates the generic class queue.
template <class QType> class queue {
  QType q[SIZE];
  int sloc, rloc;
public:
  queue() { sloc = rloc = 0; }
  void qput(QType i);
  QType qget();
};

// Put an object into the queue.
template <class QType> void queue<QType>::qput(QType i)
{
  if(sloc==SIZE) {
    cout << "Queue is full.\n";
    return;
  }
  sloc++;
  q[sloc] = i;
}

// Get an object from the queue.
template <class QType> QType queue<QType>::qget()
{
  if(rloc == sloc) {
    cout << "Queue Underflow.\n";
    return 0;
  }
  rloc++;
```

```
    return q[rloc];
}

int main()
{
  queue<int> a, b;  // create two integer queues

  a.qput(10);
  b.qput(19);
  a.qput(20);
  b.qput(1);

  cout << a.qget() << " ";
  cout << a.qget() << " ";
  cout << b.qget() << " ";
  cout << b.qget() << "\n";

  queue<double> c, d;  // create two double queues

  c.qput(10.12);
  d.qput(19.99);
  c.qput(-20.0);
  d.qput(0.986);

  cout << c.qget() << " ";
  cout << c.qget() << " ";
  cout << d.qget() << " ";
  cout << d.qget() << "\n";

  return 0;
}
```

The output is shown here.

```
10 20 19 1
10.12 -20 19.99 0.986
```

In the program, the declaration of a generic class is similar to that of a generic function. The actual type of data stored by the queue is generic in the class declaration. It is not until an object of the queue is declared that the actual data type is determined. When a specific instance of **queue** is declared, the compiler automatically generates all the functions and variables necessary for handling the actual data. In this example, two different types of queues are declared. Two are integer queues. Two are queues of **double**s. Pay special attention to these declarations:

```
queue<int> a, b;
queue<double> c, d;
```

Notice how the desired data type is passed inside the angle brackets. By changing the type of data specified when **queue** objects are created, you can change the type of data stored in that queue. For example, by using the following declaration, you can create another queue that stores character pointers:

```
queue<char *> chrptrQ;
```

You can also create queues to store data types that you create. For example, if you want to use the following structure to store address information,

```
struct addr {
  char name[40];
  char street[40];
  char city[30];
  char state[3];
  char zip[12];
};
```

then to use **queue** to generate a queue that will store objects of type **addr**, use a declaration like this:

```
queue<addr> obj;
```

As the **queue** class illustrates, generic functions and classes are powerful tools that you can use to maximize your programming efforts, because they allow you to define the general form of an object, which can then be used with any type of data. You are saved from the tedium of creating separate implementations for each data type with which you want the algorithm to work. The compiler automatically creates the specific versions of the class for you.

An Example with Two Generic Data Types

A template class can have more than one generic data type. Simply declare all the data types required by the class in a comma-separated list within the **template** specification. For example, the following program creates a class that uses two generic data types:

```
/* This example uses two generic data types in a
   class definition.
*/
#include <iostream>
using namespace std;

template <class Type1, class Type2> class myclass
{
  Type1 i;
  Type2 j;
public:
  myclass(Type1 a, Type2 b) { i = a; j = b; }
  void show() { cout << i << ' ' << j << '\n'; }
};

int main()
```

```
{
  myclass<int, double> ob1(10, 0.23);
  myclass<char, char *> ob2('X', "This is a test");

  ob1.show(); // show int, double
  ob2.show(); // show char, char *

  return 0;
}
```

This program produces the following output:

```
10 0.23
X This is a test
```

The program declares two types of objects. **ob1** uses **int** and **double** data. **ob2** uses a character and a character pointer. For both cases, the compiler automatically generates the appropriate data and functions to accommodate the way the objects are created.

Creating a Generic Array Class

Before moving on, let's look at another generic class application. As you saw in Chapter 13, you can overload the **[ ]** operator. Doing so allows you to create your own array implementations, including "safe arrays" that provide run-time boundary checking. As you know, in C++, it is possible to overrun (or underrun) an array boundary at run time, without generating a run-time error message. However, if you create a class that contains the array, and allow access to that array only through the overloaded **[ ]** subscripting operator, then you can intercept an out-of-range index.

By combining operator overloading with a generic class, it is possible to create a generic safe-array type that can be used for creating safe arrays of any data type. This type of array is created in the following program:

```
// A generic safe array example.
#include <iostream>
#include <cstdlib>
using namespace std;

const int SIZE = 10;

template <class AType> class atype {
  AType a[SIZE];
public:
  atype() {
    register int i;
    for(i=0; i<SIZE; i++) a[i] = i;
  }
  AType &operator[](int i);
};

// Provide range checking for atype.
```

```
template <class AType> AType &atype<AType>::operator[](int i)
{
  if(i<0 || i> SIZE-1) {
    cout << "\nIndex value of ";
    cout << i << " is out-of-bounds.\n";
    exit(1);
  }
  return a[i];
}

int main()
{
  atype<int> intob; // integer array
  atype<double> doubleob; // double array

  int i;

  cout << "Integer array: ";
  for(i=0; i<SIZE; i++) intob[i] = i;
  for(i=0; i<SIZE; i++) cout << intob[i] << "  ";
  cout << '\n';

  cout << "Double array: ";
  for(i=0; i<SIZE; i++) doubleob[i] = (double) i/3;
  for(i=0; i<SIZE; i++) cout << doubleob[i] << "  ";
  cout << '\n';

  intob[12] = 100; // generates runtime error

  return 0;
}
```

This program implements a generic safe-array type and then demonstrates its use by creating an array of **int**s and an array of **double**s. You should try creating other types of arrays. As this example shows, part of the power of generic classes is that they allow you to write the code once, debug it, and then apply it to any type of data, without having to re-engineer it for each specific application.

Using Non-Type Arguments with Generic Classes

In the template specification for a generic class, you may also specify non-type arguments. That is, in a template specification, you can specify what you would normally think of as a standard argument, such as an integer or a pointer. The syntax to accomplish this is essentially the same as for normal function parameters: Simply include the type and name of the argument. For example, here is a better way to implement the safe-array class presented in the preceding section:

```
// Demonstrate non-type template arguments.
#include <iostream>
#include <cstdlib>
using namespace std;
```

```
// Here, int size is a non-type argument.
template <class AType, int size> class atype {
  AType a[size]; // length of array is passed in size
public:
  atype() {
    register int i;
    for(i=0; i<size; i++) a[i] = i;
  }
  AType &operator[](int i);
};

// Provide range checking for atype.
template <class AType, int size>
AType &atype<AType, size>::operator[](int i)
{
  if(i<0 || i> size-1) {
    cout << "\nIndex value of ";
    cout << i << " is out-of-bounds.\n";
    exit(1);
  }
  return a[i];
}

int main()
{
  atype<int, 10> intob;        // integer array of size 10
  atype<double, 15> doubleob;  // double array of size 15

  int i;

  cout << "Integer array: ";
  for(i=0; i<10; i++) intob[i] = i;
  for(i=0; i<10; i++) cout << intob[i] << "  ";
  cout << '\n';

  cout << "Double array: ";
  for(i=0; i<15; i++) doubleob[i] = (double) i/3;
  for(i=0; i<15; i++) cout << doubleob[i] << "  ";
  cout << '\n';

  intob[12] = 100; // generates runtime error

  return 0;
}
```

Look carefully at the template specification for **atype**. Note that **size** is declared as an **int**. This parameter is then used within **atype** to declare the size of the array **a**. Even though **size** is depicted as a "variable" in the source code, its value is known at compile time. This allows it to be used to set the size of the array. **size** is also used in the bounds checking within the **operator[ ]( )** function. Within **main( )**, notice how the integer and floating-point arrays are created. The second parameter specifies the size of each array.

Non-type parameters are restricted to integers, pointers, or references. Other types, such as **float**, are not allowed. The arguments that you pass to a non-type parameter must consist of either an integer constant, or a pointer or reference to a global function or object. Thus, non-type parameters should, themselves, be thought of as constants, since their values cannot be changed. For example, inside **operator[ ]( )**, the following statement is not allowed:

```
size = 10; // Error
```

Since non-type parameters are treated as constants, they can be used to set the dimension of an array, which is a significant, practical benefit.

As the safe-array example illustrates, the use of non-type parameters greatly expands the utility of template classes. Although the information contained in the non-type argument must be known at compile time, this restriction is mild compared with the power offered by non-type parameters.

Programming challenge: The **queue** template class, shown earlier in this chapter, would also benefit from a non-type parameter that specifies the size of the queue. Try making this improvement on your own.

Using Default Arguments with Template Classes

A template class can have a default argument associated with a generic type. For example:

```
template <class X=int> class myclass { //...
```

Here, the type **int** will be used if no other type is specified when an object of type **myclass** is instantiated.

It is also permissible for non-type arguments to take default arguments. The default value is used when no explicit value is specified when the class is instantiated. Default arguments for non-type parameters are specified by using the same syntax as default arguments for function parameters.

Here is another version of the safe-array class that uses default arguments for both the type of data and the size of the array:

```
// Demonstrate default template arguments.
#include <iostream>
#include <cstdlib>
using namespace std;

// Here, AType defaults to int and size defaults to 10.
template <class AType=int, int size=10> class atype {
  AType a[size]; // size of array is passed in size
public:
  atype() {
    register int i;
    for(i=0; i<size; i++) a[i] = i;
  }
```

```
  AType &operator[](int i);
};

// Provide range checking for atype.
template <class AType, int size>
AType &atype<AType, size>::operator[](int i)
{
  if(i<0 || i> size-1) {
    cout << "\nIndex value of ";
    cout << i << " is out-of-bounds.\n";
    exit(1);
  }
  return a[i];
}

int main()
{
  atype<int, 100> intarray;   // integer array, size 100
  atype<double> doublearray; // double array, default size
  atype<> defarray;           // default to int array of size 10

  int i;

  cout << "int array: ";
  for(i=0; i<100; i++) intarray[i] = i;
  for(i=0; i<100; i++) cout << intarray[i] << "  ";
  cout << '\n';

  cout << "double array: ";
  for(i=0; i<10; i++) doublearray[i] = (double) i/3;
  for(i=0; i<10; i++) cout << doublearray[i] << "  ";
  cout << '\n';

  cout << "defarray array: ";
  for(i=0; i<10; i++) defarray[i] = i;
  for(i=0; i<10; i++) cout << defarray[i] << "  ";
  cout << '\n';

  return 0;
}
```

Pay close attention to this line:

```
template <class AType=int, int size=10> class atype {
```

Here, **AType** defaults to type **int**, and **size** defaults to 10. As the program illustrates, **atype** objects can be created three ways:

◆   By explicitly specifying both the type and size of the array

◆   By explicitly specifying the type, but letting the size default to 10

◆   By letting the type default to **int** and the size default to 10

The use of default arguments—especially default types—adds versatility to your template classes. You can provide a default for the type of data most commonly used, while still allowing the user of your classes to specialize them as needed.

Explicit Class Specializations

As with template functions, you can create a specialization of a generic class. To do so, use the **template<>** construct, which works the same as it does for explicit function specializations. For example:

```cpp
// Demonstrate class specialization.
#include <iostream>
using namespace std;

template <class T> class myclass {
  T x;
public:
  myclass(T a) {
    cout << "Inside generic myclass\n";
    x = a;
  }
  T getx() { return x; }
};

// Explicit specialization for int.
template <> class myclass<int> {
  int x;
public:
  myclass(int a) {
    cout << "Inside myclass<int> specialization\n";
    x = a * a;
  }
  int getx() { return x; }
};

int main()
{
  myclass<double> d(10.1);
  cout << "double: " << d.getx() << "\n\n";

  myclass<int> i(5);
  cout << "int: " << i.getx() << "\n";

  return 0;
}
```

This program displays the following output:

```
Inside generic myclass
double: 10.1

Inside myclass<int> specialization
int: 25
```

In the program, pay close attention to this line:

```
template <> class myclass<int> {
```

It tells the compiler that an explicit integer specialization of **myclass** is being created. This same general syntax is used for any type of class specialization.

Explicit class specialization expands the utility of generic classes, because it lets you easily handle one or two special cases, while allowing all others to be automatically processed by the compiler. Of course, if you find that you are creating too many specializations, then you are probably better off not using a template class in the first place.

CHAPTER 17

Exception Handling

This chapter discusses exception handling. An exception is an error that occurs at run time. Using C++'s exception-handling subsystem, you can, in a structured and controlled manner, handle run-time errors. When exception handling is employed, your program automatically invokes an error-handling routine when an exception occurs. The principal advantage of exception handling is that it automates much of the error-handling code that previously had to be entered "by hand" into any large program.

This chapter also revisits C++'s dynamic allocation operators: **new** and **delete**. As explained earlier in this book, if **new** cannot allocate the requested memory, it generates an exception. In this chapter, you will learn to handle that exception. You will also see how to overload **new** and **delete**, which allows you to define your own allocation schemes.

Exception Handling Fundamentals

Exception handling is a structured means by which your program can manage run-time errors.

throw throws an exception, which is caught by a **catch** statement.

C++ exception handling is built upon three keywords: **try**, **catch**, and **throw**. In the most general terms, program statements that you want to monitor for exceptions are contained in a **try** block. If an exception (i.e., an error) occurs within the **try** block, it is thrown (using **throw**). The exception is caught, using **catch**, and processed. The following discussion elaborates upon this general description.

Code that you want to monitor for exceptions must have been executed from within a **try** block. (A function called from within a **try** block is also monitored.) Exceptions that can be thrown by the monitored code are caught by a **catch** statement, which immediately follows the **try** statement in which the exception was thrown. The general form of **try** and **catch** are shown here:

```
try {
    // try block
}
catch (type1 arg) {
    // catch block
}
catch (type2 arg) {
    // catch block
}
catch (type3 arg) {
    // catch block
}
// ...
catch (typeN arg) {
    // catch block
}
```

The **try** block must contain the portion of your program that you want to monitor for errors. This section can be as short as a few statements within one function, or as all-encompassing as a **try** block that encloses the **main( )** function code (which would, in effect, cause the entire program to be monitored).

When an exception is thrown, it is caught by its corresponding **catch** statement, which then processes the exception. There can be more than one **catch** statement associated with a **try**. The type of the exception determines which **catch** statement is used. That is, if the data type specified by a **catch** statement matches that of the exception, then that **catch** statement is executed (and all others are bypassed). When an exception is caught, *arg* will receive its value. Any type of data can be caught, including classes that you create.

17

To catch an exception, it must be thrown from within a **try** block.

The general form of the **throw** statement is shown here:

> throw *exception*;

throw generates the exception specified by *exception*. If this exception is to be caught, then **throw** must be executed either from within a **try** block itself, or from any function called from within the **try** block (directly or indirectly).

NOTE: If you throw an exception for which there is no applicable **catch** statement, an abnormal program termination will occur. Throwing an unhandled exception will cause the **terminate( )** standard library function to be invoked. By default, **terminate( )** calls **abort( )** to stop your program, but you can specify your own termination handler, if you like. You will need to refer to your compiler's documentation for details.

Here is a very simple example that shows how C++ exception handling operates:

```
// A simple exception handling example.
#include <iostream>
using namespace std;

int main()
{
  cout << "start\n";

  try { // start a try block
    cout << "Inside try block\n";
    throw 99; // throw an error
    cout << "This will not execute";
  }
  catch (int i) { // catch an error
    cout << "Caught an exception -- value is: ";
    cout << i << "\n";
  }

  cout << "end";

  return 0;
}
```

This program displays the following output:

```
start
Inside try block
Caught an exception — value is: 99
end
```

Look carefully at this program. As you can see, there is a **try** block containing three statements, and a **catch(int i)** statement that processes an integer exception. Within the **try** block, only two of the three statements will execute: the first **cout** statement and the **throw**. Once an exception has been thrown, control passes to the **catch** expression, and the **try** block is terminated. That is, **catch** is *not* called. Rather, program execution is transferred to it. (The program's stack is automatically reset, as necessary, to accomplish this.) Thus, the **cout** statement following the **throw** will never execute.

After the **catch** statement executes, program control continues with the statements following the **catch**. Thus, it is the job of your exception handler to remedy the problem that caused the exception, so that program execution can continue normally. In cases where the error cannot be fixed, a **catch** block will usually end with a call to **exit( )** or **abort( )**, or otherwise terminate program execution. (The **exit( )** and **abort( )** functions are described in the In Depth box.)

As mentioned earlier, the type of the exception must match the type specified in a **catch** statement. For example, in the preceding program, if you change the type in the **catch** statement to **double**, then the exception will not be caught, and abnormal termination will occur. This change is shown here:

IN DEPTH

exit( ) and abort( )

The **exit( )** and **abort( )** functions are provided by the C++ library. Both cause the termination of a program, but in different ways. These functions are frequently used in C++ programming.

The **exit( )** function causes the immediate, orderly termination of a program. (Orderly termination means that the normal program shutdown sequence is followed.) It is typically used to halt a program when a fatal error has occurred that renders further execution of the program meaningless or harmful. The **exit( )** function requires the header **<cstdlib>**. It has the following prototype:

void exit(int *status*);

Because **exit( )** causes immediate termination of the program, it does not return to the calling program and does not have a return value. However, the value of *status* is returned as an exit code to the calling process. By convention, a *status* value of 0 indicates successful termination. Any other value indicates that your program terminated because of some sort of error. You may also use the constant **EXIT_SUCCESS** to indicate successful termination, or **EXIT_FAILURE** to specify an error. These constants are defined in **<cstdlib>.**

The **abort( )** function has this prototype:

```
void abort( );
```

Similar to **exit( )**, **abort( )** causes immediate program termination. However, unlike **exit( )**, it does not return status information to the operating system, nor does it perform an orderly shutdown of your program. It requires the header **<cstdlib>.** In practical terms, **abort( )** is a C++ program's "emergency stop" function. It should be used only after a catastrophic error has occurred.

```cpp
// This example will not work.
#include <iostream>
using namespace std;

int main()
{
  cout << "start\n";

  try { // start a try block
    cout << "Inside try block\n";
    throw 99; // throw an error
    cout << "This will not execute";
  }
  catch (double i) { // won't work for an int exception
    cout << "Caught an exception -- value is: ";
    cout << i << "\n";
  }

  cout << "end";

  return 0;
}
```

This program produces the following output, because the integer exception will not be caught by the **catch(double i)** statement:

```
start
Inside try block
Abnormal program termination
```

Depending upon what compiler you are using, the precise message displayed when an abnormal termination occurs may differ from the one shown above.

An exception thrown by a function called from within a **try** block can be caught by that **try** block. For example, this is a valid program:

```
/* Throwing an exception from a function called
   from within a try block.
*/
#include <iostream>
using namespace std;

void Xtest(int test)
{
  cout << "Inside Xtest, test is: " << test << "\n";
  if(test) throw test;
}

int main()
{
  cout << "start\n";

  try { // start a try block
    cout << "Inside try block\n";
    Xtest(0);
    Xtest(1);
    Xtest(2);
  }
  catch (int i) { // catch an error
    cout << "Caught an exception -- value is: ";
    cout << i << "\n";
  }

  cout << "end";

  return 0;
}
```

This program produces the following output:

```
start
Inside try block
Inside Xtest, test is: 0
Inside Xtest, test is: 1
Caught an exception — value is: 1
end
```

A **try** block can be localized to a function. When this is the case, each time the function is entered, the exception handling relative to that function is reset. Examine this sample program:

```
#include <iostream>
using namespace std;
```

```
// A try/catch is reset each time a function is entered.
void Xhandler(int test)
{
  try{
    if(test) throw test;
  }
  catch(int i) {
    cout << "Caught One!  Ex. #: " << i << '\n';
  }
}

int main()
{
  cout << "start\n";

  Xhandler(1);
  Xhandler(2);
  Xhandler(0);
  Xhandler(3);

  cout << "end";

  return 0;
}
```

This program displays the following output:

```
start
Caught One!  Ex. #: 1
Caught One!  Ex. #: 2
Caught One!  Ex. #: 3
end
```

As you can see, three exceptions are thrown. After each exception, the function returns. When the function is called again, the exception handling is reset.

In general, a **try** block is reset each time it is entered. Thus, a **try** block that is part of a loop will be reset each time the loop repeats.

Catching Class Types

An exception can be of any type, including class types that you create. Actually, in real-world programs, most exceptions will be class types, rather than built-in types. Perhaps the most common reason that you will want to define a class type for an exception is to create an object that describes the error that occured. This information can be used by the exception handler to help it process the error. The following example demonstrates this.

```
// Use an exception class.
#include <iostream>
#include <cstring>
using namespace std;
```

```
class MyException {
public:
  char str_what[80];

  MyException() { *str_what = 0; }

  MyException(char *s) {
    strcpy(str_what, s);
  }
};

int main()
{
  int a, b;

  try {
    cout << "Enter numerator and denominator: ";
    cin >> a >> b;
    if(!b)
      throw MyException("Cannot divide by zero!");
    else
      cout << "Quotient is " << a/b << "\n";
  }
  catch (MyException e) { // catch an error
    cout << e.str_what << "\n";
  }

  return 0;
}
```

Here is a sample run:

```
Enter numerator and denominator: 10 0
Cannot divide by zero!
```

The program prompts the user for a numerator and denominator. If the denominator is zero, an object of the class **MyException** is created that indicates the divide-by-zero error. Thus, **MyException** encapsulates information about the error. This information is then used by the exception handler to tell the user what happened.

Of course, most real-world exception classes will be more sophisticated than **MyException**. In general, you will want to create exception classes that encapsulate sufficient information about an error to enable the exception handler to respond effectively, possibly rectifying the situation.

Using Multiple catch Statements

As stated earlier, you can associate more than one **catch** statement with a **try**. In fact, it is common to do so. However, each **catch** must catch a different type of exception. For example, the program shown here catches both integers and character pointers:

```
#include <iostream>
using namespace std;

// Different types of exceptions can be caught.
void Xhandler(int test)
{
  try{
    if(test) throw test;
    else throw "Value is zero";
  }
  catch(int i) {
    cout << "Caught One!  Ex. #: " << i << '\n';
  }
  catch(char *str) {
    cout << "Caught a string: ";
    cout << str << '\n';
  }
}

int main()
{
  cout << "start\n";

  Xhandler(1);
  Xhandler(2);
  Xhandler(0);
  Xhandler(3);

  cout << "end";

  return 0;
}
```

This program produces the following output:

```
start
Caught One!  Ex. #: 1
Caught One!  Ex. #: 2
Caught a string: Value is zero
Caught One!  Ex. #: 3
end
```

As you can see, each **catch** statement responds only to its own type.

In general, **catch** expressions are checked in the order in which they occur in a program. Only a matching statement is executed. All other **catch** blocks are ignored.

Catching Base Class Exceptions

There is one important point about multiple **catch** statements that relates to derived classes. A **catch** clause for a base class will also match any class derived from that base. Thus, if you want to catch exceptions of both a base class type and a derived class type, put the derived class first in the **catch** sequence. If you don't, then the base class **catch** will also catch all derived classes. For example, consider the following program:

```
// Catching derived classes.
#include <iostream>
using namespace std;

class B {
};

class D: public B {
};

int main()
{
  D derived;

  try {
    throw derived;
  }
  catch(B b) {
    cout << "Caught a base class.\n";
  }
  catch(D d) {
    cout << "This won't execute.\n";
  }

  return 0;
}
```

Here, because **derived** is an object that has **B** as a base class, it will be caught by the first catch clause, and the second clause will never execute. Some compilers will flag this condition with a warning message. Others may issue an error. Either way, to fix this condition, reverse the order of the **catch** clauses.

Options for Exception Handling

There are several additional features and nuances to C++ exception handling that make it easier and more convenient to use. These attributes are discussed here.

Catching All Exceptions

In some circumstances, you will want an exception handler to catch all exceptions, instead of just a certain type. This is easy to accomplish. Simply use this form of **catch**:

```
catch(...) {
    // process all exceptions
}
```

Here, the ellipsis matches any type of data.

The following program illustrates **catch(...)**:

```
// This example catches all exceptions.
#include <iostream>
using namespace std;

void Xhandler(int test)
{
  try{
    if(test==0) throw test; // throw int
    if(test==1) throw 'a'; // throw char
    if(test==2) throw 123.23; // throw double
  }
  catch(...) { // catch all exceptions
    cout << "Caught One!\n";
  }
}

int main()
{
  cout << "start\n";

  Xhandler(0);
  Xhandler(1);
  Xhandler(2);

  cout << "end";

  return 0;
}
```

This program displays the following output:

```
start
Caught One!
Caught One!
Caught One!
end
```

As you can see, all three **throw**s were caught by using the one **catch** statement.

One very good use for **catch(...)** is as the last **catch** of a cluster of catches. In this capacity, it provides a useful default or "catch all" statement. For example, this slightly different version of the preceding program explicitly catches integer exceptions, but relies upon **catch(...)** to catch all others:

```
// This example uses catch(...) as a default.
#include <iostream>
using namespace std;

void Xhandler(int test)
{
  try{
    if(test==0) throw test;    // throw int
```

```
    if(test==1) throw 'a';     // throw char
    if(test==2) throw 123.23;  // throw double
  }
  catch(int i) { // catch an int exception
    cout << "Caught " << i << '\n';
  }
  catch(...) { // catch all other exceptions
    cout << "Caught One!\n";
  }
}

int main()
{
  cout << "start\n";

  Xhandler(0);
  Xhandler(1);
  Xhandler(2);

  cout << "end";

  return 0;
}
```

The output produced by this program is shown here:

```
start
Caught 0
Caught One!
Caught One!
end
```

As this example suggests, using **catch(...)** as a default is a good way to catch all exceptions that you don't want to handle explicitly. Also, by catching all exceptions, you prevent an unhandled exception from causing an abnormal program termination.

Restricting Exceptions Thrown by a Function

You can restrict the type of exceptions that a function can throw outside of itself. In fact, you can also prevent a function from throwing any exceptions whatsoever. To accomplish these restrictions, you must add a **throw** clause to a function definition. The general form of this clause is

```
ret-type func-name(arg-list) throw(type-list)
{
   // ...
}
```

Here, only those data types contained in the comma-separated *type-list* can be thrown by the function. Throwing any other type of expression will cause abnormal program termination. If you don't want a function to be able to throw *any* exceptions, then use an empty list.

NOTE: Attempting to throw an exception that is not supported by a function will cause the **unexpected( )** standard library function to be called. By default, this causes **abort( )** to be called, which causes abnormal program termination. However, you can specify your own termination handler, if you like. You will need to refer to your compiler's documentation for details.

The following program shows how to restrict the types of exceptions that can be thrown from a function:

```cpp
// Restricting function throw types.
#include <iostream>
using namespace std;

// This function can only throw ints, chars, and doubles.
void Xhandler(int test) throw(int, char, double)
{
  if(test==0) throw test;   // throw int
  if(test==1) throw 'a';    // throw char
  if(test==2) throw 123.23; // throw double
}

int main()
{
  cout << "start\n";

  try{
    Xhandler(0); // also, try passing 1 and 2 to Xhandler()
  }
  catch(int i) {
    cout << "Caught int\n";
  }
  catch(char c) {
    cout << "Caught char\n";
  }
  catch(double d) {
    cout << "Caught double\n";
  }

  cout << "end";

  return 0;
}
```

In this program, the function **Xhandler( )** can throw only integer, character, and **double** exceptions. If it attempts to throw any other type of exception, then an abnormal program termination will occur. (That is, **unexpected( )** will be called.) To see an example of this, remove **int** from the list and retry the program.

It is important to understand that a function can be restricted only in what types of exceptions it throws back to the **try** block that has called it. That is, a **try** block *within* a function can throw any type of exception, as long as the exception is caught *within* that function. The restriction applies only when throwing an exception outside of the function.

The following change to **Xhandler( )** prevents it from throwing any exceptions:

```
// This function can throw NO exceptions!
void Xhandler(int test) throw()
{
  /* The following statements no longer work.  Instead,
     they will cause an abnormal program termination. */
  if(test==0) throw test;
  if(test==1) throw 'a';
  if(test==2) throw 123.23;
}
```

NOTE: At the time of this writing, Visual C++ does not actually prevent a function from throwing an exception type that is not specified in a **throw** clause. This is non-standard behavior. You can still specify a **throw** clause, but such a clause is considered informational only.

Rethrowing an Exception

If you want to rethrow an exception from within an exception handler, you can do so by calling **throw** by itself, with no exception. This causes the current exception to be passed on to an outer **try/catch** sequence. The most likely reason for calling **throw** this way is to allow multiple handlers to have access to the exception. For example, perhaps one exception handler manages one aspect of an exception, and a second handler copes with another aspect. An exception can be rethrown only from within a **catch** block (or from any function called from within that block). When you rethrow an exception, it will not be recaught by the same **catch** statement. It will propagate to the immediately enclosing **try/catch** sequence.

The following program illustrates rethrowing an exception. It rethrows a **char *** exception.

```
// Example of "rethrowing" an exception.
#include <iostream>
using namespace std;

void Xhandler()
{
  try {
    throw "hello"; // throw a char *
  }
  catch(char *) { // catch a char *
    cout << "Caught char * inside Xhandler\n";
```

```
      throw ; // rethrow char * out of function
  }
}

int main()
{
  cout << "start\n";

  try{
    Xhandler();
  }
  catch(char *) {
    cout << "Caught char * inside main\n";
  }

  cout << "end";

  return 0;
}
```

This program displays the following output:

```
start
Caught char * inside Xhandler
Caught char * inside main
end
```

Handling Exceptions Thrown by new

In Chapter 9 you learned that the **new** operator throws an exception if an allocation request fails. Because exceptions had not yet been discussed, a description of how to handle that exception was deferred until later. Now the time has come for you to see the proper way to handle a **new** allocation failure.

Before beginning, it is necessary to state that the material in this section describes the behavior of **new** as specified by Standard C++. As you should recall from Chapter 9, the precise action that occurs when **new** fails has been changed several times since C++ was invented. Originally, **new** returned null on failure. Later, this was changed such that **new** caused an exception on failure. Also, the name of this exception has changed over time. Finally, it was decided that a **new** failure will generate an exception by default, but that a null pointer could be returned instead, as an option. Thus, **new** has been implemented differently, at different times. Although all modern compilers implement **new** in compliance with Standard C++, older ones may not. If the code examples shown here do not work with your compiler, check its documentation for details on how it implements **new**.

In Standard C++, when an allocation request cannot be honored, **new** throws a **bad_alloc** exception. If you don't catch this exception, then your program will be terminated. While this behavior is fine for short sample programs, in real applications, you must catch this exception and process it in some rational manner. To have access to this exception, you must include the header **<new>** in your program.

Here is an example of **new** that uses a **try/catch** block to monitor for an allocation failure:

```
// Handle exceptions thrown by new.
#include <iostream>
#include <new>
using namespace std;

int main()
{
  int *p, i;

  try {
    p = new int[32]; // allocate memory for 32-element int array
  } catch (bad_alloc xa) {
    cout << "Allocation failure.\n";
    return 1;
  }

  for(i=0; i<32; i++) p[i] = i;

  for(i=0; i<32; i++) cout << p[i] << " ";

  delete [] p; // free the memory

  return 0;
}
```

Here, if an allocation failure occurs, it is caught by the **catch** statement. This same general approach can be used to watch for allocation errors whenever **new** is used. Simply enclose each **new** statement within a **try** block.

The nothrow Alternative

In Standard C++, it is also possible to have **new** return **null**, instead of having it throw an exception when an allocation failure occurs. This form of **new** is most useful when you are compiling older code with a modern C++ compiler. It is also valuable when you are replacing calls to **malloc( )** with **new**. (This is common when updating C code to C++.) This form of **new** is shown here:

> *p_var* = new(nothrow) *type*;

Here, *p_var* is a pointer variable of type *type*. The **nothrow** form of **new** works like the original version of **new** from years ago. Since it returns null on failure, it can be "dropped into" older code, without having to add exception handling. However, for new code, exceptions provide a better alternative.

The following program shows how to use the **new(nothrow)** alternative. It reworks the preceding program.

```
// Demonstrate nothrow version of new.
#include <iostream>
```

```
#include <new>
using namespace std;

int main()
{
  int *p, i;

  p = new(nothrow) int[32]; // use nothrow option
  if(!p) {
   cout << "Allocation failure.\n";
   return 1;
  }

  for(i=0; i<32; i++) p[i] = i;

  for(i=0; i<32; i++) cout << p[i] << " ";

  delete [] p; // free the memory

  return 0;
}
```

As this program demonstrates, when using the **nothrow** approach, you must check the pointer returned by **new** after each allocation request.

Overloading new and delete

Because **new** and **delete** are operators, they too can be overloaded. Although operator overloading was discussed in Chapter 13, the overloading of **new** and **delete** was deferred until after exceptions had been discussed. This was necessary because a properly overloaded version of **new** (one that is in compliance with Standard C++) must generate a **bad_alloc** exception when it fails. You might want to create your own version of **new** for any number of reasons. For example, you may want to create allocation routines that automatically begin using a disk file as virtual memory when the heap has been exhausted. Whatever the reason, it is a simple matter to overload these operators.

The skeletons for the functions that overload **new** and **delete** are shown here:

```
// Allocate an object.
void *operator new(size_t size)
{
  /* Perform allocation.  Throw bad_alloc on failure.
     Constructor called automatically. */
  return pointer_to_memory;
}

// Delete an object.
void operator delete(void *p)
{
  /* Free memory pointed to by p.
     Destructor called automatically. */
}
```

The type **size_t** is a defined type capable of containing the largest single piece of memory that can be allocated. (**size_t** is essentially an unsigned integer.) The parameter **size** will contain the number of bytes needed to hold the object being allocated. This is the amount of memory that your version of **new** must allocate. The overloaded **new** function must return a pointer to the memory that it allocates, or throw a **bad_alloc** exception if an allocation error occurs. Beyond these constraints, the overloaded **new** function can do anything else you require. When you allocate an object using **new** (whether your own version or not), the object's constructor is automatically called.

The **delete** function receives a pointer to the region of memory to be freed. It must then release the previously allocated memory back to the system. When an object is deleted, its destructor function is automatically called.

To allocate and free arrays of objects, you must use these forms of **new** and **delete**:

```
// Allocate an array of objects.
void *operator new[](size_t size)
{
  /* Perform allocation. Throw bad_alloc exception on failure.
     Each constructor called automatically. */
  return pointer_to_memory;
}

// Delete an array of objects.
void operator delete[](void *p)
{
  /* Free memory pointed to by p.
     Destructor for each element automatically called. */
}
```

When an array is allocated, each object's constructor is automatically called. When an array is freed, each object's destructor is automatically called. You do not have to provide explicit code to accomplish these actions.

The **new** and **delete** operators are generally overloaded relative to a class. For the sake of simplicity, in the example that follows, no new allocation scheme will be used. Instead, the overloaded functions will simply invoke the C-based allocation functions **malloc( )** and **free( )**. (In your own application, you are, of course, free to implement any alternative allocation method you like.)

To overload the **new** and **delete** operators relative to a class, simply make the overloaded operator functions class members. In the following sample program, the **new** and **delete** operators are overloaded relative to the **three_d** class. Both are overloaded to allow objects and arrays of objects to be allocated and freed.

```
// Demonstrate overloaded new and delete.
#include <iostream>
#include <new>
#include <cstdlib>
using namespace std;

class three_d {
```

```
    int x, y, z; // 3-D coordinates
public:
  three_d() {
    x = y = z = 0;
    cout << "Constructing 0, 0, 0\n";
  }
  three_d(int i, int j, int k) {
    x = i; y = j; z = k;
    cout << "Constructing " << i << ", ";
    cout << j << ", " << k;
    cout << '\n';
  }
  ~three_d( ) { cout << "Destructing\n"; }
  void *operator new(size_t size);
  void *operator new[](size_t size);
  void operator delete(void *p);
  void operator delete[](void *p);
  void show() ;
};

// new overloaded relative to three_d.
void *three_d::operator new(size_t size)
{
  void *p;

  cout << "Allocating three_d object.\n";
  p = malloc(size);

  // throw an exception on failure
  if(!p) {
    bad_alloc ba;
    throw ba;
  }
  return p;
}
// new overloaded relative to arrays of three_d.
void *three_d::operator new[](size_t size)
{
  void *p;

  cout << "Allocating array of three_d objects.\n";

  // throw an exception on failure
  p = malloc(size);
  if(!p) {
    bad_alloc ba;
    throw ba;
  }
  return p;
}

// delete overloaded relative to three_d.
void three_d::operator delete(void *p)
{
```

```
    cout << "Deleting three_d object.\n";
    free(p);
}

// delete overloaded relative to arrays of three_d.
void three_d::operator delete[](void *p)
{
    cout << "Deleting array of three_d objects.\n";
    free(p);
}

// Show X, Y, Z coordinates.
void three_d::show()
{
    cout << x << ", ";
    cout << y << ", ";
    cout << z << "\n";
}

int main()
{
    three_d *p1, *p2;

    try {
        p1 = new three_d[3]; // allocate array
        p2 = new three_d(5, 6, 7); // allocate object
    } catch (bad_alloc ba) {
        cout << "Allocation error.\n";
        return 1;
    }

    p1[1].show();
    p2->show();

    delete [] p1; // delete array
    delete p2;    // delete object

    return 0;
}
```

The output produced by this program is shown here:

```
Allocating array of three_d objects.
Constructing 0, 0, 0
Constructing 0, 0, 0
Constructing 0, 0, 0
Allocating three_d object.
Constructing 5, 6, 7
0, 0, 0
5, 6, 7
Destructing
Destructing
```

```
Destructing
Deleting array of three_d objects.
Destructing
Deleting three_d object.
```

The first three **Constructing** messages are caused by the allocation of the three-element array. As stated, when an array is allocated, each element's constructor is automatically called. The last **Constructing** message is caused by the allocation of a single object. The first three **Destructing** messages are caused by the deletion of the three-element array. Each element's destructor is automatically called. No special action is required on your part. The last **Destructing** message is caused by the deletion of the single object.

It is important to understand that when **new** and **delete** are overloaded relative to a specific class, the use of these operators on any other type of data causes the original **new** or **delete** to be employed. This means that if you add the following line to **main( )**, the default **new** will be executed:

```
int *f = new int; // uses default new
```

One last point: It is also possible to overload **new** and **delete** globally. To do so, just declare their **operator** functions outside of any class. In this case, C++'s default **new** and **delete** are ignored and your versions are used for all allocation requests. Of course, if you have also defined a version of **new** and **delete** relative to a class, then the class-specific version is used when allocating/freeing an object of that class. The global **new** and **delete** are used in all other cases.

Overloading the nothrow Version of new

You can also create overloaded **nothrow** versions of **new** and **delete**. To do so, use these skeletons:

```
// Nothrow version of new.
void *operator new(size_t size, const nothrow_t &n)
{
  // Perform allocation.
  if(success) return pointer_to_memory;
  else return 0;
}

// Nothrow version of new for arrays.
void *operator new[](size_t size, const nothrow_t &n)
{
  // Perform allocation.
  if(success) return pointer_to_memory;
  else return 0;
}

// Nothrow version of delete.
void operator delete(void *p, const nothrow_t &n)
{
```

```
  // free memory
}

// Nothrow version of delete for arrays.
void operator delete[](void *p, const nothrow_t &n)
{
  // free memory
}
```

The type **nothrow_t** is defined by **<new>**. This is the type of the **nothrow** object. The **nothrow_t** parameter is unused. You might want to experiment with the **nothrow** version of **new** and **delete** on your own.

CHAPTER 18

The C++ I/O System

Since the beginning of this book, you have been using the C++ I/O system. However, you have been doing so without much formal explanation. Because the C++ I/O system is based upon a hierarchy of classes, it was not possible to present its theory and details without first discussing classes and inheritance. Now it is time to examine the C++ I/O system in detail.

This chapter discusses several features of the C++ I/O system. The I/O system is quite large, and it won't be possible to discuss every class, function, or feature, but this chapter will introduce you to those that are most important and commonly used. Specifically, it shows how to overload the << and >> operators so that you can input or output objects of classes that you design. It describes how to format output and how to use I/O manipulators. The chapter ends by discussing file I/O.

Old VS Modern C++ I/O

There are currently two versions of the C++ object-oriented I/O library in use: the older one that is based upon the original specifications for C++ and the newer one defined by Standard C++. The old I/O library is supported by the header file **<iostream.h>**. The new I/O library is supported by the header **<iostream>**. For the most part, the two libraries appear the same to the programmer. This is because the new I/O library is, in essence, simply an updated and improved version of the old one. In fact, the vast marjority of differences between the two occur beneath the surface, in the way that the libraries are implemented—not in how they are used.

From the programmer's perspective, there are two main differences between the old and new C++ I/O libraries. First, the new I/O library contains a few additional features and defines some new data types. Thus, the new I/O library is essentially a superset of the old one. Nearly all programs originally written for the old library will compile without substantive changes when the new library is used. Second, the old-style I/O library was in the global namespace. The new-style library is in the **std** namespace. (Recall that the **std** namespace is used by all of the Standard C++ libraries.) Since the old-style I/O library is now obsolete, this book describes only the new I/O library, but most of the information is applicable to the old I/O library as well.

C++ Streams

A stream is a consistent, logical interface that is linked to a physical file.

The most fundamental point to understand about the C++ I/O system is that it operates on streams. A *stream* is a common, logical interface to the various devices that comprise the computer. A stream either produces or consumes information, and is linked to a physical device by the C++ I/O system. All streams behave in the same manner, even if the actual physical devices they are linked to differ. Because all streams act the same, the same I/O functions and operators can operate on virtually any type of device. For example, the same method that you use to write to the screen can be used to write to a disk file or to the printer.

In its most common form, a stream is a logical interface to a file. As C++ defines the term "file," it can refer to a disk file, the screen, the keyboard, a port, a file on tape, and so on. Although files differ in form and capabilities, all streams are the same. The advantage to this approach is that to you, the programmer, one hardware device will look much like any other. The stream provides a consistent interface.

A stream is linked to a file through an open operation, and is disassociated from a file through a close operation.

The current location is the place within a file at which the next file access will occur.

There are two types of streams: text and binary. A text stream is used with characters. When a text stream is being used, some character translations may take place. For example, when the newline character is output, it may be converted into a carriage-return/linefeed sequence. For this reason, there might not be a one-to-one correspondence between what is sent to the stream and what is written to the file. A binary stream can be used with any type of data. No character translations will occur, and there is a one-to-one correspondence between what is sent to the stream and what is actually contained in the file.

One more concept to understand is that of the current location. The *current location* (also referred to as the *current position*) is the location in a file where the next file access will occur. For example, if a file is 100 bytes long, and half the file has been read, the next read operation will occur at byte 50, which is the current location.

To summarize: In C++, I/O is performed through a logical interface called a stream. All streams have similar properties, and every stream is operated upon by the same I/O functions, no matter what type of file it is associated with. A file is the actual physical entity that contains the data. Even though files differ, streams do not. (Of course, some devices may not support all operations, such as random-access operations, so their associated streams will not support these operations either.)

The C++ Predefined Streams

C++ contains several predefined streams that are automatically opened when your program begins execution. They are **cin, cout**, **cerr**, and **clog**. As you know, **cin** is the stream associated with standard input, and **cout** is the stream associated with standard output. The **cerr** stream is linked to standard output, and so is **clog**. The difference between these two streams is that **clog** is buffered, but **cerr** is not. This means that any output sent to **cerr** is immediately output, but output to **clog** is written only when a buffer is full. Typically, **cerr** and **clog** are streams to which program debugging or error information is written.

C++ also opens wide (16-bit) character versions of the standard streams, called **wcin**, **wcout**, **wcerr**, and **wclog**. These streams exist to support languages, such as Chinese, that require large character sets. We won't be using them in this book.

By default, the C++ standard streams are linked to the console, but they can be redirected to other devices or files by your program. They can also be redirected by the operating system.

The C++ Stream Classes

As you learned in Chapter 2, C++ provides support for its I/O system in **<iostream>**. In this header, a rather complicated set of class hierarchies is specified that supports I/O operations. The I/O classes begin with a system of template classes. As explained in the Chapter 16, a template class defines the form of a class without fully specifying the data upon which it will operate. Once a template class has been defined, specific instances of a template class can be created. As it relates to the I/O library, Standard

C++ creates two specializations of the I/O template classes: one for 8-bit characters and another for wide characters. This book will use only the 8-bit character classes since they are by far the most frequently used.

The C++ I/O system is built upon two related, but different, template class hierarchies. The first is derived from the low-level I/O class called **basic_streambuf**. This class supplies the basic, low-level input and output operations, and provides the underlying support for the entire C++ I/O system. Unless you are doing advanced I/O programming, you will not need to use **basic_streambuf** directly. The class hierarchy that you will most commonly be working with is derived from **basic_ios**. This is a high-level I/O class that provides formatting, error checking, and status information related to stream I/O. (A base class for **basic_ios** is called **ios_base**, which defines several non-template traits used by **basic_ios**.) **basic_ios** is used as a base for several derived classes, including **basic_istream**, **basic_ostream**, and **basic_iostream**. These classes are used to create streams capable of input, output, and input/output, respectively.

As explained, the I/O library creates two specializations of the template class hierarchies just described: one for 8-bit characters and one for wide characters. Here is a list of the mapping of template class names to their character-based versions.

Template Class	Character-Based Class
basic_streambuf	streambuf
basic_ios	ios
basic_istream	istream
basic_ostream	ostream
basic_iostream	iostream
basic_fstream	fstream
basic_ifstream	ifstream
basic_ofstream	ofstream

The character-based names will be used throughout the remainder of this book, since they are the names that you will use in your programs. They are also the same names that were used by the old I/O library. This is why the old and the new I/O libraries are compatible at the source code level.

One last point: The **ios** class contains many member functions and variables that control or monitor the fundamental operation of a stream. The **ios** class will be referred to frequently. Just remember that if you include **<iostream>** in your program, you will have access to this important class.

Overloading the I/O Operators

In the preceding chapters, when a program needed to output or input the data associated with a class, member functions were created whose only purpose was to output or input the class' data. While there is nothing, in itself, wrong with this approach, C++ allows a much better way of performing I/O operations on classes: by overloading the << and the >> I/O operators.

An inserter
outputs
information to
a stream. An
extractor inputs
information from
a stream.

In the language of C++, the << operator is referred to as the *insertion* operator because it inserts characters into a stream. Likewise, the >> operator is called the *extraction* operator because it extracts characters from a stream. The operator functions that overload the insertion and extraction operators are generally called *inserters* and *extractors,* respectively.

As you know, the insertion and extraction operators are already overloaded (in **<iostream>**) so that they are capable of performing stream I/O on any of C++'s built-in types. Here you will see how to define these operators relative to classes that you define.

Creating Inserters

As a simple first example, let's create an inserter for the version of the **three_d** class shown here:

```
class three_d {
public:
  int x, y, z; // 3-D coordinates
  three_d(int a, int b, int c) { x = a; y = b; z = c; }
};
```

To create an inserter function for an object of type **three_d**, you must overload the << operator. Here is one way to do this:

```
// Display X, Y, Z coordinates - three_d inserter.
ostream &operator<<(ostream &stream, three_d obj)
{
  stream << obj.x << ", ";
  stream << obj.y << ", ";
  stream << obj.z << "\n";
  return stream;  // return the stream
}
```

Let's look closely at this function, because many of its features are common to all inserter functions. First, notice that it is declared as returning a reference to an object of type **ostream**. This declaration is necessary so that several inserters of this type can be combined in a compound I/O expression. Next, the function has two parameters. The first is the reference to the stream that occurs on the left side of the << operator. The second parameter is the object that occurs on the right side. (This parameter can also be a reference to the object, if you want.) Inside the function, the three values contained in an object of type **three_d** are output, and **stream** is returned.

Here is a short program that demonstrates the inserter:

```
// Demonstrate a custom inserter.
#include <iostream>
using namespace std;
```

```
class three_d {
public:
  int x, y, z; // 3-D coordinates
  three_d(int a, int b, int c) { x = a; y = b; z = c; }
} ;

// Display X, Y, Z coordinates - three_d inserter.
ostream &operator<<(ostream &stream, three_d obj)
{
  stream << obj.x << ", ";
  stream << obj.y << ", ";
  stream << obj.z << "\n";
  return stream;  // return the stream
}

int main()
{
  three_d a(1, 2, 3), b(3, 4, 5), c(5, 6, 7);

  cout << a << b << c;

  return 0;
}
```

This program displays the following output:

```
1, 2, 3
3, 4, 5
5, 6, 7
```

If you eliminate the code that is specific to the **three_d** class, you are left with the skeleton for an inserter function, as shown here:

```
ostream &operator<<(ostream &stream, class_type obj)
{
  // class specific code goes here
  return stream;  // return the stream
}
```

Of course, it is permissible for **obj** to be passed by reference.

Within wide boundaries, what an inserter function actually does is up to you. However, good programming practice dictates that your inserter should produce reasonable output. Just make sure that you return **stream**.

Before moving on, you might be wondering why the **three_d** inserter was not coded as shown here:

```
// Limited version - don't use.
ostream &operator<<(ostream &stream, three_d obj)
{
  cout << obj.x << ", ";
```

```
    cout << obj.y << ", ";
    cout << obj.z << "\n";
    return stream;  // return the stream
}
```

In this version, the **cout** stream is hard-coded into the function. This limits the situations where it can be applied. Remember that the **<<** operator can be applied to any stream, and that the stream used in the **<<** expression is passed to **stream**. Therefore, you must use the stream passed to the function if it is to work correctly in all cases. Only in this way can you create an inserter that can be used in any I/O expression.

Using Friend Functions to Overload Inserters

In the preceding program, the overloaded inserter function is not a member of **three_d**. In fact, neither inserter nor extractor functions can be members of a class. The reason for this is that when an **operator** function is a member of a class, the left operand (implicitly passed using the **this** pointer) must be an object of the class that has generated the call to the **operator** function. There is no way to change this. However, when inserters are overloaded, the left operand is a stream, and the right operand is an object of the class being output. Therefore, overloaded inserters must be non-member functions.

The fact that inserters must not be members of the class on which they are defined to operate raises a serious question: How can an overloaded inserter access the private elements of a class? In the preceding program, the variables **x**, **y**, and **z** were made **public** so that the inserter could access them. But hiding data is an important part of OOP, and forcing all data to be public is a serious inconsistency. However, there is a solution: An inserter can be a friend of a class. As a friend of the class for which it is defined, it has access to private data. To show you an example of this, the **three_d** class and sample program are reworked here, with the overloaded inserter declared as a friend:

```
// Use a friend to overload <<.
#include <iostream>
using namespace std;

class three_d {
  int x, y, z; // 3-D coordinates - now private
public:
  three_d(int a, int b, int c) { x = a; y = b; z = c; }
  friend ostream &operator<<(ostream &stream, three_d obj);
} ;

// Display X, Y, Z coordinates - three_d inserter.
ostream &operator<<(ostream &stream, three_d obj)
{
  stream << obj.x << ", ";
  stream << obj.y << ", ";
  stream << obj.z << "\n";
  return stream;  // return the stream
}
```

```
int main()
{
  three_d a(1, 2, 3), b(3, 4, 5), c(5, 6, 7);

  cout << a << b << c;

  return 0;
}
```

Notice that the variables **x**, **y**, and **z** are now private to **three_d**, but can still be directly accessed by the inserter. Making inserters (and extractors) friends of the classes for which they are defined preserves the encapsulation principle of OOP.

Overloading Extractors

To overload an extractor, use the same general approach that you use when overloading an inserter. For example, the following extractor inputs 3-D coordinates. Notice that it also prompts the user.

```
// Get three-dimensional values - three_d extractor.
istream &operator>>(istream &stream, three_d &obj)
{
  cout << "Enter X,Y,Z values: ";
  stream >> obj.x >> obj.y >> obj.z;
  return stream;
}
```

An extractor must return a reference to an object of type **istream**. Also, the first parameter must be a reference to an object of type **istream**. This is the stream that occurs on the left side of the **>>**. The second parameter is a reference to the variable that will be receiving input. Because it is a reference, the second parameter can be modified when information is input.

The skeleton of an extractor is shown here:

```
istream &operator>>(istream &stream, object_type &obj)
{
  // put your extractor code here
  return stream;
}
```

The following program demonstrates the extractor for objects of type **three_d**:

```
// Demonstrate a custom extractor.
#include <iostream>
using namespace std;

class three_d {
```

```
    int x, y, z; // 3-D coordinates
public:
  three_d(int a, int b, int c) { x = a; y = b; z = c; }
  friend ostream &operator<<(ostream &stream, three_d obj);
  friend istream &operator>>(istream &stream, three_d &obj);
} ;

// Display X, Y, Z coordinates - three_d inserter.
ostream &operator<<(ostream &stream, three_d obj)
{
  stream << obj.x << ", ";
  stream << obj.y << ", ";
  stream << obj.z << "\n";
  return stream; // return the stream
}

// Get three dimensional values - three_d extractor.
istream &operator>>(istream &stream, three_d &obj)
{
  cout << "Enter X,Y,Z values: ";
  stream >> obj.x >> obj.y >> obj.z;
  return stream;
}

int main()
{
  three_d a(1, 2, 3);

  cout << a;

  cin >> a;
  cout << a;

  return 0;
}
```

A sample run is shown here.

```
1, 2, 3
Enter X,Y,Z values: 4 5 6
4, 5, 6
```

Like inserters, extractor functions cannot be members of the class they are designed to operate upon. They can be friends or simply independent functions.

Except for the fact that you must return a reference to an object of type **istream**, you can do anything you like inside an extractor function. However, for the sake of structure and clarity, it is best to use extractors only for input operations.

C I/O Versus C++ I/O

As you may know, C++'s predecessor, C, has one of the most flexible yet powerful I/O systems of any of the structured languages. (In fact, it may be safe to say that among the world's structured programming languages, C's I/O system is unparalleled.) Given the power of C's I/O functions, you might be asking yourself why C++ defined its own I/O system, since for the most part it duplicates the one already contained in C. The answer is that the C I/O system provides no support for user-defined objects. For example, if you create the following structure in C:

```
struct my_struct {
  int count;
  char s[80];
  double balance;
} cust;
```

there is no way to customize or extend C's I/O system so that it knows about, and can perform I/O operations directly on, an object of type **my_struct**. However, since objects are at the core of object-oriented programming, it makes sense that C++ has an I/O system that can be made aware of objects that you create. Thus, a new, object-oriented I/O system was invented for C++. As you have seen, C++'s approach to I/O allows you to overload the << and >> operators so that they know about classes that you create.

One other point: Because C++ is a superset of C, all of C's I/O system is included in C++. (See Appendix A for an overview of C-based I/O.) Therefore, if you are migrating C programs to C++, you won't have to change all the I/O statements immediately. The C-based statements will still compile and run. It is just that C-based I/O has no object-oriented capabilities.

Formatted I/O

Up to this point, the format for inputting or outputting information has been left to the defaults provided by the C++ I/O system. However, you can precisely control the format of your data in either of two ways. The first way uses member functions of the **ios** class. The second way uses a special type of function called a *manipulator*. We will begin by looking at formatting that uses the **ios** member functions.

Formatting with the ios Member Functions

Each stream has associated with it a set of format flags that control the way information is formatted by a stream. The **ios** class declares a bitmask enumeration called **fmtflags**, in which the following values are defined. (Technically, these values are defined within **ios_base**, which, as explained earlier, is a base class for **ios**.)

adjustfield	floatfield	right	skipws
basefield	hex	scientific	unitbuf
boolalpha	internal	showbase	uppercase
dec	left	showpoint	
fixed	oct	showpos	

18

These values are used to set or clear the format flags. If you are using an older compiler, then it may not define the **fmtflags** enumeration type. In this case, the format flags will be encoded into a long integer.

When the **skipws** flag is set, leading whitespace characters (spaces, tabs, and newlines) are discarded when performing input on a stream. When **skipws** is cleared, whitespace characters are not discarded.

When the **left** flag is set, output is left justified. When the **right** flag is set, output is right justified. When the **internal** flag is set, a numeric value is padded to fill a field by inserting spaces between any sign or base character. If none of these flags is set, output is right justified by default.

By default, numeric values are output in decimal. However, it is possible to change the number base. Setting the **oct** flag causes output to be displayed in octal. Setting the **hex** flag causes output to be displayed in hexadecimal. To return output to decimal, set the **dec** flag.

Setting **showbase** causes the base of numeric values to be shown. For example, if the conversion base is hexadecimal, the value 1F will be displayed as 0x1F.

By default, when scientific notation is displayed, the **e** is in lowercase. Also, when a hexadecimal value is displayed, the **x** is in lowercase. When **uppercase** is set, these characters are displayed in uppercase.

Setting **showpos** causes a leading plus sign to be displayed before positive values.

Setting **showpoint** causes a decimal point and trailing zeros to be displayed for all floating point output—whether needed or not.

By setting the **scientific** flag, floating-point numeric values are displayed using scientific notation. When **fixed** is set, floating-point values are displayed using normal notation. When neither flag is set, the compiler chooses an appropriate method.

When **unitbuf** is set, the buffer is flushed after each insertion operation.

When **boolalpha** is set, Booleans can be input or output by using the keywords **true** and **false**.

Since it is common to refer to the **oct**, **dec**, and **hex** fields, they can be collectively referred to as **basefield**. Similarly, the **left**, **right**, and **internal** fields can be referred to as **adjustfield**. Finally, the **scientific** and **fixed** fields can be referenced as **floatfield**.

To set format flags, call **setf( )**.

To set a flag, use the **setf( )** function. This function is a member of **ios**. Its most common form is shown here:

    fmtflags setf(fmtflags *flags*);

This function returns the previous settings of the format flags and turns on those flags specified by *flags*. For example, to turn on the **showbase** flag, you can use this statement:

```
stream.setf(ios::showbase);
```

Here, *stream* is the stream you want to affect. Notice the use of **ios::** to qualify **showbase**. Because **showbase** is an enumerated constant defined by the **ios** class, it must be qualified by **ios** when it is referred to. This principle applies to all of the format flags.

The following program uses **setf( )** to turn on both the **showpos** and **scientific** flags:

```
#include <iostream>
using namespace std;

int main()
{
  cout.setf(ios::showpos);
  cout.setf(ios::scientific);
  cout << 123 << " " << 123.23 << " ";

  return 0;
}
```

The output produced by this program is shown here:

```
+123 +1.232300e+002
```

You may OR together as many flags as you like in a single call. For example, by ORing together **scientific** and **showpos**, as shown next, you can change the program so that only one call is made to **setf( )**:

```
cout.setf(ios::scientific | ios::showpos);
```

To turn off a flag, use the **unsetf( )** function, whose prototype is shown here:

    void unsetf(fmtflags *flags*);

To clear format flags, call **unsetf( )**.

The flags specified by *flags* are cleared. (All other flags are unaffected.)

Sometimes it is useful to know the current flag settings. You can retrieve the current flag values by using the **flags( )** function, whose prototype is shown here:

To obtain the current flag settings, call **flags( )**.

    fmtflags flags( );

This function returns the current value of the flags relative to the invoking stream.

The following form of **flags( )** sets the flag values to those specified by *flags*, and returns the previous flag values:

fmtflags flags(fmtflags *flags*);

To see how **flags( )** and **unsetf( )** work, examine this program. It includes a function called **showflags( )** that displays the state of the flags.

```
#include <iostream>
using namespace std;

void showflags(ios::fmtflags f);

int main()
{
  ios::fmtflags f;

  f = cout.flags();

  showflags(f);
  cout.setf(ios::showpos);
  cout.setf(ios::scientific);

  f = cout.flags();
  showflags(f);

  cout.unsetf(ios::scientific);

  f = cout.flags();
  showflags(f);

  return 0;
}

void showflags(ios::fmtflags f)
{
  long i;

  for(i=0x4000; i; i = i >> 1)
    if(i & f) cout << "1 ";
    else cout << "0 ";

  cout << "\n";
}
```

When run, the program produces the following output. (The precise output that you see may differ because of implementation differences between compilers.)

```
0 0 0 0 0 1 0 0 0 0 0 0 0 0 1
0 0 1 0 0 1 0 0 0 1 0 0 0 0 1
0 0 0 0 0 1 0 0 0 1 0 0 0 0 1
```

In the foregoing program, notice that the type **fmtflags** is preceded by **ios::**. This is necessary since **fmtfags** is a type defined by **ios**. In general, whenever you use the name of a type or enumerated constant that is defined by a class, you must qualify it with the name of the class.

Setting the Field Width, Precision, and Fill Characters
In addition to the formatting flags, you can also set the field width, the fill character, and the number of digits of precision, by using these functions:

    streamsize width(streamsize *len*);

    char fill(char *ch*);

    streamsize precision(streamsize *num*);

The **width( )** function returns the current field width and sets the field width to *len*. By default, the field width varies, depending upon the number of characters it takes to hold the data. The **fill( )** function returns the current fill character, which is a space by default, and makes the current fill character the same as *ch*. The fill character is used to pad output to fill a specified field width. The **precision( )** function returns the number of digits displayed after a decimal point and sets that value to *num*. (By default, there are six digits of precision.) The **streamsize** type is defined as some form of integer.

Here is a program that demonstrates these three functions:

```
#include <iostream>
using namespace std;

int main()
{
  cout.setf(ios::showpos);
  cout.setf(ios::scientific);
  cout << 123 << " " << 123.23 << "\n";

  cout.precision(2); // two digits after decimal point
  cout.width(10);    // in a field of 10 characters
  cout << 123 << " ";
  cout.width(10);    // set width to 10
  cout << 123.23 << "\n";

  cout.fill('#');   // fill using #
  cout.width(10);   // in a field of 10 characters
  cout << 123 << " ";
  cout.width(10);   // set width to 10
  cout << 123.23;

  return 0;
}
```

The program displays this output:

```
+123 +1.232300e+002
      +123 +1.23e+002
######+123 +1.23e+002
```

In some implementations, it is necessary to reset the field width before each output operation. This is why **width( )** is called repeatedly in the preceding program.

There are overloaded forms of **width( )**, **precision( )**, and **fill( )** which obtain, but do not change the current setting. These forms are shown here.

char fill( );

streamsize width( );

streamsize precision( );

Using I/O Manipulators

You can use a manipulator to embed formatting instructions in an I/O expression.

The C++ I/O system includes a second way in which you can alter the format parameters of a stream. This method uses special functions, called *manipulators*, that can be included in an I/O expression. The standard manipulators are shown in Table 18-1.

Manipulator	Purpose	Input/Output
boolalpha	Turns on **boolapha** flag.	Input/Output
dec	Turns on **dec** flag.	Input/Output
endl	Output a newline character and flush the stream.	Output
ends	Output a null.	Output
fixed	Turns on **fixed** flag.	Output
flush	Flush a stream.	Output
hex	Turns on **hex** flag.	Input/Output
internal	Turns on **internal** flag.	Output
left	Turns on **left** flag.	Output
nobooalpha	Turns off **boolalpha** flag.	Input/Output
noshowbase	Turns off **showbase** flag.	Output
noshowpoint	Turns off **showpoint** flag.	Output
noshowpos	Turns off **showpos** flag.	Output
noskipws	Turns off **skipws** flag.	Input
nounitbuf	Turns off **unitbuf** flag.	Output

The Standard C++ I/O Manipulators
Table 18-1.

18

Manipulator	Purpose	Input/Output
nouppercase	Turns off **uppercase** flag.	Output
oct	Turns on **oct** flag.	Input/Output
resetiosflags(fmtflags *f*)	Turns off the flags specified in *f*.	Input/Output
right	Turns on **right** flag.	Output
scientific	Turns on **scientific** flag.	Output
setbase(int *base*)	Sets the number base to *base*.	Input/Output
setfill(int *ch*)	Sets the fill character to *ch*.	Output
setiosflags(fmtflags *f*)	Turns on the flags specified in *f*.	Input/Output
setprecision(int *p*)	Sets the number of digits of precision.	Output
setw(int *w*)	Sets the field width to *w*.	Output
showbase	Turns on **showbase** flag.	Output
showpoint	Turns on **showpoint** flag.	Output
showpos	Turns on **showpos** flag.	Output
skipws	Turns on **skipws** flag.	Input
unitbuf	Turns on **unitbuf** flag.	Output
uppercase	Turns on **uppercase** flag.	Output
ws	Skips leading white space.	Input

The Standard
C++ I/O
Manipulators
(continued)
Table 18-1.

To use those manipulators that take arguments, you must include **<iomanip>** in your program.

A manipulator is used as part of a larger I/O expression. Here is a sample program that uses manipulators to control the format of its output:

```
#include <iostream>
#include <iomanip>
using namespace std;

int main()
{
  cout << setprecision(2) << 1000.243 << endl;
  cout << setw(20) << "Hello there.";

  return 0;
}
```

The output is shown here.

18

```
1e+003
        Hello there.
```

Notice how the manipulators occur in the chain of I/O operations. Also, notice that when a manipulator does not take an argument, such as **endl** in the example, it is not followed by parentheses.

The following program uses **setiosflags( )** to set the **scientific** and **showpos** flags:

```
#include <iostream>
#include <iomanip>
using namespace std;

int main()
{
  cout << setiosflags(ios::showpos);
  cout << setiosflags(ios::scientific);
  cout << 123 << " " << 123.23;

  return 0;
}
```

The output is shown here.

```
+123 +1.232300e+002
```

The program shown next uses **ws** to skip any leading whitespace when inputting a string into **s**:

```
#include <iostream>
using namespace std;

int main()
{
  char s[80];

  cin >> ws >> s;
  cout << s;

  return 0;
}
```

Creating Your Own Manipulator Functions

You can create your own manipulator functions. There are two types of manipulator functions: those that take arguments and those that don't. The creation of parameterized manipulators requires the use of techniques beyond the scope of this book. However, the creation of parameterless manipulators is easily accomplished and is described here.

All parameterless manipulator output functions have this skeleton:

ostream &*manip_name*(ostream &*stream*)
{
 // *your code here*
 return *stream*;
}

Here, *manip_name* is the name of the manipulator. It is important to understand that even though the manipulator has as its single argument a pointer to the stream upon which it is operating, no argument is specified when the manipulator is used in an output expression.

The following program creates a manipulator called **setup( )** that turns on left justification, sets the field width to 10, and specifies that the dollar sign will be the fill character:

```cpp
#include <iostream>
#include <iomanip>
using namespace std;

ostream &setup(ostream &stream)
{
  stream.setf(ios::left);
  stream << setw(10) << setfill('$');
  return stream;
}

int main()
{
  cout << 10 << " " << setup << 10;

  return 0;
}
```

Custom manipulators are useful for two reasons. First, you might need to perform an I/O operation on a device for which none of the predefined manipulators applies—a plotter, for example. In this case, creating your own manipulators will make it more convenient when outputting to the device. Second, you may find that you are repeating the same sequence of operations many times. You can consolidate these operations into a single manipulator, as the foregoing program illustrates.

All parameterless input manipulator functions have this skeleton:

istream &*manip_name*(istream &*stream*)
{
 // *your code here*
 return *stream*;
}

For example, the following program creates the **prompt( )** manipulator. It displays a prompting message and then configures input to accept hexadecimal.

```
#include <iostream>
#include <iomanip>
using namespace std;

istream &prompt(istream &stream)
{
  cin >> hex;
  cout << "Enter number using hex format: ";

  return stream;
}

int main()
{
  int i;

  cin >> prompt >> i;
  cout << i;

  return 0;
}
```

18

Remember that it is crucial that your manipulator return *stream*. If this is not done, then your manipulator cannot be used in a compound input or output expression.

File I/O

You can use the C++ I/O system to perform file I/O. In order to perform file I/O, you must include the header **<fstream>** in your program. It defines several important classes and values.

Opening and Closing a File

In C++, a file is opened by linking it to a stream. As you know, there are three types of streams: input, output, and input/output. To open an input stream, you must declare the stream to be of class **ifstream**. To open an output stream, it must be declared as class **ofstream**. A stream that will be performing both input and output operations must be declared as class **fstream**. For example, this fragment creates one input stream, one output stream, and one stream capable of both input and output:

```
ifstream in;   // input
ofstream out;  // output
fstream both;  // input and output
```

open( ) *opens a file.*

Once you have created a stream, one way to associate it with a file is by using **open( )**. This function is a member of each of the three stream classes. The prototype for each is shown here:

> void ifstream::open(const char *filename,
>   ios::openmode mode = ios::in);

```
void ofstream::open(const char *filename,
          ios::openmode mode = ios::out | ios::trunc);
```

```
void fstream::open(const char *filename,
          ios::openmode mode = ios::in | ios::out);
```

Here, *filename* is the name of the file; it can include a path specifier. The value of *mode* determines how the file is opened. It must be one or more of the following values defined by **openmode**, which is an enumeration defined by **ios**.

ios::app

ios::ate

ios::binary

ios::in

ios::out

ios::trunc

You can combine two or more of these values by ORing them together.

NOTE: Depending on your compiler, the mode parameter for **fstream::open( )** may not default to **in | out**. Therefore, you might need to specify this explicitly.

Including **ios::app** causes all output to that file to be appended to the end. This value can be used only with files capable of output. Including **ios::ate** causes a seek to the end of the file to occur when the file is opened. Although **ios::ate** causes a seek to the end of the file, I/O operations can still occur anywhere within the file.

The **ios::in** value specifies that the file is capable of input. The **ios::out** value specifies that the file is capable of output.

The **ios::binary** value causes a file to be opened in binary mode. By default, all files are opened in text mode. In text mode, various character translations may take place, such as carriage return, linefeed sequences being converted into newlines. When a file is opened in binary mode, no such character translations will occur. Keep in mind that any file, whether it contains formatted text or raw data, can be opened in either binary or text mode. The only difference is whether character translations take place.

The **ios::trunc** value causes the contents of a preexisting file by the same name to be destroyed, and the file is truncated to zero length. When creating an output stream using **ofstream**, any preexisting file by that name is automatically truncated.

The following fragment opens a normal output file:

```
ofstream out;
out.open("test");
```

Since the *mode* parameter to **open( )** defaults to a value appropriate to the type of stream being opened, there is no need to specify its value in the preceding example.

If **open( )** fails, the stream will evaluate to false when used in a Boolean expression. You can make use of this fact to confirm that the open operation succeeded, by using a statement like this:

```
if(!mystream) {
  cout << "Cannot open file.\n";
  // handle error
}
```

18

In general, you should always check the result of a call to **open( )** before attempting to access the file.

You can also check to see if you have successfully opened a file by using the **is_open( )** function, which is a member of **fstream**, **ifstream**, and **ofstream**. It has this prototype:

    bool is_open( );

It returns true if the stream is linked to an open file, and false otherwise. For example, the following checks if **mystream** is currently open:

```
if(!mystream.is_open()) {
  cout << "File is not open.\n";
  // ...
```

Although it is entirely proper to use the **open( )** function for opening a file, most of the time you will not do so because the **ifstream**, **ofstream**, and **fstream** classes have constructors that automatically open the file. The constructors have the same parameters and defaults as the **open( )** function. Therefore, the most common way you will see a file opened is shown in this example:

```
ifstream mystream("myfile"); // open file for input
```

If, for some reason, the file cannot be opened, the value of the associated stream variable will be false.

To close a file, call **close( )**.

To close a file, use the member function **close( )**. For example, to close the file linked to a stream called **mystream**, you would use this statement:

```
mystream.close();
```

The **close( )** function takes no parameters and returns no value.

Reading and Writing Text Files

The easiest way to read from or write to a text file is to use the **<<** and **>>** operators. For example, this program writes an integer, a floating-point value, and a string to a file called **test**:

```
// Write to file.
#include <iostream>
#include <fstream>
using namespace std;

int main()
{
  ofstream out("test");
  if(!out) {
    cout << "Cannot open file.\n";
    return 1;
   }

  out << 10 << " " << 123.23 << "\n";
  out << "This is a short text file.";

  out.close();

  return 0;
}
```

The following program reads an integer, a **float**, a character, and a string from the file created by the previous program:

```
// Read from file.
#include <iostream>
#include <fstream>
using namespace std;

int main()
{
  char ch;
  int i;
  float f;
  char str[80];

  ifstream in("test");
  if(!in) {
    cout << "Cannot open file.\n";
    return 1;
  }

  in >> i;
  in >> f;
  in >> ch;
  in >> str;
```

```
    cout << i << " " << f << " " << ch << "\n";
    cout << str;

    in.close();
    return 0;
}
```

Keep in mind that when the **>>** operator is used for reading text files, certain character translations occur. For example, whitespace characters are omitted. If you want to prevent any character translations, you must open a file for binary access. Also remember that when **>>** is used to read a string, input stops when the first whitespace character is encountered.

18

Unformatted Binary I/O

Formatted text files (like those used in the preceding examples) are useful for a variety of situations, but they do not have the flexibility of unformatted binary files. For this reason, C++ supports a number of binary (sometimes called "raw") file I/O functions that can perform unformatted operations.

When performing binary operations on a file, be sure to open it using the **ios::binary** mode specifier. Although the unformatted file functions will work on files opened for text mode, some character translations may occur. Character translations negate the purpose of binary file operations.

get( ) reads a character from a file and put( ) writes a character to a file.

In general, there are two ways to write and read unformatted binary data to or from a file. First, you can write a byte by using the member function **put( )**, and read a byte by using the member function **get( )**. The second way uses C++'s block I/O functions: **read( )** and **write( )**. Each way is examined here.

Using get( ) and put( )

The **get( )** function has many forms, but the most commonly used version is shown next, along with that of **put( )**:

    istream &get(char &*ch*);

    ostream &put(char *ch*);

The **get( )** function reads a single character from the associated stream and puts that value in *ch*. It returns a reference to the stream. This value will be null if the end of the file is reached. The **put( )** function writes *ch* to the stream and returns a reference to the stream.

The following program will display the contents of any file on the screen. It uses the **get( )** function.

```
// Display a file using get().
#include <iostream>
#include <fstream>
using namespace std;

int main(int argc, char *argv[])
```

```
{
  char ch;

  if(argc!=2) {
    cout << "Usage: PR <filename>\n";
    return 1;
  }

  ifstream in(argv[1], ios::in | ios::binary);
  if(!in) {
    cout << "Cannot open file.\n";
    return 1;
  }

  while(in) { // in will be false when eof is reached
    in.get(ch);
    if(in) cout << ch;
  }

  in.close();

  return 0;
}
```

When **in** reaches the end of the file, it will be false, causing the **while** loop to stop.

There is actually a more compact way to code the loop that reads and displays a file, as shown here:

```
while(in.get(ch))
  cout << ch;
```

This form works because **get( )** returns the stream **in**, and **in** will be false when the end of the file is encountered.

This program uses **put( )** to write a string to a file:

```
// Use put() to write to a file.
#include <iostream>
#include <fstream>
using namespace std;

int main()
{
  char *p = "hello there";

  ofstream out("test", ios::out | ios::binary);
  if(!out) {
    cout << "Cannot open file.\n";
    return 1;
    }
```

```
while(*p) out.put(*p++);

out.close();

return 0;
}
```

Reading and Writing Blocks of Data

To read and write blocks of binary data, use the **read( )** and **write( )** member functions. Their prototypes are shown here:

>   istream &read(char *buf*, streamsize *num*);

>   ostream &write(const char *buf*, int streamsize *num*);

The **read( )** function reads *num* bytes from the associated stream and puts them in the buffer pointed to by *buf*. The **write( )** function writes *num* bytes to the associated stream from the buffer pointed to by *buf*. As mentioned earlier, **streamsize** is defined as some form of integer. It is capable of holding the largest number of bytes that can be transferred in any one I/O operation.

read( ) inputs a block of data, and **write( )** outputs a block of data.

The following program writes and then reads an array of integers:

```
// Use read() and write().
#include <iostream>
#include <fstream>
using namespace std;

int main()
{
  int n[5] = {1, 2, 3, 4, 5};
  register int i;

  ofstream out("test", ios::out | ios::binary);
  if(!out) {
    cout << "Cannot open file.\n";
    return 1;
   }

  out.write((char *) &n, sizeof n);

  out.close();

  for(i=0; i<5; i++) // clear array
    n[i] = 0;

  ifstream in("test", ios::in | ios::binary);
  if(!in) {
    cout << "Cannot open file.\n";
    return 1;
  }
```

```
    in.read((char *) &n, sizeof n);

    for(i=0; i<5; i++) // show values read from file
      cout << n[i] << " ";

    in.close();

    return 0;
}
```

Note that the type casts inside the calls to **read( )** and **write( )** are necessary when operating on a buffer that is not defined as a character array.

gcount( ) returns the number of characters read by the last input operation.

If the end of the file is reached before *num* characters have been read, then **read( )** simply stops, and the buffer will contain as many characters as were available. You can find out how many characters have been read by using another member function, called **gcount( )**, which has this prototype:

    streamsize gcount( );

gcount( ) returns the number of characters read by the last input operation.

Detecting EOF

You can detect when the end of the file is reached by using the member function **eof( )**, which has this prototype:

    bool eof( );

It returns true when the end of the file has been reached; otherwise, it returns false.

eof( ) detects when the end of the file has been reached.

The following program uses **eof( )** to display the contents of a file on the screen:

```
// Detect end-of-file using eof().
#include <iostream>
#include <fstream>
using namespace std;

int main(int argc, char *argv[])
{
  char ch;

  if(argc!=2) {
    cout << "Usage: PR <filename>\n";
    return 1;
  }

  ifstream in(argv[1], ios::in | ios::binary);
  if(!in) {
    cout << "Cannot open file.\n";
    return 1;
  }

  while(!in.eof()) { // use eof()
```

```
      in.get(ch);
      if(!in.eof()) cout << ch;
  }

  in.close();

  return 0;
}
```

A File Comparison Example

18

The following program illustrates the power and simplicity of the C++ file system. It compares two files for equality. It does so by using the binary file functions **read( )**, **eof( )**, and **gcount( )**. The program first opens the files for binary operations. (This is necessary to prevent character translations from being performed.) Next, it reads one buffer at a time from each of the files and compares the contents. Since less than a full buffer may be read, it uses the **gcount( )** function to determine precisely how many characters are in the buffers. As you can see, when using the C++ file functions, very little code is needed to perform these operations.

```
// Compare files.
#include <iostream>
#include <fstream>
using namespace std;

int main(int argc, char *argv[])
{
  register int i;

  unsigned char buf1[1024], buf2[1024];

  if(argc!=3) {
    cout << "Usage: compfiles <file1> <file2>\n";
    return 1;
  }

  ifstream f1(argv[1], ios::in | ios::binary);
  if(!f1) {
    cout << "Cannot open first file.\n";
    return 1;
  }
  ifstream f2(argv[2], ios::in | ios::binary);
  if(!f2) {
    cout << "Cannot open second file.\n";
    return 1;
   }

  cout << "Comparing files...\n";

  do {
    f1.read((char *) buf1, sizeof buf1);
    f2.read((char *) buf2, sizeof buf2);
```

```
    if(f1.gcount() != f2.gcount()) {
      cout << "Files are of differing sizes.\n";
      f1.close();
      f2.close();
      return 0;
    }

    // compare contents of buffers
    for(i=0; i<f1.gcount(); i++)
      if(buf1[i] != buf2[i]) {
        cout << "Files differ.\n";
        f1.close();
        f2.close();
        return 0;
      }

  } while(!f1.eof() && !f2.eof());

  cout << "Files are the same.\n";

  f1.close();
  f2.close();

  return 0;
}
```

Here is an experiment: The buffer size is hard-coded at 1024. As an exercise, change this value to a **const** variable, and try different buffer sizes. Find the optimal buffer size for your operating environment.

More Binary I/O Functions

In addition to the form shown earlier, the **get( )** function is overloaded several different ways. The prototypes for the three most commonly used overloaded forms are shown here:

istream &get(char *buf, streamsize *num*);

istream &get(char *buf, streamsize *num*, char *delim*);

int get( );

The first form reads characters into the array pointed to by *buf* until either *num*–1 characters have been read, a newline is found, or the end of the file has been encountered. The array pointed to by *buf* will be null-terminated by **get( )**. If the newline character is encountered in the input stream, it is *not* extracted. Instead, it remains in the stream until the next input operation.

The second form reads characters into the array pointed to by *buf* until either *num*–1 characters have been read, the character specified by *delim* has been found, or the end of the file has been encountered. The array pointed to by *buf* will be null-terminated by **get( )**. If the delimiter character is encountered in the input stream, it is *not* extracted. Instead, it remains in the stream until the next input operation.

The third overloaded form of **get( )** returns the next character from the stream. The character is contained in the low-order byte of the return value. Thus, the return value of **get( )** can be assigned to a **char** variable. The function returns **EOF** (a value that indicates end-of-file) if the end of the file is encountered. **EOF** is defined by **<iostream>**.

One good use for **get( )** is to read a string that contains spaces. As you know, when you use **>>** to read a string, it stops reading when the first whitespace character is encountered. This makes **>>** useless for reading a string containing spaces. However, you can overcome this problem by using **get(buf, num)**, as illustrated in this program:

18

```
// Use get() to read a string that contains spaces.
#include <iostream>
#include <fstream>
using namespace std;

int main()
{
  char str[80];

  cout << "Enter your name: ";
  cin.get(str, 79);

  cout << str << '\n';

  return 0;
}
```

Here, the delimiter to **get( )** is allowed to default to a newline. This makes **get( )** act much like the standard **gets( )** function. However, the advantage to **get( )** is that it enables you to prevent user input from overrunning the receiving character array because you can specify the maximum number of characters to read. This makes **get( )** much safer than **gets( )** when reading user input.

Another function that performs input is **getline( )**. It is a member of each input stream class. Its prototypes are shown here:

istream &getline(char *buf*, streamsize *num*);

istream &getline(char *buf*, streamsize *num*, char *delim*);

getline( ) is another C++ input function.

The first form reads characters into the array pointed to by *buf* until either *num*–1 characters have been read, a newline character has been found, or the end of the file has been encountered. The array pointed to by *buf* will be null-terminated by **getline( )**. If the newline character is encountered in the input stream, it is extracted, but is not put into *buf*.

The second form reads characters into the array pointed to by *buf* until either *num*–1 characters have been read, the character specified by *delim* has been found, or the end of the file has been encountered. The array pointed to by *buf* will be null-terminated by **getline( )**. If the delimiter character is encountered in the input stream, it is extracted, but is not put into *buf*.

As you can see, the two versions of **getline( )** are virtually identical to the **get(buf, num)** and **get(buf, num, delim)** versions of **get( )**. Both read characters from input and put them into the array pointed to by *buf*, until either *num*–1 characters have been read or the delimiter character is encountered. The difference between **get( )** and **getline( )** is that **getline( )** reads and removes the delimiter from the input stream; **get( )** does not.

You can obtain the next character in the input stream without removing it from that stream by using **peek( )**. It has this prototype:

    int peek( );

peek( ) obtains the next character in the input stream.

peek( ) returns the next character in the stream, or **EOF** if the end of the file is encountered. The character is returned in the low-order byte of the return value. Thus, the return value of **peek( )** can be assigned to a **char** variable.

You can return the last character read from a stream to that stream by using **putback( )**. Its prototype is shown here,

    istream &putback(char *c*);

putback( ) returns a character to the input stream.

where *c* is the last character read.

flush( ) flushes an output stream.

When output is performed, data is not immediately written to the physical device linked to the stream. Instead, information is stored in an internal buffer until the buffer is full. Only then are the contents of that buffer written to disk. However, you can force the information to be physically written to disk, before the buffer is full, by calling **flush( )**. Its prototype is shown here:

    ostream &flush( );

Calls to **flush( )** might be warranted when a program is going to be used in adverse environments (in situations where power outages occur frequently, for example).

Random Access

So far, files have always been read or written sequentially. But you can also access a file in random order. In C++'s I/O system, you perform random access using the **seekg( )** and **seekp( )** functions. Their most common forms are shown here:

    istream &seekg(off_type *offset*, seekdir *origin*);

    ostream &seekp(off_type *offset*, seekdir *origin*);

Here, **off_type** is an integer type defined by **ios** that is capable of containing the largest valid value that *offset* can have. **seekdir** is an enumeration that has these values:

Value	Meaning
ios::beg	Beginning of file
ios::cur	Current location
ios::end	End of file

seekg( ) *moves the get pointer.*
seekp( ) *moves the put pointer.*

The C++ I/O system manages two pointers associated with a file. One is the *get pointer*, which specifies where in the file the next input operation will occur. The other is the *put pointer*, which specifies where in the file the next output operation will occur. Each time an input or an output operation takes place, the appropriate pointer is automatically advanced. Using the **seekg( )** and **seekp( )** functions, it is possible to access the file in a non-sequential fashion.

The **seekg( )** function moves the associated file's current get pointer *offset* number of bytes from the specified *origin*. The **seekp( )** function moves the associated file's current put pointer *offset* number of bytes from the specified *origin*.

Generally, random access I/O should be performed only on those files opened for binary operations. The character translations that may occur on text files could cause a position request to be out of sync with the actual contents of the file.

The following program demonstrates the **seekp( )** function. It allows you to specify a file name on the command line, followed by the specific byte that you want to change in the file. The program then writes an **X** at the specified location. Notice that the file must be opened for binary read/write operations.

```
// Demonstrate random access.
#include <iostream>
#include <fstream>
#include <cstdlib>
using namespace std;

int main(int argc, char *argv[])
{
  if(argc!=3) {
    cout << "Usage: CHANGE <filename> <byte>\n";
    return 1;
  }

  fstream out(argv[1], ios::in | ios::out | ios::binary);
  if(!out) {
    cout << "Cannot open file.\n";
    return 1;
  }

  out.seekp(atoi(argv[2]), ios::beg);

  out.put('X');
  out.close();

  return 0;
}
```

The next program uses **seekg( )**. It displays the contents of a file, beginning with the location you specify on the command line.

```
// Display a file from a given starting point.
#include <iostream>
```

```
#include <fstream>
#include <cstdlib>
using namespace std;

int main(int argc, char *argv[])
{
  char ch;

  if(argc!=3) {
    cout << "Usage: NAME <filename> <starting location>\n";
    return 1;
  }

  ifstream in(argv[1], ios::in | ios::binary);
  if(!in) {
    cout << "Cannot open file.\n";
    return 1;
  }

  in.seekg(atoi(argv[2]), ios::beg);

  while(in.get(ch))
    cout << ch;

  return 0;
}
```

tellg( ) returns the current get location, and **tellp( )** returns the current put location.

You can determine the current position of each file pointer by using these functions:

pos_type tellg( );

pos_type tellp( );

Here, **pos_type** is a type defined by **ios** that is capable of holding the largest value that either function can return.

There are overloaded versions of **seekg( )** and **seekp( )** that move the file pointers to the location specified by the return values of **tellg( )** and **tellp( )**. Their prototypes are shown here:

istream &seekg(pos_type *position*);

ostream &seekp(pos_type *position*);

Checking I/O Status

The C++ I/O system maintains status information about the outcome of each I/O operation. The current status of an I/O stream is described in an object of type **iostate**, which is an enumeration defined by **ios** that includes these members:

Name	Meaning
ios::goodbit	No error bits set.
ios::eofbit	1 when end-of-file is encountered; 0 otherwise
ios::failbit	1 when a (possibly) nonfatal I/O error has occurred; 0 otherwise
ios::badbit	1 when a fatal I/O error has occurred; 0 otherwise

18

There are two ways in which you can obtain I/O status information. First, you can call the **rdstate( )** function, which is a member of **ios**. It has this prototype:

iostate rdstate( );

It returns the current status of the error flags. As you can probably guess from looking at the preceding list of flags, **rdstate( )** returns **goodbit** when no error has occurred. Otherwise, an error flag is returned.

The other way you can determine if an error has occurred is by using one or more of these **ios** member functions:

bool bad( );

bool eof( );

bool fail( );

bool good( );

The **eof( )** function was discussed earlier. The **bad( )** function returns true if **badbit** is set. The **fail( )** function returns true if **failbit** is set. The **good( )** function returns true if there are no errors. Otherwise, they return false.

Once an error has occurred, it may need to be cleared before your program continues. To do this, use the **ios** member function **clear( )**, whose prototype is shown here:

void clear(iostate *flags* = ios::goodbit);

If *flags* is **goodbit** (as it is by default), all error flags are cleared. Otherwise, set *flags* to the settings you desire.

Before moving on, you might want to experiment with these status-reporting functions by adding extended error-checking to the preceding file examples.

Customized I/O and Files

Earlier in this chapter, you learned how to overload the insertion and extraction operators relative to your own classes. You also learned how to create your own manipulators. In the examples, only console I/O was performed. However, because all C++ streams are the same, the same overloaded inserter function, for example, can be used to output to the screen or to a file with no changes whatsoever. This is one of the most important and useful features of C++'s approach to I/O.

The following program uses the overloaded **three_d** inserter to write coordinate information to a file called **threed**.

```
/* Use overloaded inserter to write three_d
   objects to a file. */
#include <iostream>
#include <fstream>
using namespace std;

class three_d {
  int x, y, z; // 3-D coordinates -- now private
public:
  three_d(int a, int b, int c) { x = a; y = b; z = c; }
  friend ostream &operator<<(ostream &stream, three_d obj);
};

// Display X, Y, Z coordinates - three_d inserter.
ostream &operator<<(ostream &stream, three_d obj)
{
  stream << obj.x << ", ";
  stream << obj.y << ", ";
  stream << obj.z << "\n";
  return stream;  // return the stream
}

int main()
{
  three_d a(1, 2, 3), b(3, 4, 5), c(5, 6, 7);
  ofstream out("threed");

  if(!out) {
    cout << "Cannot open file.";
    return 1;
  }

  out << a << b << c;

  out.close();

  return 0;
}
```

If you compare this version of the **three_d** inserter to the one shown earlier in this chapter, you will find that no changes have been made to make it accommodate disk files. Once you correctly define an inserter or extractor, it will work with any stream.

T IP: Before moving on to the next chapter, take some time to experiment with the C++ I/O system. Specifically, try creating your own class and then defining an inserter and extractor for it. Also, try creating your own manipulators.

CHAPTER 19

Run-Time Type ID
and the Casting
Operators

This chapter discusses two features of C++ that support modern, object-oriented programming: run-time type identification (or, RTTI for short) and a set of four additional casting operators. Neither of these features was part of the original specification for C++, but both were added to provide enhanced support for run-time polymorphism. RTTI allows you to identify the type of an object during the execution of your program. The casting operators give you safer, more controlled ways to cast. As you will see, one of the casting operators, **dynamic_cast**, relates directly to RTTI, so it makes sense to discuss casting operators and RTTI in the same chapter.

Run-Time Type Identification (RTTI)

Run-time type information may be new to you, because it is not found in non-polymorphic languages, such as C. In non-polymorphic languages there is no need for run-time type information because the type of each object is known at compile time (i.e., when the program is written). However, in polymorphic languages such as C++, there can be situations in which the type of an object is unknown at compile time, because the precise nature of that object is not determined until the program is executed. As you know, C++ implements polymorphism through the use of class hierarchies, virtual functions, and base class pointers. A base class pointer may be used to point to objects of the base class or *any object derived from that base*. Thus, it is not always possible to know in advance what type of object will be pointed to by a base pointer at any given moment in time. This determination must be made at run time, by using run-time type identification.

To obtain an object's type, use **typeid**. You must include the header **<typeinfo>** in order to use **typeid**. The most commonly used form of **typeid** is shown here:

typeid(*object*)

To obtain the type of an object at run time, use **typeid**.

Here, *object* is the object whose type you will be obtaining. It may be of any type, including the built-in types and class types that you create. **typeid** returns a reference to an object of type **type_info** that describes the type of *object*.

The **type_info** class defines the following public members:

bool operator==(const type_info &*ob*);

bool operator!=(const type_info &*ob*);

bool before(const type_info &*ob*);

const char *name( );

The overloaded **==** and **!=** provide for the comparison of types. The **before( )** function returns true if the invoking object is before *ob* in collation order. (This function is mostly for internal use. Its return value has nothing to do with inheritance or class hierarchies.) The **name( )** function returns a pointer to the name of the type.

19

Here is a simple example that uses **typeid**:

```
// A simple example that uses typeid.
#include <iostream>
#include <typeinfo>
using namespace std;

class myclass {
  // ...
};

int main()
{
  int i, j;
  float f;
  myclass ob;

  cout << "The type of i is: " << typeid(i).name();
  cout << endl;
  cout << "The type of f is: " << typeid(f).name();
  cout << endl;
  cout << "The type of ob is: " << typeid(ob).name();
  cout << "\n\n";

  if(typeid(i) == typeid(j))
    cout << "The types of i and j are the same\n";

  if(typeid(i) != typeid(f))
    cout << "The types of i and f are not the same\n";

  return 0;
}
```

The output produced by this program is shown here:

```
The type of i is: int
The type of f is: float
The type of ob is: class myclass

The types of i and j are the same
The types of i and f are not the same
```

Perhaps the most important use of **typeid** occurs when it is applied through a pointer of a polymorphic base class. (Recall that a polymorphic class is one that contains a virtual function.) In this case, it will automatically return the type of the actual object being pointed to, which may be a base class object or an object derived from that base. (Remember, a base class pointer can point to objects of the base class or of any class derived from that base.) Thus, by using **typeid**, you can determine at run time the type of the object that is being pointed to by a base class pointer. The following program demonstrates this principle:

```cpp
// An example that uses typeid on a polymorphic class hierarchy.
#include <iostream>
#include <typeinfo>
using namespace std;

class Base {
  virtual void f() {}; // make Base polymorphic
  // ...
};

class Derived1: public Base {
  // ...
};

class Derived2: public Base {
  // ...
};

int main()
{
  Base *p, baseob;
  Derived1 ob1;
  Derived2 ob2;

  p = &baseob;
  cout << "p is pointing to an object of type ";
  cout << typeid(*p).name() << endl;

  p = &ob1;
  cout << "p is pointing to an object of type ";
  cout << typeid(*p).name() << endl;

  p = &ob2;
  cout << "p is pointing to an object of type ";
  cout << typeid(*p).name() << endl;

  return 0;
}
```

The output produced by this program is shown here:

```
p is pointing to an object of type class Base
p is pointing to an object of type class Derived1
p is pointing to an object of type class Derived2
```

When **typeid** is applied to a base class pointer of a polymorphic type, the type of object pointed to will be determined at run time, as the output produced by the program shows.

In all cases, when **typeid** is applied to a pointer of a non-polymorphic class hierarchy, then the base type of the pointer is obtained. That is, no determination of what that pointer is actually pointing to is made. As an experiment, comment out the virtual function **f( )** in **Base** and observe the results. As you will see, the type of each object will be **Base** because that is the type of the pointer.

Since **typeid** is commonly applied to a dereferenced pointer (i.e., one to which the * operator has been applied), a special exception has been created to handle the situation in which the pointer being dereferenced is null. In this case, **typeid** throws a **bad_typeid** exception.

References to an object of a polymorphic class hierarchy work the same as pointers. When **typeid** is applied to a reference of a polymorphic class, it will return the type of the object actually being referred to, which may be a derived type. The circumstance where you will most often make use of this feature is when objects are passed to functions by reference. For example, in the following program, the function **WhatType( )** declares a reference parameter to objects of type **Base**. This means that **WhatType( )** can be passed references to objects of type **Base** or any class derived from **Base**. When the **typeid** operator is applied to this parameter, it returns the actual type of the object being passed.

```cpp
// Use a reference with typeid.
#include <iostream>
#include <typeinfo>
using namespace std;

class Base {
  virtual void f() {}; // make Base polymorphic
  // ...
};

class Derived1: public Base {
  // ...
};

class Derived2: public Base {
  // ...
};

// Demonstrate typeid with a reference parameter.
void WhatType(Base &ob)
{
  cout << "ob is referencing an object of type ";
  cout << typeid(ob).name() << endl;
}


int main()
{
  int i;
  Base baseob;
  Derived1 ob1;
```

```
  Derived2 ob2;

  WhatType(baseob);
  WhatType(ob1);
  WhatType(ob2);

  return 0;
}
```

The output produced by this program is shown here:

```
ob is referencing an object of type class Base
ob is referencing an object of type class Derived1
ob is referencing an object of type class Derived2
```

There is a second form of **typeid** that takes a type name as its argument. This form is shown here:

typeid(*type-name*)

For example, the following statement is perfectly acceptable:

```
cout << typeid(int).name();
```

The main use of this form of **typeid** is to obtain a **type_info** object that describes the specified type, so that it can be used in a type-comparison statement.

A Simple Application of Run-Time Type ID

The following program hints at the power of RTTI. It uses a modified version of the **figure** class hierarchy from Chapter 15, which defines classes that compute the area of a circle, triangle, and rectangle. In the program, the function called **factory( )** creates an instance of a circle, triangle, or rectangle, and returns a pointer to it. (A function that produces objects is sometimes called an *object factory*.) The specific type of object created is determined by the outcome of a call to **rand( )**, C++'s random-number generator. Thus, there is no way to know in advance what type of object will be generated. The program creates ten objects and counts the number of each type of figure. Since any type of figure may be generated by a call to **factory( )**, the program relies upon **typeid** to determine which type of object has actually been made.

```
// Demonstrating run-time type id.
#include <iostream>
#include <cstdlib>
using namespace std;

class figure {
protected:
  double x, y;
public:
```

```
    figure(double i, double j) {
      x = i;
      y = j;
    }
    virtual double area() = 0;
} ;

class triangle : public figure {
  public:
    triangle(double i, double j) : figure(i, j) {}
    double area() {
      return x * 0.5 * y;
    }
};

class rectangle : public figure {
  public:
    rectangle(double i, double j) : figure(i, j) {}
    double area() {
      return x * y;
    }
};

class circle : public figure {
  public:
    circle(double i, double j=0) : figure(i, j) {}
    double area() {
      return 3.14 * x * x;
    }
} ;

// A factory for objects derived from figure.
figure *factory()
{
  switch(rand() % 3 ) {
    case 0: return new circle(10.0);
    case 1: return new triangle(10.1, 5.3);
    case 2: return new rectangle(4.3, 5.7);
  }
  return 0;
}

int main()
{
  figure *p; // pointer to base class
  int i;

  int t=0, r=0, c=0;

  // generate and count objects
  for(i=0; i<10; i++) {
    p = factory(); // generate an object
```

```
    cout << "Object is " << typeid(*p).name();
    cout << ".  ";

    // count it
    if(typeid(*p) == typeid(triangle)) t++;
    if(typeid(*p) == typeid(rectangle)) r++;
    if(typeid(*p) == typeid(circle)) c++;

    // display its area
    cout << "Area is " << p->area() << endl;
  }

  cout << endl;
  cout << "Objects generated:\n";
  cout << "  Triangles: " << t << endl;
  cout << "  Rectangles: " << r << endl;
  cout << "  Circles: " << c << endl;

  return 0;
}
```

Sample output is shown here:

```
Object is class rectangle.  Area is 24.51
Object is class rectangle.  Area is 24.51
Object is class triangle.  Area is 26.765
Object is class triangle.  Area is 26.765
Object is class rectangle.  Area is 24.51
Object is class triangle.  Area is 26.765
Object is class circle.  Area is 314
Object is class circle.  Area is 314
Object is class triangle.  Area is 26.765
Object is class rectangle.  Area is 24.51

Objects generated:
  Triangles: 4
  Rectangles: 4
  Circles: 2
```

typeid Can Be Applied to Template Classes

The **typeid** operator can be applied to template classes. The type of an object that is an instance of a template class is, in part, determined by what data is used for its generic data when the object is instantiated. Two instances of the same template class that are created using different data are, therefore, different types. Here is a simple example:

```
// Using typeid with templates.
#include <iostream>
using namespace std;
```

19

```cpp
template <class T> class myclass {
  T a;
public:
  myclass(T i) { a = i; }
  // ...
};

int main()
{
  myclass<int> o1(10), o2(9);
  myclass<double> o3(7.2);

  cout << "Type of o1 is ";
  cout << typeid(o1).name() << endl;

  cout << "Type of o2 is ";
  cout << typeid(o2).name() << endl;

  cout << "Type of o3 is ";
  cout << typeid(o3).name() << endl;

  cout << endl;

  if(typeid(o1) == typeid(o2))
    cout << "o1 and o2 are the same type\n";

  if(typeid(o1) == typeid(o3))
    cout << "Error\n";
  else
    cout << "o1 and o3 are different types\n";

  return 0;
}
```

The output produced by this program is shown here:

```
Type of o1 is class myclass<int>
Type of o2 is class myclass<int>
Type of o3 is class myclass<double>

o1 and o2 are the same type
o1 and o3 are different types
```

As you can see, even though two objects are of the same template class type, if their parameterized data does not match, they are not equivalent types. In the program, **o1** is of type **myclass<int>** and **o3** is of type **myclass<double>**. Thus, they are of different types.

Here is one more example that applies **typeid** to **template** classes. It is a modified version of the figures program from the previous section. In this case, **figure** has been converted into a template class.

```cpp
// Template version of the figure hierarchy.
#include <iostream>
#include <cstdlib>
using namespace std;

template <class T> class figure {
protected:
  T x, y;
public:
  figure(T i, T j) {
    x = i;
    y = j;
  }
  virtual T area() = 0;
} ;

template <class T> class triangle : public figure<T> {
  public:
    triangle(T i, T j) : figure<T>(i, j) {}
    T area() {
      return x * 0.5 * y;
    }
};

template <class T> class rectangle : public figure<T> {
  public:
    rectangle(T i, T j) : figure<T>(i, j) {}
    T area() {
      return x * y;
    }
};

template <class T> class circle : public figure<T> {
  public:
    circle(T i, T j=0) : figure<T>(i, j) {}
    T area() {
      return 3.14 * x * x;
    }
} ;

// A factory for objects derived from figure.
figure<double> *generator()
{
  switch(rand() % 3 ) {
    case 0: return new circle<double>(10.0);
    case 1: return new triangle<double>(10.1, 5.3);
    case 2: return new rectangle<double>(4.3, 5.7);
  }
  return 0;
}

int main()
```

```
{
  figure<double> *p;
  int i;
  int t=0, c=0, r=0;

  // generate and count objects
  for(i=0; i<10; i++) {
    p = generator();

    cout << "Object is " << typeid(*p).name();
    cout << ".  ";

    // count it
    if(typeid(*p) == typeid(triangle<double>)) t++;
    if(typeid(*p) == typeid(rectangle<double>)) r++;
    if(typeid(*p) == typeid(circle<double>)) c++;

    cout << "Area is " << p->area() << endl;
  }

  cout << endl;
  cout << "Objects generated:\n";
  cout << "  Triangles: " << t << endl;
  cout << "  Rectangles: " << r << endl;
  cout << "  Circles: " << c << endl;

  return 0;
}
```

Here is sample output:

```
Object is class rectangle<double>.  Area is 24.51
Object is class rectangle<double>.  Area is 24.51
Object is class triangle<double>.  Area is 26.765
Object is class triangle<double>.  Area is 26.765
Object is class rectangle<double>.  Area is 24.51
Object is class triangle<double>.  Area is 26.765
Object is class circle<double>.  Area is 314
Object is class circle<double>.  Area is 314
Object is class triangle<double>.  Area is 26.765
Object is class rectangle<double>.  Area is 24.51

Objects generated:
  Triangles: 4
  Rectangles: 4
  Circles: 2
```

Run-time type identification is not something that every program will use. However, when you are working with polymorphic types, it allows you to know what type of object is being operated upon in any given situation.

The Casting Operators

C++ defines five casting operators. The first is the traditional-style cast, described earlier in this book. It has been part of C++ from the start. The remaining four casting operators were added a few years ago. They are **dynamic_cast**, **const_cast**, **reinterpret_cast**, and **static_cast**. These operators give you additional control over how casting takes place. Each is examined here.

dynamic_cast

dynamic_cast performs a run-time cast on polymorphic types.

Perhaps the most important of the new casting operators is the **dynamic_cast**. The **dynamic_cast** performs a run-time cast that verifies the validity of a cast. If at the time **dynamic_cast** is executed, the cast is invalid, then the cast fails. The general form of **dynamic_cast** is shown here:

dynamic_cast<*target-type*> (*expr*)

Here, *target-type* specifies the target type of the cast, and *expr* is the expression being cast into the new type. The target type must be a pointer or reference type, and the expression being cast must evaluate to a pointer or reference. Thus, **dynamic_cast** may be used to cast one type of pointer into another, or one type of reference into another.

The purpose of **dynamic_cast** is to perform casts on polymorphic types. For example, given two polymorphic classes B and D, with D derived from B, a **dynamic_cast** can always cast a D* pointer into a B* pointer. This is because a base pointer can always point to a derived object. But, a **dynamic_cast** can cast a B* pointer into a D* pointer only if the object being pointed to *actually is* a D object. In general, **dynamic_cast** will succeed if the pointer (or reference) being cast is a pointer (or reference) to either an object of the target type or an object derived from the target type. Otherwise, the cast will fail. If the cast fails, then **dynamic_cast** evaluates to null if the cast involves pointers. If a **dynamic_cast** on reference types fails, a **bad_cast** exception is thrown.

Here is a simple example. Assume that **Base** is a polymorphic class and that **Derived** is derived from **Base**.

```
Base *bp, b_ob;
Derived *dp, d_ob;

bp = &d_ob; // base pointer points to Derived object
dp = dynamic_cast<Derived *> (bp); // cast to derived pointer OK
if(dp) cout << "Cast OK";
```

Here, the cast from the base pointer **bp** to the derived pointer **dp** works because **bp** is actually pointing to a **Derived** object. Thus, this fragment displays **Cast OK**. But in the next fragment, the cast fails because **bp** is pointing to a **Base** object, and it is illegal to cast a base pointer into a derived pointer unless the object being pointed to actually is a derived object.

```
bp = &b_ob; // base pointer points to Base object
dp = dynamic_cast<Derived *> (bp); // error
if(!dp) cout << "Cast Fails";
```

Because the cast fails, this fragment displays **Cast Fails**.

The following program demonstrates the various situations that **dynamic_cast** can handle:

```
// Demonstrate dynamic_cast.
#include <iostream>
using namespace std;

class Base {
public:
  virtual void f() { cout << "Inside Base\n"; }
  // ...
};

class Derived : public Base {
public:
  void f() { cout << "Inside Derived\n"; }
};

int main()
{
  Base *bp, b_ob;
  Derived *dp, d_ob;

  dp = dynamic_cast<Derived *> (&d_ob);
  if(dp) {
    cout << "Cast from Derived * to Derived * OK.\n";
    dp->f();
  } else
    cout << "Error\n";

  cout << endl;

  bp = dynamic_cast<Base *> (&d_ob);
  if(bp) {
    cout << "Cast from Derived * to Base * OK.\n";
    bp->f();
  } else
    cout << "Error\n";

  cout << endl;

  bp = dynamic_cast<Base *> (&b_ob);
  if(bp) {
    cout << "Cast from Base * to Base * OK.\n";
    bp->f();
  } else
```

```
      cout << "Error\n";

  cout << endl;

  dp = dynamic_cast<Derived *> (&b_ob);
  if(dp)
    cout << "Error\n";
  else
    cout << "Cast from Base * to Derived * not OK.\n";

  cout << endl;

  bp = &d_ob; // bp points to Derived object
  dp = dynamic_cast<Derived *> (bp);
  if(dp) {
    cout << "Casting bp to a Derived * OK\n" <<
      "because bp is really pointing\n" <<
      "to a Derived object.\n";
    dp->f();
  } else
    cout << "Error\n";

  cout << endl;

  bp = &b_ob; // bp points to Base object
  dp = dynamic_cast<Derived *> (bp);
  if(dp)
    cout << "Error";
  else {
    cout << "Now casting bp to a Derived *\n" <<
      "is not OK because bp is really \n" <<
      "pointing to a Base object.\n";
  }

  cout << endl;

  dp = &d_ob; // dp points to Derived object
  bp = dynamic_cast<Base *> (dp);
  if(bp) {
    cout << "Casting dp to a Base * is OK.\n";
    bp->f();
  } else
    cout << "Error\n";

  return 0;
}
```

The program produces the following output:

```
Cast from Derived * to Derived * OK.
Inside Derived
```

```
Cast from Derived * to Base * OK.
Inside Derived

Cast from Base * to Base * OK.
Inside Base

Cast from Base * to Derived * not OK.

Casting bp to a Derived * OK
because bp is really pointing
to a Derived object.
Inside Derived

Now casting bp to a Derived *
is not OK because bp is really
pointing to a Base object.

Casting dp to a Base * is OK.
Inside Derived
```

19

The **dynamic_cast** operator can sometimes be used instead of **typeid** in certain cases. For example, again assuming that **Base** is a polymorphic base class for **Derived**, the following fragment will assign **dp** the address of the object pointed to by **bp** if, and only if, the object really is a **Derived** object:

```
Base *bp;
Derived *dp;
// ...
if(typeid(*bp) == typeid(Derived)) dp = (Derived *) bp;
```

In this case, a traditional-style cast is used to actually perform the cast. This is safe because the **if** statement checks the legality of the cast by using **typeid** before the cast actually occurs. However, a better way to accomplish this is to replace the **typeid** operators and the **if** statement with this **dynamic_cast**:

```
dp = dynamic_cast<Derived *> (bp);
```

Since **dynamic_cast** succeeds only if the object being cast is either already an object of the target type or an object derived from the target type, after this statement executes, **dp** will contain either a null or a pointer to an object of type **Derived**. Since **dynamic_cast** succeeds only if the cast is legal, it can simplify the logic in certain situations. The following program illustrates how a **dynamic_cast** can be used to replace **typeid**. It performs the same set of operations twice: first with **typeid**, then using **dynamic_cast**.

```
// Use dynamic_cast to replace typeid.
#include <iostream>
#include <typeinfo>
using namespace std;
```

```
class Base {
public:
  virtual void f() {}
};

class Derived : public Base {
public:
  void derivedOnly() {
    cout << "Is a Derived Object\n";
  }
};

int main()
{
  Base *bp, b_ob;
  Derived *dp, d_ob;

  // **********************************
  // use typeid
  // **********************************
  bp = &b_ob;
  if(typeid(*bp) == typeid(Derived)) {
    dp = (Derived *) bp;
    dp->derivedOnly();
  }
  else
    cout << "Cast from Base to Derived failed.\n";

  bp = &d_ob;
  if(typeid(*bp) == typeid(Derived)) {
    dp = (Derived *) bp;
    dp->derivedOnly();
  }
  else
    cout << "Error, cast should work!\n";

  // **********************************
  // use dynamic_cast
  // **********************************
  bp = &b_ob;
  dp = dynamic_cast<Derived *> (bp);
  if(dp) dp->derivedOnly();
  else
    cout << "Cast from Base to Derived failed.\n";

  bp = &d_ob;
  dp = dynamic_cast<Derived *> (bp);
  if(dp) dp->derivedOnly();
  else
```

```
        cout << "Error, cast should work!\n";

    return 0;
}
```

As you can see, the use of **dynamic_cast** simplifies the logic required to cast a base pointer into a derived pointer. The output from the program is shown here:

```
Cast from Base to Derived failed.
Is a Derived Object
Cast from Base to Derived failed.
Is a Derived Object
```

19

One last point: The **dynamic_cast** operator can also be used with template classes.

const_cast

const_cast casts away const and/or volatile attributes.

The **const_cast** operator is used to explicitly override **const** and/or **volatile** in a cast. The target type must be the same as the source type, except for the alteration of its **const** or **volatile** attributes. The most common use of **const_cast** is to remove **const**-ness. The general form of **const_cast** is shown here:

const_cast<*type*> (*expr*)

Here, *type* specifies the target type of the cast, and *expr* is the expression being cast into the new type.

The following program demonstrates **const_cast**:

```
// Demonstrate const_cast.
#include <iostream>
using namespace std;

void f(const int *p)
{
  int *v;

  // cast away const-ness.
  v = const_cast<int *> (p);

  *v = 100; // now, modify object through v
}

int main()
{
  int x = 99;
```

```
  cout << "x before call: " << x << endl;
  f(&x);
  cout << "x after call: " << x << endl;

  return 0;
}
```

The output produced by this program is shown here:

```
x before call: 99
x after call: 100
```

As you can see, **x** was modified by **f( )**, even though the parameter to **f( )** was specified as a **const** pointer.

It must be stressed that the use of **const_cast** to cast away **const**-ness is a potentially dangerous feature. Use it with care.

One other point: Only **const_cast** can cast away **const**-ness. That is, neither **dynamic_cast**, **static_cast**, nor **reinterpret_cast** can alter the **const**-ness of an object.

static_cast

`static_cast` *performs a non-polymorphic cast.*

The **static_cast** operator performs a non-polymorphic cast. It can be used for any standard conversion. No run-time checks are performed. Its general form is

static_cast<*type*> (*expr*)

Here, *type* specifies the target type of the cast, and *expr* is the expression being cast into the new type.

The **static_cast** operator is essentially a substitute for the original cast operator. It simply performs a non-polymorphic cast. For example, the following casts a **float** into an **int**:

```
// Use static_cast.
#include <iostream>
using namespace std;

int main()
{
  int i;
  float f;
```

```
    f = 199.22F;

    i = static_cast<int> (f);

    cout << i;

    return 0;
}
```

reinterpret_cast

reinterpret_cast
performs a
fundamental
type change.

The **reinterpret_cast** operator converts one type into a fundamentally different type. For example, it can change a pointer into an integer, and an integer into a pointer. It can also be used for casting inherently incompatible pointer types. Its general form is

   reinterpret_cast<*type*> (*expr*)

Here, *type* specifies the target type of the cast, and *expr* is the expression being cast into the new type.

The following program demonstrates the use of **reinterpret_cast**:

```
// An example that uses reinterpret_cast.
#include <iostream>
using namespace std;

int main()
{
  int i;
  char *p = "This is a string";

  i = reinterpret_cast<int> (p); // cast pointer to integer

  cout << i;

  return 0;
}
```

Here, **reinterpret_cast** converts the pointer **p** into an integer. This conversion represents a fundamental type change and is a good use of **reinterpret_cast**.

19

The Traditional Cast Versus the Four Casting Operators

It may have occurred to you that the four casting operators described in this chapter fully replace the need for the traditional cast. This realization usually gives rise to the question: "Should I use the traditional cast or one of the four newer casting operators?" The trouble is that there is no general rule that all programmers currently accept. Because the additional casts were created to add an element of safety to the inherently risky act of casting one type of data into another, many C++ programmers feel that they should be used exclusively. Certainly, nothing would be wrong with using this approach. Other programmers feel that the traditional cast has served programmers well over many years and should not be abandoned lightly. For example, some would argue that in the case of simple, relatively safe casts (such as those required by the **read( )** and **write( )** I/O functions described in the preceding chapter), the traditional cast is fully appropriate.

There is one point upon which there is no disagreement: When performing casts on polymorphic types, **dynamic_cast** should definitely be employed.

CHAPTER 20

Namespaces and Other Advanced Topics

This chapter describes namespaces and several other advanced features, including explicit constructors, function pointers, **static** members, **const** member functions, an alternative member initialization syntax, the pointer-to-member operators, the **asm** keyword, linkage specification, and conversion functions.

Namespaces

A namespace defines a declarative region.

Namespaces were briefly introduced in Chapter 2. Their purpose is to localize the names of identifiers to avoid name collisions. In the C++ programming environment, there has been an explosion of variable, function, and class names. Prior to the invention of namespaces, all of these names competed for slots in the global namespace, and many conflicts arose. For example, if your program defined a function called **toupper( )**, it could (depending upon its parameter list) override the standard library function **toupper( )**, because both names would be stored in the global namespace. Name collisions were compounded when two or more third-party libraries were used by the same program. In this case, it was possible—even likely—that a name defined by one library would conflict with the same name defined by the other library. The situation can be particularly troublesome for class names. For example, if your program defines a class called **VideoMode**, and a library used by your program defines a class by the same name, a conflict will arise.

The creation of the **namespace** keyword was a response to these problems. Because it localizes the visibility of names declared within it, a namespace allows the same name to be used in different contexts, without conflicts arising. Perhaps the most noticeable beneficiary of **namespace** is the C++ standard library. Prior to **namespace**, the entire C++ library was defined within the global namespace (which was, of course, the only namespace). With the addition of **namespace**, the C++ library is now defined within its own namespace, called **std**, which reduces the chance of name collisions. You can also create your own namespaces within your program to localize the visibility of any names that you think may cause conflicts. This is especially important if you are creating class or function libraries.

Namespace Fundamentals

The **namespace** keyword allows you to partition the global namespace by creating a declarative region. In essence, a **namespace** defines a scope. The general form of **namespace** is shown here:

```
namespace name {
  // declarations
}
```

Anything defined within a **namespace** statement is within the scope of that namespace.

The following program is an example of a **namespace**. It localizes the names used to implement a simple countdown counter class. In the namespace are defined the **counter** class, which implements the counter, and the variables **upperbound** and **lowerbound**, which contain the upper and lower bounds that apply to all counters.

```
namespace CounterNameSpace {
  int upperbound;
  int lowerbound;

  class counter {
     int count;
   public:
     counter(int n) {
       if(n <= upperbound) count = n;
       else count = upperbound;
     }

     void reset(int n) {
       if(n <= upperbound) count = n;
     }

     int run() {
       if(count > lowerbound) return count--;
       else return lowerbound;
     }
  };
}
```

20

Here, **upperbound**, **lowerbound**, and the class **counter** are part of the scope defined by the **CounterNameSpace** namespace.

Inside a namespace, identifiers that are declared within that namespace can be referred to directly, without any namespace qualification. For example, within **CounterNameSpace,** the **run( )** function can refer directly to **lowerbound** in the statement:

```
if(count > lowerbound) return count--;
```

However, since **namespace** defines a scope, you need to use the scope resolution operator to refer to objects declared within a namespace from outside that namespace. For example, to assign the value 10 to **upperbound** from code outside **CounterNameSpace**, you must use this statement:

```
CounterNameSpace::upperbound = 10;
```

Or, to declare an object of type **counter** from outside **CounterNameSpace**, you use a statement like this:

```
CounterNameSpace::counter ob;
```

In general, to access a member of a namespace from outside its namespace, precede the member's name with the name of the namespace, followed by the scope resolution operator.

Here is a program that demonstrates the use of the **CounterNamespace**:

```
// Demonstrate a namespace.
#include <iostream>
using namespace std;

namespace CounterNameSpace {
  int upperbound;
  int lowerbound;

  class counter {
      int count;
    public:
      counter(int n) {
        if(n <= upperbound) count = n;
        else count = upperbound;
      }

      void reset(int n) {
        if(n <= upperbound) count = n;
      }

      int run() {
        if(count > lowerbound) return count--;
        else return lowerbound;
      }
  };
}

int main()
{
  CounterNameSpace::upperbound = 100;
  CounterNameSpace::lowerbound = 0;

  CounterNameSpace::counter ob1(10);
  int i;

  do {
    i = ob1.run();
    cout << i << " ";
  } while(i > CounterNameSpace::lowerbound);
  cout << endl;

  CounterNameSpace::counter ob2(20);

  do {
    i = ob2.run();
    cout << i << " ";
  } while(i > CounterNameSpace::lowerbound);
  cout << endl;

  ob2.reset(100);
  CounterNameSpace::lowerbound = 90;
```

```
  do {
    i = ob2.run();
    cout << i << " ";
  } while(i > CounterNameSpace::lowerbound);

  return 0;
}
```

Notice that the declaration of a **counter** object and the references to **upperbound** and **lowerbound** are qualified by **CounterNameSpace**. However, once an object of type **counter** has been declared, it is not necessary to further qualify it or any of its members. Thus, **ob1.run( )** can be called directly; the namespace has already been resolved.

There may be more than one namespace declaration of the same name. This allows a namespace to be split over several files, or even to be separated within the same file. For example:

```
namespace NS {
  int i;
}

// ...

namespace NS {
  int j;
}
```

Here, **NS** is split into two pieces. However, the contents of each piece are still within the same namespace, i.e., **NS**.

A namespace must be declared outside of all other scopes. This means that you cannot declare namespaces that are localized to a function, for example. However, one namespace can be nested within another.

using

using brings a namespace into view.

As you can imagine, if your program includes frequent references to the members of a namespace, having to specify the namespace and the scope resolution operator each time you need to refer to one quickly becomes a tedious chore. The **using** statement was invented to alleviate this problem. The **using** statement has these two general forms:

using namespace *name;*

using *name::member;*

In the first form, *name* specifies the name of the namespace you want to access. All of the members defined within the specified namespace are brought into view (i.e., they become part of the current namespace) and may be used without qualification. In the second form, only a specific member of the namespace is made visible. For example, assuming **CounterNameSpace**, as shown above, the following **using** statements and assignments are valid:

```
using CounterNameSpace::lowerbound; // only lowerbound is visible
lowerbound = 10; // OK because lowerbound is visible

using namespace CounterNameSpace; // all members are visible
upperbound = 100; // OK because all members are now visible
```

The following program illustrates **using** by reworking the counter example from the previous section:

```cpp
// Demonstrate using.
#include <iostream>
using namespace std;

namespace CounterNameSpace {
  int upperbound;
  int lowerbound;

  class counter {
    int count;
   public:
    counter(int n) {
      if(n <= upperbound) count = n;
      else count = upperbound;
    }

    void reset(int n) {
      if(n <= upperbound) count = n;
    }

    int run() {
      if(count > lowerbound) return count--;
      else return lowerbound;
    }
  };
}

int main()
{
  // use only upperbound from CounterNameSpace
  using CounterNameSpace::upperbound;

  // now, no qualification needed to set upperbound
  upperbound = 100;

  // qualification still needed for lowerbound, etc.
  CounterNameSpace::lowerbound = 0;
```

```
      CounterNameSpace::counter ob1(10);
      int i;

      do {
        i = ob1.run();
        cout << i << " ";
      } while(i > CounterNameSpace::lowerbound);
      cout << endl;

      // Now, use entire CounterNameSpace
      using namespace CounterNameSpace;

      counter ob2(20);

      do {
        i = ob2.run();
        cout << i << " ";
      } while(i > lowerbound);
      cout << endl;

      ob2.reset(100);
      lowerbound = 90;
      do {
        i = ob2.run();
        cout << i << " ";
      } while(i > lowerbound);

      return 0;
    }
```

This program illustrates one other important point: Using one namespace does not override another. When you bring a namespace into view, it simply adds its names to whatever other namespaces are currently in effect. Thus, by the end of the program, both **std** and **CounterNameSpace** have been added to the global namespace.

Unnamed Namespaces

An unnamed namespace restricts identifiers to the file in which they are declared.

There is a special type of namespace, called an *unnamed namespace,* that allows you to create identifiers that are unique within a file. It has this general form:

> namespace {
> // *declarations*
> }

Unnamed namespaces allow you to establish unique identifiers that are known only within the scope of a single file. That is, within the file that contains the unnamed namespace, the members of that namespace may be used directly, without qualification. But outside the file, the identifiers are unknown.

As mentioned earlier in this book, using **static** is one way to restrict the scope of a global name to the file in which it is declared. For example, consider the following two files that are part of the same program:

File One	File Two

static int k;
void f1( ) {
  k = 99; // OK
}
	extern int k;
	void f2( ) {
	  k = 10; // error
	}

Because **k** is defined in File One, it may be used in File One. In File Two, **k** is specified as **extern**, which means that its name and type are known, but that **k** itself is not actually defined. When these two files are linked, the attempt to use **k** within File Two results in an error because there is no definition for **k**. By preceding **k** with **static** in File One, its scope is restricted to that file and it is not available to File Two.

Although the use of **static** global declarations is still allowed in C++, a better way to localize an identifier to a file is to use an unnamed namespace. For example:

File One	File Two

namespace {
  int k;
}
void f1( ) {
  k = 99; // OK
}
	extern int k;
	void f2( ) {
	  k = 10; // error
	}

Here, **k** is also restricted to File One. The use of the unnamed namespace rather than **static** is recommended for new code.

Typically, you will not need to create namespaces for most small to medium sized programs. However, if you will be creating libraries of reusable code, or if you want to ensure the widest portability, then consider wrapping your code within a namespace.

The std Namespace

Standard C++ defines its entire library in its own namespace, called **std**. This is the reason that most of the programs in this book have included the following statement:

```
using namespace std;
```

*The **std** namespace is the one used by the C++ library.*

This causes the **std** namespace to be brought into the current namespace, which gives you direct access to the names of the functions and classes defined within the library, without having to qualify each one with **std::**.

Of course, you can explicitly qualify each name with **std::**, if you like. For example, the following program does not bring the library into the global namespace:

```
// Use explicit std:: qualification.
#include <iostream>

int main()
{
  double val;

  std::cout << "Enter a number: ";

  std::cin >> val;

  std::cout << "This is your number: ";
  std::cout << val;

  return 0;
}
```

20

Here, **cout** and **cin** are both explicitly qualified by their namespace. That is, to write to standard output, you must specify **std::cout**, and to read from standard input, you must use **std::cin**.

You may not want to bring the standard C++ library into the global namespace if your program will be making only limited use of it. However, if your program contains hundreds of references to library names, then including **std** in the current namespace is far easier than qualifying each name individually.

If you are using only a few names from the standard library, it may make more sense to specify a **using** statement for each individually. The advantage to this approach is that you can still use those names without an **std::** qualification, but you will not be bringing the entire standard library into the global namespace. For example:

```
// Bring only a few names into the global namespace.
#include <iostream>

// gain access to cout and cin
using std::cout;
using std::cin;

int main()
{
  double val;

  cout << "Enter a number: ";

  cin >> val;
  cout << "This is your number: ";
  cout << val;
```

```
  return 0;
}
```

Here, **cin** and **cout** may be used directly, but the rest of the **std** namespace has not been brought into view.

As explained, the original C++ library was defined in the global namespace. If you will be converting older C++ programs, then you will need to either include a **using namespace std** statement or qualify each reference to a library member with **std::**. This is especially important if you are replacing old **.h** header files with the modern headers. Remember, the old **.h** headers put their contents into the global namespace. The modern headers put their contents into the **std** namespace.

Pointers to Functions

A particularly confusing, yet powerful, feature of C++ is the *function pointer*. Even though a function is not a variable, it still has a physical location in memory that can be assigned to a pointer. The address assigned to the pointer is the entry point of the function. (This is the address that is used when the function is called.) Once a pointer points to a function, the function can be called through that pointer. Function pointers also allow functions to be passed as arguments to other functions.

A function pointer points to the entry point of the function.

The address of a function is obtained by using the function's name, without any parentheses or arguments. (This is similar to the way an array's address is obtained when only the array name, without indices, is specified.) If you assign the address of a function to a pointer, then you can call that function through the pointer. For example, study the following program. It contains two functions, **vline( )** and **hline( )**, which draw vertical and horizontal lines of a specified length on the screen.

```
#include <iostream>
using namespace std;

void vline(int i), hline(int i);

int main()
{
  void (*p)(int i);

  p = vline; // point to vline()

  (*p)(4); // call vline()

  p = hline; // point to hline()

  (*p)(3); // call hline()

  return 0;
}

void hline(int i)
```

```
{
    for( ;i; i--) cout << "-";
    cout << "\n";
}

void vline(int i)
{
    for( ; i; i--) cout << "|\n";
}
```

Here is the output.

```
|
|
|
|
---
```

Let's examine this program in detail. The first line after **main( )** declares **p** as a pointer to a function that takes one integer argument and returns no value. It does not in any way specify what that function is. All it does is create a pointer that can be used to point to a function of that type. Because of the C++ precedence rules, the parentheses around the ***p** are necessary.

The next line assigns to **p** the address of **vline( )**. The line after that actually calls **vline( )** with an argument of 4. The program then assigns the address of **hline( )** to **p** and calls **hline( )** by using the pointer.

In the program, when a function is called through a pointer, the following form is used:

```
(*p)(4);
```

However, the function pointed to by **p** can be called using the simpler syntax, shown here:

```
p(4);
```

The only reason that you will frequently see the first style is that it tips off anyone reading your code that a function is being called through a pointer called **p**, rather a function named **p** being called. Other than that, they are equivalent.

Although the preceding example uses a function pointer in a trivial manner for the sake of illustration, function pointers have very important uses. One of these uses is to allow a function to be passed the address of another function. An important example of this is the **qsort( )** function, which is found in C++'s standard library. The **qsort( )** function is a sorting function, based upon the Quicksort algorithm, that sorts the contents of an array. Its prototype is shown here:

```
void qsort(void *start, size_t length, size_t size,
           int (*compare) (const void *, const void *));
```

The prototype for **qsort( )** is in **<cstdlib>**, which also defines the type **size_t**, which is essentially an **unsigned int**. To use **qsort( )**, you must pass a pointer to the start of the array of objects that you want sorted in *start*, the length of the array in *length*, the width of each element (in bytes) in *size*, and a pointer to a comparison function.

The comparison function used by **qsort( )** compares two elements. It must return less than zero if the first argument points to a value that is less than the second, zero if they are equal, and greater than zero if the first argument points to a value greater than the second.

To see how **qsort( )** can be used, try this program:

```
#include <iostream>
#include <cstdlib>
#include <cstring>
using namespace std;

int comp(const void *a, const void *b);

int main()
{
  char str[] = "Function pointers provide flexibility.";

  qsort(str, strlen(str), 1, comp);
  cout << "sorted string: " << str;

  return 0;
}

int comp(const void *a, const void *b)
{
  return * (char *) a - * (char *) b;
}
```

Here is the output.

```
sorted string:     .Fbcdeeefiiiiiiillnnnooopprrstttuvxy
```

This program sorts the string **str** into ascending order. Since **qsort( )** is passed all the information it needs, including a pointer to the comparison function, it can be used to sort any type of data. For example, the following program sorts an array of integers. To ensure portability, it uses **sizeof** to find the width of an integer.

```
#include <iostream>
#include <cstdlib>
using namespace std;

int comp(const void *a, const void *b);

int main()
{
```

```
    int num[] = {10, 4, 3, 6, 5 ,7 ,8};
    int i;

    qsort(num, 7, sizeof(int), comp);

    for(i=0; i<7; i++)
      cout << num[i] << ' ';

    return 0;
}

int comp(const void *a, const void *b)
{
    return * (int *) a - * (int *) b;
}
```

Although function pointers may still be somewhat confusing to you, with a little practice and thought, you should have no trouble using them. There is one more aspect to function pointers, however, that you need to know about; it concerns overloaded functions.

Finding the Address of an Overloaded Function

Finding the address of an overloaded function is a bit more complex than obtaining the address of a single function. Since there are two or more versions of an overloaded function, there must be some mechanism that determines which specific version's address is obtained. The solution is both elegant and effective. When obtaining the address of an overloaded function, it is *the way the pointer is declared* that determines which overloaded function's address will be obtained. In essence, the pointer's declaration is compared to those of the overloaded functions. The function whose declaration matches is the one whose address is obtained.

The following sample program contains two versions of a function called **space( )**. The first version outputs **count** number of spaces to the screen. The second version outputs **count** number of whatever type of character is passed to **ch**. In **main( )**, two function pointers are declared. The first one is specified as a pointer to a function having only one integer parameter. The second is declared as a pointer to a function taking two parameters.

```
/* Illustrate assigning function pointers to
   overloaded functions. */
#include <iostream>
using namespace std;

// Output count number of spaces.
void space(int count)
{
  for( ; count; count--) cout << ' ';
}
```

20

```
// Output count number of chs.
void space(int count, char ch)
{
  for( ; count; count--) cout << ch;
}

int main()
{
  /* Create a pointer to void function with
     one int parameter. */
  void (*fp1)(int);

  /* Create a pointer to void function with
     one int parameter and one character parameter. */
  void (*fp2)(int, char);

  fp1 = space; // gets address of space(int)

  fp2 = space; // gets address of space(int, char)

  fp1(22);   // output 22 spaces - same as (*fp1)(22)
  cout << "|\n";

  fp2(30, 'x'); // output 30 xs - same as (*fp2)(30, 'x')
  cout << "|\n";

  return 0;
}
```

The output is shown here.

```
                              |
xxxxxxxxxxxxxxxxxxxxxxxxxxxxxx|
```

As the comments illustrate, the compiler is able to determine which overloaded function to obtain the address of, based upon how **fp1** and **fp2** are declared.

To review: When you assign the address of an overloaded function to a function pointer, it is the declaration of the pointer that determines which function's address is assigned. Further, the declaration of the function pointer must exactly match one, and only one, of the overloaded functions. If it does not, ambiguity will be introduced, causing a compile-time error.

Static Class Members

*A single **static** class member is shared by all objects of that class.*

The keyword **static** can be applied to members of a class. When you declare a member of a class as **static**, you are telling the compiler that no matter how many objects of the class are created, there is only one copy of the **static** member. That is, a **static** member is *shared* by all objects of the class. All **static** data is initialized to zero when the first object is created, if no other initialization is present.

When you declare a **static** data member within a class, you are *not* defining it. Instead, you must provide a global definition for it elsewhere, outside the class. This is done by redeclaring the **static** variable, using the scope resolution operator to identify which class it belongs to. This causes storage to be allocated for the **static** variable.

Here is an example that uses a **static** member. Examine the program and try to understand how it works.

```
#include <iostream>
using namespace std;

class ShareVar {
  static int num;
public:
  void setnum(int i) { num = i; };
  void shownum() { cout << num << " "; }
};

int ShareVar::num; // define num

int main()
{
  ShareVar a, b;

  a.shownum(); // prints 0
  b.shownum(); // prints 0

  a.setnum(10); // set static num to 10

  a.shownum(); // prints 10
  b.shownum(); // also prints 10

  return 0;
}
```

20

Notice that the static integer **num** is both declared inside the **ShareVar** class and defined as a global variable. As stated earlier, this is necessary because the declaration of **num** inside **ShareVar** does *not* allocate storage for the variable. C++ initializes **num** to 0 since no other initialization is given. This is why the first calls to **shownum( )** both display 0. Next, object **a** sets **num** to 10. Next, both **a** and **b** use **shownum( )** to display its value. Because there is only one copy of **num** shared by **a** and **b**, both cause the value 10 to be displayed.

REMEMBER: When you declare a member of a class as **static**, you are causing only one copy of that member to be created; it will then be shared by all objects of the class.

When a **static** variable is public, it can be referred to directly through its class name, without reference to any specific object. (Of course, it can still be referred to through an object, too.) For example, consider this version of **ShareVar**:

```
class ShareVar {
public:
  static int num;
  void setnum(int i) { num = i; };
  void shownum() { cout << num << " "; }
};
```

In this verison, **num** is public. This enables you to access **num** directly, as the following statement shows.

```
ShareVar::num = 100;
```

Here, the value of **num** is set independently of any object by using its class name and the scope resolution operator. Furthermore, this statement is valid even before any objects of type **ShareVar** exist! Thus, you can obtain or set the value of a **static** class member before creating any objects.

Although you may not see an immediate need for **static** members, as you continue to write programs in C++, you will find them very useful in certain situations, because they allow you to avoid the use of global variables.

It is also possible for a member function to be declared as **static**, but this usage is not common. A member function declared as **static** may only access other **static** members of its class. (Of course, a **static** member function may access non-**static** global data and functions.) A **static** member function does not have a **this** pointer. Virtual **static** member functions are not allowed. Also, they cannot be declared as **const** or **volatile**. A **static** member function can be invoked by an object of its class, or it may be called independently of any object, using the class name and the scope resolution operator.

const Member Functions and mutable

A **const** member function cannot modify the object that invoked it.

Class member functions may be declared as **const**, which causes **this** to be treated as a **const** pointer. This means that a **const** function cannot modify the object on which it is called. Also, a **const** object may not invoke a non-**const** member function. However, a **const** member function can be called by either **const** or non-**const** objects.

To specify a member function as **const**, use the form shown in the following example:

```
class X {
  int some_var;
public:
  int f1() const; // const member function
};
```

As you can see, the **const** follows the function's parameter declaration.

The purpose of declaring a member function as **const** is to prevent it from modifying the object that invokes it. For example, consider the following program:

```
/*
   Demonstrate const member functions.
   This program won't compile.
*/
#include <iostream>
using namespace std;

class Demo {
  int i;
public:
  int geti() const {
    return i; // ok
  }

  void seti(int x) const {
    i = x; // error!
  }
};

int main()
{
  Demo ob;

  ob.seti(1900);
  cout << ob.geti();

  return 0;
}
```

This program will not compile because **seti( )** is declared as **const**. This means that it is not allowed to modify the invoking object. Since it attempts to change **i**, the program is in error. In contrast, since **geti( )** does not attempt to modify **i**, it is perfectly acceptable.

Sometimes there will be one or more members of a class that you want a **const** function to be able to modify, even though you don't want the function to be able to modify any of its other members. You can accomplish this through the use of **mutable**. It overrides **const**-ness. That is, a **mutable** member can be modified by a **const** member function. For example:

```
// Demonstrate mutable.
#include <iostream>
using namespace std;

class Demo {
  mutable int i;
```

20

```
    int j;
public:
  int geti() const {
    return i; // ok
  }

  void seti(int x) const {
    i = x; // now, OK.
  }

/* The following function won't compile.
  void setj(int x) const {
    j = x; // Still Wrong!
  }
*/
};

int main()
{
  Demo ob;

  ob.seti(1900);
  cout << ob.geti();

  return 0;
}
```

Here, **i** is specified as **mutable**, so it may be changed by the **seti( )** function. However, **j** is not **mutable** and **setj( )** is unable to modify its value.

Explicit Constructors

To create a
non-converting
constructor,
use **explicit**.

C++ defines the keyword **explicit**, which is used to handle a special-case condition that can occur when certain types of constructors are used. To understand the purpose of **explicit**, consider the following program:

```
#include <iostream>
using namespace std;

class myclass {
  int a;
public:
  myclass(int x) { a = x; }
  int geta() { return a; }
};

int main()
{
  myclass ob(4);

  cout << ob.geta();
```

```
        return 0;
}
```

Here, the constructor for **myclass** takes one parameter. Pay special attention to how **ob** is declared in **main( )**. The value 4, specified in the parentheses following **ob**, is the argument that is passed to **myclass( )**'s parameter **x**, which is used to initialize **a**. This is the form of initialization that we have been using since the start of this book. However, there is an alternative. For example, the following statement also initializes **a** to 4:

```
myclass ob = 4; // automatically converts into myclass(4)
```

As the comment suggests, this form of initialization is automatically converted into a call to the **myclass** constructor, with 4 being the argument. That is, the preceding statement is handled by the compiler as if it were written like this:

```
myclass ob(4);
```

In general, any time that you have a constructor that requires only one argument, you can use either *ob(x)* or *ob = x* to initialize an object. The reason for this is that whenever you create a constructor that takes one argument, you are also implicitly creating a conversion from the type of that argument to the type of the class.

If you do not want implicit conversions to be made, you can prevent them by using **explicit**. The **explicit** specifier applies only to constructors. A constructor specified as **explicit** will be used only when an initialization uses the normal constructor syntax. It will not perform any automatic conversion. For example, by declaring the **myclass** constructor as **explicit**, the automatic conversion will not be supplied. Here is **myclass( )** declared as **explicit**:

```
#include <iostream>
using namespace std;

class myclass {
   int a;
public:
   explicit myclass(int x) { a = x; }
   int geta() { return a; }
};
```

Now, only constructors of the form

```
myclass ob(110);
```

will be allowed.

20

An Interesting Benefit from Implicit Constructor Conversion

The automatic conversion from the type of a constructor's argument into a call to the constructor, itself, has interesting implications. For example consider the following:

```cpp
#include <iostream>
using namespace std;

class myclass {
  int num;
public:
  myclass(int i) { num = i; }
  int getnum() { return num; }
};

int main()
{
  myclass o(10);

  cout << o.getnum() << endl; // displays 10

  // now, use implicit conversion to assign new value
  o = 1000;

  cout << o.getnum() << endl; // displays 1000

  return 0;
}
```

Notice that **o** is assigned a new value using the statement:

```cpp
o = 1000;
```

This works because of the implicit conversion that is created from type **int** to type **myclass** by the **myclass** constructor. Of course, if **myclass( )** had been declared **explicit**, then the preceding statement would not work.

The Member Initialization Syntax

Example code throughout the preceding chapters has initialized member variables inside the constructor for their class. For example, the following program contains the **myclass** class, which has two integer data members called **numA** and **numB**. These member variables are initialized inside **myclass'** constructor.

```
#include <iostream>
using namespace std;

class myclass {
  int numA;
  int numB;
public:
  /* Initialize numA and numB inside the myclass constructor
     using normal syntax. */
  myclass(int x, int y) {
    numA = x;
    numB = y;
  }

  int getNumA() { return numA; }
  int getNumB() { return numB; }
};

int main()
{
  myclass ob1(7, 9), ob2(5, 2);

  cout << "Values in ob1 are " << ob1.getNumB() <<
          " and " << ob1.getNumA() << endl;

  cout << "Values in ob2 are " << ob2.getNumB() <<
          " and " << ob2.getNumA() << endl;

  return 0;
}
```

20

The output is shown here.

```
Values in ob1 are 9 and 7
Values in ob2 are 2 and 5
```

Assigning initial values to member variables **numA** and **numB** inside the constructor, as **myclass( )** does, is the usual approach, and is the way that member initialization is accomplished for many, many classes. However, this approach won't work in all cases. For example, if **numA** and **numB** were specified as **const**, like this

```
class myclass {
  const int numA; // const member
  const int numB; // const member
```

then they could not be given values by the **myclass** constructor because **const** variables must be initialized and cannot be assigned values after the fact. Similar problems arise when using reference members, which must be initialized, and when using class members that don't have default constructors. To solve these types of problems, C++ supports an alternative member initialization syntax, which gives a class member an initial value when an object of the class is created.

The member initialization syntax is similar to that used to call a base class constructor. Here is the general form.

> *constructor(arg-list)* : *member1(initializer),*
> *member2(initializer),*
> *// ...*
> *memberN(initializer)*
> {
>   // body of construcor
> }

The members that you want to initialize are specified after the class' constructor, separated from the constructor's name and argument list by a colon. You can mix calls to base class constructors with member initializations in the same list.

Here is **myclass** rewritten so that **numA** and **numB** are **const** members which are given values using the member initialization syntax.

```
#include <iostream>
using namespace std;

class myclass {
  const int numA; // const member
  const int numB; // const member
public:
  // Initialize numA and numB using initialization syntax.
  myclass(int x, int y) : numA(x), numB(y) { }

  int getNumA() { return numA; }
  int getNumB() { return numB; }
};

int main()
{
  myclass ob1(7, 9), ob2(5, 2);

  cout << "Values in ob1 are " << ob1.getNumB() <<
          " and " << ob1.getNumA() << endl;

  cout << "Values in ob2 are " << ob2.getNumB() <<
          " and " << ob2.getNumA() << endl;

  return 0;
}
```

This program produces the same output as the preceding verison. However, notice how **numA** and **numB** are initialized by this statement:

```
myclass(int x, int y) : numA(x), numB(y) { }
```

Here, **numA** is initialized with the value passed in **x**, and **numB** is initialized with the value passed in **y**. Even though **numA** and **numB** are now **const**, they can be given initial values when a **myclass** object is created because the member initialization syntax is used.

Using the asm Keyword

Assembly code
is embedded
directly into a
C++ program
by using the
asm keyword.

Although C++ is a comprehensive and powerful programming language, there are a few highly specialized situations that it cannot handle. (For example, there is no C++ statement that disables interrupts.) To accommodate special situations, C++ provides a "trap door" that allows you to drop into assembly code at any time, bypassing the C++ compiler entirely. This "trap door" is the **asm** statement. Using **asm**, you can embed assembly language directly into your C++ program. This assembly code is compiled without any modification, and it becomes part of your program's code at the point at which the **asm** statement occurs.

20

The general form of the **asm** keyword is shown here,

asm ("*op-code*");

where *op-code* is the assembly language instruction that will be embedded in your program. However, several compilers also allow the following forms of **asm**:

asm *instruction* ;

asm *instruction newline*

asm {
   instruction sequence
}

Here, *instruction* is any valid assembly language instruction. Because of the implementation-specific nature of **asm**, you must check the documentation that came with your compiler for details.

At the time of this writing, Microsoft's Visual C++ uses _ _**asm** for embedding assembly code. It is otherwise similar to **asm**.

CAUTION: A thorough working knowledge of assembly language programming is required for using the **asm** statement. If you are not proficient with assembly language, it is best to avoid using **asm**, because very nasty errors may result.

Linkage Specification

In C++, you can specify how a function is linked into your program. By default, functions are linked as C++ functions. However, by using a *linkage specification*, you can cause a function to be linked for a different type of language. The general form of a linkage specifier is shown here,

    extern *"language" function-prototype*

where *language* denotes the desired language. All C++ compilers support both C and C++ linkage. Some will also allow linkage specifiers for Fortran, Pascal, or BASIC. (You will need to check the documentation for your compiler.)

This program causes **myCfunc( )** to be linked as a C function:

```
#include <iostream>
using namespace std;

extern "C" void myCfunc();

int main()
{
  myCfunc();

  return 0;
}

// This will link as a C function.
void myCfunc()
{
  cout << "This links as a C function.\n";
}
```

NOTE: The **extern** keyword is a necessary part of the linkage specification. Further, the linkage specification must be global; it cannot be used inside of a function.

You can specify more than one function at a time by using this form of the linkage specification:

    extern *"language"* {
       prototypes
    }

Linkage specifications are rare, and you will probably not need to use one. Its main use is to allow third-party routines that are written in another language to be used by a C++ program.

The .* and –>* Pointer-to-Member Operators

The pointer-to-member operators allow you to access a class member through a pointer to that member.

C++ allows you to generate a special type of pointer that "points" generically to a member of a class, not to a specific instance of that member in an object. This sort of pointer is called a pointer to a class member or a *pointer-to-member*, for short. A pointer to a member is not the same as a normal C++ pointer. Instead, a pointer to a member provides only an offset into an object of the member's class at which that member can be found. Since member pointers are not true pointers, the **.** and **–>** cannot be applied to them. To access a member of a class given a member pointer, you must use the special pointer-to-member operators **.*** and **–>***.

If the preceding paragraph seems a bit confusing, the following example should help clear things up. This program displays the summation of the number 7. It accesses the function **sum_it( )** and the variable **sum** by using member pointers.

```
// Pointer-to-member example.
#include <iostream>
using namespace std;

class myclass {
public:
  int sum;
  void myclass::sum_it(int x);
};

void myclass::sum_it(int x) {
  int i;

  sum = 0;
  for(i=x; i; i--) sum += i;
}

int main()
{
  int myclass::*dp;  // pointer to an integer class member
  void (myclass::*fp)(int x); // pointer to member function
  myclass c;

  dp = &myclass::sum;  // get address of data
  fp = &myclass::sum_it; // get address of function

  (c.*fp)(7);  // compute summation of 7
  cout << "summation of 7 is " << c.*dp;

  return 0;
}
```

The output is shown here.

```
summation of 7 is 28
```

Inside **main( )**, this program creates two member pointers: **dp**, which will point to the variable **sum**, and **fp**, which will point to the function **sum_it( )**. Note carefully the syntax of each declaration. The scope resolution operator is used to specify which class is being referred to. The program also creates an object of **myclass**, called **c**.

Next, the program obtains the addresses of **sum** and **sum_it( )** and assigns them to **dp** and **fp**, respectively. As stated earlier, these addresses are really just offsets into an object of **myclass**, at which point **sum** and **sum_it( )** will be found. Next, the program uses the function pointer **fp** to call the **sum_it( )** function of **c**. The extra parentheses are necessary in order to correctly associate the **.*** operator. Finally, the program displays the summed value by accessing **c**'s **sum** through **dp**.

When you are accessing a member of an object using an object or a reference, you must use the **.*** operator. However, if you are using a pointer to the object, you need to use the **–>*** operator, as illustrated in this version of the preceding program:

```
#include <iostream>
using namespace std;

class myclass {
public:
  int sum;
  void myclass::sum_it(int x);
};

void myclass::sum_it(int x) {
  int i;

  sum = 0;
  for(i=x; i; i--) sum += i;
}

int main()
{
  int myclass::*dp;  // pointer to an integer class member
  void (myclass::*fp)(int x); // pointer to member function
  myclass *c, d; // c is now a pointer to an object

  c = &d; // give c the address of an object

  dp = &myclass::sum;  // get address of data
  fp = &myclass::sum_it; // get address of function

  (c->*fp)(7);  // now, use ->* to call function
  cout << "summation of 7 is " << c->*dp; // use ->*

  return 0;
}
```

In this version, **c** is now a pointer to an object of type **myclass**, and the **–>*** operator is used to access **sum** and **sum_it( )**.

Remember that the pointer-to-member operators are designed for special-case applications. You will not need them in your normal, day-to-day programming tasks.

Creating Conversion Functions

Sometimes you will want to freely mix a class that you have created with other types of data in an expression. Although overloaded operator functions can provide a means of mixing types, sometimes a simple type conversion is all that is needed. In this case, you can use a type conversion function to convert your class into a type that is compatible with that of the rest of the expression. The general format of a type conversion function is

> operator *type*( ) {return *value*;}

20

Here, *type* is the target type that you are converting to, and *value* is the value after conversion. A conversion function must be a member of the class for which it is defined.

A conversion function automatically converts a class type into another type.

To illustrate how to create a conversion function, let's use the **three_d** class once again. Suppose that you want to be able to convert an object of type **three_d** into an integer so that it can be used in an integer expression. Further, the conversion will take place by using the product of the three dimensions. To accomplish this, you will use a conversion function that looks like this:

```
operator int() { return x * y * z; }
```

Here is a program that illustrates how the conversion function works:

```
#include <iostream>
using namespace std;

class three_d {
  int x, y, z; // 3-D coordinates
public:
  three_d(int a, int b, int c) { x = a; y = b; z = c; }

  three_d operator+(three_d op2) ;
  friend ostream &operator<<(ostream &stream, three_d &obj);

  operator int() {return x * y * z; }
} ;

// Display X, Y, Z coordinates - three_d inserter.
ostream &operator<<(ostream &stream, three_d &obj)
{
  stream << obj.x << ", ";
  stream << obj.y << ", ";
  stream << obj.z << "\n";
  return stream;  // return the stream
}
```

```
three_d three_d::operator+(three_d op2)
{
  three_d temp(0, 0, 0);

  temp.x = x+op2.x;
  temp.y = y+op2.y;
  temp.z = z+op2.z;
  return temp;
}

int main()
{
  three_d a(1, 2, 3), b(2, 3, 4);

  cout << a << b;

  cout <<  b+100;  // displays 124 because of conversion to int
  cout << "\n";

  a = a + b; // add two three_d objects - no conversion

  cout << a;  // displays 3, 5, 7

  return 0;
}
```

The program displays this output:

```
1, 2, 3
2, 3, 4
124
3, 5, 7
```

As the program illustrates, when a **three_d** object is used in an integer expression, such as **cout << b+100**, the conversion function is applied to the object. In this specific case, the conversion function returns the value 24, which is then added to 100. However, when no conversion is needed, as in **a = a+b**, the conversion function is not called.

Once you have created a conversion function, it will be called whenever that conversion is required, including when an object is passed as a parameter to a function. For example, the **three_d**-to-**int** conversion function is also called if a **three_d** object is passed to the standard **abs( )** function, because **abs( )** requires an integer argument.

REMEMBER: You can create different conversion functions to meet different needs. You could define one that converts **three_d** to **double** or **long**, for example. Each will be applied automatically. Conversion functions further help you integrate new class types that you create into your C++ programming environment.

CHAPTER 21

Introducing the Standard Template Library

T his chapter explores what is considered by many to be the most important feature added to C++ in recent years: the Standard Template Library. The inclusion of the *Standard Template Library*, or *STL*, was one of the major efforts that took place during the standardization of C++. The STL provides general-purpose, templatized classes and functions that implement many popular and commonly used algorithms and data structures. For example, it includes support for vectors, lists, queues, and stacks. It also defines various functions that access them. Because the STL is constructed from template classes, the algorithms and data structures can be applied to nearly any type of data.

The STL is a set of general-purpose template classes.

The STL is a complex piece of software engineering that uses some of C++'s most sophisticated features. To understand and use the STL, you must be comfortable with all of the material in the preceding chapters. Specifically, you must feel at home with templates. Frankly, the template syntax that describes the STL can seem quite intimidating—although it looks more complicated than it actually is. While there is nothing in this chapter that is any more difficult than the material in the rest of this book, don't be surprised or dismayed if you find the STL confusing at first. Just be patient, study the examples, and don't let the unfamiliar syntax override the STL's basic simplicity.

The STL is a large library and not all of its features can be described in this chapter. In fact, a full description of the STL and all of its features, nuances, and programming techniques fill an entire book. The overview presented here is intended to familiarize you with its basic operation, design philosophy, and programming fundamentals. After working through this chapter, you will be able to easily explore the remainder of the STL on your own.

This chapter also describes another important C++ class: **string**. The **string** class defines a string data type which allows you to work with character strings much like you do with other data types: using operators. The **string** class is closely related to the STL.

An Overview of the STL

Although the Standard Template Library is large and its syntax is, at times, rather intimidating, it is actually quite easy to use once you understand how it is constructed and what elements it employs. Therefore, before looking at any code examples, an overview of the STL is warranted.

At the core of the Standard Template Library are three foundational items: *containers*, *algorithms*, and *iterators*. These items work in conjunction with one another to provide off-the-shelf solutions to a variety of programming problems.

Containers are objects that hold other objects.

Containers are objects that hold other objects. There are several different types of containers. For example, the **vector** class defines a dynamic array, **queue** creates a queue, and **list** provides a linear list. In addition to the basic containers, the STL also defines *associative containers*, which allow efficient retrieval of values based on keys. For example, a **map** provides access to values with unique keys. Thus, a **map** stores a key/value pair and allows a value to be retrieved given its key.

Each container class defines a set of functions that may be applied to the container. For example, a list container includes functions that insert, delete, and merge elements. A stack includes functions that push and pop values.

Algorithms act
on the contents
of containers.

Algorithms act on the contents of containers. They include capabilities for initializing, sorting, searching, and transforming the contents of containers. Many algorithms operate on a *range* of elements within a container.

Iterators
are similar
to pointers.

Iterators are objects that act, more or less, like pointers. They give you the ability to cycle through the contents of a container in much the same way that you would use a pointer to cycle through an array. There are five types of iterators:

Iterator	Access Allowed
Random Access	Store and retrieve values. Elements may be accessed randomly.
Bidirectional	Store and retrieve values. Forward and backward moving.
Forward	Store and retrieve values. Forward moving only.
Input	Retrieve, but not store values. Forward moving only.
Output	Store, but not retrieve values. Forward moving only.

In general, an iterator that has greater access capabilities can be used in place of one that has lesser capabilities. For example, a forward iterator can be used in place of an input iterator.

21

Iterators are handled just like pointers. You can increment and decrement them. You can apply the ***** operator to them. Iterators are declared using the **iterator** type defined by the various containers.

The STL also supports reverse iterators. *Reverse iterators* are either bidirectional or random-access iterators that move through a sequence in the reverse direction. Thus, if a reverse iterator points to the end of a sequence, incrementing that iterator will cause it to point to one element before the end.

When referring to the various iterator types in template descriptions, this book will use the following terms:

Term	Represents
BiIter	Bidirectional iterator
ForIter	Forward iterator
InIter	Input iterator
OutIter	Output iterator
RandIter	Random access iterator

In addition to containers, algorithms, and iterators, the STL relies upon several other standard components for support. Chief among these are allocators, predicates, and comparison functions.

An allocator
manages memory
allocation for
a container.

Each container has an allocator defined for it. *Allocators* manage memory allocation for a container. The default allocator is an object of class **allocator**, but you can define your own allocators, if needed, for specialized applications. For most uses, the default allocator is sufficient.

A predicate
returns a true/
false result.

Several of the algorithms and containers use a special type of function called a *predicate*. There are two variations of predicates: unary and binary. A *unary predicate* takes one argument. A *binary predicate* has two arguments. These functions return true/false results, but the precise conditions that make them return true or false are defined by you. For the rest of this chapter, when a unary predicate function is required, it will be notated using the type **UnPred**. When a binary predicate is required, the type **BinPred** will be used. In a binary predicate, the arguments are always in the order of *first,second*. For both unary and binary predicates, the arguments will contain values of the type of objects being stored by the container.

A comparison
function compares
two elements of a
sequence.

Some algorithms and classes use a special type of binary predicate that compares two elements. *Comparison functions* return true if their first argument is less than their second. Comparison functions will be notated using the type **Comp**.

In addition to the headers required by the various STL classes, the C++ standard library includes the **<utility>** and **<functional>** headers, which provide support for the STL. For example, in **<utility>** is defined the template class **pair**, which can hold a pair of values. We will make use of **pair** later in this chapter.

The templates in **<functional>** help you to construct objects that define **operator( )**. These are called *function objects*, and they may be used in place of function pointers in many places. There are several predefined function objects declared within **<functional>**. Some are shown here:

plus	minus	multiplies	divides	modulus
negate	equal_to	not_equal_to	greater	greater_equal
less	less_equal	logical_and	logical_or	logical_not

Perhaps the most widely used function object is **less,** which determines when one object is less than another. Function objects can be used in place of actual function pointers in the STL algorithms, described later. Using function objects rather than function pointers allows the STL to generate more efficient code in some cases. However, for the purposes of this chapter, function objects are not needed and we won't be using them directly. Although function objects are not inherently difficult, a detailed discussion of function objects is beyond the scope of this book. (Complete coverage of function objects can be found in my book *C++: The Complete Reference, 4th Edition*, McGraw-Hill/Osborne).

The Container Classes

As explained, containers are the STL objects that actually store data. The containers defined by the STL are shown in Table 21-1. Also shown are the headers necessary to use each container. The **string** class, which manages character strings, is also a container, but it is discussed later in this chapter.

Container	Description	Required Header
bitset	A set of bits.	\<bitset\>
deque	A double-ended queue.	\<deque\>
list	A linear list.	\<list\>
map	Stores key/value pairs in which each key is associated with only one value.	\<map\>
multimap	Stores key/value pairs in which one key may be associated with two or more values.	\<map\>
multiset	A set in which each element is not necessarily unique.	\<set\>
priority_queue	A priority queue.	\<queue\>
queue	A queue.	\<queue\>
set	A set in which each element is unique.	\<set\>
stack	A stack.	\<stack\>
vector	A dynamic array.	\<vector\>

The Containers Defined by the STL
Table 21-1.

21

Since the names of the placeholder types in a template class declaration are arbitrary, the container classes declare **typedef**ed versions of these types. This makes the type names concrete. Some of the most common **typedef** names are shown here:

size_type	Some type of integer.
reference	A reference to an element.
const_reference	A **const** reference to an element.
iterator	An iterator.
const_iterator	A **const** iterator.
reverse_iterator	A reverse iterator.
const_reverse_iterator	A **const** reverse iterator.
value_type	The type of a value stored in a container.
allocator_type	The type of the allocator.
key_type	The type of a key.
key_compare	The type of a function that compares two keys.
value_compare	The type of a function that compares two values.
mapped_type	The type of value stored in a map. (Same as the generic type T.)

While it is not possible to examine each container in this chapter, the next sections explore three representative containers: **vector, list**, and **map**. Once you understand how these containers work, you will have no trouble using the others.

Vectors

Perhaps the most general-purpose of the containers is **vector**. The **vector** class supports a dynamic array. This is an array that can grow as needed. As you know, in C++, the size of an array is fixed at compile time. While this is, by far, the most efficient way to implement arrays, it is also the most restrictive because the size of the array cannot be adjusted at run time to accommodate changing program conditions. A vector solves this problem by allocating memory as needed. Although a vector is dynamic, you can still use the standard array subscript notation to access its elements.

The template specification for **vector** is shown here:

template <class T, class Allocator = allocator<T> > class vector

Here, **T** is the type of data being stored, and **Allocator** specifies the allocator, which defaults to the standard allocator. **vector** has the following constructors:

explicit vector(const Allocator &*a* = Allocator( ));

explicit vector(size_type *num*, const T &*val* = T ( ),
        const Allocator &*a* = Allocator( ));

vector(const vector<T, Allocator> &*ob*);

template <class InIter> vector(InIter *start*, InIter *end*,
        const Allocator &*a* = Allocator( ));

The first form constructs an empty vector. The second form constructs a vector that has *num* elements with the value *val*. The value of *val* may be allowed to default. The third form constructs a vector that contains the same elements as *ob*. The fourth form constructs a vector that contains the elements in the range specified by the iterators *start* and *end*.

For maximum flexibility and portability, any object that will be stored in a **vector** should define a default constructor. It should also define the **<** and **==** operations. Some compilers may require that other comparison operators be defined. (Since implementations vary, consult your compiler's documentation for precise information.) All of the built-in types automatically satisfy these requirements.

Although the template syntax looks rather complex, there is nothing difficult about declaring a vector. Here are some examples:

```
vector<int> iv;            // create zero-length int vector
vector<char> cv(5);        // create 5-element char vector
vector<char> cv(5, 'x');   // initialize a 5-element char vector
vector<int> iv2(iv);       // create int vector from an int vector
```

The following comparison operators are defined for **vector**:

==, <, <=, !=, >, >=

The subscripting operator **[ ]** is also defined for **vector**. This allows you to access the elements of a vector by using standard array subscripting notation.

The member functions defined by **vector** are shown in Table 21-2. (Again, it is important not to be put off by the syntax.) Some of the most important member functions are **size( )**, **begin( )**, **end( )**, **push_back( )**, **insert( )**, and **erase( )**. The **size( )** function returns the current size of the vector. This function is quite useful because it allows you to determine the size of a vector at run time. Remember, vectors will increase in size as needed, so the size of a vector must be determined during execution, not during compilation.

Member	Description
template <class InIter> void assign(InIter *start*, InIter *end*);	Assigns the vector the sequence defined by *start* and *end*.
void assign(size_type *num*, const T &*val*);	Assigns the vector *num* elements of value *val*.
reference at(size_type *i*); const_reference at(size_type *i*) const;	Returns a reference to an element specified by *i*.
reference back( ); const_reference back( ) const;	Returns a reference to the last element in the vector.
iterator begin( ); const_iterator begin( ) const;	Returns an iterator to the first element in the vector.
size_type capacity( ) const;	Returns the current capacity of the vector. This is the number of elements it can hold before it will need to allocate more memory.
void clear( );	Removes all elements from the vector.
bool empty( ) const;	Returns true if the invoking vector is empty and false otherwise.
iterator end( ); const_iterator end( ) const;	Returns an iterator to the end of the vector.
iterator erase(iterator *i*);	Removes the element pointed to by *i*. Returns an iterator to the element after the one removed.
iterator erase(iterator *start*, iterator *end*);	Removes the elements in the range *start* to *end*. Returns an iterator to the element after the last element removed.
reference front( ); const_reference front( ) const;	Returns a reference to the first element in the vector.
allocator_type get_allocator( ) const;	Returns vector's allocator.
iterator insert(iterator *i*, const T &*val*);	Inserts *val* immediately before the element specified by *i*. An iterator to the element is returned.

The Member
Functions
Defined by
vector
Table 21-2.

Member	Description
void insert(iterator *i*, size_type *num*, const T & *val*);	Inserts *num* copies of *val* immediately before the element specified by *i*.
template <class InIter> void insert(iterator *i*, InIter *start*, InIter *end*);	Inserts the sequence defined by *start* and *end* immediately before the element specified by *i*.
size_type max_size( ) const;	Returns the maximum number of elements that the vector can hold.
reference operator[ ](size_type *i*) const; const_reference operator[ ](size_type *i*) const;	Returns a reference to the element specified by *i*.
void pop_back( );	Removes the last element in the vector.
void push_back(const T &*val*);	Adds an element with the value specified by *val* to the end of the vector.
reverse_iterator rbegin( ); const_reverse_iterator rbegin( ) const;	Returns a reverse iterator to the end of the vector.
reverse_iterator rend( ); const_reverse_iterator rend( ) const;	Returns a reverse iterator to the start of the vector.
void reserve(size_type *num*);	Sets the capacity of the vector so that it is equal to at least *num*.
void resize(size_type *num*, T val = T ( ));	Changes the size of the vector to that specified by *num*. If the vector must be lengthened, then elements with the value specified by *val* are added to the end.
size_type size( ) const;	Returns the number of elements currently in the vector.
void swap(vector<T, Allocator> &*ob*);	Exchanges the elements stored in the invoking vector with those in *ob*.

The Member
Functions
Defined
by **vector**
(continued)
Table 21-2.

The **begin( )** function returns an iterator to the start of the vector. The **end( )** function returns an iterator to the end of the vector. As explained, iterators are similar to pointers, and it is through the use of the **begin( )** and **end( )** functions that you obtain an iterator to the beginning and end of a vector.

The **push_back( )** function puts a value onto the end of the vector. If necessary, the vector is increased in length to accommodate the new element. You can add elements to the middle by using **insert( )**. A vector can also be initialized. In any event, once a vector contains elements, you can use array subscripting to access or modify those elements. You can remove elements from a vector by using **erase( )**.

Here is a short example that illustrates the basic operation of a vector:

```
// Vector basics.
#include <iostream>
#include <vector>
using namespace std;

int main()
{
  vector<int> v; // create zero-length vector
  unsigned int i;

  // display original size of v
  cout << "Size = " << v.size() << endl;

  /* put values onto end of vector --
     vector will grow as needed */
  for(i=0; i<10; i++) v.push_back(i);

  // display current size of v
  cout << "Current contents:\n";
  cout << "Size now = " << v.size() << endl;

  // display contents of vector
  for(i=0; i<v.size(); i++) cout << v[i] << " ";
  cout << endl;

  /* put more values onto end of vector --
     again, vector will grow as needed */
  for(i=0; i<10; i++) v.push_back(i+10);

  // display current size of v
  cout << "Size now = " << v.size() << endl;

  // display contents of vector
  cout << "Current contents:\n";
  for(i=0; i<v.size(); i++) cout << v[i] << " ";
  cout << endl;

  // change contents of vector
  for(i=0; i<v.size(); i++) v[i] = v[i] + v[i];

  // display contents of vector
  cout << "Contents doubled:\n";
  for(i=0; i<v.size(); i++) cout << v[i] << " ";
  cout << endl;

  return 0;
}
```

21

The output of this program is shown here:

```
Size = 0
Current contents:
Size now = 10
0 1 2 3 4 5 6 7 8 9
Size now = 20
Current contents:
0 1 2 3 4 5 6 7 8 9 10 11 12 13 14 15 16 17 18 19
Contents doubled:
0 2 4 6 8 10 12 14 16 18 20 22 24 26 28 30 32 34 36 38
```

Let's look at this program carefully. In **main( )**, an integer vector called **v** is created. Since no initialization is used, it is an empty vector with an initial capacity of zero. That is, it is a zero-length vector. This is confirmed by calling the **size( )** member function. Next, 10 elements are added to the end of **v** by using the member function **push_back( )**. This causes **v** to grow in order to accommodate the new elements. As the output shows, its size after these additions is 10. Next, the contents of **v** are displayed. Notice that the standard array subscripting notation is employed. Next, 10 more elements are added, and **v** is automatically increased in size to handle them. Finally, the values of **v**'s elements are altered by using standard subscripting notation.

There is one other point of interest in this program: Notice that the loops that display the contents of **v** use as their target **v.size( )**. One of the advantages that vectors have over arrays is that it is possible to find the current size of a vector. As you can imagine, this is quite useful in a variety of situations.

Accessing a Vector Through an Iterator

As you know, arrays and pointers are tightly linked in C++. An array can be accessed through either subscripting or a pointer. The parallel to this in the STL is the link between vectors and iterators. You can access the members of a vector using either subscripting or an iterator. The following example shows how:

```cpp
// Access a vector using an iterator.
#include <iostream>
#include <vector>
using namespace std;

int main()
{
  vector<char> v; // create zero-length vector
  int i;

  // put values into a vector
  for(i=0; i<10; i++) v.push_back('A' + i);

  // can access vector contents using subscripting
  for(i=0; i<10; i++) cout << v[i] << " ";
  cout << endl;
```

```
  // access via iterator
  vector<char>::iterator p = v.begin();
  while(p != v.end()) {
    cout << *p << " ";
    p++;
  }

  return 0;
}
```

The output from this program is

```
A B C D E F G H I J
A B C D E F G H I J
```

In this program, the vector is initially created with zero length. The **push_back( )** member function puts characters onto the end of the vector, expanding its size as needed.

Notice how the iterator **p** is declared. The type **iterator** is defined by the container classes. Thus, to obtain an iterator for a particular container, you will use a declaration similar to that shown in the example: Simply qualify **iterator** with the name of the container. In the program, **p** is initialized to point to the start of the vector by using the **begin( )** member function. This function returns an iterator to the start of the vector. This iterator can then be used to access the vector an element at a time by incrementing it as needed. This process is directly parallel to the way a pointer can be used to access the elements of an array. To determine when the end of the vector has been reached, the **end( )** member function is employed. This function returns an iterator to the location that is one past the last element in the vector. Thus, when **p** equals **v.end( )**, the end of the vector has been reached.

21

Inserting and Deleting Elements in a Vector

In addition to putting new values on the end of a vector, you can insert elements into the middle by using the **insert( )** function. You can also remove elements by using **erase( )**. The following program demonstrates **insert( )** and **erase( )**:

```
// Demonstrate insert and erase.
#include <iostream>
#include <vector>
using namespace std;

int main()
{
  vector<char> v;
  unsigned int i;

  for(i=0; i<10; i++) v.push_back('A' + i);
```

```
// display original contents of vector
cout << "Size = " << v.size() << endl;
cout << "Original contents:\n";
for(i=0; i<v.size(); i++) cout << v[i] << " ";
cout << endl << endl;

vector<char>::iterator p = v.begin();
p += 2; // point to 3rd element

// insert 10 X's into v
v.insert(p, 10, 'X');

// display contents after insertion
cout << "Size after insert = " << v.size() << endl;
cout << "Contents after insert:\n";
for(i=0; i<v.size(); i++) cout << v[i] << " ";
cout << endl << endl;

// remove those elements
p = v.begin();
p += 2; // point to 3rd element
v.erase(p, p+10); // remove next 10 elements

// display contents after deletion
cout << "Size after erase = " << v.size() << endl;
cout << "Contents after erase:\n";
for(i=0; i<v.size(); i++) cout << v[i] << " ";
cout << endl;

  return 0;
}
```

This program produces the following output:

```
Size = 10
Original contents:
A B C D E F G H I J

Size after insert = 20
Contents after insert:
A B X X X X X X X X X X C D E F G H I J

Size after erase = 10
Contents after erase:
A B C D E F G H I J
```

Storing Class Objects in a Vector

Although the preceding examples have stored objects of only the built-in types in a vector, **vector**s are not limited to this. They can store any type of objects, including those of classes that you create. Here is an example that uses a **vector** to store **three_d** objects.

Notice that the class defines the default constructor, and that overloaded versions of < and == are provided. Remember, depending upon how your compiler implements the STL, other comparison operators may need to be defined.

```cpp
// Store a class object in a vector.
#include <iostream>
#include <vector>
using namespace std;

class three_d {
  int x, y, z;
public:
  three_d() { x = y = z = 0; }
  three_d(int a, int b, int c) { x = a; y = b; z = c; }

  three_d &operator+(int a) {
    x += a;
    y += a;
    z += a;
    return *this;
  }

  friend ostream &operator<<(ostream &stream, three_d obj);
  friend bool operator<(three_d a, three_d b);
  friend bool operator==(three_d a, three_d b);
} ;

// Display X, Y, Z coordinates - three_d inserter.
ostream &operator<<(ostream &stream, three_d obj)
{
  stream << obj.x << ", ";
  stream << obj.y << ", ";
  stream << obj.z << "\n";
  return stream;  // return the stream
}

bool operator<(three_d a, three_d b)
{
  return (a.x + a.y + a.z) < (b.x + b.y + b.z);
}

bool operator==(three_d a, three_d b)
{
  return (a.x + a.y + a.z) == (b.x + b.y + b.z);
}

int main()
{
  vector<three_d> v;
  unsigned int i;
```

21

```
  // add objects to a vector
  for(i=0; i<10; i++)
    v.push_back(three_d(i, i+2, i-3));

  // display contents of vector
  for(i=0; i<v.size(); i++)
    cout << v[i];

  cout << endl;

  // modify objects in a vector
  for(i=0; i<v.size(); i++)
    v[i] = v[i] + 10;

  // display modified vector
  for(i=0; i<v.size(); i++)
    cout << v[i];

  return 0;
}
```

The output from this program is shown here:

```
0, 2, -3
1, 3, -2
2, 4, -1
3, 5, 0
4, 6, 1
5, 7, 2
6, 8, 3
7, 9, 4
8, 10, 5
9, 11, 6

10, 12, 7
11, 13, 8
12, 14, 9
13, 15, 10
14, 16, 11
15, 17, 12
16, 18, 13
17, 19, 14
18, 20, 15
19, 21, 16
```

Vectors offer great power, safety, and flexibility, but they are less efficient than normal arrays. Thus, for most programming tasks, normal arrays will still be your first choice. But watch for situations in which the benefits of using **vector** outweighs the costs.

IN DEPTH

The Power of Iterators

Part of the power of the STL comes from the fact that many of its functions operate on iterators. This fact allows operations on two containers at the same time. For example, consider this form of **vector**'s **insert( )** function:

template <class InIter> void insert(iterator *i,* InIter *start,* InIter *end*);

This function inserts the sequence defined by *start* and *end* into the target sequence beginning at *i.* There is no requirement that *i* point into the same vector as *start* and *end.* Thus, using this version of **insert( )**, you can insert one vector into another. For example:

```cpp
// Insert one vector into another.
#include <iostream>
#include <vector>
using namespace std;

int main()
{
  vector<char> v, v2;
  unsigned int i;

  for(i=0; i<10; i++) v.push_back('A' + i);

  // display original contents of vector
  cout << "Original contents:\n";
  for(i=0; i<v.size(); i++) cout << v[i] << " ";
  cout << endl << endl;

  // initialize second vector
  char str[] = "-STL Power-";
  for(i = 0; str[i]; i++) v2.push_back(str[i]);

  /* get iterators to the middle of v and
     the start and end of v2 */
  vector<char>::iterator p = v.begin()+5;
  vector<char>::iterator p2start = v2.begin();
  vector<char>::iterator p2end = v2.end();

  // insert v2 into v
  v.insert(p, p2start, p2end);

  // display result
  cout << "Contents of v after insertion:\n";
  for(i=0; i<v.size(); i++) cout << v[i] << " ";

  return 0;
}
```

21

The output produced by this program is the following:

```
Original contents:
A B C D E F G H I J

Contents of v after insertion:
A B C D E - S T L   P o w e r - F G H I J
```

As you can see, the contents of vector **v2** are inserted into the middle of vector **v**.

As you learn more about the STL, you will find that interators are the glue that holds it together. They offer a convenient means of working with two or more STL objects at the same time. They are especially useful to the algorithms described later in this chapter.

Lists

A **list** is a bidirectional linear list.

The **list** class supports a bidirectional, linear list. Unlike a vector, which supports random access, a list can be accessed sequentially only. Since lists are bidirectional, they may be accessed front-to-back or back-to-front.

A **list** has this template specification:

> template <class T, class Allocator = allocator<T> > class list

Here, **T** is the type of data stored in the list. The allocator is specified by **Allocator**, which defaults to the standard allocator. It has the following constructors:

> explicit list(const Allocator &*a* = Allocator( ));

> explicit list(size_type *num*, const T &*val* = T ( ),
> const Allocator &*a* = Allocator( ));

> list(const list<T, Allocator> &*ob*);

> template <class InIter>list(InIter *start*, InIter *end*,
> const Allocator &*a* = Allocator( ));

The first form constructs an empty list. The second form constructs a list that has *num* elements with the value *val*, which can be allowed to default. The third form constructs a list that contains the same elements as *ob*. The fourth form constructs a list that contains the elements in the range specified by the iterators *start* and *end*.

The following comparison operators are defined for **list**:

> ==, <, <=, !=, >, >=

The member functions defined for **list** are shown in Table 21-3. Like a vector, elements may be put into a list by using the **push_back( )** function. You can put elements on the front of the list by using **push_front( )**. An element may also be inserted into the middle of a list by using **insert( )**. Two lists may be joined by using **splice( )**. One list may be merged into another by using **merge( )**.

Member	Description
template <class InIter> void assign(InIter *start*, InIter *end*);	Assigns the list the sequence defined by *start* and *end*.
void assign(size_type *num*, const T &*val*);	Assigns the list *num* elements of value *val*.
reference back( ); const_reference back( ) const;	Returns a reference to the last element in the list.
iterator begin( ); const_iterator begin( ) const;	Returns an iterator to the first element in the list.
void clear( );	Removes all elements from the list.
bool empty( ) const;	Returns true if the invoking list is empty and false otherwise.
iterator end( ); const_iterator end( ) const;	Returns an iterator to the end of the list.
iterator erase(iterator *i*);	Removes the element pointed to by *i*. Returns an iterator to the element after the one removed.
iterator erase(iterator *start*, iterator *end*);	Removes the elements in the range *start* to *end*. Returns an iterator to the element after the last element removed.
reference front( ); const_reference front( ) const;	Returns a reference to the first element in the list.
allocator_type get_allocator( ) const;	Returns list's allocator.
iterator insert(iterator *i*, const T &*val* = T( ));	Inserts *val* immediately before the element specified by *i*. An iterator to the element is returned.
void insert(iterator *i*, size_type *num*, const T & *val*);	Inserts *num* copies of *val* immediately before the element specified by *i*.

template <class InIter>
    void insert(iterator *i*,
          InIter *start*, InIter *end*);
	Inserts the sequence defined by *start* and *end* immediately before the element specified by *i*.

size_type max_size( ) const;	Returns the maximum number of elements that the list can hold.

The **list** Member Functions
Table 21-3.

21

Member	Description

void merge(list<T, Allocator> &*ob*);
template <class Comp>
   void merge(<list<T, Allocator> &*ob*,
         Comp *cmpfn*);
	Merges the ordered list contained in *ob* with the ordered invoking list. The result is ordered. After the merge, the list contained in *ob* is empty. In the second form, a comparison function can be specified that determines when one element is less than another.

void pop_back( );	Removes the last element in the list.
void pop_front( );	Removes the first element in the list.
void push_back(const T &*val*);	Adds an element with the value specified by *val* to the end of the list.
void push_front(const T &*val*);	Adds an element with the value specified by *val* to the front of the list.
reverse_iterator rbegin( ); const_reverse_iterator rbegin( ) const;	Returns a reverse iterator to the end of the list.
void remove(const T &*val*);	Removes elements with the value *val* from the list.
template <class UnPred> void remove_if(UnPred *pr*);	Removes elements for which the unary predicate *pr* is true.
reverse_iterator rend( ); const_reverse_iterator rend( ) const;	Returns a reverse iterator to the start of the list.
void resize(size_type *num*, T *val* = T ( ));	Changes the size of the list to that specified by *num*. If the list must be lengthened, then elements with the value specified by *val* are added to the end.
void reverse( );	Reverses the invoking list.
size_type size( ) const;	Returns the number of elements currently in the list.

void sort( );
template <class Comp>
   void sort(Comp *cmpfn*);
	Sorts the list. The second form sorts the list using the comparison function *cmpfn* to determine when one element is less than another.

void splice(iterator *i*, list<T, Allocator> &*ob*);	The contents of *ob* are inserted into the invoking list at the location pointed to by *i*. After the operation, *ob* is empty.

void splice(iterator *i*,
       list<T, Allocator> &*ob*,
       iterator *el*);
	The element pointed to by *el* is removed from the list *ob* and stored in the invoking list at the location pointed to by *i*.

The **list** Member
Functions
(continued)
Table 21-3.

Member	Description

void splice(iterator *i*,
        list<T, Allocator> &*ob*,
        iterator *start*, iterator *end*);
	The range defined by *start* and *end* is removed from *ob* and stored in the invoking list beginning at the location pointed to by *i*.

void swap(list<T, Allocator> &*ob*);	Exchanges the elements stored in the invoking list with those in *ob*.

void unique( );
template <class BinPred>
  void unique(BinPred *pr*);
	Removes duplicate elements from the invoking list. The second form uses *pr* to determine uniqueness.

The **list** Member
Functions
(continued)
Table 21-3.

For maximum flexibility and portability, any object that will be held in a list should define a default constructor. It should also define the < operator, and possibly other comparison operators. The precise requirements for an object that will be stored in a list vary from compiler to compiler, so you will need to check your compiler's documentation.

21

Here is a simple example of **list**:

```
// List basics.
#include <iostream>
#include <list>
using namespace std;

int main()
{
  list<char> lst; // create an empty list
  int i;

  for(i=0; i<10; i++) lst.push_back('A'+i);

  cout << "Size = " << lst.size() << endl;

  cout << "Contents: ";
  list<char>::iterator p = lst.begin();
  while(p != lst.end()) {
    cout << *p;
    p++;
  }

  return 0;
}
```

The output produced by this program is shown here:

```
Size = 10
Contents: ABCDEFGHIJ
```

This program creates a list of characters. First, an empty **list** object is created. Next, ten characters, the letters A through J, are put into the list. This is accomplished by using the **push_back( )** function, which puts each new value on the end of the existing list. Next, the size of the list is displayed. Finally, the list is displayed. The code that does this is shown here:

```
list<char>::iterator p = lst.begin();
while(p != lst.end()) {
  cout << *p;
  p++;
}
```

Here, the iterator **p** is initialized to point to the start of the list. Each time through the loop, **p** is incremented, causing it to point to the next element. The loop ends when **p** points to the end of the list. Loops like this are common when using the STL. For example, a similar loop was used to display the contents of a vector in the previous section.

Because lists are bidirectional, elements can be put on a list at either the front or the back. For example, the following program creates two lists, with the first being the reverse of the second:

```
// Elements can be put on the front or end of a list.
#include <iostream>
#include <list>
using namespace std;

int main()
{
  list<char> lst;
  list<char> revlst;
  int i;

  for(i=0; i<10; i++) lst.push_back('A'+i);

  cout << "Size of lst = " << lst.size() << endl;
  cout << "Original contents: ";

  list<char>::iterator p;

  /* Remove elements from lst and put them
     into revlst in reverse order. */
  while(!lst.empty()) {
    p = lst.begin();
    cout << *p;
    lst.pop_front();
    revlst.push_front(*p);
  }
  cout << endl << endl;

  cout << "Size of revlst = ";
  cout << revlst.size() << endl;
```

```
  cout << "Reversed contents: ";
  p = revlst.begin();
  while(p != revlst.end()) {
    cout << *p;
    p++;
  }

  return 0;
}
```

This program produces the following output:

```
Size of lst = 10
Original contents: ABCDEFGHIJ

Size of revlst = 10
Reversed contents: JIHGFEDCBA
```

In the program, the list is reversed by removing elements from the start of **lst** and pushing them onto the front of **revlst**. This causes the elements to be stored in reverse order in **revlst**.

21

Sort a List

A list can be sorted by calling the **sort( )** member function. The following program creates a list of random integers and then puts the list into sorted order:

```
// Sort a list.
#include <iostream>
#include <list>
#include <cstdlib>
using namespace std;

int main()
{
  list<int> lst;
  int i;

  // create a list of random integers
  for(i=0; i<10; i++)
    lst.push_back(rand());

  cout << "Original contents:\n";
  list<int>::iterator p = lst.begin();
  while(p != lst.end()) {
    cout << *p << " ";
    p++;
  }
  cout << endl << endl;

  // sort the list
  lst.sort();
```

```
  cout << "Sorted contents:\n";
  p = lst.begin();
  while(p != lst.end()) {
    cout << *p << " ";
    p++;
  }

  return 0;
}
```

Here is sample output produced by the program:

```
Original contents:
41 18467 6334 26500 19169 15724 11478 29358 26962 24464

Sorted contents:
41 6334 11478 15724 18467 19169 24464 26500 26962 29358
```

Merging One List with Another

One ordered list can be merged with another. The result is an ordered list that contains the contents of the two original lists. The new list is left in the invoking list, and the second list is left empty. The next example merges two lists. The first contains the letters ACEGI and the second contains BDFHJ. These lists are then merged to produce the sequence ABCDEFGHIJ.

```
// Merge two lists.
#include <iostream>
#include <list>
using namespace std;

int main()
{
  list<char> lst1, lst2;
  int i;

  for(i=0; i<10; i+=2) lst1.push_back('A'+i);
  for(i=1; i<11; i+=2) lst2.push_back('A'+i);

  cout << "Contents of lst1: ";
  list<char>::iterator p = lst1.begin();
  while(p != lst1.end()) {
    cout << *p;
    p++;
  }
  cout << endl << endl;

  cout << "Contents of lst2: ";
  p = lst2.begin();
  while(p != lst2.end()) {
    cout << *p;
    p++;
```

```
  }
  cout << endl << endl;

  // now, merge the two lists
  lst1.merge(lst2);
  if(lst2.empty())
    cout << "lst2 is now empty\n";

  cout << "Contents of lst1 after merge:\n";
  p = lst1.begin();
  while(p != lst1.end()) {
    cout << *p;
    p++;
  }

  return 0;
}
```

The output produced by this program is shown here:

```
Contents of lst1: ACEGI

Contents of lst2: BDFHJ

lst2 is now empty
Contents of lst1 after merge:
ABCDEFGHIJ
```

Storing Class Objects in a List

Here is an example that uses a list to store objects of type **myclass**. Notice that the <, >, !=, and == are overloaded for objects of type **myclass**. (For some compilers, you will not need to define all of these operators, or you might need to define additional ones.) The STL uses these functions to determine the ordering and equality of objects in a container. Even though a list is not an ordered container, it still needs a way to compare elements when searching, sorting, or merging.

```
// Store class objects in a list.
#include <iostream>
#include <list>
#include <cstring>
using namespace std;

class myclass {
  int a, b;
  int sum;
public:
  myclass() { a = b = 0; }
  myclass(int i, int j) {
    a = i;
    b = j;
    sum = a + b;
```

```
    }
    int getsum() { return sum; }

    friend bool operator<(const myclass &o1,
                          const myclass &o2);
    friend bool operator>(const myclass &o1,
                          const myclass &o2);
    friend bool operator==(const myclass &o1,
                           const myclass &o2);
    friend bool operator!=(const myclass &o1,
                           const myclass &o2);
};

bool operator<(const myclass &o1, const myclass &o2)
{
  return o1.sum < o2.sum;
}

bool operator>(const myclass &o1, const myclass &o2)
{
  return o1.sum > o2.sum;
}

bool operator==(const myclass &o1, const myclass &o2)
{
  return o1.sum == o2.sum;
}

bool operator!=(const myclass &o1, const myclass &o2)
{
  return o1.sum != o2.sum;
}

int main()
{
  int i;

  // create first list
  list<myclass> lst1;
  for(i=0; i<10; i++) lst1.push_back(myclass(i, i));

  cout << "First list: ";
  list<myclass>::iterator p = lst1.begin();
  while(p != lst1.end()) {
    cout << p->getsum() << " ";
    p++;
  }
  cout << endl;

  // create a second list
  list<myclass> lst2;
  for(i=0; i<10; i++) lst2.push_back(myclass(i*2, i*3));

  cout << "Second list: ";
```

```
  p = lst2.begin();
  while(p != lst2.end()) {
    cout << p->getsum() << " ";
    p++;
  }
  cout << endl;

  // now, merge lst1 and lst2
  lst1.merge(lst2);

  // display merged list
  cout << "Merged list: ";
  p = lst1.begin();
  while(p != lst1.end()) {
    cout << p->getsum() << " ";
    p++;
  }

  return 0;
}
```

21

This program creates two lists of **myclass** objects and displays the contents of each list. It then merges the two lists and displays the result. The output from this program is shown here:

```
First list: 0 2 4 6 8 10 12 14 16 18
Second list: 0 5 10 15 20 25 30 35 40 45
Merged list: 0 0 2 4 5 6 8 10 10 12 14 15 16 18 20 25 30 35 40 45
```

Maps

A **map** is an associative container.

The **map** class supports an associative container in which unique keys are mapped with values. In essence, a *key* is simply a name that you give to a value. Once a value has been stored, you can retrieve it by using its key. Thus, in its most general sense, a map is a list of key/value pairs. The power of a map is that you can look up a value if you know its key. For example, you could define a map that uses a person's name as its key and stores that person's telephone number as its value. Associative containers are becoming more popular in programming.

As mentioned, a map may hold only unique keys. Duplicate keys are not allowed. To create a map that allows non-unique keys, use **multimap**.

The **map** container has the following template specification:

    template <class Key, class T, class Comp = less<Key>,
            class Allocator = allocator<pair<const Key, T> > > class map

Here, **Key** is the data type of the keys, **T** is the data type of the values being stored (mapped), and **Comp** is a function that compares two keys. This defaults to the standard **less** utility function object. **Allocator** is the allocator (which defaults to **allocator**).

A **map** has the following constructors:

explicit map(const Comp &*cmpfn* = Comp( ),
const Allocator &*a* = Allocator( ));

map(const map<Key, T, Comp, Allocator> &*ob*);

template <class InIter> map(InIter *start*, InIter *end*,
const Comp &*cmpfn* = Comp( ), const Allocator &*a* = Allocator( ));

The first form constructs an empty map. The second form constructs a map that contains the same elements as *ob*. The third form constructs a map that contains the elements in the range specified by the iterators *start* and *end*. The function specified by *cmpfn*, if present, determines the ordering of the map.

In general, any object used as a key should define a default constructor and overload the < operator, and any other necessary comparison operators. The specific requirements vary from compiler to compiler.

The following comparison operators are defined for **map**:

==, <, <=, !=, >, >=

The member functions contained by **map** are shown in Table 21-4. In the descriptions, **key_type** is the type of the key, and **value_type** represents **pair<Key, T>**.

Key/value pairs are stored in a map as objects of type **pair**, which has the following template specification:

```
template <class Ktype, class Vtype> struct pair {
  typedef Ktype first_type; // type of key
  typedef Vtype second_type; // type of value
  Ktype first; // contains the key
  Vtype second; // contains the value

  // constructors
  pair();
  pair(const Ktype &k, const Vtype &v);
  template<class A, class B> pair(const<A, B> &ob);
}
```

As the comments suggest, the value in **first** contains the key, and the value in **second** contains the value associated with that key.

Member	Description
iterator begin( ); const_iterator begin( ) const;	Returns an iterator to the first element in the map.
void clear( );	Removes all elements from the map.
size_type count(const key_type &k) const;	Returns the number of times *k* occurs in the map (1 or zero).
bool empty( ) const;	Returns true if the invoking map is empty and false otherwise.
iterator end( ); const_iterator end( ) const;	Returns an iterator to the end of the map.

pair<iterator, iterator>
    equal_range(const key_type &k);
pair<const_iterator, const_iterator>
    equal_range(const key_type &k) const;
	Returns a pair of iterators that point to the first and last elements in the map that contain the specified key.

void erase(iterator *i*);	Removes the element pointed to by *i*.
void erase(iterator *start*, iterator *end*);	Removes the elements in the range *start* to *end*.
size_type erase(const key_type &k);	Removes from the map elements that have keys with the value *k*.
iterator find(const key_type &k); const_iterator find(const key_type &k) const;	Returns an iterator to the specified key. If the key is not found, then an iterator to the end of the map is returned.
allocator_type get_allocator( ) const;	Returns map's allocator.
iterator insert(iterator *i*, const value_type &*val*);	Inserts *val* at or after the element specified by *i*. An iterator to the element is returned.
template <class InIter> void insert(InIter *start*, InIter *end*);	Inserts a range of elements.
pair<iterator, bool> insert(const value_type &*val*);	Inserts *val* into the invoking map. An iterator to the element is returned. The element is inserted only if it does not already exist. If the element was inserted, **pair<iterator, true>** is returned. Otherwise, **pair<iterator, false>** is returned.
key_compare key_comp( ) const;	Returns the function object that compares keys.

iterator lower_bound(const key_type &k);
const_iterator
    lower_bound(const key_type &k) const;
	Returns an iterator to the first element in the map with the key equal to or greater than *k*.

The **map** Member Functions **Table 21-4.**

21

Member	Description
size_type max_size( ) const;	Returns the maximum number of elements that the map can hold.
mapped_type & operator[ ] (const key_type &i);	Returns a reference to the element specified by *i*. If this element does not exist, it is inserted.
reverse_iterator rbegin( ); const_reverse_iterator rbegin( ) const;	Returns a reverse iterator to the end of the map.
reverse_iterator rend( ); const_reverse_iterator rend( ) const;	Returns a reverse iterator to the start of the map.
size_type size( ) const;	Returns the number of elements currently in the map.
void swap(map<Key, T, Comp, Allocator> &ob);	Exchanges the elements stored in the invoking map with those in *ob*.

iterator upper_bound(const key_type &k);
const_iterator
upper_bound(const key_type &k) const;
	Returns an iterator to the first element in the map with the key greater than *k*.

value_compare value_comp( ) const;	Returns the function object that compares values.

The **map**
Member
Functions
(continued)
Table 21-4.

You can construct a pair by using either one of **pair**'s constructors, or by using **make_pair( )**, which constructs a pair object based upon the types of the data used as parameters. **make_pair( )** is a generic function that has this prototype:

```
template <class Ktype, class Vtype>
    pair<Ktype, Vtype> make_pair(const Ktype &k, const Vtype &v);
```

As you can see, it returns a pair object consisting of values of the types specified by *Ktype* and *Vtype*. The advantage of **make_pair( )** is that the types of the objects being stored are determined automatically by the compiler, rather than being explicitly specified by you.

The following program illustrates the basics of using a map. It stores 10 key/value pairs. The key is a character and the value is an integer. The key/value pairs stored are

A   0

B   1

C   2

and so on. Once the pairs have been stored, you are prompted for a key (i.e., a letter between A and J), and the value associated with that key is displayed.

```
// A simple map demonstration.
#include <iostream>
#include <map>
using namespace std;

int main()
{
  map<char, int> m;
  int i;

  // put pairs into map
  for(i=0; i<10; i++) {
    m.insert(pair<char, int>('A'+i, i));
  }

  char ch;
  cout << "Enter key: ";
  cin >> ch;

  map<char, int>::iterator p;

  // find value given key
  p = m.find(ch);
  if(p != m.end())
    cout << p->second;
  else
    cout << "Key not in map.\n";

  return 0;
}
```

21

Notice the use of the **pair** template class to construct the key/value pairs. The data types specified by **pair** must match those of the **map** into which the pairs are being inserted.

Once the map has been initialized with keys and values, you can search for a value, given its key, by using the **find( )** function. **find( )** returns an iterator to the matching element or to the end of the map if the key is not found. When a match is found, the value associated with the key is contained in the **second** member of **pair**.

In the preceding example, key/value pairs were constructed explicitly, using **pair<char, int>**. While there is nothing wrong with this approach, it is often easier to use **make_pair( )**, which constructs a **pair** object based upon the types of the data used as parameters. For example, assuming the previous program, this line of code will also insert key/value pairs into **m**:

```
m.insert(make_pair((char)('A'+i), i));
```

Here, the cast to **char** is needed to override the automatic conversion to **int** when **i** is added to 'A'. Otherwise, the type determination is automatic.

Storing Class Objects in a Map

Like all of the containers, you can use a map to store objects of types that you create. For example, the next program creates a simple dictionary. That is, it creates a map of words with their meanings. To do this, it creates two classes, called **word** and **meaning**. Since a map maintains a sorted list of keys, the program also defines the < operator for objects of type **word**. In general, you should define the < operator for any classes that you will use as keys. (Some compilers may require that additional comparison operators be defined.)

```cpp
// Use a map to create a dictionary.
#include <iostream>
#include <map>
#include <cstring>
using namespace std;

class word {
  char str[20];
public:
  word() { strcpy(str, ""); }
  word(char *s) { strcpy(str, s); }
  char *get() { return str; }

};

// must define less than relative to word objects
bool operator<(word a, word b)
{
    return strcmp(a.get(), b.get()) < 0;
}

class meaning {
  char str[80];
public:
  meaning() { strcmp(str, ""); }
  meaning(char *s) { strcpy(str, s); }
  char *get() { return str; }
};


int main()
{
  map<word, meaning> dictionary;

  // put words and meanings into map
  dictionary.insert(pair<word, meaning>(word("house"),
                    meaning("A place of dwelling.")));
  dictionary.insert(pair<word, meaning>(word("keyboard"),
                    meaning("An input device.")));
  dictionary.insert(pair<word, meaning>(word("programming"),
              meaning("The act of writing a program.")));
  dictionary.insert(pair<word, meaning>(word("STL"),
                    meaning("Standard Template Library")));
```

```
// given a word, find meaning
char str[80];
cout << "Enter word: ";
cin >> str;

map<word, meaning>::iterator p;

p = dictionary.find(word(str));
if(p != dictionary.end())
   cout << "Definition: " <<  p->second.get();
else
   cout << "Word not in dictionary.\n";

return 0;
}
```

Here is a sample run:

```
Enter word: house
Definition: A place of dwelling.
```

21

In the program, each entry in the map is a character array that holds a null-terminated string. Later in this chapter, you will see an easier way to write this program that uses the standard **string** type.

Algorithms

Algorithms act on containers. Although each container provides support for its own basic operations, the standard algorithms provide more extended or complex actions. They also allow you to work with two different types of containers at the same time. To have access to the STL algorithms, you must include **<algorithm>** in your program.

The STL defines a large number of algorithms, which are summarized in Table 21-5. All of the algorithms are template functions. This means that they can be applied to any type of container. The following sections explore a representative sample.

Algorithm	Purpose
adjacent_find	Searches for adjacent matching elements within a sequence and returns an iterator to the first match.
binary_search	Performs a binary search on an ordered sequence.
copy	Copies a sequence.
copy_backward	Same as **copy( )** except that it moves the elements from the end of the sequence first.
count	Returns the number of elements in the sequence.
count_if	Returns the number of elements in the sequence that satisfy some predicate.
equal	Determines if two ranges are the same.

The STL
Algorithms
Table 21-5.

Algorithm	Purpose
equal_range	Returns a range in which an element can be inserted into a sequence without disrupting the ordering of the sequence.
fill and fill_n	Fills a range with the specified value.
find	Searches a range for a value and returns an iterator to the first occurrence of the element.
find_end	Searches a range for a subsequence. It returns an iterator to the end of the subsequence within the range.
find_first_of	Finds the first element within a sequence that matches an element within a range.
find_if	Searches a range for an element for which a user-defined unary predicate returns true.
for_each	Applies a function to a range of elements.
generate and generate_n	Assign elements in a range the values returned by a generator function.
includes	Determines if one sequence includes all of the elements in another sequence.
inplace_merge	Merges a range with another range. Both ranges must be sorted in increasing order. The resulting sequence is sorted.
iter_swap	Exchanges the values pointed to by its two iterator arguments.
lexicographical_compare	Alphabetically compares one sequence with another.
lower_bound	Finds the first point in the sequence that is not less than a specified value.
make_heap	Constructs a heap from a sequence.
max	Returns the maximum of two values.
max_element	Returns an iterator to the maximum element within a range.
merge	Merges two ordered sequences, placing the result into a third sequence.
min	Returns the minimum of two values.
min_element	Returns an iterator to the minimum element within a range.
mismatch	Finds first mismatch between the elements in two sequences. Iterators to the two elements are returned.
next_permutation	Constructs next permutation of a sequence.
nth_element	Arranges a sequence such that all elements less than a specified element *E* come before that element and all elements greater than *E* come after it.
partial_sort	Sorts a range.
partial_sort_copy	Sorts a range and then copies as many elements as will fit into a resulting sequence.

The STL
Algorithms
(continued)
Table 21-5.

Algorithm	Purpose
partition	Arranges a sequence such that all elements for which a predicate returns true come before those for which the predicate returns false.
pop_heap	Exchanges the first and last −1 elements and then rebuilds the heap.
prev_permutation	Constructs previous permutation of a sequence.
push_heap	Pushes an element onto the end of a heap.
random_shuffle	Randomizes a sequence.
remove, remove_if, remove_copy, and remove_copy_if	Removes elements from a specified range.
replace, replace_copy, replace_if, and replace_copy_if	Replaces elements within a range.
reverse and reverse_copy	Reverses the order of a range.
rotate and rotate_copy	Left-rotates the elements in a range.
search	Searches for subsequence within a sequence.
search_n	Searches for a sequence of a specified number of similar elements.
set_difference	Produces a sequence that contains the difference between two ordered sets.
set_intersection	Produces a sequence that contains the intersection of the two ordered sets.
set_symmetric_difference	Produces a sequence that contains the symmetric difference between the two ordered sets.
set_union	Produces a sequence that contains the union of the two ordered sets.
sort	Sorts a range.
sort_heap	Sorts a heap within a specified range.
stable_partition	Arranges a sequence such that all elements for which a predicate returns true come before those for which the predicate returns false. The partitioning is stable. This means that the relative ordering of the sequence is preserved.
stable_sort	Sorts a range. The sort is stable. This means that equal elements are not rearranged.
swap	Exchanges two values.
swap_ranges	Exchanges elements in a range.
transform	Applies a function to a range of elements and stores the outcome in a new sequence.
unique and unique_copy	Eliminates duplicate elements from a range.
upper_bound	Finds the last point in a sequence that is not greater than some value.

21

The STL
Algorithms
(continued)
Table 21-5.

Counting

One of the most basic operations that you can perform on a sequence is to count its contents. To do this, you can use either **count( )** or **count_if( )**. Their general forms are shown here:

    template <class InIter, class T>
        ptrdiff_t count(InIter *start*, InIter *end*, const T &*val*);

    template <class InIter, class UnPred>
        ptrdiff_t count_if(InIter *start*, InIter *end*, UnPred *pfn*);

The **count( )** algorithm returns the number of elements in the sequence, beginning at *start* and ending at *end*, that match *val*. The **count_if( )** algorithm returns the number of elements in the sequence, beginning at *start* and ending at *end*, for which the unary predicate *pfn* returns true. The type **ptrdiff_t** is defined as some form of integer.

The following program demonstrates **count( )** and **count_if( )**:

```
// Demonstrate count and count_if.
#include <iostream>
#include <vector>
#include <algorithm>
#include <cctype>
using namespace std;

/* This is a unary predicate that determines
   if character is a vowel. */
bool isvowel(char ch)
{
  ch = tolower(ch);
  if(ch=='a' || ch=='e' || ch=='i'
      || ch=='o' || ch=='u' || ch=='y') return true;

  return false;
}

int main()
{
  char str[] = "STL programming is powerful.";
  vector<char> v;
  unsigned int i;

  for(i=0; str[i]; i++) v.push_back(str[i]);

  cout << "Sequence: ";
  for(i=0; i<v.size(); i++) cout << v[i];
  cout << endl;

  int n;
  n = count(v.begin(), v.end(), 'p');
  cout << n << " characters are p\n";
```

```
  n = count_if(v.begin(), v.end(), isvowel);
  cout << n << " characters are vowels.\n";

  return 0;
}
```

This program displays the following output:

```
Sequence: STL programming is powerful.
2 characters are p
7 characters are vowels.
```

The program begins by creating a vector that contains the string "STL programming is powerful.". Next, **count( )** is used to count the number of **p**'s in the vector. Then, **count_if( )** counts the number of characters that are vowels, specifying **isvowel( )** as its predicate. Notice how the unary predicate **isvowel( )** is coded. All unary predicates receive as a parameter an object that is of the same type as that stored in the container upon which the predicate is operating. The predicate must then return a true or false result based upon this object.

21

Removing and Replacing Elements

Sometimes it is useful to generate a new sequence that consists of only certain items from an original sequence. One algorithm that does this is **remove_copy( )**. Its general form is shown here:

> template <class InIter, class OutIter, class T>
>   OutIter remove_copy(InIter *start*, InIter *end*,
>   OutIter *result*, const T &*val*);

The **remove_copy( )** algorithm copies elements from the specified range, removing those that are equal to *val*. It puts the result into the sequence pointed to by *result* and returns an iterator to the end of the result. The output container must be large enough to hold the result.

To replace one element in a sequence with another element when a copy is made, use **replace_copy( )**. Its general form is shown here:

> template <class InIter, class OutIter, class T>
>   OutIter replace_copy(InIter *start*, InIter *end*,
>   OutIter *result*, const T &*old,* const T &*new*);

The **replace_copy( )** algorithm copies elements from the specified range, replacing elements equal to *old* with *new*. It puts the result into the sequence pointed to by *result* and returns an iterator to the end of the result. The output container must be large enough to hold the result.

The following program demonstrates **remove_copy( )** and **replace_copy( )**. It creates a sequence of characters. It then removes all of the **i**'s from the sequence. Next, it replaces all **s**'s with **X**'s.

```
// Demonstrate remove_copy and replace_copy.
#include <iostream>
#include <vector>
#include <algorithm>
using namespace std;

int main()
{
  char str[] = "This is a test.";
  vector<char> v, v2(20);
  unsigned int i;

  for(i=0; str[i]; i++) v.push_back(str[i]);

  // **** demonstrate remove_copy ****

  cout << "Input sequence: ";
  for(i=0; i<v.size(); i++) cout << v[i];
  cout << endl;

  // Remove all i's
  remove_copy(v.begin(), v.end(), v2.begin(), 'i');

  cout << "Result after removing i's: ";
  for(i=0; i<v2.size(); i++) cout << v2[i];
  cout << endl << endl;

  // **** now, demonstrate replace_copy ****

  cout << "Input sequence: ";
  for(i=0; i<v.size(); i++) cout << v[i];
  cout << endl;

  // Replace s's with X's
  replace_copy(v.begin(), v.end(), v2.begin(), 's', 'X');

  cout << "Result after replacing s's with X's: ";
  for(i=0; i<v2.size(); i++) cout << v2[i];
  cout << endl << endl;

  return 0;
}
```

The output produced by this program is shown here:

```
Input sequence: This is a test.
Result after removing i's: Ths s a test.

Input sequence: This is a test.
Result after replacing s's with X's: ThiX iX a teXt.
```

Reversing a Sequence

An often useful algorithm is **reverse( )**, which reverses a sequence. Its general form is

        template <class BiIter> void reverse(BiIter *start*, BiIter *end*);

The **reverse( )** algorithm reverses the order of the range specified by *start* and *end*.

The following program demonstrates **reverse( )**:

```
// Demonstrate reverse.
#include <iostream>
#include <vector>
#include <algorithm>
using namespace std;

int main()
{
  vector<int> v;
  unsigned int i;

  for(i=0; i<10; i++) v.push_back(i);

  cout << "Initial: ";
  for(i=0; i<v.size(); i++) cout << v[i] << " ";
  cout << endl;

  reverse(v.begin(), v.end());

  cout << "Reversed: ";
  for(i=0; i<v.size(); i++) cout << v[i] << " ";

  return 0;
}
```

The output from this program is shown here:

```
Initial: 0 1 2 3 4 5 6 7 8 9
Reversed: 9 8 7 6 5 4 3 2 1 0
```

Transforming a Sequence

One of the more interesting algorithms is **transform( )** because it modifies each element in a range according to a function that you provide. The **transform( )** algorithm has these two general forms:

        template <class InIter, class OutIter, class Func)
            OutIter transform(InIter *start*, InIter *end*, OutIter *result*, Func *unaryfunc*);

        template <class InIter1, class InIter2, class OutIter, class Func)
            OutIter transform(InIter1 *start1*, InIter1 *end1*, InIter2 *start2*,
                            OutIter *result*, Func *binaryfunc*);

21

The **transform( )** algorithm applies a function to a range of elements and stores the outcome in *result*. In the first form, the range is specified by *start* and *end*. The function to be applied is specified by *unaryfunc*. This function receives the value of an element in its parameter, and it must return its transformation. In the second form, the transformation is applied by using a binary operator function that receives the value of an element from the sequence to be transformed in its first parameter, and an element from the second sequence as its second parameter. Both versions return an iterator to the end of the resulting sequence.

The following program uses a simple transformation function, called **xform( )**, to square the contents of a list. Notice that the resulting sequence is stored in the same list that provided the original sequence.

```cpp
// An example of the transform algorithm.
#include <iostream>
#include <list>
#include <algorithm>
using namespace std;

// A simple transformation function.
int xform(int i) {
  return i * i; // square original value
}

int main()
{
  list<int> xl;
  int i;

  // put values into list
  for(i=0; i<10; i++) xl.push_back(i);

  cout << "Original contents of xl: ";
  list<int>::iterator p = xl.begin();
  while(p != xl.end()) {
    cout << *p << " ";
    p++;
  }

  cout << endl;

  // transform xl
  p = transform(xl.begin(), xl.end(), xl.begin(), xform);

  cout << "Transformed contents of xl: ";
  p = xl.begin();
  while(p != xl.end()) {
    cout << *p << " ";
    p++;
  }

  return 0;
}
```

The output produced by the program is shown here:

```
Original contents of x1: 0 1 2 3 4 5 6 7 8 9
Transformed contents of x1: 0 1 4 9 16 25 36 49 64 81
```

As you can see, each element in the **x1** has been squared.

Exploring the Algorithms

Although the algorithms just described are representative of those provided by the STL, they only scratch the surface. You will want to explore the others on your own. Some of the most interesting algorithms are those that operate on sets, such as **set_union( )** and **set_difference( )**. Two other fascinating algorithms are **next_permutation( )** and **prev_permutation( )**. They construct the next and previous permutation of elements from a sequence. The time you spend exploring the STL algorithms is time well spent.

The string Class

The **string** class provides an alternative to null-terminated strings.

As you know, C++ does not support a built-in string type, per se. It does, however, provide for two ways of handling strings. First, you may use the traditional, null-terminated character array, with which you are already familiar. This is sometimes referred to as a *C string*. The second way is as a class object of type **string**, and this approach is examined here.

Actually, the **string** class is a specialization of a more general template class called **basic_string**. In fact, there are two specializations of **basic_string**: **string**, which supports 8-bit character strings, and **wstring**, which supports wide-character strings. Since 8-bit characters are, by far, the most commonly used in normal programming, it is the version of **basic_string** that is examined here.

Before looking at the **string** class, it is important to understand why it is part of the C++ library. Standard classes have not been casually added to C++. In fact, a significant amount of thought and debate has accompanied each new addition. Given that C++ already contains some support for strings as null-terminated character arrays, it may at first seem that the inclusion of the **string** class is an exception to this rule. However, this is actually far from the truth. Here is why: Null-terminated strings cannot be manipulated by any of the standard C++ operators. Nor can they take part in normal C++ expressions. For example, consider this fragment:

```
char s1[80], s2[80], s3[80];

s1 = "one"; // can't do
s2 = "two"; // can't do
s3 = s1 + s2; // error, not allowed
```

As the comments show, in C++, it is not possible to use the assignment operator to give a character array a new value (except during initialization), nor is it possible to

21

use the + operator to concatenate two strings. These operations must be written using library functions, as shown here:

```
strcpy(s1, "one");
strcpy(s2, "two");
strcpy(s3, s1);
strcat(s3, s2);
```

Since null-terminated character arrays are not technically data types in their own right, the C++ operators cannot be applied to them. This makes even the most rudimentary string operations clumsy. More than anything else, it is the inability to operate on null-terminated strings using the standard C++ operators that has driven the development of a standard string class. Remember, when you define a class in C++, you are defining a new data type that can be fully integrated into the C++ environment. This, of course, means that the operators can be overloaded relative to the new class. Therefore, by adding a standard string class, it becomes possible to manage strings in the same way as any other type of data: through the use of operators.

There is, however, one other reason for the standard string class: safety. In the hands of an inexperienced or careless programmer, it is very easy to overrun the end of an array that holds a null-terminated string. For example, consider the standard string copy function, **strcpy( )**. This function contains no provision for checking the boundary of the target array. If the source array contains more characters than the target array can hold, then a program error or system crash is possible (likely). As you will see, the standard **string** class prevents such errors.

In the final analysis, there are three reasons for the inclusion of the standard **string** class: consistency (a string now defines a data type), convenience (you can use the standard C++ operators), and safety (array boundaries will not be overrun). Keep in mind that there is no reason that you should altogether abandon normal, null-terminated strings. They are still the most efficient way in which to implement strings. However, when speed is not an overriding concern, using the new **string** class gives you access to a safe and fully integrated way to manage strings.

Although not traditionally thought of as part of the STL, **string** is another container class defined by C++. This means that it supports the algorithms described in the previous section. However, strings have additional capabilities. To have access to the **string** class, you must include **<string>** in your program.

The **string** class is very large, with many constructors and member functions. Also, many member functions have multiple overloaded forms. For this reason, it is not possible to look at the entire contents of **string** in this chapter. Instead, we will examine several of its most commonly used features. Once you have a general understanding of how **string** works, you will be able to easily explore the rest of **string**'s features on your own.

The prototypes for three of **string**'s most commonly used constructors are shown here:

string( );

string(const char *str);

string(const string &str);

The first form creates an empty **string** object. The second creates a **string** object from the null-terminated string pointed to by *str*. This form provides a conversion from null-terminated strings to **string** objects. The third form creates a **string** from another **string**.

A number of operators are defined for **string** objects, including:

Operator	Meaning
=	Assignment
+	Concatenation
+=	Concatenation assignment
= =	Equality
!=	Inequality
<	Less than
<=	Less than or equal
>	Greater than
>=	Greater than or equal
[]	Subscripting
<<	Output
>>	Input

21

These operators allow the use of **string** objects in normal expressions and eliminate the need for calls to functions such as **strcpy( )** or **strcat( )**. In general, you can mix **string** objects with null-terminated strings in expressions. For example, a **string** object can be assigned a null-terminated string.

The + operator can be used to concatenate a string object with another string object, or a string object with a C-style string. That is, the following variations are supported:

> string + string
>
> string + C-string
>
> C-string + string

The + operator can also be used to concatenate a character onto the end of a string.

The **string** class defines the constant **npos**, which is –1. This constant represents the length of the longest possible string.

The C++ string classes make string handling extraordinarily easy. For example, by using **string** objects, you can use the assignment operator to assign a quoted string to a **string**, the + operator to concatenate strings, and the comparison operators to compare strings. The following program illustrates these operations:

```
// A short string demonstration.
#include <iostream>
#include <string>
using namespace std;

int main()
{
```

```
string str1("The string class gives ");
string str2("C++ high-powered string handling.");
string str3;

// assign a string
str3 = str1;
cout << str1 << "\n" << str3 << "\n";

// concatenate two strings
str3 = str1 + str2;
cout << str3 << "\n";

// compare strings
if(str3 > str1) cout << "str3 > str1\n";
if(str3 == str1+str2)
  cout << "str3 == str1+str2\n";

/* A string object can also be
   assigned a normal string. */
str1 = "This is a null-terminated string.\n";
cout << str1;

// create a string object using another string object
string str4(str1);
cout << str4;

// input a string
cout << "Enter a string: ";
cin >> str4;
cout << str4;

return 0;
}
```

This program produces the following output:

```
The string class gives
The string class gives
The string class gives C++ high-powered string handling.
str3 > str1
str3 == str1+str2
This is a null-terminated string.
This is a null-terminated string.
Enter a string: Hello
Hello
```

Notice the ease with which the string handling is accomplished. For example, the + is used to concatenate strings, and the > is used to compare two strings. To accomplish these operations using C-style, null-terminated strings, less convenient calls to the **strcat( )** and **strcmp( )** functions would be required. Because C++ **string** objects can be freely mixed with C-style strings, there is no disadvantage to using them in your program—and there are considerable benefits to be gained.

There is one other thing to notice in the preceding program: The size of the strings are not specified. **string** objects are automatically sized to hold the string that they are given. Thus, when assigning or concatenating strings, the target string will grow as needed to accommodate the size of the new string. It is not possible to overrun the end of the string. This dynamic aspect of **string** objects is one of the ways that they are better than null-terminated strings (which *are* subject to boundary overruns).

Some string Member Functions

Although most simple string operations can be accomplished by using the string operators, more complex or subtle ones are accomplished by using **string** member functions. While **string** has far too many member functions to discuss them all, we will examine several of the most common.

T IP: Because **string** is a container, it also supports the common container functions, such as **begin( )**, **end( )**, and **size( )**.

21

Basic String Manipulations

To assign one string to another, use the **assign( )** function. Two of its forms are shown here:

    string &assign(const string &*strob*, size_type *start*, size_type *num*);

    string &assign(const char **str*, size_type *num*);

In the first form, *num* characters from *strob*, beginning at the index specified by *start*, will be assigned to the invoking object. In the second form, the first *num* characters of the null-terminated string *str* are assigned to the invoking object. In each case, a reference to the invoking object is returned. Of course, it is much easier to use the = to assign one entire string to another. You will need to use the **assign( )** function only when assigning a partial string.

You can append part of one string to another by using the **append( )** member function. Two of its forms are shown here:

    string &append(const string &*strob*, size_type *start*, size_type *num*);

    string &append(const char **str*, size_type *num*);

Here, *num* characters from *strob*, beginning at the index specified by *start*, will be appended to the invoking object. In the second form, the first *num* characters of the null-terminated string *str* are appended to the invoking object. In each case, a reference to the invoking object is returned. Of course, it is much easier to use the + to append one entire string to another. You will need to use the **append( )** function only when appending a partial string.

You can insert or replace characters within a string by using **insert( )** and **replace( )**. The prototypes for their most common forms are shown here:

    string &insert(size_type *start*, const string &*strob);*

    string &insert(size_type *start*, const string &*strob*,
                size_type *insStart*, size_type *num*);

    string &replace(size_type *start*, size_type *num*, const string &*strob);*

    string &replace(size_type *start*, size_type *orgNum*, const string &*strob*,
                size_type *replaceStart*, size_type *replaceNum*);

The first form of **insert( )** inserts *strob* into the invoking string at the index specified by *start*. The second form of the **insert( )** function inserts *num* characters from *strob*, beginning at *insStart*, into the invoking string at the index specified by *start*.

Beginning at *start*, the first form of **replace( )** replaces *num* characters from the invoking string, with *strob*. The second form replaces *orgNum* characters, beginning at *start*, in the invoking string with *replaceNum* characters from the string specified by *strob*, beginning at *replaceStart*. In both cases, a reference to the invoking object is returned.

You can remove characters from a string by using **erase( )**. One of its forms is shown here:

    string &erase(size_type *start* = 0, size_type *num* = npos);

This removes *num* characters from the invoking string, beginning at *start*. A reference to the invoking string is returned.

The following program demonstrates the **insert( )**, **erase( )**, and **replace( )** functions:

```
// Demonstrate insert(), erase(), and replace().
#include <iostream>
#include <string>
using namespace std;

int main()
{
  string str1("This is a test");
  string str2("ABCDEFG");

  cout << "Initial strings:\n";
  cout << "str1: " << str1 << endl;
  cout << "str2: " << str2 << "\n\n";

  // demonstrate insert()
  cout << "Insert str2 into str1:\n";
  str1.insert(5, str2);
  cout << str1 << "\n\n";

  // demonstrate erase()
  cout << "Remove 7 characters from str1:\n";
```

```
      str1.erase(5, 7);
      cout << str1 <<"\n\n";

      // demonstrate replace
      cout << "Replace 2 characters in str1 with str2:\n";
      str1.replace(5, 2, str2);
      cout << str1 << endl;

      return 0;
   }
```

The output produced by this program is shown here:

```
Initial strings:
str1: This is a test
str2: ABCDEFG

Insert str2 into str1:
This ABCDEFGis a test

Remove 7 characters from str1:
This is a test

Replace 2 characters in str1 with str2:
This ABCDEFG a test
```

Searching a String

The **string** class provides several member functions that search a string, including **find( )** and **rfind( )**. Here are the prototypes for the most common versions of these functions:

  size_type find(const string &*strob*, size_type *start*=0) const;

  size_type rfind(const string &*strob*, size_type *start*=npos) const;

Beginning at *start*, **find( )** searches the invoking string for the first occurrence of the string contained in *strob*. If found, **find( )** returns the index at which the match occurs within the invoking string. If no match is found, then **npos** is returned. **rfind( )** is the opposite of **find( )**. Beginning at *start*, it searches the invoking string in the reverse direction for the first occurrence of the string contained in *strob* (i.e., it finds the last occurrence of *strob* within the invoking string). If found, **rfind( )** returns the index at which the match occurs within the invoking string. If no match is found, **npos** is returned.

Here is a short example that uses **find( )**:

```
#include <iostream>
#include <string>
using namespace std;

int main()
{
   int i;
```

21

```
string s1 =
  "The string class makes string handling easy.";
string s2;

i = s1.find("class");
if(i!=string::npos) {
  cout << "Match found at " << i << endl;
  cout << "Remaining string is: ";
  s2.assign(s1, i, s1.size());
  cout << s2;
}

return 0;
}
```

The output produced by this program is shown here:

```
Match found at 11
Remaining string is: class makes string handling easy.
```

Comparing Strings

To compare the entire contents of one string object with another, you will normally use the overloaded relational operators, described earlier. However, if you want to compare a portion of one string with another, then you will need to use the **compare( )** member function, shown here:

int compare(size_type *start*, size_type *num*, const string &*strob*) const;

Here, *num* characters in *strob*, beginning at *start*, will be compared against the invoking string. If the invoking string is less than *strob*, **compare( )** will return less than zero. If the invoking string is greater than *strob*, it will return greater than zero. If *strob* is equal to the invoking string, **compare( )** will return zero.

Obtaining a Null-Terminated String

Although **string** objects are useful in their own right, there will be times when you will need to obtain a null-terminated character-array version of the string. For example, you might use a **string** object to construct a file name. However, when opening a file, you will need to specify a pointer to a standard, null-terminated string. To solve this problem, the member function **c_str( )** is provided. Its prototype is shown here:

const char *c_str( ) const;

This function returns a pointer to a null-terminated version of the string contained in the invoking **string** object. The null-terminated string must not be altered. It is also not guaranteed to be valid after any other operations have taken place on the **string** object.

Putting Strings into Other Containers

Since **string** defines a data type, it is possible to create containers that hold objects of type **string**. For example, here is a better way to write the dictionary program shown earlier:

```cpp
// Use a map of strings to create a dictionary.
#include <iostream>
#include <map>
#include <string>
using namespace std;

int main()
{
  map<string, string> dictionary;

  dictionary.insert(pair<string, string>("house",
                   "A place of dwelling."));
  dictionary.insert(pair<string, string>("keyboard",
                   "An input device."));
  dictionary.insert(pair<string, string>("programming",
                   "The act of writing a program."));
  dictionary.insert(pair<string, string>("STL",
                   "Standard Template Library"));

  string s;
  cout << "Enter word: ";
  cin >> s;

  map<string, string>::iterator p;

  p = dictionary.find(s);
  if(p != dictionary.end())
    cout << "Definition: " << p->second;
  else
    cout << "Word not in dictionary.\n";

  return 0;
}
```

21

Final Thoughts on the STL

The STL is an important, integral part of the C++ language. Many programming tasks can (and will) be framed in terms of it. The STL combines power with flexibility, and while its syntax is a bit complex, its ease-of-use is remarkable. No C++ programmer can afford to neglect the STL, because it will play an important role in the way future programs are written.

CHAPTER 22

The C++
Preprocessor

This final chapter concludes our examination of C++ by discussing the C++ preprocessor. The *preprocessor* is that part of the compiler that performs various text manipulations on your program prior to the actual translation of your source code into object code. You can give text-manipulation commands to the preprocessor. These commands are called *preprocessor directives* and, although not technically part of the C++ language, they expand the scope of its programming environment.

The C++ preprocessor contains the following directives:

#define	#error	#include
#if	#else	#elif
#endif	#ifdef	#ifndef
#undef	#line	#pragma

As is apparent, all preprocessor directives begin with a **#** sign. Each will be examined here in turn.

NOTE: The C++ preprocessor is a holdover from C and some of its features have been rendered redundant by newer and better C++ language elements. However, it is still an important part of the C++ programming environment.

#define

#define defines a macro name.

#define is used to define an identifier and a character sequence that will be substituted for the identifier each time it is encountered in the source file. The identifier is called a *macro name* and the replacement process is called *macro substitution*. The general form of the directive is

    #define *macro-name character-sequence*

Notice that there is no semicolon in this statement. There can be any number of spaces between the identifier and the character sequence, but once the sequence begins, it is terminated only by a newline.

For example, if you want to use the word UP for the value 1 and the word DOWN for the value 0, you could declare these two **#define**s:

```
#define UP 1
#define DOWN 0
```

These statements will cause the compiler to substitute a 1 or a 0 each time the name **UP** or **DOWN** is encountered in your source file. For example, the following will print **1 0 2** on the screen:

```
cout << UP << ' ' << DOWN << ' ' << UP + UP;
```

Once a macro name has been defined, it can be used as part of the definition of other macro names. For example, the following code defines the names **ONE**, **TWO**, and **THREE** to their respective values:

```
#define ONE    1
#define TWO    ONE+ONE
#define THREE  ONE+TWO
```

It is important to understand that the macro substitution is simply the replacing of an identifier with its associated string. Therefore, if you want to define a standard message, you might write something like this:

```
#define GETFILE "Enter File Name"
// ...
cout << GETFILE;
```

The preprocessor will substitute the string "Enter File Name" when the identifier **GETFILE** is encountered. To the compiler, the **cout** statement will actually appear to be

```
cout << "Enter File Name";
```

No text substitutions will occur if the identifier occurs within a quoted string. For example:

```
#define GETFILE "Enter File Name"
// ...
cout << "GETFILE is a macro name\n";
```

will not display

```
Enter File Name is a macro name
```

but rather

```
GETFILE is a macro name
```

If the string is longer than one line, you can continue it on the next line by placing a backslash at the end of the line, as shown in this example:

```
#define LONG_STRING "this is a very long \
string that is used as an example"
```

It is common practice among C++ programmers to use capital letters for macro names. This convention helps anyone reading the program to know at a glance that a macro substitution will take place. Also, it is best to put all **#define**s at the start of the file, or perhaps in a separate include file, rather than sprinkling them throughout the program.

Macro substitutions are often used to define "magic numbers" that occur in a program. For example, you may have a program that defines an array and has several routines that access that array. Instead of "hard-coding" the array's size with a constant, it is better to define a name that represents the size, and then use that name whenever the size of the array is needed. Therefore, if the size of the array changes, you have to change it in only one place in the file, and then recompile. For example:

```
#define MAX_SIZE 100
// ...
float balance[MAX_SIZE];
double index[MAX_SIZE];
int num_emp[MAX_SIZE];
```

TIP: It is important to remember that C++ provides a better way of defining constants. This is to use the **const** specifier. However, many C++ programmers have migrated from C, where **#define** is commonly used for this purpose. Thus, you will likely see it frequently in C++ code, too.

Function-Like Macros

The **#define** directive has another feature: The macro name can have arguments. Each time the macro name is encountered, the arguments associated with it are replaced by the actual arguments found in the program. This creates a *function-like* macro. Here is an example:

```
// Use a function-like macro.
#include <iostream>
using namespace std;

#define MIN(a,b)   (((a)<(b)) ? a : b)

int main()
{
  int x, y;

  x = 10;
  y = 20;
  cout << "The minimum is " << MIN(x, y);

  return 0;
}
```

When this program is compiled, the expression defined by **MIN(a,b)** will be substituted, except that **x** and **y** will be used as the operands. That is, the **cout** statement will be substituted to look like this:

```
cout << "The minimum is: " << (((x)<(y)) ? x : y);
```

A function-like
macro is one
that takes an
argument.

In essence, the function-like macro is a way to define a function that has its code expanded in line rather than called.

The apparently redundant parentheses surrounding the **MIN** macro are necessary to ensure proper evaluation of the substituted expression, because of the relative precedence of the operators. In fact, the extra parentheses should be applied in virtually all function-like macros. In general, you must be very careful how you define function-like macros; otherwise, there can be surprising results. For example, consider this short program, which uses a macro to determine whether a value is even or odd:

```
// This program will give the wrong answer.
#include <iostream>
using namespace std;

#define EVEN(a) a%2==0 ? 1 : 0

int main()
{
  if(EVEN(9+1)) cout << "is even";
  else cout << "is odd";

  return 0;
}
```

22

This program will not work correctly because of the way the macro substitution is made. When compiled, the **EVEN(9+1)** is expanded to

```
9+1%2==0 ? 1 : 0
```

As you should recall, the **%** (modulus) operator has higher precedence than the plus operator. This means that the **%** operation is first performed on the 1 and then the result is added to 9, which (of course) does not equal 0. To fix the problem, there must be parentheses around **a** in the macro definition of **EVEN**, as is shown in this corrected version of the program:

```
// This program is now fixed.
#include <iostream>
using namespace std;

#define EVEN(a) (a)%2==0 ? 1 : 0

int main()
{
  if(EVEN(9+1)) cout << "is even";
  else cout << "is odd";

  return 0;
}
```

Now, the **9+1** is evaluated prior to the modulus operation. In general, it is a good idea to surround macro parameters with parentheses, to avoid unforeseen troubles like the one just described.

The use of macro substitutions in place of real functions has one major benefit: Because macro substitution code is expanded in line, no overhead for a function call is incurred, so the speed of your program increases. However, this increased speed might be paid for with an increase in the size of the program, due to duplicated code.

TIP: Although still commonly seen in C++ code, the use of function-like macros has been rendered completely redundant by the **inline** specifier, which accomplishes the same goal better and more safely. (Remember, **inline** causes a function to be expanded in line rather than called.) Also, **inline** functions do not require the extra parentheses needed by most function-like macros. However, function-like macros will almost certainly continue to be a part of C++ programs for some time to come, because many longtime C/C++ programmers continue to use them out of habit.

#error

#error displays an error message.

When the **#error** directive is encountered, it forces the compiler to stop compilation. This directive is used primarily for debugging. The general form of the directive is

#error *error-message*

Notice that the *error-message* is not between double quotes. When the compiler encounters this directive, it displays the error message and other information, and then terminates compilation. Your implementation determines what information will actually be displayed. (You might want to experiment with your compiler to see what is shown.)

#include

#include includes a header or another source file.

The **#include** preprocessor directive instructs the compiler to include either a standard header or another source file with the file that contains the **#include** directive. The name of the standard headers are enclosed between angle brackets, as shown in the programs throughout this book. For example,

```
#include <vector>
```

includes the standard header for vectors.

When including another source file, its name can be enclosed between double quotes or angle brackets. For example, the following two directives both cause C++ to read and compile a file called **sample.h**:

```
#include <sample.h>
#include "sample.h"
```

When including a file, whether the filename is enclosed by quotes or angle brackets determines how the search for the specified file is conducted. If the filename is enclosed between angle brackets, the compiler searches for it in one or more implementation-defined directories. If the filename is enclosed between quotes, then the compiler searches for it in some other implementation-defined directory, which is typically the current working directory. If the file is not found in this directory, the search is restarted as if the filename had been enclosed between angle brackets. Since the search path is implementation defined, you will need to check your compiler's documentation for details.

Conditional Compilation Directives

There are several directives that allow you to selectively compile portions of your program's source code. This process, called *conditional compilation*, is widely used by commercial software houses that provide and maintain many customized versions of one program.

#if, #else, #elif, and #endif

#if, #ifdef, #ifndef, #elif, and #else are the conditional compilation directives.

The general idea behind the **#if** directive is that if the constant expression following the **#if** is true, then the code between it and an **#endif** will be compiled; otherwise, the code will be skipped over. **#endif** is used to mark the end of an **#if** block.

22

The general form of **#if** is

```
#if constant-expression
    statement sequence
#endif
```

If the constant expression is true, the block of code will be compiled; otherwise, it will be skipped. For example:

```
// A simple #if example.
#include <iostream>
using namespace std;

#define MAX 100
int main()
{
#if MAX>10
  cout << "Extra memory required.\n";
#endif

  // ...
  return 0;
}
```

This program will display the message on the screen because, as defined in the program, **MAX** is greater than 10. This example illustrates an important point: The expression that follows the **#if** is *evaluated at compile time*. Therefore, it must contain only identifiers that have been previously defined or constants. No variables can be used.

The **#else** directive works in much the same way as the **else** statement that forms part of the C++ language: It establishes an alternative if the **#if** directive fails. The previous example can be expanded to include the **#else** directive, as shown here:

```
// A simple #if/#else example.
#include <iostream>
using namespace std;

#define MAX 6
int main()
{
#if MAX>10
  cout << "Extra memory required.\n");
#else
  cout << "Current memory OK.\n";
#endif

  // ...

  return 0;
}
```

In this program, **MAX** is defined to be less than 10, so the **#if** portion of the code is not compiled, but the **#else** alternative is. Therefore, the message **Current memory OK.** is displayed.

Notice that the **#else** is used to mark both the end of the **#if** block and the beginning of the **#else** block. This is necessary because there can be only one **#endif** associated with any **#if**.

The **#elif** means "else if" and is used to establish an if-else-if ladder for multiple compilation options. The **#elif** is followed by a constant expression. If the expression is true, then that block of code is compiled, and no other **#elif** expressions are tested or compiled. Otherwise, the next **#elif** expression in the series is checked. The general form is

```
#if expression
   statement sequence
#elif expression 1
   statement sequence
#elif expression 2
   statement sequence
#elif expression 3
   statement sequence
// ...
#elif expression N
   statement sequence
#endif
```

For example, this fragment uses the value of **COMPILED_BY** to define who compiled the program:

```
#define JOHN 0
#define BOB 1
#define TOM 2

#define COMPILED_BY JOHN

#if COMPILED_BY == JOHN
  char who[] = "John";
#elif COMPILED_BY == BOB
  char who[] = "Bob";
#else
  char who[] = "Tom";
#endif
```

#ifs and **#elif**s can be nested. In this case, the **#endif**, **#else**, or **#elif** associate with the nearest **#if** or **#elif**. For example, the following is perfectly valid:

```
#if COMPILED_BY == BOB
   #if DEBUG == FULL
      int port = 198;
   #elif DEBUG == PARTIAL
      int port = 200;
   #endif
#else
   cout << "Bob must compile for debug output.\n";
#endif
```

#ifdef and #ifndef

Another method of conditional compilation uses the directives **#ifdef** and **#ifndef**, which mean "if defined" and "if not defined," respectively, and refer to macro names.

The general form of **#ifdef** is

> #ifdef *macro-name*
>   *statement sequence*
> #endif

If the *macro-name* has been previously defined in a **#define** statement, the statement sequence between the **#ifdef** and **#endif** will be compiled.

The general form of **#ifndef** is

> #ifndef *macro-name*
>   *statement sequence*
> #endif

22

If *macro-name* is currently undefined by a **#define** statement, then the block of code is compiled.

Both the **#ifdef** and **#ifndef** directives can have an **#else** or **#elif** statement. For example:

```
#include <iostream>
using namespace std;

#define TOM

int main()
{
#ifdef TOM
  cout << "Programmer is Tom.\n";
#else
  cout << "Programmer is unknown.\n";
#endif
#ifndef RALPH
  cout << "RALPH not defined.\n";
#endif
  return 0;
}
```

This program displays

```
Programmer is Tom.
RALPH not defined.
```

However, if **TOM** were not defined, then the output would be

```
Programmer is unknown.
RALPH not defined.
```

One other point: You can nest **#ifdef**s and **#ifndef**s in the same way as **#if**s.

#undef

The **#undef** directive is used to remove a previously defined definition of a macro name. The general form is

> #undef *macro-name*

Consider this example:

```
#define TIMEOUT 100
#define WAIT 0

// ...
```

```
#undef TIMEOUT
#undef WAIT
```

Here, both **TIMEOUT** and **WAIT** are defined until the **#undef** statements are encountered.

The principal use of **#undef** is to allow macro names to be localized to only those sections of code that need them.

Using defined

In addition to **#ifdef**, there is a second way to determine whether a macro name is defined. You can use the **#if** directive in conjunction with the **defined** compile-time operator. For example, to determine whether the macro **MYFILE** is defined, you can use either of these two preprocessing commands:

```
#if defined MYFILE
```

or

```
#ifdef MYFILE
```

You can also precede **defined** with the **!** to reverse the condition. For example, the following fragment is compiled only if **DEBUG** is not defined:

```
#if !defined DEBUG
  cout << "Final version!\n";
#endif
```

IN DEPTH

The Diminishing Role of the Preprocessor

The C++ preprocessor is directly derived from the C preprocessor, and it offers no enhancements over its C counterpart. However, the role of the preprocessor in C++ is much smaller than it is in C. One reason for this is that many of the chores that are performed by the preprocessor in C are performed by language elements in C++. Stroustrup has stated his desire to render the preprocessor redundant, so that, ultimately, it could be removed from the language entirely.

At this time, the preprocessor is already partially redundant. For example, two of the most common uses for **#define** have been replaced by C++ statements. Specifically, its abilities to create a constant value and to define a function-like macro are now redundant. In C++, there are better ways of doing both of these jobs. To create a constant, simply define a **const** variable. To create an inline function, use the **inline** specifier. Both of these procedures are better ways of accomplishing what has been done using **#define**.

Another example of the replacement of preprocessor elements with language elements is the single-line comment. One of the reasons this element was created was to allow comments to be commented-out. As you know, the /*...*/ style comment cannot be nested. This means that you cannot comment-out a fragment of code that includes /*...*/ comments. However, you can comment-out // comments by surrounding them with a /*...*/ comment. The ability to comment-out code renders some uses of the conditional compilation directives, such as **#ifdef**, partially redundant.

#line

#line changes the contents of the _ _LINE_ _ and _ _FILE_ _macros.

The **#line** directive is used to change the contents of _ _**LINE**_ _ and _ _**FILE**_ _, which are predefined macro names. _ _**LINE**_ _ contains the line number of the line currently being compiled, and _ _**FILE**_ _ contains the name of the file being compiled. The basic form of the **#line** command is

#line *number "filename"*

Here, *number* is any positive integer, and the optional *filename* is any valid file identifier. The line number becomes the number of the current source line, and the filename becomes the name of the source file. **#line** is primarily used for debugging purposes and for special applications.

For example, the following program specifies that the line count will begin with 200. The **cout** statement displays the number 202 because it is the third line in the program after the **#line 200** statement.

```
#include <iostream>
using namespace std;

#line 200             // set line counter to 200
int main()            // now this is line 200
{                     // this is line 201
  cout <<  _ _LINE_ _; // outputs 202

  return 0;
}
```

#pragma

The **#pragma** directive is an implementation-defined directive that allows various instructions, defined by the compiler's creator, to be given to the compiler. The general form of the **#pragma** directive is

    #pragma *name*

Here, *name* is the name of the **#pragma** you want. If the *name* is unrecognized by the compiler, then the **#pragma** directive is simply ignored and no error results.

TIP: Check the documentation that came with your compiler to see what types of **#pragma**s it supports. You might find some that are valuable to your programming efforts. Typical **#pragma**s include those that determine what compiler warning messages are issued, how code is generated, and what library is linked.

The # and ## Preprocessor Operators

22

C++ supports two preprocessor operators: **#** and **##**. These operators are used in conjunction with **#define**. The **#** operator causes the argument it precedes to become a quoted string. For example, consider this program:

```
#include <iostream>
using namespace std;

#define mkstr(s)  # s

int main()
{
  cout << mkstr(I like C++);

  return 0;
}
```

The C++ preprocessor turns the line

```
cout << mkstr(I like C++);
```

into

```
cout << "I like C++";
```

The **##** operator is used to concatenate two tokens. Here is an example:

```
#include <iostream>
using namespace std;

#define concat(a, b)  a ## b

int main()
{
  int xy = 10;

  cout << concat(x, y);

  return 0;
}
```

The preprocessor transforms

```
cout << concat(x, y);
```

into

```
cout << xy;
```

If these operators seem strange to you, keep in mind that they are not needed or used in most programs. They exist primarily to allow some special cases to be handled by the preprocessor.

Predefined Macro Names

C++ specifies six built-in predefined macro names. They are

> _ _LINE_ _
> _ _FILE_ _
> _ _DATE_ _
> _ _TIME_ _
> _ _STDC_ _
> _ _cplusplus

Each will be described here, in turn.

The _ _**LINE**_ _ and _ _**FILE**_ _ macros were introduced in the discussion of **#line**. Briefly, they contain the current line number and filename of the program when it is being compiled.

The _ _**DATE**_ _ macro contains a string of the form *month/day/year* that is the date of the translation of the source file into object code.

The _ _**TIME**_ _ macro contains the time at which the program was compiled. The time is represented in a string having the form *hour:minute:second*.

The meaning of _ _**STDC**_ _ is implementation-defined. Generally, if _ _**STDC**_ _ is defined, then the compiler will accept only standard C/C++ code that does not contain any non-standard extensions.

A compiler conforming to ANSI/ISO Standard C++ will define _ _**cplusplus** as a value containing at least 6 digits. Non-conforming compilers will use a value with 5 or less digits.

Final Thoughts

You have come a long way since Chapter 1. If you have read and worked through all the examples in this book, then you can call yourself a C++ programmer. Like many things, programming is best learned by doing, so the best way to reinforce what you have learned is to write programs. Also, look at examples of C++ programs written by other people. If possible, study the C++ code written by several different programmers, paying attention to how the program is designed and implemented. Look for shortcomings as well as strong points. This will expand the way you think about programming. Also, consider ways existing code can be improved through use of STL containers and algorithms. These items offer great potential to improve the readability and maintainability of large programs. Finally, experiment. Push your limits. You will be surprised at how quickly you become an expert C++ programmer!

To continue your study of C++, I suggest my book *C++: The Complete Reference*, published by McGraw-Hill/Osborne. It contains in-depth descriptions of the C++ language and its libraries.

22

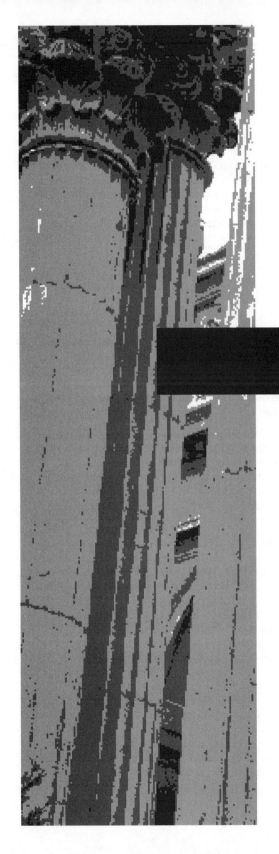

APPENDIX A

C-Based I/O

This appendix presents a brief overview of the C I/O system. Even though you will normally use the C++ I/O system, there are several reasons why you may need to understand the fundamentals of C-based I/O. First, if you will be working on C code (especially if you are converting it to C++), then you will need to understand how the C I/O system works. Second, it is common to find both C and C++ I/O within the same program. This is true especially when the program is very large and has been written by multiple programmers over a long period of time. Third, a great number of existing C programs continue to be used and maintained. Finally, many books and periodicals contain programs written in C. To understand these programs, you need to understand the basics of the C I/O system.

REMEMBER: For C++ programs, you should use the C++ object-oriented I/O system.

This appendix covers the most commonly used C-based I/O functions. However, the C standard library contains a very rich and diverse assortment of I/O functions—more than can be covered here. If you will be doing extensive work in C, you will want to explore its I/O system in detail.

The C-based I/O system requires either the header file **stdio.h** or the new-style header **<cstdio>**. A C program must use the **stdio.h** since C does not support C++-style headers. A C++ program uses either one. The header **<cstdio>** puts its contents into the **std** namespace. The header file **stdio.h** puts its contents into the global namespace, which is in keeping with C. The examples in this appendix are C programs, so they use the C-style header **stdio.h**, and no namespace statement is required.

One other point: As explained in Chapter 1, the C language standard was updated in 1999, resulting in the C99 standard for C. At that time, a few enhancements were made to the C I/O system. However, because C++ is built on C89, it does not support any features added by C99. (Furthermore, at the time of this writing, no widely available compiler supports C99, nor is there any widely distributed code that uses the C99 features.) Thus, none of the features added to the C I/O system by C99 are described here. If you are interested in the C language, including a complete description of its I/O system and those features added by the C99 standard, I recommend my book *C: The Complete Reference, 4th edition*, McGraw-Hill/Osborne.

C I/O Uses Streams

Like the C++ I/O system, the C-based I/O system operates on streams. At the beginning of a program's execution, three predefined text streams are opened. They are **stdin**, **stdout**, and **stderr**. (Some compilers also open other, implementation-dependent streams.) These streams are the C versions of **cin**, **cout**, and **cerr**, respectively. They each refer to a standard I/O device connected to the system, as shown here:

Stream	Device
stdin	keyboard
stdout	screen
stderr	screen

Remember that most operating systems, including Windows, allow I/O redirection, so functions that read or write to these streams may be redirected to other devices. You should never try to explicitly open or close these streams.

Each stream that is associated with a file has a file control structure of type **FILE**. This structure is defined in **stdio.h**. You must not make modifications to this file control block.

Understanding printf( ) and scanf( )

The two most commonly used C-based I/O functions are **printf( )** and **scanf( )**. The **printf( )** function writes data to the console; **scanf( )**, its complement, reads data from the keyboard. Because the C language does not support operator overloading, or the use of << and >> as I/O operators, it relies on **printf( )** and **scanf( )** for console I/O. Both **printf( )** and **scanf( )** can operate on any of the built-in data types, including characters, strings, and numbers. However, since these functions are not object-oriented, they cannot operate directly upon class types that you create.

A

printf( )

The **printf( )** function has this prototype:

    int printf(const char *fmt_string, ...);

The first argument, *fmt_string*, defines the way any subsequent arguments are displayed. This argument is often called the *format string*. It contains two things: text and format specifiers. Text is printed on the screen and has no other effect. The format specifiers define the way arguments that follow the format string are displayed. A format specifier begins with a percent sign, and is followed by the format code. The format specifiers are shown in Table A-1. There must be exactly the same number of arguments as there are format specifiers, and the format specifiers and the arguments are matched in order. For example, this **printf( )** call,

    printf("Hi %c %d %s", 'c', 10, "there!");

displays: **Hi c 10 there!**.

The **printf( )** function returns the number of characters output. It returns a negative value if an error occurs.

The format specifiers may have modifiers that specify the field width, the number of decimal places, and a left-justification flag. An integer placed between the % sign

Code	Format
%c	Character
%d	Signed decimal integers
%i	Signed decimal integers
%e	Scientific notation (lowercase e)
%E	Scientific notation (uppercase E)
%f	Decimal floating point
%g	Uses %e or %f, whichever is shorter
%G	Uses %E or %F, whichever is shorter
%o	Unsigned octal
%s	String of characters
%u	Unsigned decimal integers
%x	Unsigned hexadecimal (lowercase letters)
%X	Unsigned hexadecimal (uppercase letters)
%p	Displays a pointer
%n	The associated argument is a pointer to an integer into which the number of characters written so far is placed
%%	Displays a % sign

The **printf( )** Format Specifiers **Table A-1.**

and the format specifier acts as a minimum-field-width specifier. This pads the output with spaces to ensure that it is at least a certain minimum length. If the string or number is greater than that minimum, it will be printed in full, even if it overruns the minimum. If you want to pad with 0s, place a 0 before the field-width specifier. For example, %05d will pad a number of less than five digits with 0s so that its total length is five.

To specify the number of decimal places printed for a floating-point number, place a decimal point after the field-width specifier, followed by the number of decimal places you want to display. For example, %10.4f will display a number at least ten characters wide, with four decimal places. When this is applied to strings or integers, the number following the period specifies the maximum field length. For example, %5.7s will display a string that is at least five characters long, but that does not exceed seven characters. If the string is longer than the maximum field width, the characters will be truncated from the end.

By default, all output is right-justified: If the field width is larger than the data printed, the data will be placed on the right edge of the field. You can force the information to be left-justified by placing a minus sign directly after the %. For example, %–10.2f will left-justify a floating-point number, with two decimal places in a ten-character field. Here is a program that demonstrates field-width specifiers and left-justification:

```
#include <stdio.h>

int main()
{
  printf("|%10.5f|\n", 123.23);
  printf("|%-10.5f|\n", 123.23);
  printf("|%10.5s|\n", "Hello there");
  printf("|%-10.5s|\n", "Hello there");

  return 0;
}
```

This program displays the following output:

```
|  123.23000|
|123.23000  |
|     Hello|
|Hello      |
```

There are two format specifier modifiers that allow **printf( )** to display **short** and **long** integers. These modifiers can be applied to the **d**, **i**, **o**, **u**, and **x** type specifiers. The **l** (*ell*) modifier tells **printf( )** that a **long** data type follows. For example, **%ld** means that a **long int** is to be displayed. The **h** modifier instructs **printf( )** to display a **short int**. Therefore, **%hu** indicates that the data is of the short, unsigned integer type.

The **l** and **h** modifiers can also be applied to the **n** specifier, to indicate that the corresponding argument is a pointer to a **long** or **short** integer, respectively.

If your compiler fully complies with Standard C++, then you can use the **l** modifier with the **c** format to indicate a wide character. You can also use the **l** modifier with the **s** format to indicate a wide-character string.

The **L** modifier can prefix the floating-point specifiers **e**, **f**, and **g**. In this context, it indicates that a **long double** follows.

A

scanf( )

C's general-purpose console input function is **scanf( )**. It can read all the built-in data types and automatically convert numbers into the proper internal format. It is much like the reverse of **printf( )**. The general form of **scanf( )** is

int scanf(const char *fmt_string,...);

The format string consists of three classifications of characters:

◆   Format specifiers
◆   Whitespace characters
◆   Non-whitespace characters

The **scanf( )** function returns the number of fields that are input. It returns **EOF** (defined in **stdio.h**) if an error occurs.

The input format specifiers are preceded by a % sign. They tell **scanf( )** what type of data is to be read next. For example, **%s** reads a string, while **%d** reads an integer. These codes are listed in Table A-2.

A whitespace character in the control string causes **scanf( )** to skip over one or more whitespace characters in the input stream. A whitespace character is either a space, a tab, or a newline. In essence, one whitespace character in the control string will cause **scanf( )** to read, but not store, any number (including zero) of whitespace characters up to the first non-whitespace character.

A non-whitespace character causes **scanf( )** to read and discard a matching character. For example, **"%d,%d"** causes **scanf( )** to first read an integer, then read and discard a comma, and finally read another integer. If the specified character is not found, **scanf( )** will terminate.

Code	Meaning
%c	Read a single character
%d	Read a decimal integer
%i	Read an integer in either decimal, octal, or hexadecimal format.
%e	Read a floating-point number
%f	Read a floating-point number
%g	Read a floating-point number
%o	Read an octal number
%s	Read a string
%x	Read a hexadecimal number
%p	Read a pointer
%n	Receives an integer value equal to the number of characters read so far
%u	Read an unsigned decimal integer
%[ ]	Scan for a set of characters
%%	Read a percent sign

The **scanf( )**
Format
Specifiers
Table A-2.

All the variables used to receive values through **scanf( )** must be passed by their addresses. This means that all arguments must be pointers to the variables used as arguments. (C does not support references or the reference parameter.) Passing pointers allows **scanf( )** to alter the contents of an argument. For example, if you want to read an integer into the variable **count**, use the following **scanf( )** call:

```
scanf("%d", &count);
```

Strings will be read into character arrays, and the array name, without any index, is the address of the first element in an array. So, to read a string into the character array **address**, you would use

```
char address[80];
scanf("%s", address);
```

In this case, **address** is already a pointer, and need not be preceded by the **&** operator.

The data items read by **scanf( )** must be separated by spaces, tabs, or newlines. Punctuation such as commas, semicolons, and the like do not count as separators. This means that

```
scanf("%d%d", &r, &c);
```

will accept an input of **10 20**, but will fail with **10,20**. As in **printf( )**, the **scanf( )** format codes are matched, in order, with the variables receiving input in the argument list.

A

An ***** placed after the **%** and before the format code will read data of the specified type, but will not assign it to any variable. Thus,

```
scanf("%d%*c%d", &x, &y);
```

when given the input **10/20**, will place the value 10 into **x**, discard the division sign, and give **y** the value 20.

The format specifiers can specify a maximum-field-length modifier. This is an integer number placed between the % and the format-specifier code that limits the number of characters read for any field. For example, if you want to read no more than 20 characters into **str**, then you would write

```
scanf("%20s", str);
```

If the input stream is greater than 20 characters, then a subsequent call to input begins where this call leaves off. For example, if

ABCDEFGHIJKLMNOPQRSTUVWXYZ

is entered as the response to the **scanf( )** call in this example, then only the first 20 characters, or up to the 'T,' are placed into **str**, because of the maximum-size specifier.

This means that the remaining characters, "UVWXYZ," have not yet been used. If another **scanf( )** call is made, such as

```
scanf("%s", str);
```

then the characters "UVWXYZ" are placed into **str**. If a whitespace is encountered, input for a field may terminate before the maximum field length is reached. In this case, **scanf( )** will move on to the next field.

Although spaces, tabs, and newlines are used as field separators, they are read like any other characters when single characters are being read. For example, with an input stream of "x y,"

```
scanf("%c%c%c", &a, &b, &c);
```

will return with the character 'x' in **a**, a space in **b**, and the character 'y' in **c**.

Another feature of **scanf( )** is the scanset. A *scanset* defines a set of characters that will be matched by **scanf( )** and stored in a character-array. The **scanf( )** function continues to input characters as long as they are members of the scanset. When a character is entered that does not match any in the scanset, **scanf( )** null-terminates the corresponding array and moves on to the next (if any) field.

You define a scanset by putting a list of the characters you want to scan for inside square brackets. The beginning square bracket must be prefixed by a percent sign. For example, this scanset tells **scanf( )** to read only the letters X, Y, and Z.

```
%[XYZ]
```

The argument corresponding to the scanset must be a pointer to a character array. Upon return from **scanf( )**, the array will contain a null-terminated string composed of the characters read. For example, the following program uses a scanset to read digits into **s1**. As soon as a non-digit is entered, **s1** is null-terminated, and characters are read into **s2** until the next whitespace character is entered.

```
/* A simple scanset example. */
#include <stdio.h>

int main()
{
  char s1[80], s2[80];

  printf("Enter numbers, then some letters\n");
  scanf("%[0123456789]%s", s1, s2);
  printf("%s %s", s1, s2);

  return 0;
}
```

In most implementations, you can specify a range inside a scanset by using a hyphen. For example, the following scanset tells **scanf( )** to accept the characters A through Z:

```
%[A-Z]
```

You can specify more than one range within a scanset. For example, this program reads digits and then letters:

```
/* A scanset example using ranges. */
#include <stdio.h>

int main()
{
  char s1[80], s2[80];

  printf("Enter numbers, then some letters\n");
  scanf("%[0-9]%[a-zA-Z]", s1, s2);
  printf("%s %s", s1, s2);

  return 0;
}
```

You can specify an inverted set if the first character in the set is a ^. When the ^ is present, it tells **scanf( )** to accept any character that *is not* defined by the scanset. The following modification of the preceding example uses the ^ to invert the type of characters the scanset will read:

A

```
/* A scanset example using inverted ranges. */
#include <stdio.h>

int main()
{
  char s1[80], s2[80];

  printf("Enter non-numbers, then some non-letters\n");
  scanf("%[^0-9]%[^a-zA-Z]", s1, s2);
  printf("%s %s", s1, s2);

  return 0;
}
```

One important point to remember is that the scanset is case-sensitive. Therefore, if you want to scan for both uppercase and lowercase letters, they must be specified individually.

Several of the format specifiers can take modifiers which precisely specify the type of variable that receives the data. To assign data to a **long** integer, put an **l** (*ell*) in front of the format specifier. To assign data to a **short** integer, put an **h** in front of the format specifier. These modifiers can be used with the **d**, **i**, **o**, **u**, **x,** and **n** format codes.

By default, the **f**, **e**, and **g** specifiers tell **scanf( )** to assign data to a **float**. If you put an **l** (*ell*) in front of one of these specifiers, **scanf( )** assigns the data to a **double**. Using an **L** tells **scanf( )** that the variable receiving the data is a **long double**.

The **l** (*ell*) modifier can also be used with the **c** and **s** format codes as long as your compiler fully complies with Standard C++. Preceding **c** with an **l** indicates a pointer to an object of type **wchar_t**. Preceding **s** with an **l** indicates a pointer to a **wchar_t** array. The **l** can also be used to modify a scanset for use with wide characters.

The C File System

Although the C file system differs from that used by C++, it largely parallels it. The C file system is composed of several interrelated functions. The most commonly used are listed in Table A-3.

The common thread that ties the C I/O system together is the file pointer. A *file pointer* is a pointer to information that defines various things about the file, including its name, status, and current position. In essence, the file pointer identifies a specific disk file, and is used by the stream to tell each of the C I/O functions where to perform operations. A file pointer is a pointer variable of type **FILE**, which is defined in **stdio.h**.

The remainder of this appendix discusses the basic file functions.

Function	Purpose
fopen( )	Opens a stream
fclose( )	Closes a stream
fputc( )	Writes a character to a stream
fgetc( )	Reads a character from a stream
fwrite( )	Writes a block of data to a stream
fread( )	Reads a block of data from a stream
fseek( )	Seeks to specified byte in a stream
fprintf( )	Is to a stream what **printf( )** is to the console
fscanf( )	Is to a stream what **scanf( )** is to the console
feof( )	Returns true if end-of-file is reached
ferror( )	Returns true if an error has occurred
rewind( )	Resets the file position indicator to the beginning of the file
remove( )	Erases a file

The Most Commonly used C File System Functions

Table A-3.

fopen( )

fopen( ) serves three functions:

1. It opens a stream for use
2. It links a file with that stream
3. It returns a **FILE** pointer to that stream

Most often, and for the rest of this discussion, the file is a disk file. The **fopen( )** function has this prototype:

FILE *fopen(const char *filename, const char *mode);

where *filename* points to the name of the file that is being opened, and *mode* points to a string containing the desired open status. The legal values for *mode* are shown in Table A-4. The filename must be a string of characters that comprise a filename valid in the operating system; it may also include a path specification.

The **fopen( )** function returns a pointer of type **FILE**. This pointer identifies the file, and is used by most other file system functions. It should never be altered by your code. On failure, **fopen( )** returns null.

As Table A-4 shows, a file can be opened in either text mode or binary mode. In text mode, carriage-return/linefeed sequences are translated into newline characters on input. On output, the reverse occurs: newlines are translated into carriage-return/linefeeds. No such translations occur on binary files.

A

Mode	Meaning
"r"	Open a text file for reading
"w"	Create a text file for writing
"a"	Append to a text file
"rb"	Open a binary file for reading
"wb"	Create a binary file for writing
"ab"	Append to a binary file
"r+"	Open a text file for read/write
"w+"	Create a text file for read/write
"a+"	Append to or create a text file for read/write
"r+b"	Open a binary file for read/write
"w+b"	Create a binary file for read/write
"a+b"	Append to or create a binary file for read/write

The Legal
Values for **mode**
Table A-4.

If you want to open a file for writing with the name **test**, then you could write

```
fp = fopen("test", "w");
```

where **fp** is a variable of type **FILE ***. However, you will usually see it written like this:

```
if((fp = fopen("test", "w"))==NULL) {
  printf("Cannot open file.");
  exit(1);
}
```

This method detects any error in opening a file, such as a write-protected or full disk, before attempting to write to it. **NULL** is a macro defined in **stdio.h**.

If you use **fopen( )** to open a file for output, then any preexisting file by that name will be erased and a new file started. If no file by that name exists, then one will be created. If you want to add to the end of an existing file, then you must use mode "a". If the file does not exist, it will be created. Opening a file for read operations requires that the file exists. If it does not, an error will be returned. Finally, if a file is opened for read/write operations, it will not be erased if it exists; however, if it does not exist, it will be created.

fputc( )

The **fputc( )** function is used to write characters to a stream that was previously opened for writing by using the **fopen( )** function. Its prototype is:

int fputc(int *ch*, FILE **fp*);

Here, *fp* is the file pointer returned by **fopen( )**, and *ch* is the character to be output. The file pointer tells **fputc( )** which disk file to write to. Although *ch* is an **int**, only the low-order byte is used.

If an **fputc( )** operation is a success, then it will return the character written. Upon failure, an **EOF** is returned.

fgetc( )

The **fgetc( )** function is used to read characters from a stream opened in read mode by **fopen( )**. Its prototype is

int fgetc(FILE **fp*);

Here, *fp* is a file pointer of type **FILE** returned by **fopen( )**. Although **fgetc( )** returns an integer, the high-order byte is zero.

The **fgetc( )** function will return **EOF** when an error occurs or the end of the file has been reached. Therefore, to read to the end of a text file you could use the following code:

```
ch = fgetc(fp);
```

```
while(ch!=EOF) {
  ch = fgetc(fp);
}
```

feof( )

The C file system can also operate on binary data. When a file is opened for binary input, it is possible that an integer value equal to **EOF** may be read. This would cause the code shown above to indicate an end-of-file condition, even though the physical end of the file had not been reached. To solve this problem, C includes the function **feof( )**, which is used to determine end-of-file when reading binary data. It has the prototype

> int feof(FILE *fp);

where *fp* identifies the file. The **feof( )** function returns non-zero if the end of the file has been reached; otherwise, zero is returned. Therefore, the following reads a binary file until end-of-file is encountered:

```
while(!feof(fp)) ch = fgetc(fp);
```

Of course, this same method can be applied to text files, as well.

fclose( )

The **fclose( )** function closes a stream that was opened by a call to **fopen( )**. It writes any data still remaining in the disk buffer to the file, and does a formal operating-system-level close on the file. A call to **fclose( )** frees the file control block associated with the stream and makes it available for reuse. As you probably know, there is an operating system limit to the number of open files you can have at any one time, so it may be necessary to close one file before opening another.

The **fclose( )** function has the following prototype:

> int fclose(FILE *fp);

where *fp* is the file pointer returned by the call to **fopen( )**. A return value of zero signifies a successful close operation; **EOF** is returned if an error occurs. Generally, the only time **fclose( )** will fail is when a disk has been prematurely removed from the drive or there is no more space on the disk.

Using fopen( ), fgetc( ), fputc( ), and fclose( )

The functions **fopen( )**, **fget( )**, **fputc( )**, and **fclose( )** comprise a minimal set of file routines. The following program demonstrates these functions by using them to copy a file. Notice that the files are opened in binary mode, and that **feof( )** is used to check for end-of-file.

```
/* This program will copy one file to another. */
#include <stdio.h>
```

```
int main(int argc, char *argv[])
{
  FILE *in, *out;
  char ch;

  if(argc!=3) {
    printf("You forgot to enter a filename\n");
    return 1;
  }

  if((in=fopen(argv[1], "rb")) == NULL) {
    printf("Cannot open source file.\n");
    return 1;
  }
  if((out=fopen(argv[2], "wb")) == NULL) {
    printf("Cannot open destination file.\n");
    return 1;
  }

  /* This code actually copies the file. */
  while(!feof(in)) {
     ch = fgetc(in);
     if(!feof(in)) fputc(ch, out);
  }

  fclose(in);
  fclose(out);

  return 0;
}
```

ferror( ) and rewind( )

The **ferror( )** function is used to determine whether a file operation has produced an error. It has the prototype

   int ferror(FILE *fp);

where *fp* is a valid file pointer. **ferror( )** returns true if an error has occurred during the last file operation; it returns false otherwise. Because each file operation sets the error condition, **ferror( )** should be called immediately after each file operation; otherwise, an error may be lost.

The **rewind( )** function will reset the file position indicator to the beginning of the file specified as its argument. The prototype is

   void rewind(FILE *fp);

where *fp* is a valid file pointer.

fread( ) and fwrite( )

The C file system provides two functions, **fread( )** and **fwrite( )**, that allow the reading and writing of blocks of data. These functions are similar to C++'s **read( )** and **write( )** functions. Their prototypes are

size_t fread(void *buffer*, size_t *num_bytes*, size_t *count*, FILE *fp*);

size_t fwrite(const void *buffer*, size_t *num_bytes*, size_t *count*, FILE *fp*);

In the case of **fread( )**, *buffer* is a pointer to a region of memory that will receive the data read from the file. The function reads *count* number of objects, each object being *num_bytes* in length, from the stream pointed to by *fp*. **fread( )** returns the number of objects read, which may be less than *count* if an error or the end of the file is encountered.

For **fwrite( )**, *buffer* is a pointer to the information that will be written to the file. The function writes *count* number of objects, each object being *num_bytes* in length, to the stream pointed to by *fp*. **fwrite( )** returns the number of objects written, which will be equal to *count*, unless an error occurs.

As long as the file has been opened for binary operations, **fread( )** and **fwrite( )** can read and write any type of information. For example, this program writes a **float** to a disk file:

A

```
/* Write a floating point number to a disk file. */
#include <stdio.h>

int main()
{
  FILE *fp;
  float f = 12.23F;

  if((fp=fopen("test","wb"))==NULL) {
    printf("Cannot open file.\n");
    return 1;
  }

  fwrite(&f, sizeof(float), 1, fp);

  fclose(fp);
  return 0;
}
```

As this program illustrates, the buffer can be, and often is, simply a variable.

One of the most useful applications of **fread( )** and **fwrite( )** involves the reading and writing of arrays or structures. For example, the following program writes the contents of the floating-point array **balance** to the file "balance" by using a single **fwrite( )** statement. Next, it reads the array, using a single **fread( )** statement, and displays its contents.

```c
#include <stdio.h>

int main()
{
  register int i;
  FILE *fp;
  float balance[100];

  /* open for write */
  if((fp=fopen("balance","w"))==NULL) {
    printf("Cannot open file.\n");
    return 1;
  }

  for(i=0; i<100; i++) balance[i] = (float) i;

  /* This saves the entire balance array in one step. */
  fwrite(balance, sizeof balance, 1, fp);
  fclose(fp);

  /* zero array */
  for(i=0; i<100; i++) balance[i] = 0.0;

  /* open for read */
  if((fp=fopen("balance","r"))==NULL) {
    printf("Cannot open file.\n");
    return 1;
  }

  /* This reads the entire balance array in one step. */
  fread(balance, sizeof balance, 1, fp);

  /* display contents of array */
  for(i=0; i<100; i++) printf("%f ", balance[i]);

  fclose(fp);
  return 0;
}
```

Using **fread( )** and **fwrite( )** to read or write blocks of data is more efficient than using repeated calls to **fgetc( )** and **fputc( )**.

fseek( ) and Random-Access I/O

You can perform random read and write operations using the C I/O system with the help of **fseek( )**, which sets the file position indicator. Its prototype is

   int fseek(FILE *fp, long numbytes, int origin);

where *fp* is a file pointer returned by a call to **fopen( )**, *numbytes* is the number of bytes from *origin* to seek to, and *origin* is one of the following macros (defined in **stdio.h**):

Origin	Macro
Beginning of file	SEEK_SET
Current position	SEEK_CUR
End of file	SEEK_END

Therefore, to seek *numbytes* from the start of the file, *origin* should be **SEEK_SET**. To seek from the current position, use **SEEK_CUR**, and from the end of the file, use **SEEK_END**.

The **fseek( )** function returns zero on success, and non-zero if a failure occurs.

As a general rule, the use of **fseek( )** on files opened in text mode is not recommended, because the character translations will cause position errors to result. Therefore, its use is suggested only for files opened in binary mode. For example, if you want to read the 234th byte in a file called **test**, you could use the following code:

```
int func1()
{
  FILE *fp;

  if((fp=fopen("test", "rb")) == NULL) {
    printf("cannot open file\n");
    exit(1);
  }

  fseek(fp, 234L, SEEK_SET);
  return getc(fp);    /* read one character */
                      /* at 234th position */
}
```

fprintf( ) and fscanf( )

In addition to the basic I/O functions discussed above, the C I/O system includes **fprintf( )** and **fscanf( )**. These functions behave exactly like **printf( )** and **scanf( )**, except that they operate on files. For this reason, these functions are commonly found in C programs. The prototypes of **fprintf( )** and **fscanf( )** are

int fprintf(FILE *fp*, const char *fmt_string*, ...);

int fscanf(FILE *fp*, const char *fmt_string*, ...);

where *fp* is a file pointer returned by a call to **fopen( )**. Except for directing their focus to the file defined by *fp*, they operate exactly like **printf( )** and **scanf( )**, respectively.

Erasing Files

The **remove( )** function erases the specified file. Its prototype is

```
int remove(const char *filename);
```

It returns zero upon success, and non-zero if it fails.

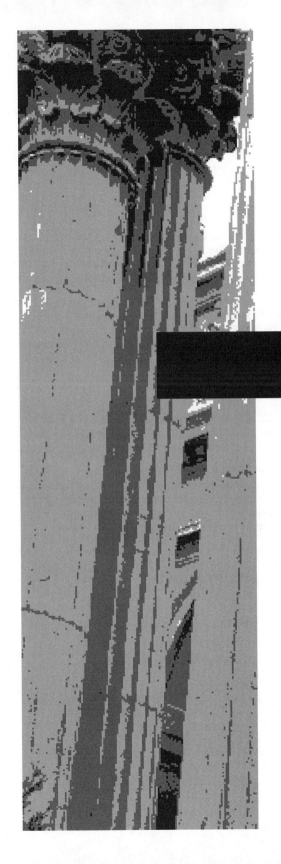

APPENDIX B

Working with an Older C++ Compiler

The programs in this book fully conform to the ANSI/ISO standard for C++ and can be compiled by nearly any modern C++ compiler, including Microsoft's Visual C++ and Borland's C++ Builder. Therefore, if you are using a modern compiler, you had no trouble compiling the programs in this book. If this is the case, then you won't need the information presented in this appendix. Simply use the programs exactly as they are shown.

However, if you are using a compiler that was created several years ago, then it might report a number of errors when you try to compile the examples because it does not recognize a few of C++'s newer features. If this is the case, don't worry. Only minor changes are required to modify the example programs so that they will work with old compilers. Most often, the differences between old-style and modern code involve the use of two features: new-style headers and the **namespace** statement. Each is examined here.

As explained in Chapter 2, the **#include** statement includes a header into your program. For early versions of C++, all headers were files that used the file extension **.h**. For example, in an old-style program you would use a statement like this to include the **iostream** header.

```
#include <iostream.h>
```

This caused the file **iostream.h** to be included in your program. Thus, in an old-style program, when you included a header, you specified its filename which had the **.h** extension. This is not the case today.

Modern C++ uses a different kind of header, which was developed when the ANSI/ISO Standard for C++ was created. The modern headers *do not* specify filenames. Instead, they specify standard identifiers, which may be mapped to files by the compiler, but need not be. The modern C++ headers are an abstraction that simply guarantee that the appropriate information required by your program is included.

Because the modern headers are not filenames, they do not have a **.h** extension. They consist solely of the header name contained between angle brackets. For example, here are two of the modern headers supported by Standard C++.

<iostream>

<fstream>

To convert these new-style headers into old-style header files, simply add a **.h** extension.

When you include a modern header in your program, the contents of that header are contained in the **std** namespace. As explained, a namespace is simply a declarative region. Its purpose is to localize the names of identifiers to avoid name collisions. Older versions of C++ put the names of library functions, etc., into the global namespace, not the **std** namespace used by modern compilers. Thus, when working with an old-style compiler, there is no need for this statement

```
using namespace std;
```

In fact, most older compilers won't accept the **using namespace** statement at all.

Two Simple Changes

If your compiler does not support namespaces and modern-style headers then it will report one or more errors when it tries to compile the first few lines of the sample programs in this book. If this is the case, then for many of the programs in this book you need only make two simple changes: use an old-style header and delete the **namespace** statement. For example, just replace

```
#include <iostream>
using namespace std;
```

with

```
#include <iostream.h>
```

This change transforms a modern program into a old-style one. Since the old-style header reads all of its contents into the global namespace, there is no need for a **using namespace** statement. After making these changes, the sample program can be compiled by an older compiler.

There is one other change that you will occasionally need to make. C++ inherits a few headers from the C language. The C language does not support the modern, C++-style headers. Instead, C uses **.h** header files. To allow for backward compatibility, Standard C++ still supports the C-style header files. However, Standard C++ also defines modern headers that you can use in place of the C header files. The C++ versions of the C standard headers simply add a 'c' prefix to the C filename and drop the **.h**. For example, the C++ header for **math.h** is **<cmath>**. The one for **string.h** is **<cstring>**. Although it is currently permissible to include a C-style header file, this approach is deprecated by Standard C++ (that is, it is not recommended). For this reason, this book uses modern C++ headers in all **#include** statements. If your compiler does not support C++-style headers for the C headers, then simply substitute the old-style header files.

B

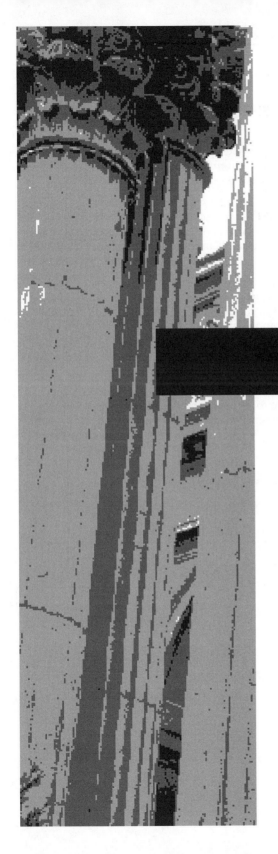

APPENDIX C

The .NET Managed Extensions to C++

Microsoft's .NET Framework defines an environment that supports the development and execution of highly-distributed, component-based applications. It enables differing computer languages to work together, and provides for security, program portability, and a common programming model for the Windows platform. Although the .NET Framework is a relatively recent addition to computing, it is an environment in which many C++ programmers will likely be working in the near future.

Microsoft's .NET Framework provides a managed environment that oversees program execution. A program targeted for the .NET Framework is not compiled into executable object code. Rather, it is compiled into Microsoft Intermediate Language (MSIL), which is then executed under the control of the Common Language Runtime (CLR). Managed execution is the mechanism that supports the key advantages offered by the .NET Framework.

To take advantage of .NET managed execution, it is necessary for a C++ program to use a set of non-standard, extended keywords and preprocessor directives that have been defined by Microsoft. It is important to understand that these extensions are not defined by ANSI/ISO standard C++. Thus, code in which they are used is not portable to other environments.

It is far beyond the scope of this book to describe the .NET Framework, or the C++ programming techniques necessary to utilize it. (A thorough explanation of the .NET Framework and how to create C++ code for it would easily fill a large book!) However, a brief synopsis of the .NET managed extensions to C++ is given here for the benefit of those programmers working in the .NET environment. A basic understanding of the .NET Framework is assumed.

The .NET Keyword Extensions

To support the .NET managed execution environment, Microsoft adds the following keywords to the C++ language.

_ _abstract	_ _box	_ _delegate
_ _event	_ _finally	_ _gc
_ _identifier	_ _interface	_ _nogc
_ _pin	_ _property	_ _sealed
_ _try_cast	_ _typeof	_ _value

Each of these is briefly described in the following sections.

_ _abstract

_ _**abstract** is used in conjuction with _ _**gc** to specify an abstract managed class. No object of an _ _**abstract** class can be created. A class specified as _ _**abstract** is not required to contain pure virtual functions.

_ _box

_ _**box** wraps a value within an object. Boxing enables a value type to be used by code that requires an object derived from **System::Object**, which is the base class of all .NET objects.

_ _delegate

_ _**delegate** specifies a delegate, which encapsulates a pointer to a function within a managed class (that is, a class modified by _ _**gc**).

_ _event

_ _**event** specifies a function that represents an event. Only the prototype for the function is specified.

_ _finally

_ _**finally** is an addition to the standard C++ exception handling mechanism. It is used to specify a block of code that will be executed when a **try/catch** block is left. It does not matter what conditions cause the **try/catch** block to terminate. In all cases, the _ _**finally** block will be executed.

_ _gc

_ _**gc** specifies a managed class. Here, "gc" stands for "garbage collection" and indicates that objects of the class are automatically garbage collected when they are no longer needed. An object is no longer needed when no references to the object exist. Objects of a _ _**gc** class must be created using **new**. Arrays, pointers, and interfaces can also be specified as _ _**gc**.

_ _identifier

_ _**identifier** allows a C++ keyword to be used as an identifier. This is a special-purpose extension that will not be used by most programs.

_ _interface

_ _**interface** specifies a class that will act as an interface. In an interface, no function can include a body. Thus, all functions in an interface are implicitly pure virtual functions. An interface is essentially an abstract class in which no function has an implementation.

_ _nogc

_ _**nogc** specifies a non-managed class. Since this is the type of class created by default, the _ _**nogc** keyword is not usually used.

_ _pin

_ _**pin** is used to specify a pointer that fixes the location in memory of the object to which it points. Thus, an object that is "pinned" will not be moved in memory by the garbarge collector. As a result, garbage collection does not invalidate a pointer modified by _ _**pin**.

_ _property

_ _**property** specifies a property, which is a member function that gets or sets the value of a member variable. Properties provide a convenient means to control access to private or protected data.

_ _sealed

_ _**sealed** prevents the class that it modifies from being inheritied. It can also be used to specify that a virtual function cannot be overridden.

_ _try_cast

_ _**try_cast** attempts to cast one type of expression into another. If the cast fails, an exception of type **System::InvalidCastException** is thrown.

_ _typeof

_ _**typeof** obtains an object that encapsulates type information for a given type. This object is an instance of **System::Type**.

_ _value

_ _**value** specifies a class that is represented as a value type. A value type holds its own values. This differs from a _ _**gc** type, which must allocate storage through the use of **new**. Value types are not subject to garbage collection.

Preprocessor Extensions

To support .NET, Microsoft defines the **#using** preprocessor directive, which is used to import metadata into your program. Metadata contains type and member information in a form that is indepedent of a specific computer language. Thus, metadata helps support mixed-language programming. All managed C++ programs must import **<mscorlib.dll>**, which contains the metadata for the .NET Framework.

Microsoft defines two pragmas that relate to the .NET Framework. (Pragmas are used with the **#pragma** preprocessing directive.) The first is **managed**, which specifies managed code. The second is **unmanaged**, which specifies unmanaged (that is, native) code. These pragmas can be used within a program to selectively create managed and unmanaged code.

The attribute Attribute

Microsoft defines **attribute**, which is the attribute used to declare another attribute.

Compiling Managed C++

At the time of this writing, the only commonly available compiler that can target the .NET Framework is the one supplied by Microsoft's Visual Studio .NET. To compile a managed code program, you must use the **/clr** option, which targets code for the Common Language Runtime.

C

Index

D

E

INTERNATIONAL CONTACT INFORMATION

AUSTRALIA
McGraw-Hill Book Company Australia Pty. Ltd.
TEL +61-2-9900-1800
FAX +61-2-9878-8881
http://www.mcgraw-hill.com.au
books-it_sydney@mcgraw-hill.com

CANADA
McGraw-Hill Ryerson Ltd.
TEL +905-430-5000
FAX +905-430-5020
http://www.mcgraw-hill.ca

GREECE, MIDDLE EAST, & AFRICA
(Excluding South Africa)
McGraw-Hill Hellas
TEL +30-210-6560-990
TEL +30-210-6560-993
TEL +30-210-6560-994
FAX +30-210-6545-525

MEXICO (Also serving Latin America)
McGraw-Hill Interamericana Editores S.A. de C.V.
TEL +525-117-1583
FAX +525-117-1589
http://www.mcgraw-hill.com.mx
fernando_castellanos@mcgraw-hill.com

SINGAPORE (Serving Asia)
McGraw-Hill Book Company
TEL +65-863-1580
FAX +65-862-3354
http://www.mcgraw-hill.com.sg
mghasia@mcgraw-hill.com

SOUTH AFRICA
McGraw-Hill South Africa
TEL +27-11-622-7512
FAX +27-11-622-9045
robyn_swanepoel@mcgraw-hill.com

SPAIN
McGraw-Hill/Interamericana de España, S.A.U.
TEL +34-91-180-3000
FAX +34-91-372-8513
http://www.mcgraw-hill.es
professional@mcgraw-hill.es

UNITED KINGDOM, NORTHERN, EASTERN, & CENTRAL EUROPE
McGraw-Hill Education Europe
TEL +44-1-628-502500
FAX +44-1-628-770224
http://www.mcgraw-hill.co.uk
computing_europe@mcgraw-hill.com

ALL OTHER INQUIRIES Contact:
Osborne/McGraw-Hill
TEL +1-510-549-6600
FAX +1-510-883-7600
http://www.osborne.com
omg_international@mcgraw-hill.com